MW00718084

Social Psychology 05/06

Sixth Edition

EDITOR

Karen G. Duffy

SUNY at Geneseo (Emerita)

Karen G. Duffy holds a doctorate in psychology from Michigan State University, and she is an emerita Distinguished Service Professor of State University of New York at Geneseo. Dr. Duffy continues to work on her books and research, and she is also involved in several community service projects both in the United States and Russia.

McGraw-Hill/Dushkin

2460 Kerper Blvd., Dubuque, IA 52001

Visit us on the Internet
http://www.dushkin.com

Credits

1. **Research Issues**
   Unit photo—© Getty Images/Don Farrall
2. **The Self**
   Unit photo—© Getty Images/PhotoLink
3. **Social Cognition and Social Perception**
   Unit photo—© Getty Images/Keith Brofsky
4. **Attitudes**
   Unit photo—© Getty Images/Ryan McVay
5. **Social Influence**
   Unit photo—Photo courtesy of Dept. of Defense, by Tech. Sgt. Jerry Morrison Jr., U.S. Air Force
6. **Social Relationships**
   Unit photo—© Cindy Brown/Sweet By & By
7. **Social Biases**
   Unit photo—© CORBIS/Royalty-Free
8. **Violence and Aggression**
   Unit photo—© CORBIS/Royalty-Free
9. **Altruism, Helping and Cooperation**
   Unit photo—© Getty Images/Doug Menuez
10. **Group Processes**
    Unit photo—© Getty Images/Keith Brofsky

Copyright

Cataloging in Publication Data
Main entry under title: Annual Editions: Social Psychology 2005/2006.
1. Psychology—Periodicals. I. Duffy, Karen, *comp.* II. Title: Social psychology.
ISBN 0–07–310214–8   302'.05   ISSN 0730–6962

Sixth Edition

Cover image © Doub Menuez/Getty Images
Printed in the United States of America   1234567890QPDQPD987654   Printed on Recycled Paper

Editors/Advisory Board

Members of the Advisory Board are instrumental in the final selection of articles for each edition of ANNUAL EDITIONS. Their review of articles for content, level, currentness, and appropriateness provides critical direction to the editor and staff. We think that you will find their careful consideration well reflected in this volume.

Preface

In publishing ANNUAL EDITIONS we recognize the enormous role played by the magazines, newspapers, and journals of the public press in providing current, first-rate educational information in a broad spectrum of interest areas. Many of these articles are appropriate for students, researchers, and professionals seeking accurate, current material to help bridge the gap between principles and theories and the real world. These articles, however, become more useful for study when those of lasting value are carefully collected, organized, and reproduced in a low-cost format, which provides easy and permanent access when the material is needed. That is the role played by ANNUAL EDITIONS.

Social psychology is one of the most fascinating fields in all of psychology. Its rapid and continued strong growth attest to its interest level, contributions to science, and applicability.

Just what is social psychology? There are as many different definitions as there are authors. Most definitions of social psychology are similar to the following—*social psychology is the scientific study of how others affect our thoughts and behaviors.* In other words, individual "action" (behavior) may be the domain of all of psychology, but social *inter*action is the province of social psychology.

What does this definition mean for you? First, as stated in the definition, other people's actions and thoughts have an impact on you. You, however, have just as important an influence on them. If someone else is angry with you, you will certainly feel the effects—direct or indirect. On the other hand, if you are angry with someone, that person may also experience the repercussions.

All types of groups—large and small—are of interest to social psychologists. Loving couples, angry friends, and mothers and infants make up some of the smallest groups social psychologists study. Medium sized groups also fall under the scrutiny of social psychologists, including but not limited to work groups, committees, and even a gang of bank robbers. Large groups and sometimes whole organizations also captivate the attention of social psychologists. Such groups as students in a classroom, whole corporations, crowds at a sporting event, and chat room participants are within a social psychologist's purview.

On the other hand, there are some marked similarities between social psychologists and other psychologists. All psychologists base their knowledge and practices on science. Most research psychologists call upon the scientific method in their investigations. As in other fields of psychology, the inspiration for research in social psychology is a theory—to be supported or not. Finally, most psychologists hope that their theories and research can be employed to help improve the human condition.

The first unit, *Research Issues,* is new to this edition. Social psychologists are more likely to utilize deception than are many other types of psychologists. Thus, they greatly worry about research ethics, research design, and protection of human participants.

Unit 2 pertains to the self-concept. Self-concept, most psychologists would argue, originates because of social interactions with significant others (namely parents). Culture also plays a key role in determining who we think we are and what we think of ourselves. Unit 3 relates to social cognition and social perception. It is divided into a subunit on each topic. Your interpretation of others' behaviors, motives, feel-ings, and attitudes is as important as their construal of yours. Misperception can sometimes spell disaster, especially at the international level.

Children appear to be born without attitudinal biases. Attitudes form during childhood from exchanges with others. If Mom and Dad practice a particular religion, join a certain political party, and root for a specific team, chances are their child will soon hold the same attitudes, beliefs, and values. Attitudes, attitude formation, and resistance to attitude change, then, are important aspects of social psychology and are covered in Unit 4—Attitudes.

There exist myriad methods to influence or persuade others, known as social influence. The three main techniques are conformity, compliance, and obedience—in order of the intensity of influence. These topics are covered in Unit 5. Unit 6 is equally important because it contains articles on social relationships. There are two subunits once again, one on interpersonal relationships such as friendships and another on more intimate relationships such as marriage.

Unit 7 on prejudice affords you the opportunity to examine social biases in detail. Prejudice is an attitude that can cause discrimination as well as stereotypes. Each of these topics is explored in its own subunit. Additionally, any social psychology text would be incomplete without a presentation of on the matter of violence—societal, within and between groups, or inter-individual. In Unit 8 several articles explore a variety of related issues including conflict, hostility, and aggressiveness. A more positive side of human nature is considered in Unit 9. Humans can also use their energy to benefit others. This part of the anthology includes articles on altruism and helping.

This collection ends with Unit 10—Group Processes. Because this subject is last does not mean it is least important. In fact, group (and leader) dynamics are one of the oldest areas of social psychology, in part spawned by army brigades in World War II and further nurtured by the need to know about groups and leaders, such as mangers and their employees.

Annual Editions: Social Psychology 05/06 will challenge and interest you in a plethora of topics. It will provide you with many answers and also stimulate many questions. As has been true in the past, your feedback on this edition would be valuable for future revisions. Please take a moment to fill out and return the postage-paid article rating form on the last page. Thank you.

Karen Grover Duffy
Editor

Contents

UNIT 1
Research Issues

UNIT 2
The Self

The concepts in bold italics are developed in the article. For further expansion, please refer to the Topic Guide.

UNIT 3
Social Cognition and Social Perception

The concepts in bold italics are developed in the article. For further expansion, please refer to the Topic Guide.

UNIT 4
Attitudes

UNIT 5
Social Influence

The concepts in bold italics are developed in the article. For further expansion, please refer to the Topic Guide.

UNIT 6
Social Relationships

UNIT 7
Social Biases

The concepts in bold italics are developed in the article. For further expansion, please refer to the Topic Guide.

UNIT 8
Violence and Aggression

The concepts in bold italics are developed in the article. For further expansion, please refer to the Topic Guide.

UNIT 9
Altruism, Helping and Cooperation

UNIT 10
Group Processes

The concepts in bold italics are developed in the article. For further expansion, please refer to the Topic Guide.

The concepts in bold italics are developed in the article. For further expansion, please refer to the Topic Guide.

Topic Guide

This topic guide suggests how the selections in this book relate to the subjects covered in your course. You may want to use the topics listed on these pages to search the Web more easily.

On the following pages a number of Web sites have been gathered specifically for this book. They are arranged to reflect the units of this *Annual Edition*. You can link to these sites by going to the DUSHKIN ONLINE support site at *http://www.dushkin.com/online/*.

ALL THE ARTICLES THAT RELATE TO EACH TOPIC ARE LISTED BELOW THE BOLD-FACED TERM.

Abuse
14. Abu Ghraib Brings A Cruel Reawakening
26. How Psychology Can Help Explain The Iraqi Prisoner Abuse

Aggression
14. Abu Ghraib Brings A Cruel Reawakening
25. Prime-Time Violence 1993–2001: Has The Picture Really Changed?
26. How Psychology Can Help Explain The Iraqi Prisoner Abuse
27. Bullying: It Isn't What It Used to Be

Altruism
29. The Nature of Human Altruism
30. Cause of Death: Uncertain(ty)

Attitudes
11. Sources of Implicit Attitudes
12. The Science and Practice of Persuasion

Attribution
9. How Culture Molds Habits of Thought

Bullying
27. Bullying: It Isn't What It Used to Be

Cognition
7. How Social Perception Can Automatically Influence Behavior
8. Make-Believe Memories
9. How Culture Molds Habits of Thought

Conflict
28. Influencing, Negotiating Skills, and Conflict-Handling: Some Additional Research and Reflections

Cooperation
31. Trends in the Social Psychological Study of Justice

Culture
4. Self-Concordance and Subjective Well-Being in Four Cultures
9. How Culture Molds Habits of Thought

Deception (in research)
14. Abu Ghraib Brings A Cruel Reawakening

Discrimination
23. Change of Heart

Eyewitnesses
8. Make-Believe Memories

Groups and group dynamics
32. Putting Leaders on the Couch
33. When Followers Become Toxic
35. Senate Intelligence Report: Groupthink Viewed as Culprit in Move to War

Groupthink
35. Senate Intelligence Report: Groupthink Viewed as Culprit in Move to War

Helping
29. The Nature of Human Altruism
30. Cause of Death: Uncertain(ty)

Human subjects
1. Stupid Human Tricks
2. Research Synthesis: Protection of Human Subjects of Research: Recent Developments and Future Prospects for the Social Sciences

Impression management and impression formation
10. More Than One Way to Make an Impression: Exploring Profiles of Impression Management

Institutional review boards
2. Research Synthesis: Protection of Human Subjects of Research: Recent Developments and Future Prospects for the Social Sciences

Internet
18. Linking Up Online
20. If It's Easy Access That Really Makes You Click, Log On Here

Interpersonal relationships
10. More Than One Way to Make an Impression: Exploring Profiles of Impression Management
17. Beyond Shyness and Stage Fright: Social Anxiety Disorder
34. Interpersonal Skills: What They Are, How to Improve Them, and How to Apply Them

Intimate relationships
19. Isn't She Lovely?
20. If It's Easy Access That Really Makes You Click, Log On Here
21. The Marriage Savers

Justice and equity
31. Trends in the Social Psychological Study of Justice

Leaders
32. Putting Leaders on the Couch
33. When Followers Become Toxic

Loneliness
18. Linking Up Online

Marriage
21. The Marriage Savers

Media and media violence
25. Prime-Time Violence 1993–2001: Has The Picture Really Changed?

World Wide Web Sites

The following World Wide Web sites have been carefully researched and selected to support the articles found in this reader. The easiest way to access these selected sites is to go to our DUSHKIN ONLINE support site at *http://www.dushkin.com/online/*.

AE: Social Psychology 05/06

The following sites were available at the time of publication. Visit our Web site—we update DUSHKIN ONLINE regularly to reflect any changes.

General Sources

Journals Related to Social Psychology
http://www.socialpsychology.org/journals.htm

Maintained by Wesleyan University, this site is a link to journals related to the study of psychology, social psychology, and sociology.

Social Psychology Network
http://www.socialpsychology.org

The Social Psychology Network is the most comprehensive source of social psychology information on the Internet, including resources, programs, and research.

Society of Experimental Social Psychology
http://www.sesp.org

SESP is a scientific organization dedicated to the advancement of social psychology.

UNIT 1: Research Issues

American Educational Research Association (AERA)
http://www.aera.net/

AERA is concerned with improving the educational process by encouraging scholarly inquiry related to education and by promoting the dissemination and practical application of research results.

Office of Science and Technology Policy (OSTP)
http://www.ostp.gov/

The National Science and Technology Council's Committee on Science provides advice and assistance to the National Science and Technology Council on significant science policy matters that cross federal agencies.

UNIT 2: The Self

FreudNet
http://www.psychoanalysis.org

FreudNet is part of the Abraham A. Brill Library of the New York Psychoanalytic Institute. This site provides information on mental health, Sigmund Freud, and psychoanalysis.

UNIT 3: Social Cognition and Social Perception

Cognitive and Psychological Sciences on the Internet
http://www-psych.stanford.edu/cogsci/

This site, maintained by Ruediger Oehlmann, is a detailed listing of cognitive psychology Web sites. Information on programs, organizations, journals, and groups is at this site.

Nonverbal Behavior and Nonverbal Communication
http://www3.usal.es/~nonverbal/

This fascinating site has a detailed listing of nonverbal behavior and nonverbal communication sites on the Web, including the work of historical and current researchers.

UNIT 4: Attitudes

Propaganda and Psychological Warfare Research Resource
http://ww2.lafayette.edu/~mcglonem/prop.html

This Web site provides links to sites that use propaganda to influence and change attitudes. At this site, you can link to contemporary fascist, political, religious, and Holocaust revisionist propaganda.

The Psychology of Cyberspace
http://www.rider.edu/users/suler/psycyber/psycyber.html

This site studies the psychological dimensions of environments created by computers and online networks.

UNIT 5: Social Influence

AFF Cult Group Information
http://www.csj.org

AFF's mission is to study psychological manipulation and cult groups, to assist those who have been adversely affected by a cult experience, and to educate.

Center for Leadership Studies
http://www.situational.com

The Center for Leadership Studies (CLS) is organized for the research and development of the full range of leadership in individuals, teams, organizations, and communities.

Social Influence Website
http://www.influenceatwork.com/

This Web site is devoted to social influence—the modern scientific study of persuasion, compliance, and propaganda.

UNIT 6: Social Relationships

American Association of University Women
http://www.aauw.org

The AAUW is a national organization that promotes education and equity for all women and girls.

Coalition for Marriage, Family, and Couples Education
http://www.smartmarriages.com

CMFCE is dedicated to bringing information about and directories of skill-based marriage education courses to the public. It hopes to lower the rate of family breakdown through couple-empowering preventive education.

GLAAD: Gay and Lesbian Alliance Against Defamation
http://www.glaad.org

GLAAD was formed in New York in 1985. Its mission is to improve the public's attitudes toward homosexuality and put an end to discrimination against lesbians and gay men.

www.dushkin.com/online/

The Kinsey Institute for Reasearch in Sex, Gender, and Reproduction
http://www.indiana.edu/~kinsey/

The purpose of the Kinsey Institute's Web site is to support interdisciplinary research and the study of human sexuality. The institute was founded by Dr. Alfred Kinsey, 1894–1956.

Marriage and Family Therapy
http://www.aamft.org/index_nm.asp

This site has links to numerous marriage and family therapy topics. Online directories, books and articles are also available.

The National Organization for Women (NOW) Home Page
http://www.now.org

NOW is the largest organization of feminist activists in the United States. It has 250,000 members and 600 chapters in all 50 states and the District of Columbia. NOW's goal has been "to take action" to bring about equality for all women.

The Society for the Scientific Study of Sexuality
http://www.ssc.wisc.edu/ssss/

The Society for the Scientific Study of Sexuality is an international organization dedicated to the advancement of knowledge about sexuality.

UNIT 7: Social Biases

NAACP Online: National Association for the Advancement of Colored People
http://www.naacp.org

The principal objective of the NAACP is to ensure the political, educational, social, and economic equality of minority group citizens in the United States.

National Civil Rights Museum
http://www.civilrightsmuseum.org

The National Civil Rights Museum, located at the Lorraine Motel, where Dr. Martin Luther King Jr. was assassinated April 4, 1968, is the world's first and only comprehensive overview of the civil rights movement in exhibit form.

United States Holocaust Memorial Museum
http://www.ushmm.org

The United States Holocaust Memorial Museum is America's national institution for the documentation, study, and interpretation of Holocaust history, and serves as this country's memorial to the millions of people murdered during the Holocaust.

Yahoo—Social Psychology
http://www.yahoo.com/Social_Science/Psychology/disciplines/social_psychology/

This link takes you to Yahoo!'s social psychology Web sites. Explore prejudice, discrimination, and stereotyping from this site.

UNIT 8: Violence and Aggression

MINCAVA: Minnesota Center Against Violence and Abuse
http://www.mincava.umn.edu

The Minnesota Center Against Violence and Abuse operates an electronic clearinghouse via the World Wide Web with access to thousands of Gopher servers, interactive discussion groups, newsgroups, and Web sites around the world. Its goal is to provide quick, user-friendly access to the extensive electronic resources on the topic of violence and abuse.

National Consortium on Violence Research
http://www.ncovr.heinz.cmu.edu/docs/data_mission.htm

The National Consortium on Violence Research is a newly established research and training institute that is dedicated to the scientific and advanced study of the factors contributing to interpersonal violence.

UNIT 9: Altruism, Helping and Cooperation

Americans With Disabilities Act Document Center
http://www.jan.wvu.edu/links/adalinks.htm

This Web site contains copies of the Americans With Disabilities Act of 1990 (ADA) and ADA regulations. This Web site also provides you with links to other Internet sources of information concerning disability issues.

Give Five
http://www.independentsector.org/give5/givefive.html

The Give Five Web site is a project of Independent Sector, a national coalition of foundations, voluntary organizations, and corporate giving programs working to encourage giving, volunteering, not-for-profit initiatives, and citizen action.

University of Maryland Diversity Database
http://www.inform.umd.edu/EdRes/Topic/Diversity/

The University of Maryland's Diversity Database is sponsored by the Diversity Initiative Program. It contains campus, local, national, and international academic material relating to age, class, disability, ethnicity, gender, national origin, race, religion, and sexual orientation.

UNIT 10: Group Processes

Center for the Study of Group Processes
http://www.uiowa.edu/~grpproc/

The mission of the Center for the Study of Group Processes includes promoting basic research in the field of group processes and enhancing the professional development of faculty and students in the field of group processes.

Collaborative Organizations
http://www.workteams.unt.edu

The Center for Collaborative Organizations is a nonprofit organization whose vision is to become the premier center for research on collaborative work systems to create learning partnerships that support the design, implementation, and development of collaborative work systems.

We highly recommend that you review our Web site for expanded information and our other product lines. We are continually updating and adding links to our Web site in order to offer you the most usable and useful information that will support and expand the value of your Annual Editions. You can reach us at: *http://www.dushkin.com/annualeditions/*.

UNIT 1

Research Issues

Unit Selections

1. **Stupid Human Tricks**, Ana Marie Cox
2. **Research Synthesis: Protection of Human Subjects of Research: Recent Developments and Future Prospects for the Social Sciences**, Eleanor Singer and Felice J. Levine

Key Points to Consider

- Have you ever participated in any research? What was the nature of the research (medical, educational, psychological, etc.)? Why did you choose to participate? Were you asked to sign a consent form? Did you guess the hypotheses? Were you informed after participation about the true nature of the research? Did the researcher influence you in any subtle or obvious ways? If you did not consent, why not?

- Do you think deception should be allowed in research? Why or why not? Do you think such deception can harm or can change an individual, especially if he or she is to participate in other projects? If you were on an institutional review board for human subjects, what types of research and research techniques would you allow? How could you measure whether the information learned offsets any detrimental effects of the research?

- Have you heard of past research that critics say did harm to participants? Can you describe the study and the results? Why was this research harmful or unethical? Would you allow the research again? Why? How would you alter the research to come into compliance with today's standards?

 **Links: www.dushkin.com/online/**
These sites are annotated in the World Wide Web pages.

American Educational Research Association (AERA)
http://www.aera.net/
Office of Science and Technology Policy (OSTP)
http://www.ostp.gov/

Social psychologists believe firmly in the scientific method. Interestingly, because of social psychology's breadth, the arsenal of research methods available to social psychologists is very broad, although controlled experiments remain highly respected. Interviews, questionnaires, observations, and analysis of historical data are just a few of the research techniques from which social psychologists choose. You should recognize, though, that these alternate methods are borrowed from a variety of related fields, including but not limited to anthropology, education, sociology, political science, and others. As you can see, social psychologists have many intellectual brothers and sisters outside their own field. Likewise, many of these siblings share a huge interest in the results and applications of social psychological research.

Research in social psychology has one or two primary purposes. One purpose is to confirm or disconfirm a theory and related hypotheses. The second purpose is to eventually apply results to practical solutions, especially for compelling social problems, be they school bullying, gang violence, student-teacher conflict, or marital strife.

In their scientific endeavors, social psychologists regularly collide with a multitude of problems, not the least of which is sheer human vagary. For example, some people do not wish to participate in psychological research. Others participate but are not especially cooperative when they do. Yet others are too young, too inexperienced, or too inarticulate to contribute. Finally, some participants may be busy guessing the researcher's hypothesis, which can drastically alter research results and subsequent interpretations.

Even the investigator can alter his or her own results. If a researcher knows in advance the hypothesis or theory, holds biases against certain groups, or possesses some unusual attribute (e.g. extraordinarily tall), the results might be compromised. In fact, research on research processes has demonstrated that the mere presence of a white lab coat or of ominous looking electrical equipment can skew results.

In addition, social psychologists eventually have to move from their laboratories to the "real" world, the world of everyday social interaction. Once any researcher heads outside the lab, she or he inevitably loses some essential control over events as well as participants. Such control is valued because by containing the influence of some factors (i.e. variables), the researcher can be more certain that other factors, and only those factors, account for the results. A rainy day in the park has ruined many an observational study due to lack of park attendees, while gaps in public records have spoiled many an archival study.

While the research design is of crucial importance, another pressing issue for social psychologists is to do no harm to those they investigate. Reviewing of research proposals by an institutional review board, obtaining a participant's *informed* consent, and debriefing them are part of the ethical principles of conducting human research.

Compared to other scientists, social psychologists frequently include deception in their research. Justifying the deception and ultimately revealing it to participants are paramount pieces of our ethical principles. In order to justify deception, researchers need to be able to demonstrate that the information gleaned far outweighs the damage any deception might generate.

The first article in this unit relates to just this issue—the ethics of deception. Several famous studies such as Asch's conformity studies, Milgram's obedience research, and Zimbardo's prison simulation are first reviewed. Then, author Mike Cardwell weighs the balance of the harm of deception against the advancement of our psychological knowledge.

The authors of the second article, Eleanor Singer and Felice Levine, discuss why the National Research Act was passed. This legislation established the requirement for review of *all* human research—especially medical and psychological investigations. The authors also attend to what the future holds for social and behavioral scientists given our history with this mandate.

Stupid Human Tricks

Ana Marie Cox

Even if you don't know the names of the scientists featured in Opening Skinner's Box, you've probably heard about their experiments—and not necessarily in school. Lauren Slater, a psychologist and the author of several memoirs, writes that her subjects "deserve to be not only reported on as research, but also celebrated as story." Popular culture, however, has already done that for her: many of the psychological experiments she discusses have had the contagious staying power of urban legends or ghost stories.

There's B. F. Skinner, of course, whose experiments with squirrels produced the theory of behaviorism. Skinner kept his squirrels in boxes equipped with levers, which they had to pull in order to get a treat. It seems like the simplest sort of stupid pet trick, but the experiments proved the extraordinary power of positive reinforcement. And their results influence our daily lives intimately, from the employee-of-the-month program at your grocery store to the gold stars on your child's homework. But Skinner went even further, turning his results into an ideology that considered autonomy and even emotion to be illusions. No wonder his work has spawned dark legends: Slater records a rumor that Skinner's daughter was kept in a box, grew up psychotic, and committed suicide in a bowling alley in Billings, Montana.

Other experiments in Opening Skinner's Box have entered popular culture on the strength of their internal grisliness or their tantalizingly dismal significance. Harry Harlow, for instance, is the scientist who built fake monkey mothers out of wire mesh, designed to test the limits of infantile attachment. And people who have never heard of Stanley Milgram know about his experiments, in which people agreed to torture strangers because a man in a lab coat told them to.

But this familiarity does not mean that Slater's book is redundant; she has uncovered stories within the stories we thought we knew. For instance, Skinner's daughter is actually alive and well—though she did spend time in an especially luxurious Skinner box. Slater even uncovers a playful streak in Skinner one wouldn't expect from the man who wanted "behavioral engineers" to manage everything from child rearing to global government. He used the techniques of behaviorism to teach his family's beagle to play hide-and-seek and the cat to play the piano (though probably not very well).

Even Slater's more obscure subjects turn out to have a surprising relevance. Shortly after the September 11 attacks, she looked into John Darley and Bibbe Latane's experiments on altruism—the likelihood that we will help a stranger or do something to prevent a crime. The altruism experiments were conducted in the wake of the infamous Kitty Genovese attack in 1964, in an attempt to explain how thirty-eight neighbors could have witnessed a brutal rape and murder and not done anything about it. The results were—and are—sobering. Presented with a stranger who appeared to be in the midst of an epileptic seizure, most people did nothing to help. The disinclination grew with the number of people witnessing the event, a phenomenon the researchers called "diffusion of responsibility." But the outpouring of generosity and concern after 9/11, Slater suggests, reminds us that psychological experiments-unlike experiments in, say, physics—do not reveal unalterable laws. They can help us understand our behavior, but they do not necessarily predict it.

Slater freely admits her intention to write about her experiments as stories, using the devices of fiction to color in spaces that lab notebooks leave bare. "He leaned way out on the window ledge and smelled squirrel," she writes of Skinner, "a musky odor of night and scat, of fur and flowers." Of Milgram's childhood she writes: "He grew into adolescence with this as his background music-bombs and burns—and meanwhile his body was doing its own detonations. How confusing: sex and terror." Beyond such literary flourishes, sometimes Slater's stories themselves have a novelistic depth and pattern. Take, for instance, the plot that springs forth from the life of psychologist Elizabeth Loftus, who demonstrated the astonishing and frightening ease with which people will accept fictional traumas as their own personal experience. Loftus's subjects came to believe, based solely on her suggestion, that they had been lost in a mall in childhood.

In a twist so neat it would make a Hollywood screenwriter blush, Slater discovers that, as a child, Loftus kept a fake diary designed to thwart her mother's attempts at spying. Loftus would write "acceptable" entries in the diary proper; events she wanted to keep secret she wrote on loose sheets that she attached with paper clips. She called these her "removable truths." No wonder Loftus grew up fascinated by the boundary between the imaginary and the real, "story truth and happening-truth. "

When Slater first conceived of Opening Skinner's Box, she writes, she intended to use these experiments to tell the story of psychology's evolution, from its roots in philosophy to its current alliance with medicine and pharmacology. But she discovered, to her surprise, that psychology has pretty much always spun like a dynamo between the poles of speculative thought and clinical science. In the early twentieth century, William James's metaphysical reflections about the mind were followed by Antonio Egas Moniz's invention of the lobotomy as a crudely physical way to manipulate the brain. (Slater attempts to understand the procedure's acceptance in the 1920s, if not exactly to defend it.) The 1960s saw both Milgram's existentialist parody of torture and Harlow's brutally tangible experiments on love. Today's research shows the same Janus face: Loftus pokes her fingers into the loose weave of our memories, even as the scientist Eric Kandel moves around the very molecules of which memory is made.

Yet I think there may be a thread running through Slater's stories, after all. As she moves toward the present, one cannot help noticing that commercial motivations loom larger and larger in psychological experiments. In the 1970s, Bruce Alexander lost funding for his whimsical experiment on the nature of addiction based on its "publicity failure." (Using a laboratory wonderland called "Rat Park," his research suggested that rats, and maybe even humans, prefer a natural high to a chemical one.) In 1990, Loftus began a high-profile career as an expert witness, thanks to the emergence of the recovered-memory industry and its head-line-grabbing trials. And in 1997, Kandel founded the for-profit company Memory Pharmaceuticals. He plans to market a cognition-enhancing pill (still in development)—not to Alzheimer's patients, but to "you and me, the bulk of the baby boomers who can't recall the location of their car keys, or that tip-of-the-tongue word."

Finally, however, it dawned on me that there was an even bigger moneymaking potential here. Almost all of Slater's experiments could succeed as reality television game shows—in fact, variations of them are already on the air. What could be more "Punk'd" than a hidden camera documenting neighbors' reactions to the staged murder of a stranger? And once Fear Factor begins to bore, wouldn't audiences lap up the sight of a celebrity turning the knobs in a glitzy version of Stanley Milgram's lab?

In fact, Slater makes a similar point, arguing that psychological experiments are themselves, after a fashion, entertainments: "There are similar aesthetic demands in terms of structure, pacing, revelation, lesson learned." But when experiments are nothing more than entertainment—when simply watching human beings do strange and painful things becomes an end in itself—it begins to feel as though we are not watching a test of human psychology, but tailing one.

Ana Marie Cox is the editor of Wonkette (www.wonkette.com). a daily Web journal covering Washington, D.C.

Research Synthesis

Protection of Human Subjects of Research: Recent Developments and Future Prospects for Future Prospects for the Social Sciences

ELEANOR SINGER and FELICE J. LEVINE

Introduction

The National Research Act of 1974 (P.L. 93-348, 88 Stat. 342, July 12, 1974) established the human research protections system to ensure the rights of human participants in biomedical and behavioral research. The act prompted the development of regulations that require colleges, universities, and other institutions receiving federal funds to establish institutional review boards (IRBs) to protect the rights of research volunteers. The legislation also created the National Commission for the Protection of Human Subjects of Biomedical and Behavioral Research and required this commission to identify principles underlying the ethical conduct of biomedical and behavioral research. The high-profile Belmont Report, published in 1979, was the key product of the commission's effort (National Commission for the Protection of the Human Subjects of Biomedical and Behavioral Research 1979).

As can be seen in the enabling legislation and the work of the National Commission, social and behavioral sciences research was from the outset part of the human subjects protection system. Although the system has been defined and dominated by biomedical and clinical concerns, for over 25 years it has included social and behavioral research within its domain. Despite the pervasive use of biomedical language, the Code of Federal Regulations for the Protection of Human Subjects—the well-known 45 CFR 46—is readily translatable to research involving human subjects in the social and behavioral sciences. (The code is available on line at http://www.med.umich.edu/irbmed/FederalDocuments/hhs/HHS45CFR46.html.)

Over time, IRBs have become more conversant with human research protection issues in the social sciences. During the past several years, however, the human research protection system has been under considerable stress. With much of that stress emanating from concerns about the adequacy of protections in biomedical and clinical areas, IRBs have increasingly tended to apply the rules from a biomedical and clinical perspective. This situation has worked to the detriment of assessing best ethical practices and is seen by some as unnecessarily burdening social and behavioral science research.

This article presents the contemporary situation in the context of this history. In recent years, national advisory bodies, federal agencies, and the U.S. Congress have attempted to address key concerns in the human subjects protection arena. Their work contains many similar themes and some novel approaches to improve the operation of the system. In this article, we provide an overview of the current actors and activities, as well as their recommendations. It is still too early to know whether these recommendations will be implemented and, if they are, how they will affect the conduct of social and behavioral science research. Nevertheless, we provide a snapshot and analysis of the current situation and the prospects that lie ahead.

Background

The current system of protection for human subjects of research can be traced to gross violations of subjects' rights by biomedical researchers, especially by German scientists during the Nazi era, but also by American scientists in the Tuskegee syphilis study (Faden and Beauchamp 1986; Katz 1972; Tuskegee Syphilis Study Ad Hoc Advisory Panel 1973). The Tuskegee study recruited poor black southern men with syphilis for a longitudinal study of the course of the disease. Begun at a time when no effective treatment for syphilis was available, it was continued by government scientists even after the discovery of penicillin, without informing subjects of the existence of a new and effective treatment. The U.S. government did not formally acknowledge responsibility for scientific misconduct or apologize to the victims until the Clinton administration did so in 1993, and the Tuskegee study has been a major reason for distrust of the government and the medical establishment on the part of African Americans.

Although these early violations of human rights occurred in biomedical studies, some social science research (e.g., research by Laud Humphreys [1970], the Milgram studies [1974], as well as other social psychological research involving deception) also aroused public concern about potential harm to subjects. All of these concerns led to the eventual codification and adoption of the Federal Regulations in 1974. In 1991, the various rules of 17 federal agencies were reconciled and integrated as Subpart A of 45 CFR 46—otherwise known as the Common Rule.

The Federal Regulations are based on the three ethical principles set forth in the Belmont Report (National Commission 1979): beneficence, respect for persons, and justice. The principle of beneficence gives rise to the requirement that the risk of harm to research subjects should be balanced by potential benefits. The principle of respect for persons gives rise to the requirement for informed consent, regardless of the risk of harm involved. The principle of justice asserts that the burdens of research should not fall unduly on any one class or group of persons.

Although the Federal Regulations for the Protection of Human Subjects specify the general procedures that must be followed, their application is left to the IRBs at the institutions that fund or carry out the research. The establishment of a human research protection system is mandated by the Federal Regulations as a condition for the institution's receiving federal funding for research. All research involving human subjects that receives federal funding from agencies that are signatories to the Common Rule must be reviewed by an IRB. In practice, however, research and educational institutions have increasingly required IRB review of almost all research involving human subjects, whether it is funded by the federal government or not.

This system for protecting human subjects is, in principle, subject to the oversight of the Office of Human Research Protections (OHRP), located in the Office of the Secretary of the Department of Health and Human Services (DHHS). Until June 2000, OHRP's functions were carried out by the Office for Protection from Research Risks (OPRR), located at the National Institutes of Health (NIH). The move in 2000 to DHHS and the appointment of a federal advisory committee signaled the administration's intent to give greater visibility and voice to human research protection issues.

Recent Causes for Attention and Concern

In the last several years, some highly visible failures of the system of human subjects protection have resulted in the deaths of several volunteers in clinical trials at well-known universities. These deaths and the ensuing public outrage and government shutdown of research at the universities involved (beginning in May of 1999) have placed the system under renewed and intense scrutiny by various government agencies and federal panels. Partly in response to these events, OHRP and IRBs have also increased their scrutiny of research protocols and the documentation they require from researchers.

Not only have IRBs begun to tighten their procedures, but these procedures also vary across institutions. Early evidence of such variability appears in a 25-year-old study of human subject review committees, as IRBs were then called, by Bradford Gray and his colleagues (1977, 1978). This variability does not appear to have been much reduced over time, according to a new survey of IRB practices by Bell, Whiton, and Connelly (1998), as well as informal anecdotes from researchers.

Operating in the shadow of troubled cases has led IRBs to become more absolute and literal in their interpretation and implementation of the federal regulations. As a result, the fault lines have widened between the intent of 45 CFR 46 "on the books" and how they are administered by IRBs in everyday practice. There is, by design, a great deal of flexibility in the regulations. Variability and flexibility of IRBs was intentionally built into the system in order to maximize the meaningful protection of research participants. The new hurdles risk interfering with the goals of science without adding protections for human subjects. While this is potentially the case for all areas of human research, these negative effects are particularly evident in the social and behavioral sciences, because the regulations, built on a biomedical model, do not always fit well with the requirements of research in the social and behavioral sciences.

Transcending the Biomedical Framework

The Federal Regulations were designed primarily with clinical medicine in mind. As a result, IRB members unfamiliar with the work of social and behavioral scientists often relied on a model that did not reflect an understanding of human research protection issues as they relate to different methodologies and contexts of research. A divergence in perspective between behavioral and biomedical scientists was documented in Gray's report 25 years ago. On a variety of measures used in Gray's study, for example, behavioral scientists who were members of review boards differed from their biomedical colleagues. They were twice as likely to approve of withholding information from subjects about the design or purpose of the study if this was likely to affect the validity of measurements; almost twice as likely to say that, in studies with little risk and no benefit, it was permissible to withhold from participants the fact that they were subjects; and more likely to agree that high-risk research of no direct benefit to subjects could be done if subjects were capable of giving consent. Behavioral scientists who were members of review boards were also less likely than biomedical members to disapprove of giving compensation to subjects to induce participation or compensate them for the risks to which they were exposed. Behavioral science investigators who were not members of review boards had the least favorable attitudes toward the performance of IRBs.

These differences in perspective do not reflect differences in ethical standards regarding the treatment of humans (indeed, there is considerable similarity in the ethical guidance specified across scientific fields that engage in human subjects research). Rather, they appear to reflect differences in the modes of inquiry in these sciences and in researchers' conception of the level and kinds of risk that they entail for human subjects. Research designed to clarify the reasons for these different perspectives could be used to illuminate the processes by which different parties—investigators, IRB members, the public at large, and patients with specific diseases—balance the various "goods" that come into play when ethical decisions involving human subjects have to be made.

Criticisms of the operation of the system of human subjects protection have come both from those who see the system as being insufficiently protective and from those who see it as unnecessarily hampering scientific goals without enhancing human subjects protection. This renewed scrutiny may be an opportunity for further improvements, even if the heightened attention thus far has produced more rigidity than reform. In the remainder of this article, we focus on some of the proposals and recommendations tendered by groups with varying perspectives on the issues involved.

Actors and Proposed Remedies

Federal Advisory Bodies

National Bioethics Advisory Commission. In October 1995, the National Bioethics Advisory Commission (NBAC) was established by Executive Order to identify principles for the ethical conduct of research and to provide advice and recommendations to the federal entities regarding bioethical issues in biological and behavioral research. Over a period of 6 years, NBAC produced a number of reports and recommendations, including *Ethical and Policy Issues in Research Involving Human Participants.* (National Bioethics Advisory Commission 2001), which was devoted to reviewing the oversight system as a whole. Among its many recommendations for improving the efficiency and effectiveness of the oversight system for human subjects were (1) the creation of a new independent oversight office that would have under its purview research sponsored and conducted by all federal agencies and private sector entities—both domestic and international; (2) the creation and implementation of a uniform set of regulations that would cover all government agencies, academic settings, and the private sector, while maintaining flexibility for application in a variety of research settings; (3) federal policies that ensure research ethics review is commensurate with the nature and level of risk in the study; (4) that at least 25 percent of the IRB membership be comprised of persons who represent the perspectives of participants, are unaffiliated with the institution, and whose primary concerns are nonscientific; (5) independent evaluation of the risks and potential benefits for each component of a study; (6) that federal policy distinguish minimal and more than minimal risk research and that minimal risk be defined as "the probability and magni-

tude of harms that are normally encountered in the daily lives of the general population"; (7) that federal policy emphasize the process of informed consent (rather than its documentation), the comprehension of such information, voluntary consent throughout the research process, and flexibility with respect to how informed consent is documented; and (8) that mechanisms be developed to equip investigators and institutions with tools to reduce threats to privacy and confidentiality.

Since NBAC issued its last report in 2001, its charter has expired. Any implementation of these recommendations lies in the hands of the U.S. Congress (see the section on federal legislation) and DHHS. Meanwhile, the recommendations have been widely disseminated, and institutions, local IRBs, and investigators are considering how to change the culture of the oversight system and its operation within the flexibility and limits allowed by law.

National Human Research Protections Advisory Committee. In the last year of NBAC's work, the secretary of the Department of Health and Human Services created a 17-member advisory committee whose goal was to provide advice and recommendations to the secretary, the assistant secretary for Health, the director of the Office for Human Research Protections, and other federal officials on a range of issues relating to the protection of human subjects in research. In February 2001, the National Human Research Protections Advisory Committee (NHRPAC) established a number of working groups, the very first of which was for the social and behavioral sciences. Over an 18-month period, the Social and Behavioral Sciences Working Group systematically addressed areas of concern to researchers in these fields, including confidentiality and research data protection, public use data files, third parties in research, informed consent, risk and harm, and student research. Three of the reports of this working group (regarding public use data files, third parties, and confidentiality) shaped the recommendations that NHRPAC forwarded to the secretary of DHHS. In the other areas, the working group's efforts are still under way. (See http://www.aera.net for updates on the working group's activities and copies of the completed reports.)

The report and recommendations on public use data files made clear to IRBs and others what public use data files are, that producers and suppliers of data sets are responsible for having them reviewed by IRBs before making them publicly available, and that, once something is certified as a public use data file, no additional review by IRBs should be required. Also, the recommendations addressed how IRBs can make the determination that data files can be classified as being for public use.

The controversial topic of third parties (persons referenced by human subjects in the course of their interaction with investigators) was taken up by two NHRPAC working groups. In the end, NHRPAC agreed to a one-page statement that makes clear that the determination of who is a research subject rests with the IRB; third parties who are referenced in research are not necessarily considered human subjects; third parties may become human subjects if they can be identified and if the IRB, through careful analysis of a number of factors, determines that the focus of the research is really on the third party and not on (or not only on) the originally designated human subject. The recommendations clarify that the requirement of consent, or waiver of consent, pertains only to human subjects and not to third parties unless IRBs determine that these third parties are subjects as well.

Finally, the NHRPAC report on confidentiality and research data protection also grew out of the Social and Behavioral Sciences Working Group. It aimed to (1) convey to IRBs that the degree of confidentiality protection required in research should be commensurate with the degree of risk, while allowing a good data protection plan to reduce or eliminate the risk; (2) encourage OHRP to examine existing confidentiality protections in certificates of confidentiality offered by federal agencies and in various statutes; (3) encourage OHRP to provide guidance to IRBs and investigators regarding limitations in confidentiality protections and how this information can be conveyed effectively during the consent process; (4) emphasize the research institution's role in supporting investigators' attempts to protect confidential information from compelled disclosure; and (5) clarify for IRBs and investigators that, when identifiable data are shared between investigators, the original confidentiality protections are transferred with the data.

As in other areas where NHRPAC has offered recommendations, NHRPAC submitted all three reports to the DHHS. The Office of Human Research Protections may or may not choose to act on the recommendations in issuing guidance for IRBs and investigators. The next steps remain with OHRP. At the time of this writing, OHRP has been working on the issue of third parties, and it is expected to release proposed draft guidance for public comment soon. In August 2002, the administration allowed NHRPAC's charter to expire. The possible elimination of the only federal advisory committee for the protection of human subjects was covered in the media and was the subject of a letter from Senators Edward Kennedy (D-MA) and Hillary Clinton (D-NY) to DHHS Secretary Tommy Thompson. Scientific societies and organizations also weighed in with their concerns about the demise of NHRPAC. In particular, the Consortium of Social Science Associations and the Federation of Behavioral, Psychological, and Cognitive Sciences wrote Secretary Thompson specifically calling for the reestablishment of such a committee and the presence of social and behavioral scientists on it.

During September 2002, the Department of Health and Human Services signaled its intent to create another scientific advisory body with a broader charge to address human subjects protection issues. While Secretary Thompson signed off on a charter to establish the Secretary's Advisory Committee on Human Research Protections (SACHRP) on October 1, news of it did not become public until the end of that month. The SACHRP charter is at once broader in scope, yet much more specific, than NHRPAC's in terms of topics of emphasis and responsibility for reviewing the ongoing work of OHRP. The highest profile change—with considerable potential for politicizing the committee—is the inclusion of embryos within the scope of a committee otherwise charged with advising on human research subjects.

By mid-January 2003, Secretary Thompson completed making appointments to this committee. With 11 members, SACHRP is smaller in size than NHRPAC. The final composition includes two persons who had previously served on NHRPAC. Efforts of social and behavioral science societies to ensure the appointment of members of these disciplines may have helped to shape the final configuration. The committee includes developmental psychologist Celia Fisher, who is a professor at Fordham University and director of its Center for Ethics Education, as well as Susan Weiner, president and founder of Children's Cause, who is trained in developmental psychology. It is far too early to know what role this committee will play or whether it will reconstitute working groups to help expand its capacity for input and work. Despite the end of NHRPAC, the Social and Behavioral Science Working Group decided to continue operating as an independent body in September 2002. After a meeting in late October to take stock and plan an agenda of work, the working group moved ahead with a number of activities, including identifying persistent gaps in the oversight system, further piloting a "model" human subjects protection course for the social and behavioral sciences, completing work on previously identified critical issues, and initiating consideration of new but unaddressed topics (e.g., ethnographic and qualitative research and research in educational settings). Perhaps most important, the working group will convene a workshop and prepare a compendium of "best practices" by IRBs in an effort to improve the operation of the human research protection system. In addition to executing its agenda of work through 2003, the group also aims during this period to facilitate consideration of how best to assure an ongoing presence for the social and behavioral sciences on human research protections issues. Felice Levine, Executive Director of the American Educational Research Association and co-author of this article, will continue to chair the working group and oversee its activities. In February 2003, Celia Fisher accepted an invitation to join this group.

The Institute of Medicine (IOM) reports. Since December 2000, the Institute of Medicine has produced three reports aimed at improving the human subjects protections system and the overall environment in which research is conducted. Two reports grew out of a request from the DHHS's Office of Human Research Protections (with support provided by five DHHS agencies and the Greenwall Foundation) and were focused on the oversight system for human research protections. A third report, not discussed in detail here, was developed in response to a request from DHHS's Office of Research Integrity and aimed to address more broadly issues of research integrity and responsible conduct in science. That report, titled *Integrity in Scientific Research: Creating an Environment that Promotes Responsible Conduct*, was issued in July 2002 (Institute of Medicine 2002a) and contained initiatives to enhance integrity that could be administered by the research institution. A key conclusion was that implementing policies and procedures is necessary but not sufficient to ensure integrity in research. The committee suggested institutional self-assessment as one promising avenue for evaluating and promoting the responsible conduct of research, and it recommended that institutional self-assessment of research integrity be included in the accreditation process.

The findings of each of the other two reports are described briefly below.

"Preserving Public Trust: Accreditation and Human Research Participant Protection Program." The IOM was asked

to "review and consider proposed performance standards, recommend standards for accreditation, and recommend an approach to monitoring and evaluating the system." Its first report (Institute of Medicine 2001) dealt primarily with possible accreditation of human research review systems as a way of assuring the quality of the review process. The committee reviewed draft standards developed independently by Public Responsibility in Medicine and Research (PRIM&R) and the National Committee for Quality Assurance (NCCQA), which is under contract to the U.S. Department of Veteran Affairs (VA). The committee concluded that the standards proposed by NCQA for VA facilities appeared promising for pilot testing in the accreditation of IRBs not only at VA institutions but also, with modification, for the accreditation of IRBs elsewhere. The committee therefore recommended that pilot accreditation programs start with the NCQA standards but that they strengthen them in several ways, including addressing "how investigators will be reviewed … how sponsors will be assessed; how participants will be involved in setting performance standards; and how oversight mechanisms can ensure participants' safety" ("Executive Summary" of Institute of Medicine 2001, p. 2). It recommended that the organizations doing the accreditation be independent, nongovernmental organizations and that participants be involved in all aspects of the process.

The committee acknowledged the daunting nature of its task in two respects. First, many institutions performing research with humans are not primarily engaged in clinical research, yet the standards have clearly been formulated with medical research in mind. Second, the accreditation system, in IOM's view, must cover all types of research organizations, yet a large fraction of clinical research is privately sponsored and conducted outside traditional medical research institutions. As the committee notes, "failure to include privately sponsored research … would not only exclude a significant fraction of research with humans but would also call into question whether the accreditation process was skewed in favor of academic health centers" (Institute of Medicine 2001, p. 7).

From the perspective of the behavioral sciences, one feature of the IOM document on accreditation is of particular interest. Recommendation 6 notes that, although accreditation standards should start from federal regulations for protecting human research participants, they should seek to augment those regulations. This conflicts with the view taken by another panel, also constituted by the National Academy of Sciences, which argues that the federal regulations provide an adequate basis for protecting human subjects and that IRBs should not seek to go beyond them.

"Responsible Research: A Systems Approach to Protecting Research Participants." The IOM committee's second report was released in October 2002 (Institute of Medicine 2002b). While acknowledging the absence of good information about the extent of harm to human participants in research and stressing the need to collect such data, the report nevertheless concludes that "there is abundant evidence of significant strains and weakness in the current system, and this committee has reached the conclusion that major reforms are in order" (p. 4). Although in his preface, Committee Chairman Daniel Federman stated that the committee does not urge "a permanent accretion of new regulations and bureaucracy" (p. ix) and recommends that the proposed new system be reexamined when better data are in hand, that clearly remains an aspiration rather than a prescription.

A number of the committee's recommendations would, if carried out, have major impact on the conduct of research in this country. First, the committee recommends that all research be "subject to a responsible Human Research Participant Protection Program (HRPPP) under federal oversight" and that Congress should enact legislation to assure this (Institute of Medicine 2002b, p. 6). Potentially, this would include not only scientific research carried out under government and private sponsorship but also market and commercial research of all kinds. Second, it recommends a major refocusing of the informed consent process to assure better comprehension by participants and to move away from legalistic documentation of consent that primarily protects institutions. Third, it envisions much broader participation by research participants in all phases of the review process, including research design and operation. It proposes that a certain proportion of IRB members be composed of participants and that decisions be reached by "consensus." Fourth, it recommends better safety monitoring, including continual review and monitoring of risk-prone studies, and it also recommends "reasonable" financial compensation "in legitimate instances of research harm."

The committee recognizes that not all research is high-risk research, and it recommends "federal intervention and guidance" in developing a consistent and rational system for classifying research at varying levels of risk. This recommendation, however, is not very specific, and its recognition of varying levels of research risk is not well reflected in the rest of the committee's recommendations, which appear to be aimed primarily at high-risk clinical research.

Panel on Institutional Review Boards, Surveys, and Social Science Research. The Institute of Medicine committee had only two social scientists (one a biostatistician and one a psychologist) among its 11 members, together with five expert advisers and four "liaisons." To try to ensure that the special circumstances and concerns of social and behavioral science research would not go unrecognized, the National Research Council (NRC; part of the National Academy of Sciences) appointed a "sister panel" to the IOM committee to specifically address these concerns. The panel's preliminary letter report is included as appendix B of the IOM report, *Responsible Research,* and the panel is completing its final report as this article is being written. Despite the shared concerns of both groups, there are ways in which their emphases differ. Whereas the IOM committee's chief focus was on improving the oversight system to protect subjects in high-risk clinical research from harm, the chief aim of the NRC panel might be described as identifying ways in which minimal risk research can proceed without burdensome regulation. Despite these differences, however, the NAS panel shares certain specific recommendations with the IOM committee. Like that committee, it urges a better definition of research involving minimal risk and thus eligible for expedited review. Like the IOM committee, it urges less attention to the formal documentation of informed consent and greater emphasis on how to improve comprehension. Also like the IOM committee, it recommends continuing research to study the actual operation of the system for the protection of human subjects.

The NAS panel differs fundamentally from the IOM Committee in its image of what the most pervasive, and most harmful, risks emerging from social and behavioral research are likely to be. Unlike clinical research, which at times involves the risk of physical injury and even death as a direct result of a research intervention, the most severe harms likely to befall subjects in social science research arise from potential breaches of the confidentiality of the data collected. Thus, for example, loss of job, criminal prosecution, and public humiliation are all potential consequences of revealing damaging information that a research subject has disclosed to an investigator. In light of this fact, the panel recommends ongoing research on ways to protect the confidentiality of data, as well as the dissemination of principles of "best practices" to researchers. Unlike the IOM committee, as already noted, the NAS panel sees the current system of regulations as adequate to the task of protecting human subjects, but it recommends more guidance from OHRP in the uniform application of these regulations by local IRBs and more use of the provisions for exempting certain categories of research from review and for modifying or waiving requirements for obtaining or documenting informed consent. The divergences between the two sets of recommendations can best be understood in light of the different images of research risks that underlie them.

Federal Government

Office of Science and Technology Policy's National Science and Technology Council. The National Science and Technology Council's Committee on Science provides advice and assistance to the National Science and Technology Council on significant science policy matters that cross federal agencies. Its work is accomplished through a number of interagency subcommittees and work groups, including the Human Subjects Research Subcommittee (HSRS). Of special interest to the *Public Opinion Quarterly* audience is the work of the HSRS Non-Biomedical Working Group. The principal activities of this working group have centered on developing a web-based decision tree to guide investigators who conduct human subjects research, creating a public use data files document based largely upon the recommendations of NHRPAC, and developing a document on participant confidentiality. Given the interagency nature of the working group and its parent groups, any recommendations for changes or clarification in the human subjects protections system are likely to carry a great deal of weight. Although the suggested guidance is not yet public, the recommendations build upon many of those made by NHRPAC and its Social and Behavioral Sciences Working Group, and any guidance that results will be posted on the individual web sites of the 17 departments, agencies, and offices that adopted the Common Rule and make up the HSRS. For updates, refer to http://www.ostp.gov.

The National Science Foundation. In June 2001, the National Science Foundation (NSF) began to address the rapid changes in the human subjects protections system. The Directorate for Social, Behavioral, and Economic Sciences convened a group of social and behavioral scientists from universities across the country to discuss the changes in the human subjects protections system, efforts under way to bring all research under the DHHS umbrella, the use of the biomedical/clinical model in reviewing social and behavioral science research, and the resulting impact on numerous federally funded research programs. The aim of the workshop was to produce guidance for NSF funded social and behavioral science investigators regarding the flexibility that exists in the Common Rule. The National Science Foundation has created a web site, http://www.nsf.gov/bfa/cpo/policy/hsfaqs.htm, to provide such guidance and will be revising this periodically.

Congressional initiatives. Some of the recommendations reviewed in the preceding section clearly have legislative implications. In fact, two pieces of legislation were introduced in the last Congress, one in the House of Representatives and the other in the Senate. Although they are, of course, likely to undergo change, their provisions are briefly reviewed here. "A Bill to Amend the Public Health Service Act with Respect to the Protection of Human Subjects in Research" ("Human Research Subject Protections Act of 2002"), or HR 4697, was introduced by Representatives Diana DeGette (D-CO) and James Greenwood (R-PA) on May 9, 2002. It contains the following major provisions:

- It would make human subjects in all clinical research subject to the Common Rule.
- It would require giving a written copy of the documentation of consent to every participant, as well as a written explanation of the elements of consent, but would not require written consent in all circumstances.
- It would require that 20 percent of the members of an IRB be nonscientists, and 20 percent be unaffiliated with the institution.
- If the proposal includes vulnerable populations or minority groups, members of these groups must participate as voting members of the IRB.
- The bill would exempt research involving written records, even if these contain identifiable information.
- Although the bill refers to high-risk research, it does not clearly distinguish levels of risk in its provisions.

The full text of the "Human Research Subject Protections Act of 2002" for the second session of the 107th Congress (H.R. 4697) is available through the Library of Congress on line at http://thomas.loc.gov. Given that there is now a new Congress, this bill will have to be reintroduced.

The "Research Revitalization Act of 2002," or S. 3060, was introduced in the U.S. Senate by Senator Edward Kennedy on October 7, 2002. Its aims are to provide a comprehensive set of protections for human participants in research, promote effective oversight of such research, prevent financial conflicts of interest by those conducting or overseeing research, require that all IRBs be accredited, and provide oversight for research conducted outside the United States but subject to the regulatory authority of the United States. To accomplish these aims, the bill:

- further codifies the DHHS Office of Human Research Protections;

- makes the Common Rule, and other subparts of 45 CFR 46, the basis for regulating participation in research;
- includes all research involving human participants;
- allows the director of OHRP to promulgate regulations (after consulting with specified entities) that amend the Common Rule, and specifically authorizes him to define whether research is covered research and whether covered research involves greater than minimal risk;
- finds that much, though not all, of social science research, as well a other specified categories of research, involves minimal risk and is therefore entitled to administrative review;
- authorizes the OHRP director to require Data Safety Monitoring Boards for all research deemed to involve greater than minimal risk;
- requires the director to promulgate rules for paying incentives to participants, and would require IRBs to consider compliance with these rules;
- requires IRBs at all institutions that conduct "covered" research to review all research involving human participants, and would require accreditation of such IRBs;
- allows institutions to recover the costs of complying with human subjects protections as direct costs; and
- allocates funds for research into, and improvement of, such protections.

The bill contains many other provisions, for example, those dealing with financial conflicts of interest, multisite reviews, and international oversight, but those listed above are of most relevance for social scientists and public opinion researchers. The full text of the "Research Revitalization Act of 2002" for the second session of the 107th Congress (S. 3060) is available through the Library of Congress on line at `http://thomas.loc.gov`. This bill also will need to be reintroduced.

Emerging Organizations

One organization that has the potential to influence the field significantly is the relatively new Association for the Accreditation of Human Research Protection Programs (AAHRPP). After a long development period, it was formally established in Spring 2001 by seven nonprofit organizations representing the full spectrum of educational and research societies, including the Consortium of Social Science Associations. The AAHRPP aims to advance research consistent with the best human research protection practices by supporting a voluntary program of self-assessment, confidential peer review, and education. The first executive director, Marjorie Speers, is trained in psychology as well as epidemiology, and she brings to the task a strong appreciation of the research and ethical aspects of the social and behavioral sciences.

As a creation of the research, education, and human research protection communities, AAHRPP is likely to become central to research institutions' own efforts to promote the best practices for protecting research volunteers. Of importance to social and behavioral science researchers, three social scientists sit on the 21-member board of directors. In addition, AAHRPP's

Council on Accreditation is made up of an equal number of social and biomedical scientists, and social scientists are represented on site visit teams when an entity conducts and reviews proposals from these areas. Finally, the accreditation standards were developed to apply to different types of research, including clinical, social and behavioral sciences, law, business, and the humanities.

The organization is committed to examining closely those issues of concern to the social and behavioral sciences, including the composition of IRBs, informed consent processes and documentation, analysis of risks and potential benefits, confidentiality protections, and determination of exempt categories of research. With encouragement and engagement from the social and behavioral sciences, AAHRPP can be an important contributor to improving human research protection nationally as well as at the local level.

The Shape of Things to Come

With actors changing and with new and emerging groups coming on the scene, the "crystal ball" is far from clear. However, unless some changes currently under way radically alter the direction in which the human subjects protection system is moving, we see several developments that are likely to affect the current system and how researchers relate to it.

First, the move toward accrediting all elements of an institution's human subjects protection system, including institutional review boards, is likely to accelerate. While accreditation is being introduced slowly and on a voluntary basis, it is likely to become more pervasive, if not mandatory. In that case, it will be important for AAHRPP or other such entities to resist a "one-size-fits-all" uniformity in the application of human subjects regulations.

Second, the likelihood that additional legislation bearing on the human subjects protection system will be passed by Congress in the next year or two also implies greater national uniformity in the system. The challenge is to prevent national standards from compromising the flexibility and discretion now permissible under 45 CFR 46. The fact that the Kennedy bill would allow institutions to recover the costs of complying with human subjects protections as direct costs may also spur a movement toward standardization and bureaucratization, with the potential for increasing the time and burden involved in the process. The goal, of course, is to avoid the fault lines that have come with great variability in practices, while permitting appropriate translation of the Federal Regulations for the Protection of Human Subjects to different research contexts.

Third, a feature of virtually all the proposals currently on the table is a call for greater involvement by participants in all phases of the research, including its design and oversight. Social scientists have even less experience with such a requirement than do biomedical researchers, and providing for meaningful participant involvement is likely to pose a challenge to the conduct of social and behavioral research. The social and behavioral science community must consider how best to introduce public members to the ethical dimensions of different research methods and subjects of inquiry. This topic is important from the vantage of both research and professional responsibility.

Finally, there are a number of areas where the protection of human participants would benefit from empirical research. In the social and behavioral sciences, for example, such research is clearly needed to help resolve the tension between giving researchers greater access to data collected by others and protecting the confidentiality of those providing the data. Research is also needed into the informed consent process. How can subjects be given enough information to permit an informed choice about participation, without at the same time creating undue fear or concern? How can information about confidentiality protections, for example, be communicated without arousing greater concern about disclosure? How can researchers assure that such information is actually understood by participants? Another area that would benefit greatly from research attention is the perception of risk and harm. At present, IRBs tend to make judgments about the risks, harms, and benefits of research on the basis of their own experience. Almost nothing is known about how these are actually viewed by participants. The Kennedy bill would allocate funds for research into, and improvement of, human subjects protection. Some government agencies, such as the National Institutes of Health, are already investing funds in such research. Social and behavioral researchers should become much more active in this process than they currently are.

In addition to these potential developments, which are likely to affect all social and behavioral research, different areas face specialized problems. For market and commercial researchers, for example, the big issue is likely to be whether or not their activities will fall under the revamped human subjects protection system, and if so, how their operations can best be accommodated to the requirements of such a system. For government agencies, the big issue is likely to be the tension between access to data and confidentiality protection, and the development of methods to further both of these goals. For academics, the big issues are likely to involve informed consent—how best to obtain it and from whom it must be obtained (e.g., the potential classification of "third parties" as human subjects).

As we have already indicated above, many changes are under way in the human subjects protection system. The IOM panel completed its work and made numerous recommendations to improve the oversight system. The Panel on Institutional Review Boards, Surveys, and Social Science Research is completing its final report. NHRPAC's charter expired in August 2002, but by January 2003, SACHRP had been launched. A number of NBAC's recommendations have surfaced in proposed federal legislation, but any final bill remains for a future session of Congress. DHHS/OHRP may choose to act on any of the multitude of recommendations coming out of NHRPAC, NBAC, IOM, or the Panel on IRBs, but, given the administration's interest in wholesale overhaul of several scientific advisory committees, it is uncertain whether OHRP will be given the authority to act or otherwise would do so. Adding to the un-

certainty is the resignation on November 30, 2002, of the first director of OHRP, Greg Koski, and the apppointment on January 31, 2003 of Bernard Schwetz as interim director. With Schwetz just starting and SACHRP not yet convened at the time of this writing, there are many unknowns about how OHRP will operate and what role the new advisory body will play.

Despite these ambiguities in the current climate, there are opportunities for progress. The very fact that groups are being convened to address the issue of human research protection that would be more attentive to social and behavioral sciences research is an indicator of progress. Also, much more discussion is occurring among individual researchers on campuses, at research institutes and organizations, and at research society meetings, both about the human subjects protection system and about ethical considerations in the conduct of human research more generally. Even in an environment that is in flux, developments over the past 2 years may bring better protection for research subjects, as well as more flexibility in the procedures followed by researchers.

References

Bell, J., J. Whiton, and S. Connelly. 1998. *Evaluation of NIH Implementation of Section 491 of the Public Health Service Act, Mandating a Program of Protection for Research Subjects.* Report prepared under NIH contract N01-OD-2-2109. Washington, DC: U.S. Department of Health and Human Services.

Faden, R. R., and T. L. Beauchamp. 1986. *A History and Theory of Informed Consent.* New York: Oxford University Press.

Gray, B. H., R. A. Cooke, and A. S. Tannenbaum. 1978. "Research Involving Human Subjects." *Science* 201:1094–1101.

Gray, B. H., R. A. Cooke, A. S. Tannenbaum, and D. H. McCulloch. 1977. "Research Involving Human Subjects: An Empirical Report on Human Subjects Review Committees." Paper presented at the annual meeting of the American Sociological Association, Chicago.

Humphreys, L. 1970. *Tearoom Trade: Impersonal Sex in Public Places.* Chicago: Aldine.

Institute of Medicine. 2001. *Preserving Public Trust: Accreditation and Human Research Participant Protection Programs.* Washington, DC: National Academy.

———. 2002a. *Integrity in Scientific Research: Creating an Environment That Promotes Responsible Conduct.* Washington, DC: National Academy.

———. 2002b. *Responsible Research: A Systems Approach to Protecting Research Participants.* Washington, DC: National Academy.

Katz, J. *Experimenting with Human Beings.* 1972. New York: Sage.

Milgram, S. 1974. *Obedience to Authority: An Experimental View.* New York: Harper & Row.

National Bioethics Advisory Commission. 2001. *Ethical and Policy Issues in Research Involving Human Participants.* Vol. 1, *Report and Recommendations.* Bethesda, MD: Advisory Commission.

National Commission for the Protection of Human Subjects of Biomedical and Behavioral Research (National Commission). 1979. *Belmont Report: Ethical Principles and Guidelines for the Protection of Human Subjects of Research.* Washington, DC: U.S. Government Printing Office.

Tuskegee Syphilis Study Ad Hoc Advisory Panel. 1973. *Final Report.* Washington, DC: U.S. Department of Health, Education, and Welfare.

UNIT 2
The Self

Unit Selections

3. **Something From Nothing: Seeking a Sense of Self**, Lance Strate
4. **Self-Concordance and Subjective Well-Being in Four Cultures**, Kennon M. Sheldon et. al.
5. **Making Sense of Self-Esteem**, Mark R. Leary
6. **Why We Overestimate Our Competence**, Tori DeAngelis

Key Points to Consider

- How do you know you possess a self-concept? Do you recall childhood experiences, or even recent incidents, that have had a formative impact on your self-concept? What is your earliest memory of your having interacted with someone else? Do you think self-concept is ever-evolving or rather stable over a lifetime?

- Do you think animals have a sense of self? Is it possible that a baby is born with a self-concept? How so? What role do you think language plays in the development of self-concept? In self-esteem?

- What do you know about autism? Can you imagine what it would be like to be autistic? Can you conceive of life without a self-concept?

- How does culture impact self-concept? Self-esteem? Have you ever visited other cultures where people's sense of self was quite different from your own? Do you agree that self-concordance is a universal human value? When people diverge from their personal values and opinions, why do they do so? What are their motives? How do people who deviate from personal principles justify their actions?

- What is self-esteem; how does it differ from self-concept? What other aspects of self-concept are important besides self-esteem? From where does self-esteem come? Does a sense of self or self-esteem serve an evolutionary function?

- Why are some people so arrogant and other so self-deprecating? Do you think their childhoods differed significantly? How so? Why do some people overestimate their capabilities? When is overestimation dangerous? Is underestimation also hazardous?

 **Links: www.dushkin.com/online/**
These sites are annotated in the World Wide Web pages.

FreudNet
http://www.psychoanalysis.org

Joaquin looks at himself in the mirror. He is 14 years old. His parents were divorced when he was a baby. As he stares into the mirror, he wonders if he is handsome, will he ever marry, and will he make a good father? He assures himself that his new girlfriend really likes him, although they are both young.

Have you ever pondered yourself in the mirror? Do you wonder how you stack up compared to other college students? Are you smarter? Better looking? More successful? Babies cannot and do not ask themselves these questions.

Philosophizing about oneself appears to be quintessentially human. Other animals high on the evolutionary scale may recognize their own self-images and be able to communicate with others of their own specie. They do not appear, however, to experience existential crises and self-doubts as do humans. Neither are they egotistical nor their psyches as fragile as ours.

From where do our questions about ourselves come? Better yet, where does self-concept, itself, originate? Both psychologists and sociologists have examined these issues and have pronounced that our sense of self—our self-concept—develops by means of interaction with oth-ers. Our parents and significant others, such as teachers, play an especially important role in this development.

Scientists believe that it is through *reflected appraisal* from others that we form our own self-impressions. Reflected appraisal means that we detect others' reactions to us in their faces, mannerisms and comments and, thus, begin to incorporate these mirrored evaluations into our own self-concepts. Here's an example: if as a child Joaquin repeatedly spilled his milk and his mother frequently labeled him "clumsy," Joaquin would probably think of himself as clumsy, in spite of his gracefulness and athleticism on the basketball court.

Self-concept, then, is probably established at an early age, but as many social psychologists hypothesize, the perception of the self can be modified by experience. Suppose that in late adolescence Joaquin is accepted to college, participates in intramural basketball, and the head coach seated in the grandstand takes notice. After Joaquin tries out for the varsity team and is accepted and becomes the team's star in his senior year, Joaquin may well begin to think of himself as anything but clumsy.

Besides significant others, the culture in which we are reared also plays a powerful role in the promulgation of self-concept. For example, some individuals live in collective cultures, where the goals of others take precedence over the advancement of the individual. On the other hand, in individualistic societies, individual achievement regularly occurs at the expense of others or at least ahead of others' wants and needs. Individualism versus collectivism is but one way in which cultures differ and hence affect the development of self-concept.

There are many aspects or components of self-concept, including but not limited to *ideal self* (the self we'd like to be), the *real self* (the self we think we are), and the *negative self* (aspects of the self which you would like to change). Perhaps the most important facet of self-concept, though, is *self-esteem.* Self-esteem, briefly, is your feeling of self-worth. Some individuals have high esteem, now and then to the point of overconfidence; others have low self-esteem, which can lead to depression, even suicide.

In this second unit, the articles presented offer information on the self-concept and self-esteem. The first article, "Something from Nothing," is an introspective essay about the sense of self and some of the theories about its development. The article also provides a poignant example of the lack of self-concept in autistic children and clarifies the reasons for their aloneness, lack of self-identity, and inability to communicate with others.

In "Self-Concordance and Subjective Well-Being in Four Cultures," the authors investigate how committed to one's personal values and interests individuals in various cultures are. (Some of these cultures are collective and others are individualistic as described above.) Despite a few assorted differences, the authors conclude that self-concordance ("be true to thyself") must be a universal human value.

In "Making Sense of Self-Esteem," psychologist Mark Leary proposes that self and self-esteem evolved to help us understand others' valuation of us. We need to know how others appraise us so that we can adjust our self-concept and avoid rejection, the latter of which would be disastrous, evolutionarily speaking (i.e. safety in numbers). In a companion article, Tori DeAngelis, writing for the *Monitor on Psychology,* suggests that we have a self-protective mechanism which inspires us to overestimate our own competence. In some instances, as in the case of new doctors' over-confidence, misjudgments and miscalculations can be lethal.

Something from Nothing

Seeking a sense of self.

by Lance Strate

THE TOPIC I wish to take up here is the relationship between communication and the sense of self. In doing so, I intend to communicate to you a little bit about myself, and will thereby run the risk of narcissism. At the same time, I will run the risk of echolalia, as most of what I have to say is merely a repetition of what has been said before. And I want to begin by echoing a story taken from a children's book by Phoebe Gilman entitled *Something From Nothing* (1992), a book that my son Benjamin and I enjoy reading together. The text is itself an echo, as it is adapted from a Jewish folk tale, and I in turn will adapt and paraphrase Gilman's story.

It is about a tailor who made his newborn grandson a wonderful blanket out of some rare and beautiful material. Joseph, his grandson, loved that blanket, but as time passed and the blanket got worn and frazzled, his mother wanted to throw it out. But Joseph took it to his grandfather, who said, "There's just enough material here to make a wonderful jacket." When, in time, Joseph outgrew the jacket and his mother wanted to throw it out, he took it to his grandfather, who said, "There's just enough material here to make a wonderful vest." When the vest grew old, and his mother wanted to throw it out he took it to his grandfather, who said, "There's just enough material here to make a wonderful tie." The tie in turn became worn and stained, and Joseph's mother wanted to throw it out, but he again took it to his grandfather, who said, "There's just enough material here to make a wonderful handkerchief." But over time the handkerchief grew dirty and tattered, and his mother said, now, finally, it's time to

throw it out. But Joseph believed in his grandpa, and brought it to him, and his grandfather said, "There's just enough material here to make a wonderful button." But one day Joseph lost the button. Distraught, he ran to his grandfather's house. His mother, running after him said, "Joseph! Even your grandfather can't make something from nothing," and his grandfather sadly agreed. The next day Joseph went to school, where he put pen to paper, and said, "There's just enough material here to make a wonderful story."

The theme of material is a natural one for a writer and artist like Gilman, who used a folk tale as source material for a wonderful children's book. For my part, I am using *Something for Nothing* (1992) as material for this essay. Material is a concern for anyone engaged in acts of creation and communication: public speakers need material for their speeches, stand-up comics need material to get their laughs, teachers need material for their classes.

The humor of Gilman's story revolves around the double meaning of the word material. On the one hand, it refers to physical substance, on the other to communication content. This pun is part of a larger metaphor through which communication is compared to cloth, tale-tellers are linked to tailors, and text is turned into textile. Across various cultures, stories are woven like fabric, yarns are spun, accounts embroidered, and falsehoods are manufactured out of whole cloth. The thrust of this ancient motif, in Gilman's folk tale and elsewhere, is to ground the abstract concept of communication in the concreteness of the human life-world. It reminds us that

both form and information are rooted in physical matter.

We therefore should not forget that even the social construction of reality requires raw materials, and that common sense and scientific knowledge alike are rooted in our physical existence; they are not simply a result of political decision-making. Spiritual approaches to communication need to take this into account as well. After all, the theologians tell us that only God creates ex nihlo, out of absolutely nothing. All the rest of us have to make do with the materials at hand.

I believe that an understanding of the materiality of communication leads naturally to the study of media, and to Marshall McLuhan's (1964) famous maxim, "the medium is the message" (p.7). For what is the common denominator that links medium and message, but material? The material is the message; it is the material that communicators draw upon for their content. And the material is the medium; it is the substance through which we exchange messages, and it is the environment within which we communicate. We draw upon our material environment, including the technological, the biological, and the purely physical, to construct our messages and meanings.

Returning to Gilman's (1992) book, I think it crucial to note that her title, *Something From Nothing,* is not entirely accurate. Joseph does not fabricate something out of absolutely nothing. His material is pen and paper, and it is language and experience. He makes this material into something new, and this I would argue is the significance of human communication. Through the magic of sounds and scribbles we alter our environment, and create things that never were. Alfred Korzybski (1958), Kenneth Burke (1945, 1950), Susanne K. Langer (1951), Paul Watzlawick (in Watzlawick, Weakland, & Fisch, 1974), and Marshall McLuhan (1964; see also McLuhan & Zingrone, 1995), all have discussed the link between communication and change. I want to echo these seminal scholars in suggesting that communication is not so much about creation as it is about mutation, and that the process of representation, signification, symbolization, and yes, mediation, is in fact a process of transformation.

The phrase "something from nothing" is a wonderful way to express the power of symbolic communication as the most radical form of change we know. But Joseph's act of written communication is only the last in a series of transformations, as the original piece of cloth goes through periodic alterations at the hands of his grandfather. The story begins with the making of a blanket, but the blanket's cloth was made from raw material, which was the product of living organisms, which arose out of a particular physical environment. The universe is a material environment that is characterized by continuous transformation. And somehow, despite the tendency of change to move in the direction of disorder and entropy, some of those changes result in increased organization, complexity, and life. Organisms not only modify themselves to meet the demands of the environment, they also transform their environment to make it more favorable to their own survival and prosperity. This process is called ecology. Sometimes organism s alter their environments through the use of technologies and symbolic forms, and this process is called media ecology (Nystrom, 1973; Postman, 1970).

Through communication as information, physical systems defy entropy, organize themselves, and become increasingly more complex. Through communication as social action, social systems maintain themselves in space and modify themselves over time. Through communication as a system of meanings, cultures are established and evolve. Through communication as a system of thought, minds are born and grow. Through communication as a system of symbols, we construct worlds, and we transcend them, just as Joseph transcended the limitations of needle and thread. We may not escape material reality, but we are able to change and to improve upon our environment, and ourselves. The media ecology approach to communication focuses on the means and

methods, the techniques and technologies that bring about change. It therefore is concerned with the pragmatics of change, in addition to the substance of transformation. In a human context, change may occur as a result of conscious choice and planning, rather than as a product of automatic processes. But our modifications and manipulations often lead to unanticipated and undesirable changes—this is one of media ecology's primary lessons.

⸰ It is worth emphasizing at this point that the primary medium of human communication is language, and the field of media ecology is an outgrowth in many ways of general semantics, with its analysis of the social and psychological effects of symbols, and its links with the linguistic relativism of Edward Sapir (1921) and Benjamin Lee Whorf (1956) and the theory of symbolic forms put forth by Susanne K. Langer (1951). Christine Nystrom (2000) has examined the relationship between media ecology and both Langer and Whorf, while Louis Forsdale (1981) identified the connection between the Sapir-Whorf hypothesis and McLuhan's perspective on media. Neil Postman, who coined the term "media ecology" (Nystrom 1973), has written some of the fundamental works in this field (e.g., Postman, 1979, 1982, 1985, 1992; Postman & Weingartner, 1969), while at the same time making substantial contributions to general semantics (e.g., Postman, 1976; Postman & Weingartner, 1966; Postman, Weingartner, & Moran, 1969). More recently, Raymond Gozzi, Jr. (1999) has brought media ecology together with general semantics and the study of the metaphor. These are associations that I share, as well.

Having now provided you with some sense of myself as a communication scholar, I would like to turn to a second folk tale, one whose theme is also transformation. What I am referring to is the myth of Echo and Narcissus, as related by the Roman poet Ovid, in his masterpiece, Metamorphoses (1955). The myth is no doubt familiar, and therefore I will only touch on the highlights. Echo was a talkative nymph who had been punished by Juno, so that she could only repeat back whatever she heard. Narcissus was a youth so beautiful that everyone he met fell in love with him, including Echo. He was callous, however, and coldly rejected Echo as he did all of his admirers. Brokenhearted, the poor nymph faded away until nothing was left of her but her voice. Narcissus was eventually punished when he saw his own image in a pool

of water. Not recognizing himself, he was mesmerized by his own beauty. Even after he realized it was only his own reflection, Narcissus could not leave, and slowly wasted away until he finally turned into the flower that bears his name.

Sigmund Freud (e.g., 1966) saw in Narcissus an ego that thinks itself super, and named a character disorder after him, narcissism. Narcissists exhibit selflove and a sense of superiority entirely out of line with reality; they devalue others or exhibit disinterest in them, while clinging to a "grandiose conception of the self" (Lasch, 1979, p.84). My treatment of narcissism here is necessarily superficial; in essence, I wish to follow the lead of Christopher Lasch (1979) and use narcissism to refer to the problem of too much self.

Perhaps in his own way reflecting the myth, Freud acted as if Echo were invisible, and only had eyes for Narcissus in his writings. Still, Echo's name managed to make its way into the psychology literature as echolalia, which refers to a type of language use in which speakers repeat back what they have heard without understanding its meaning. Echolalia is a normal facet of early language development, and also a symptom of various types of brain disorders and disabilities. Here too, I will not take up all of the specifics of this type of behavior, but rather use it as a metaphor for the problem of too little self. Thus narcissism and echolalia represent two extremes in the development of a sense of self, against which we struggle to find a balance.

It is, by the same token, a struggle to find a balance between self and other, a point that is essential in Freud's psychoanalytic tradition, as well as the symbolic interactionist approach of George Herbert Mead (1934), Erving Goffman (1959), and others. Underlying these perspectives is the notion that we are not born with a sense of self, but rather construct one with the raw material of body and brain, and by means of human communication. As we learn to use our senses and make sense out of our surroundings, we begin to separate ourselves from our environment. We develop a concept of self as we develop a concept of other, a process that is intimately tied to language acquisition. Language gives us a name, and therefore a singular identity. The pronoun "me" provides us with a self that is situated within an environment. And the pronoun "I" is the perfect expression of the ego acting upon its surroundings (see, for example, Becker, 1971). Symbolic communication gives us the ability to become our own material , allowing us to construct a sense of self. It follows, I would argue, that changes in our mode of symbolic communication would, in turn, change our sense of self.

Echo and Narcissus represent two different extremes in the construction of the self, but they also represent two different modes of sense perception and symbolic communication (and, as Eric McLuhan, 1998, notes, the two different brain hemispheres). As media ecology theorists such as Marshall McLuhan (1962, 1964), Harold Innis (1951, 1972), Eric Havelock (1963, 1986), and Walter Ong (1967, 1982, 1986) have noted, one of the major divisions in perception and culture is that of the ear and the eye. Echo represents hearing and sound, and therefore the sort of media environment marked by the absence of literacy, by reliance on speech and song, and by emphasis on oral tradition. Such oral cultures lack a storage medium outside of human memory, and therefore rely upon repetition to keep knowledge alive. Just as individual memory acts as a neural echo chamber, the collective memory of an oral society functions as an echo-system. In contrast to Echo, Narcissus represents sight and visual imagery, and therefore stands for the type of media environment characterized by writing systems and literate habits of mind. Like Narcissus, readers become engrossed in the object of their attention, lured into a life of solitary study, trapped by the process of reflection. Writing freezes language, freeing people from the necessity of memorization, thereby rendering the oral tradition obsolescent. Oral cultures have difficulty surviving when they are thrust into competition with literate cultures, just as Echo fades from view after encountering Narcissus.

The interpretations of this myth as being about sense perception and about senses of self fit together quite nicely. In the same way as Echo represents the extreme of too little self, members of oral cultures have a weak sense of self in comparison to literates (Ong, 1967, 1982, 1986). Collective, tribal identity dominates, as the preservation of knowledge requires a group effort. Likewise, conformity and tradition are required for cultural survival. The very mode of aural communication is biased towards the group, as audiences listen as a whole, bound together by the simultaneity of sound; this is in contrast to readers who must read as isolated individuals (Ong, 1967, 1982). Of course, from an oral perspective, members of literate cultures, like Narcissus, develop too much self. They are freed from the pressures of conformity and

tradition, and encouraged by this mode of visual communication to view themselves as individuals.

Now that we have moved into a postliterate, electronic culture, what has happened to our sense of self? There is at once the fear of a return to echolaha in the form of a "technological society" (Ellul, 1964) in which the individual seeks to "escape from freedom" (Fromm, 1965), gives "obedience to authority" (Milgram, 1974), becomes "the organization man" (Whyte, 1956), is manipulated by "the mind managers" (Schiller, 1973), who use the media for the purpose of "manufacturing consent" (Herman & Chomsky, 1988). At the same time, there is the fear that we live in a "culture of narcissism (Lasch, 1979) in which we are members of "the lonely crowd" (Riesman, Denney, & Glazer, 1950), isolated by our "habits of the heart" (Bellah, Madsen, Sullivan, Swidler, & Tipton, 1985), and reduced to either "bowling alone" (Putnam, 2000) or finding some other way of "amusing ourselves to death" (Postman, 1985). And the truth is that both extremes of narcissism and echolalia seem to coexist today, at the expense of a balanced sense of self. This crisis of the self has gone by many names: we have been told about the divided self (Laing, 1965), the need to find oneself, and the need to find self esteem. We have endured identity crises (Erikson, 1950, 1980), identity politics (Gitlin, 1995), and even identity theft (U.S. Federal Trade Commission, 2000). We have observed the disappearance of childhood, and of adulthood (Meyrowitz, 1985; Postman, 1982). We have been informed of the decentering of the subject (Jameson, 1991, Poster, 1990), the death of the author (Barthes, 1977), and the saturation of the self (Gergen, 1991). We have been told that we are now transhuman (Dewdney, 1998) or posthuman (Hayles, 1999). And we have heard calls for character education rooted in nostalgia for our lost sense of self (Bennett, 1996). This crisis of the self has led to a struggle over what kind of self will prevail in the electronic media environment, and educational institutions are one of the principal battlegrounds for this conflict.

• With this in mind, I now want to turn to an example from my personal life. It is neither a folk tale, nor a myth, nor a story with a happy ending. Rather, it is the story of my daughter Sarah and her disability. In June of 1998, when Sarah was two and a half years old, my wife and I received the diagnosis that Sarah is autistic. We had some concerns about her development dur-

ing her first year, and began to understand that something was seriously wrong during her second year, as she suffered from a series of seizures when she was twenty-one months old, often appeared withdrawn, and failed to develop language. She did exhibit echolalia, repeating back words and phrases like "thank you" and "big" without any regard for their meaning, and showed a remarkable ability to memorize songs such as Raffi's "Baby Beluga" and Barney's "I Love You" song. As it turns out, this echolalia is a symptom of autism, but among autistic children it is a positive indication of their potential for linguistic and cognitive development.

I do not want to dwell on the devastating impact Sarah's diagnosis had on my family. But, as you no doubt know, reading is one of the coping mechanisms that we literates employ in times of trouble. And so I immediately set out to read as much as I could about autism, as a parent of course, not a scholar. And yet, I could not help but notice the many ways that this disorder intersects with my own intellectual background. As the name of the syndrome implies, autism is a disorder of the self, and it is a disorder profoundly linked to problems in communication and perception. But let me begin with some facts.

• Autism is the product of a neurological abnormality, present before birth, which affects the development of the brain. While it is a biological condition, no medical tests have yet been developed to identify it, and diagnosis depends upon behavioral observation. Autism therefore is a fuzzy category; first identified in 1943 by Leo Kanner, it has come to be understood as a spectrum disorder, meaning that there is a continuum between the severest cases, through the mildest which may go undiagnosed, and perhaps extending into nonautistic normalcy. And it is a syndrome, meaning that it encompasses a wide variety of traits, some of which may or may not be present in any given case, and which may appear in any number of combinations. Autism is a pervasive developmental disorder which occurs in males four times as often as it does in females, and affects approximately half a million people in the United States with a rate of occurrence somewhere between 1 in 500 and 1 in 1000 (for more information see Baron-Cohen & Bolton, 1993; Cohen, 1998; Frith, 1989; Siegel, 1996).

• This disorder is diagnosed by three main criteria. The first has to do with impairments in social interaction; Kanner referred to this as "autistic aloneness" (quoted in Frith, 1989, p.10). There are problems developing relationships, reciprocating emotions, and sharing interests with others, as well as a blindness to nonverbal social cues. The autistic may seem lost in his or her own world, and an alien in our own. The second impairment is in communication, both verbal and nonverbal, and often includes delays in language acquisition or a complete lack of speech. Also, there may be a lack of imaginative play, and of interest in narrative, as well as problems with the processing of sensory information. The third criterion is described as "restricted, repetitive, and stereotyped patterns of behavior, interests, or activity" (Siegel, 1996, p.18). Both simple motions like hand flapping and complex behavioral patterns may be enacted repeatedly. There is a tendency to favor ritual and routine, and to behave obsessively and compulsively. Even in mild cases, interests may be pursued with unusual focus and intensity.

The majority of autistics are categorized as mentally retarded, but of course assessing intelligence is highly problematic when dealing with individuals who may be unable or unwilling to speak. Only 20% attain a relatively typical level of intelligence, and are referred to as high functioning. Some autistics have savant skills, highly developed abilities in one specialized area, such as mathematics, computer science, music, art, architecture, mechanics, biology, or simply memorization, visualization, or manual dexterity. These savants are well below normal in other areas, however, and autistics in general are particularly handicapped in regards to social and emotional intelligence. The unevenness of autistic intelligence is in part what inspired Howard Gardner's (1983, 1993, 1997) theory of multiple intelligences.

Many of you are no doubt familiar with Dustin Hoffman's portrayal of an autistic adult in the film *Rain Man*. Often unacknowledged is the fact that Pete Townsend of *The Who* drew upon his experiences with autistic children in constructing the title character of the rock opera Tommy. In any discussion of unacknowledged autistics, the name of Albert Einstein inevitably comes up, insofar as he did not speak until the age of five, had a great deal of difficulty with social interaction, and possessed savant skills in mathematics and visualization. Vincent Van Gogh's seizures and psychological difficulties may also have been the result of the syndrome, and others who have been identified as mildly autistic

include Thomas Jefferson, Thomas Edison, Ludwig Wittgenstein, Andy Warhol, Béla Bartók, Glenn Gould, and Bill Gates. A more severe case may have been the 18th century wild boy of Aveyron, the subject of a film by Francois Truffaut, who was said to have been raised by wolves, but may have been an autistic child who had been abandoned or had run away.

Contemporary high functioning autistics have been able to communicate something about their condition. Donna Williams, for example, has written five books about her experiences (1992, 1994, 1996, 1998, 1999); consider this passage from Autism and Sensing: The Unlost Instinct (1998):

> Up to the age of four, I sensed according to pattern and shifts in pattern. My ability to interpret what I saw was impaired because I took each fragment in without understanding its meaning in the context of its surroundings. I'd see the nostril but lose the nose, see the nose but lose the face, see the fingernail but lose the finger. My ability to interpret what I heard was equally impaired. I heard the intonation but lost the meaning of the words, got a few of the words but lost the sentences. I couldn't consistently process the meaning of my own body messages if I was focusing in on something with my eyes or ears. I didn't know myself in relation to other people because when I focused on processing information about "other," I lost "self," and when I focused on "self," I lost "other." I could either express something in action or make some meaning of some of the information coming in but not both at once. So crossing the room to do something meant I'd probably lose the experience of walking even though my body did it. Speaking, I'd lose the meaning of my own sounds whilst moving. The deaf-blind may have lost their senses; I had my senses but lost the sense. I was meaning deaf, meaning blind. (p.33)

What Williams describes is a world of fleeting and fragmentary perceptions, an inability to organize sensory data and construct a meaningful reality. It was only with difficulty that she was able to build a world in which she could understand self and other, but not simultaneously. Either she would shut out her environment and turn inward, or give up her sense of self and become lost in her perceptions.

Her world is also concrete to an extreme. Language use for the autistic child may be so concrete that a word learned with a particular individual, in a particular

place, and during a particular activity, may not be generalized to other people, places, or situations. Among the most difficult words for autistics to learn to use appropriately are the highly abstract pronouns I and you, which may also reflect problems in forming a sense of self and other. Even savant skills may be based on autistic concreteness. Many do quite well at jigsaw puzzles, because they pay close attention to shape rather than picture—in fact, it is just as easy for them to put the pieces together when they are turned picture-side down. Memorization, one of the more common savant abilities, is also a concrete operation, as is visualization. Consider how one such person describes her thought processes:

> I think in pictures. Words are like a second language to me. I translate both spoken and written words into full-color movies, complete with sound, which run like a VCR tape in my head. When somebody speaks to me, his words are instantly translated into pictures. Language-based thinkers often find this phenomenon difficult to understand, but in my job as an equipment designer for the livestock industry, visual thinking is a tremendous advantage. (Grandin, 1995, p.19)

This passage was written by Temple Grandin, who holds a Ph.D. in animal science, and is on the faculty at Colorado State University (see also Grandin & Scariano, 1986). It is no secret that academia is much more forgiving of such autistic traits as absentmindedness, intense and single-minded interests, and social impairment as compared with other sectors of society.

Concreteness, delays in language acquisition, and social impairment are all interrelated. For example, seeing eye to eye is one of the most basic forms of relating to others, but autistics tend not to make eye contact, and have trouble making meaning from such nonverbal cues. The gesture of pointing, normally developed very early in childhood, often needs to be taught to autistic children. It implies an awareness of self and other, a shared gaze, a shared attention, a shared meaning. And it is a key step in language acquisition, as we ultimately replace our fingers with words that "point" to things in our environment. Meaning making is thus linked to empathy, a trait that is also impaired among autistics. A lack of empathy, by the way, in no way leads to inmoral conduct, as researcher Uta Frith (1989) explains, "Some of the perceived abnormalities of autistic social behavior can be seen not so much as impairments, but as unusually positive qualities. These qualities can be captured by terms such as innocence, honesty and guilelessness" (p. 140).

What Frith (1989) believes to be the ultimate impairment of autism is the failure to form a theory of mind, that is, an understanding that others have a mind like one's own. Rather than thinking in terms of mental states and motivations, autistics tend to view others concretely, as objects and behaviors. They essentially rely on an extensional orientation rather than an intensional one, and while this insulates them from some of the problems brought on by the process of abstracting (see Korzybski, 1958, on extension and intension, and abstracting), it also means that they suffer from "mind-blindness" (Baron-Cohen, 1995, p. xxiii). Without a theory of mind, it is impossible to see oneself as others do, leading to social impairment; it is also very difficult to understand deception. Julian Jaynes (1976) posited that theory of mind was a fairly recent evolutionary development. No doubt, our ancestors could have survived without it, as have other forms of life. Perhaps the Neanderthals lacked it, depending instead on skills such as memory and visualization. Perhaps they disappeared because their mind-blindness made them vulnerable to our own ancestors. It is possible that the development of theory of mind led to the creative explosion of art and ritual that occurred sometime between twenty and thirty thousand years ago (Pfeiffer, 1982), or it may be that it developed much earlier among our evolutionary ancestors (Dunbar, 1996). Whenever it appeared, theory of mind would have tremendous survival value, as it leads us to make inferences about the mental states of others, and thereby predict their behavior; applied to the natural environment as anthropomorphism, it even is an efficient form of theory-building, and therefore would be favored by natural selection (Baron-Cohen, 1995).

Lacking theory of mind, autistics would be at a decided disadvantage in early human societies, and their social impairment would no doubt collide with oral societies' emphasis on cohesion and conformity. But the autistic would work well with the structure, formality, and emphasis on ritual found in these traditional cultures. No doubt, savant skills, and in particular a strong memory, would be highly valued, and would probably hold enough survival value to overlook individual idiosyncrasies. We do know that autistics can thrive in a literate culture, and that they have a certain affinity for the liter-

ate mindset. To note just a few of the parallels: Where autistics may perceive the world in fragments, literacy is biased towards fragmentation and analysis (Carpenter & Heyman, 1970; Goody, 1977; Logan, 1986; McLuhan, 1962, 1964). Where savant skills are isolated islands of ability, literacy favors specialization (Eisenstein, 1980; Innis, 1951; McLuhan, 1962, 1964; Meyrowitz, 1985). Where autistics are socially impaired, literacy favors privacy and individualism (Havelock, 1963, 1986; Logan, 1986; McLuhan, 1962, 1964; Ong, 1967, 1982). Where some autistics excel at visual thinking, reading relies on the sense of vision alone as opposed to the multisensory nature of face-to-face communication (Goody, 1977; Innis, 1951, 1971; McLuhan, 1962, 1964; Ong, 1967, 1982). In fact, some autistic children can draw in perspective without training (e.g., Selfe, 1977), a skill McLuhan (1962, 1964) thought purely a product of reading's fixed point of view (see also Romanyshyn, 1989; Wachtel, 1995). Actually, autistics are naturally capable of a kind of detachment and objectivity that has for long been an ideal of western literate cultures (McLuhan, 1962, 1964; Ong, 1967, 1982). It therefore makes perfect sense that some autistics are hyperlexic, that is, they learn to read at a much younger age than typical children (although comprehension is difficult to assess).

In our electronic age, high functioning autistics find a niche in the solitary activity of computer programming. But more often than not, what all autistics encounter is a hostile media environment. From the fluorescent lighting which many find painful, to the sensory bombardment and information overload which disrupt the thought processes of us all, our culture offers neither the routine predictability and slow pace of primary orality, nor the quiet concentration of traditional literacy. As one autistic argues, "… the way of life of this age is ever more demanding of a certain way of living that is the WORST case of living, for many autistic people, and there are fewer and fewer places to hide, to be sheltered from the media Storms … and even the "normal" kid may become mind-fractured into Autism … under all the sense stress and overloads!" (Wilson, 2000, no pagination).

More and more there is talk of an epidemic of autism, and it is unclear to what degree this is due to the stresses of our environment, or contaminants and pollutants, or diet and allergies, or infections and vaccinations, or genetic predisposition, or simply improved diagnostic procedures.

At present, there is no cure for autism, but early intervention can help, and some who are diagnosed with the disability are later mainstreamed, and sometimes declassified. The most effective form of treatment begins with Applied Behavioral Analysis, and the breaking down of activities into their smallest units. Through a process of discrete trials involving drill and rewards, each unit of behavior is taught until mastered, a technique that was pioneered by Anne Sullivan, Helen Keller's teacher. Research indicates that this method is effective if the program is begun during early childhood, and the intervention is intensive —preferably forty hours a week of one-on-one behavioral treatment (Lovaas, 1981; Maurice, 1993; Smith, Groen, & Wynn, 2000). The goal is to jump start neural self-organization by working through the interface of human communication.

Autism cuts across the extremes of narcissism and echolalia, and presents us with a sense of self that is at the same time too little and too much. More than anything else, it is an incomplete sense of self, one cut off from a sense of other. Can autistic individuals develop an integrated sense of self? From what I gather, the raw material is there, but it involves a tremendous struggle to construct a coherent and meaningful sense of the world. Can autistic individuals develop a theory of mind? There is some indication that the answer is yes, but only for some, and only with great difficulty (Howlin, Baron-Cohen, & Hadwin, 1999).

As for my daughter, we are fighting to provide her with the best possible life chances, and her teachers are the heroes who are out on the front lines. But what she has taught me is that the self we take for granted is in fact the product of a struggle. It is the most important struggle of our lives, despite the fact that we are largely unaware of it. Through our efforts from early childhood on, we take the raw material we are born with, and we build ourselves. And having done so, we continue to transform ourselves. The self is a product of metamorphosis, not a static entity. There are many kinds of selves we can construct with the materials at hand, but they are not all of equal worth. Some may be too easily overwhelmed by others, some too insensitive. Moreover, different media environments tend to favor or discourage different types of selves. As the materials we work with change, our sense of self may also be altered. Thus, for example, we move from oral cultures' tendency to develop too little self to literate cultures' too much self.

Donna Williams (1998) writes of how she moved past the stage of "no self, no other," but could exist either as "all self, no other," or "all other, no self." It is only with difficulty that she could develop a "simultaneous sense of self and other." In a similar way, electronic culture seems to oscillate between the extremes of echolalia and narcissism. And I would suggest that on the cultural level this is just as much a disability as it is on the individual level, and that our current crisis of the self represents a struggle of the greatest import.[It is a struggle over the kinds of selves we want to produce and reproduce.]

Ovid's tale of metamorphosis is a tragic one. But the story of Joseph, the tailor's grandson, is a human comedy of survival, transformation, and transcendence. It shows us that it is possible to work with the material at hand, and make something that never was. We might begin by retrieving oral culture's selflessness, community-mindedness, and the ability to sacrifice oneself for the sake of others. And we could add to it literate culture's self-fullness, its emphasis on individual rights and responsibilities, and the idea of integrity and moral character. Both narcissism and echolalia can be positive traits if exhibited in moderation and balance. Changes in our media environment may have destabilized our culture's established sense of self, but we have the raw materials and the understanding of media and communication necessary to build a new, integrated sense of self. The struggle now falls to us, as parents and as citizens, as scholars and as communicators, and above all, as teachers, to make something from nothing.

REFERENCES

Baron-Cohen, S. (1995). *Mindblindness: An essay on autism and theory of mind.* Cambridge, MA: MIT Press.

Baron-Cohen, S., & Bolton, P. (1993). *Autism: The facts.* Oxford: Oxford University Press.

Barthes, R. (1977). *Image, music, text* (S. Heath, Trans.). New York : Hill and Wang.

Becker, E. (1971). *The birth and death of meaning: An interdisciplinary perspective on the problem of man* (2nd. ed.). New York: The Free Press.

Bellah, R. N., Madsen, R., Sullivan, W. M., Swidler, A., & Tipton, S. M. (1985). *Habits of the heart: Individualism and commitment in American life.* New York: Perennial Library.

Bennett, W. J. (Ed.). (1996). *The book of virtues for young people: A treasury of great moral stories.* Parsippany, NJ: Silver Burdett Press.

Burke, K. (1965). *Permanence and change: An anatomy of purpose* (2nd rev. ed.). Indianapolis: Bobbs-Merrill.

Carpenter, E., & Heyman, K. (1970). *They became what they beheld.* New York: Outerbridge & Dienstfrey.

Cohen, S. (1998). *Targeting autism: What we know, don't know, and can do to help young children with autism and related disorders.* Berkeley: University of California Press.

Dewdney, C. (1998). *Last flesh: Life in the transhuman era.* Toronto: HarperCollins.

Dunbar, R. (1996). *Grooming, gossip, and the evolution of language.* Cambridge, MA: Harvard University Press.

Eisenstein, E. L. (1980). *The printing press as an agent of change.* New York: Cambridge University Press.

Ellul, J. (1964). *The technological society* (J. Wilkinson, Trans.). New York: Knopf.

Erikson, E. H. (1950). *Childhood and society.* New York: W. W. Norton.

Erikson, E. H. (1980). *Identity and the life cycle.* New York: W. W. Norton.

Forsdale, L. (1981). *Perspectives on communication.* Reading, MA: Addison-Wesley.

Freud, S. (1966). *Introductory lectures on psychoanalysis* (J. Strachey, Trans.). New York: W. W. Norton.

Frith, U. (1989). *Autism: Explaining the enigma.* Oxford: Blackwell.

Fromm, E. (1965). *Escape from freedom.* New York: Avon Books.

Gardner, H. (1983). *Frames of mind: The theory of multiple intelligences.* New York: BasicBooks.

Gardner, H. (1993). *Multiple intelligences: The theory in practice.* New York: BasicBooks.

Gardner, H. (1997). *Extraordinary minds: Portraits of exceptional individuals and an examination of our own extraordinariness.* New York: BasicBooks.

Gergen, K. J. (1991). *The saturated self.* New York: BasicBooks.

Gilman, P. (1992). *Something from nothing.* New York: Scholastic.

Gitlin, T. (1995). *The twilight of common dreams: Why America is wracked by culture wars.* New York: Metropolitan Books.

Goffman, E. (1959). *The presentation of self in everyday life.* Garden City, NY: Doubleday Anchor.

Goody, J. (1977). *The domestication of the savage mind.* Cambridge: Cambridge University Press.

Gozzi, R., Jr. (1999). *The power of metaphor in the age of electronic media.* Cresskill, NJ: Hampton Press.

Grandin, T. (1995). *Thinking in pictures and other reports from my life with autism.* New York: Random House.

Grandin, T., & Scariano, M. M. (1986). *Emergence: Labeled autistic.* Novato, CA: Arena Press.

Havelock, E. A. (1963). *Preface to Plato.* Cambridge, MA: The Belknap Press of Harvard University Press.

Havelock, E. A. (1986). *The muse learns to write: Reflections on orality and literacy from antiquity to the present.* New Haven, CT: Yale University Press.

Hayles, N. K. (1999). *How we became posthuman: Virtual bodies in cybernetics, literature, and informatics.* Chicago: University of Chicago Press.

Herman, E. S., & Chomsky, N. (1988). *Manufacturing consent: The political economy of the mass media.* New York: Pantheon.

Howlin, P., Baron-Cohen, S., & Hadwin, J. (1999). *Teaching children with autism to mind-read: A practical guide.* Chichester: John Wiley & Sons.

Innis, H. A. (1951). *The bias of communication.* Toronto: University of Toronto Press.

Innis, H. A. (1972). *Empire and communication* (rev. ed.). Toronto: University of Toronto Press.

Jameson, F. (1991). *Postmodernism, or, the cultural logic of late capitalism.* Durham, NC: Duke University Press.

Jaynes, J. (1976). *The origin of consciousness in the breakdown of the bicameral mind.* Boston: Houghton Muffin.

Korzybski, A. (1958). *Science and sanity: An introduction to non-Aristotelian systems and general semantics* (4th ed.). Lakeville, CT: The International Non-Aristotelian Library.

Laing, R. D. (1965). *The divided self: An existential study in sanity and madness.* Harmondsworth: Penguin.

Laing, R. D. (1969). *Self and others* (2nd ed.). Harmondsworth: Penguin.

Langer, S. K. (1951). *Philosophy in a new key: A study in the symbolism of reason, rite and art.* Cambridge, MA: Harvard University Press.

Lasch, C. (1979). *The culture of narcissism: American life in an age of diminishing expectations.* New York: Warner Books.

Logan, R. K. (1986). *The alphabet effect: The impact of the phonetic alphabet on the development of Western civilization.* New York: William Morrow.

Lovaas, O. I. (1981). *Teaching developmentally disabled children: The ME book.* Austin, TX: Pro-Ed.

Maurice, C. (Ed.). (1993). *Behavioral intervention for young children with autism: A manual for parents and professionals.* Austin, TX: Pro-Ed.

McLuhan, E. (1998). *Electric language: Understanding the message.* New York: Buzz Books.

McLuhan, E., & Zingrone, F. (1995). *Essential McLuhan.* New York: BasicBooks.

McLuhan, M. (1962). *The Gutenberg galaxy: The making of typographic man.* Toronto: University of Toronto Press.

McLuhan, M. (1964). *Understanding media: The extensions of man.* New York: McGraw-Hill.

Mead, G. H. (1934). *Mind, self and society, from the standpoint of a social behaviorist.* Chicago: University of Chicago Press.

Meyrowitz, J. (1985). *No sense of place.* New York: Oxford University Press.

Milgram, S. (1974). *Obedience to authority: An experimental view.* New York: Harper & Row.

Nystrom, C. L. (1973). Toward a science of media ecology: The formulation of integrated conceptual paradigms for the study of human communication systems. Unpublished doctoral dissertation, New York University.

Nystrom, C. L. (2000). Symbols, thought, and reality: The contributions of Benjamin Lee Whorf and Susanne K. Langer to media ecology. *New Jersey Journal of Communication* 8(1), pp.8-33.

Ong, W. J. (1967). *The presence of the word: Some prolegomena for cultural and religious history.* Minneapolis, MN: University of Minnesota Press.

Ong, W. J. (1982). *Orality and literacy: The technologizing of the word.* London: Methuen.

Ong, W. J. (1986). *Hopkins, the self and God.* Toronto: University of Toronto Press.

Ovid. (1955). *Metamorphoses (R. Humphries, Trans.).* Bloomington: Indiana University Press.

Pfeiffer, I. E. (1982). *The creative explosion: An inquiry into the origins of art and religion.* New York: Harper & Row.

Poster, M. (1990). *The mode of information.* Chicago: University of Chicago Press.

Postman, N. (1970). The reformed English curriculum. In A. C. Eurich (Ed.), *High school 1980: The shape of the future in American secondary education* (pp.160-168). New York: Pitman.

Postman, N. (1976). *Crazy talk stupid talk.* New York: Delacorte.

Postman, N. (1979). *Teaching as a conserving activity.* New York: Delacorte.

Postman, N. (1982). *The disappearance of childhood.* New York: Delacorte.

Postman, N. (1985). *Amusing ourselves to death: Public discourse in the age of show business.* New York: Knopf.

Postman, N. (1992). *Technopoly: The surrender of culture to technology.* New York: Alfred A. Knopf.

Postman, N. & Weingartner, C. (1966). *Linguistics: A revolution in teaching.* New York: Delta.

Postman, N. & Weingartner, C. (1969). *Teaching as a subversive activity.* New York: Delta.

Postman, N., Weingartner, C., & Moran, T. P. (eds.). (1969). *Language in America.* New York: Pegasus.

Putnam, R. D. (2000). *Bowling alone: The collapse and revival of American community.* New York: Simon & Schuster.

Romanyshyn, R. D. (1989). *Technology as symptom and dream.* London: Routledge.

Riesman, D., Denney, R., & Glazer, N. (1950). *The lonely crowd: A study of the changing American character.* New Haven: Yale University Press.

Sapir, E. (1921). *Language: An introduction to the study of speech.* New York: Harcourt, Brace.

Schiller, H. I. (1973). *The mind managers.* Boston: Beacon Press.

Selfe, L. (1977). *A case of extraordinary drawing ability in an autistic child.* London: Academic Press.

Siegel, B. (1996). *The world of the autistic child: Understanding and treating autistic spectrum disorders.* New York: Oxford University Press.

Smith, T., Groen, A. D., & Wynn, J. W. (2000). Randomized trial of intensive early intervention for children with pervasive developmental disorder. *American Journal on Mental Retardation* 105(4), pp. 269-285.

U.S. Federal Trade Commission. (2000). ID theft: When bad things happen to your good name. Retrieved from http://www.consumer.gov/idtheft/

Wachtel, E. (1995). To an eye in a fixed position: Glass, art, and vision. In J. C. Pitt (Ed.), *New directions in the philosophy of technology* (pp. 41-61). Amsterdam: Kluwer

Watzlawick, P., Weakland, J., & Fisch, R. (1974). Change: Principles of problem formation and problem resolution. New York: W. W. Norton.

Whorf, B. L. (1956). *Language, thought, and reality: Selected writings* (J. B. Carroll, Ed.). Cambridge, MA: MIT Press.

Whyte, W. H., Jr. (1956). *The organization man.* New York: Touchstone.

Williams, D. (1992). *Nobody, nowhere: The extraordinary autobiography of an autistic:* New York: Times Books.

Williams, D. (1994). *Somebody, somewhere: Breaking free from the world of autism.* New York: Times Books.

Williams, D. (1996). *Autism: An inside-out approach.* London: Jessica Kingsley.

Williams, D. (1998). *Autism and sensing: The unlost instinct.* London: Jessica Kingsley.

Williams, D. (1999). *Like colour to the blind: Soul searching and soul finding.* London: Jessica Kingsley.

Wilson, F. (2000, August 29). *Why is there so much autism in kids today today?!* 2worlds Listserv. Retrieved from http://groups.yahoo.com/group/2worlds/message/79

Lance Strate is Associate Professor of Communication and Media Studies, Fordham University, Bronx, New York, and President of the Media Ecology Association. Earlier versions of this lecture were presented as the John F. Wilson Fellow Address at the 57th Annual Convention of the New York State Communication Association, Monticello, NY, Oct. 8-10, 1999, and at the 45th Media Ecology Conference, Rosendale, NY, Nov. 3-5, 2000, and an expanded version was published in the Speech Communication Annual (Vol. 14, 2000, pp. 14-62), all under the title "Narcissism and Echolalia: Sense and the Struggle for the Self."

Self-Concordance and Subjective Well-Being in Four Cultures

Sheldon and colleagues have recently focused research attention on the concept of self-concordance, in which people feel that they pursue their goals because the goals fit with their underlying interests and values rather than because others say they should pursue them. Self-concordant individuals typically evidence higher subjective well-being (SWB). But is this also true in non-Western cultures, which emphasize people's duty to conform to societal expectations and group-centered norms? To address this question, this study assessed goal self-concordance and SWB in four different cultures. U.S., Chinese, and South Korean samples evidenced equal levels of self-concordance, whereas a Taiwanese sample evidenced somewhat less self-concordance. More importantly, self-concordance predicted SWB within every culture. It appears that "owning one's actions"—that is, feeling that one's goals are consistent with the self—may be important for most if not all humans.

KENNON M. SHELDON, ANDREW J. ELLIOT, RICHARD M. RYAN, VALERY CHIRKOV, YOUNGMEE KIM, CINDY WU, MELIKSAH DEMIR, and ZHIGANG SUN

Recently, Sheldon and colleagues (Sheldon, 2002; Sheldon & Elliot, 1999; Sheldon & Houser-Marko, 2001) have proposed the idea of *self-concordance* as a way of conceptualizing optimal goal-striving. Self-concordant individuals are people who pursue life goals with a sense that they express their authentic choices rather than with a sense that they are controlled by external forces over which they have little say. Thus, self-concordant goals are ones that represent people's actual interests and passions as well as their central values and beliefs. In contrast, nonconcordant goals are ones that are pursued with a sense of "having to," as the person does not really enjoy or believe in the goals. For example, a student's goal of learning to play the piano may be self-concordant; that is, the student has an interest in music and a genuine desire to master the instrument. Or, it may be non-self-concordant; that is, the student has little natural inclination or interest for the piano and practices only because his or her parents insist.

To measure self-concordance, Sheldon (2002) has drawn from self-determination theory (SDT; Deci & Ryan, 1985, 1991, 2000) and its concept of the "perceived locus of causality continuum" (PLOC). The question is, does a person engage in goal-pursuits with a sense that "I" chose them (an internal perceived locus of causality, or I-PLOC)? Or does a person pursue goals with a sense that his or her situation is the source of the goals (an external perceived locus of causality, or E-PLOC)? Research focusing on Western samples has shown that self-concordance (i.e., greater I-PLOC than E-PLOC) is associated with concurrent subjective well-being (SWB; Sheldon & Kasser, 1995). In addition, self-concordance also predicts longitudinal increases in SWB by way of the greater goal-attainment inspired by self-concordance (Sheldon & Elliot, 1999; Sheldon & Houser-Marko, 2001; Sheldon & Kasser, 1998). In terms of the aforementioned example, the student who practices piano with a sense of interest and conviction is typically a happier person than the student who practices with a sense of pressure and obligation, and this student would also tend to improve his or her playing more rapidly, perhaps becoming an even happier person. Based on such findings, Sheldon (2002) suggested that self-concordance—that is, the sense of "owning" one's personal goals—might be a culturally invariant need or benefit for human beings. However, Sheldon reported no cross-cultural goal data to support this idea.

Relevant to Sheldon's claim, researchers working within the SDT tradition have now published considerable data demonstrating the importance of internal motivation within non-Western samples. For example, Chirkov, Ryan, Kim, and Kaplan (2003) showed that although different types of social behaviors were differently internalized within four different cultures, having an I-PLOC regarding behavior predicted SWB in every culture. Hayamizu (1997) found that in a sample of Japanese high school students, internal motivation was related to positive coping, whereas external or "controlled" motivation was associated with maladaptive coping. Yamaguchi and Tanaka (1998) recently reported more adaptive learning styles and positive experiences in Japanese students with an I-PLOC for academic behavior. In addition, Deci et al. (2001) found in a sample of Bulgarian adults that I-PLOC on the job predicted work engagement, job performance, and psychological well-being (see Deci & Ryan, 2000, for a more comprehensive consideration of this emerging literature).

In the current work, we sought to generalize these cross-cultural results to the case of self-generated personal goals. Indeed, there is reason to suspect that the above-cited effects may not generalize to personal goal constructs. Idiographic goals represent people's self-generated initiatives for positive change and life improvement, and it may be that not all cultures support such proactive initiatives. For example, Markus and Kitayama (1994) suggested that in interdependent or collectivist cultures (Triandis, 1997), goals undertaken to "fit in" and have harmonious relationships with others should be most conducive to SWB, whereas goals undertaken to advance self-interests or achievements may actually be harmful to SWB. Similarly, Oishi (2000) has also argued that goals associated with independence and self-expression may be less beneficial within collectivist cultures than in individualist cultures. In this vein, Oishi and Diener (2001) reported that relative to European American college students, Asian college students did not benefit as much emotionally by attaining goals pursued "for fun and enjoyment," whereas achieving goals undertaken to "please friends and parents" resulted in greater emotional benefits for participants within collectivist cultures.

In sum, although some theoretical perspectives and cross-cultural data suggest that pursuing self-concordant personal goals should be beneficial within any cultural context, other perspectives and data suggest that it may always not be the case (Markus, Kitayama, & Heiman, 1996).[1] The current research sought to shed new light on these issues by assessing personal goals, self-concordance, and SWB within four different cultures: the United States, China, Taiwan, and South Korea. Based on past findings concerning the current measure of self-concordance, our primary hypothesis was that self-concordance would be positively associated with SWB in many, if not all, of these cultures. However, we also believed that the effects of self-concordance might to some extent be moderated by culture; we sought to uncover any such cultural differences. In addition, we wished to examine cultural mean differences in self-concordance. However, we had no theoretical reasons for making hypotheses concerning mean differences.

SECONDARY ISSUES

Below, we briefly consider each of the four types of motivation that together constitute the self-concordance concept and measure; we will also present data regarding each type separately. According to SDT, motivations can be located on a continuum of internalization, ranging from external motivation (the person acts with a feeling of being controlled by external pressures or contingencies) to introjected motivation (the person acts with a feeling of being controlled by his or her own internal processes) to identified motivation (the person acts with a sense of choice and volition, even if he or she does not enjoy the action) to intrinsic motivation (the person acts because the activity is inherently interesting and challenging). External and introjected motivations are classified as nonconcordant and potentially problematic motivations because the person does not fully assent to his or her own behavior. In contrast, identified and intrinsic motivations are classified as concordant and more beneficial motivations (Deci & Ryan, 2000; Ryan & Connell, 1989) because the person fully accepts them and because these motivations typically represent more central and stable aspects of the person.

According to SDT, intrinsic motivation is the prototypical self-concordant motivation as it represents the organism's self-initiated attempts to learn about the world and master new skills. We believed it might be very illuminating to examine this motivation by itself as some cross-cultural research calls into question the invariant association of intrinsic motivation with positive outcomes (Iyengar & Lepper, 1999; Oishi & Diener, 2001). Nevertheless, we hypothesized that intrinsic goal motivation, defined in terms of people's sense of interest and engagement in their personal goals as well as the enjoyment associated with those goals, should tend to be beneficial in every culture. We ventured no hypotheses concerning cultural differences in intrinsic motivation as we believe that people can find ways to be intrinsically motivated in almost any context.

Identified motivation, the second form of self-concordant motivation, may be a particularly important motivation to examine in a cross-cultural context because it represents the extent to which external prescriptions have been internalized into the self. In fact, SDT maintains that people can follow tradition, obey rules, and defer to others to no harmful effect as long as they identify with the behavior and enact it willingly—indeed, in this case, pursuing externally-mandated goals may even be positive (Chirkov et al., 2003). Based on this reasoning, we hypothesized that identified motivation should tend to be beneficial in every culture. We ventured no hypotheses concerning cultural differences in mean levels of identified motivation.

Introjected motivation, the sense that "I must force myself" to do a behavior, is also an important motivation to examine in a cross-cultural context, given likely cultural differences in the strength of social pressures, obligations, and expectations. Although one might expect greater introjection in more traditional or collectivist cultures, it is also possible that prosocial norms in such cultures help people to more fully internalize imposed motivations, leading to less introjection overall. Thus, although we expected introjection to be associated with lower SWB in most if not all cultures, we ventured no hypotheses regarding cultural mean differences in introjection.

Finally, external motivation is also worthy of examination in its own right. Although Oishi and Diener (2001) assumed that "striving to please my parents" is an external motivation, again, we believe it depends on the person's PLOC for the behavior. According to SDT, one might strive to please one's parents with a sense of being controlled by unassimilated forces or with a sense of wholeheartedly wanting to please them; as noted earlier, positive relations with SWB are expected to the extent that the latter is true. Again, because the internalization process might actually be better supported in non-Western than in Western cultures, we ventured no hypotheses regarding cultural mean differences in external motivation. However, we did expect that external motivation would be associated with lower SWB in most if not all cultures.

Finally, as an additional measure, in each culture we also asked participants to rate the extent their goals are self-focused (undertaken primarily to serve the needs and preferences of the self) versus other-focused (undertaken primarily to serve the needs and preferences of social groups, such as family, team, club, or friends). This allowed us to directly assess the extent to which goals are perceived as addressing individual interests and achievements, relative to collective interests and achievements—an important distinction according to Markus and Kitayama (1994) and many other cultural theorists. Notably, however, selfdetermination theorists have argued that the individualism/collectivism distinction is largely independent of the concordance/nonconcordance distinction (Chirkov et al., 2003; Deci & Ryan, 2000). In other words, one might engage in either collectivist or individualist behaviors with either a sense of self-ownership or with a sense of being controlled by nonassimilated forces. Thus, we expected few or weak correlations of self-focus with self-concordance. If a positive association emerged, we intended to control for self-focused goals in the self-concordance-to-SWB analyses to ensure that self-concordance effects involve more than a tendency to pursue primarily self-interests.

SUMMARY OF HYPOTHESES

Again, our primary hypothesis was that self-concordant motivation would be associated with SWB in most, if not all, of the cultural groups studied. In terms of the four constituent dimensions of self-concordance, external and introjected motivation should tend to be negatively associated with SWB, and intrinsic and identified motivation should tend to be positively associated with SWB. We ventured no a priori hypotheses regarding cultural mean differences for either the aggregate self-concordance measure or for the four individual motivation measures.

METHODS

PARTICIPANTS AND PROCEDURE

Five hundred and fifty-one college undergraduates participated in the study, all of them students at large universities. There were 194 South Korean students from Hanyang University in

Seoul, South Korea;[2] 153 U.S. students from the University of Missouri in Columbia, Missouri); 163 Taiwanese students from the National SunYat-Sen University, in Kaohsiung, Taiwan; and 41 Chinese students from the Guangdon Commercial College in Guangzhou, South China).[3] Participants were drawn from a variety of majors and courses of study. All participants were volunteers, although Missouri participants received credit toward their introductory psychology experimental requirement for participating. The data collections occurred between November 1999 and December 2001. Participants attended small group questionnaire sessions. During these sessions participants first completed SWB measures, then goal measures, then demographic measures.

An English version of the questionnaire was created for use with the U.S. sample. Chinese, Taiwanese, and South Korean versions were created by a process in which a bilingual psychologist/native to the country translated the questionnaire into the appropriate language, after which it was translated back by a second individual proficient in both English and the language in question. The equivalence of the original and the back-translated versions of the questionnaire was evaluated, and minor revisions were made to arrive at the final versions of the questionnaire.

MEASURES

Personal goals. All participants completed a standard personal-strivings assessment (Emmons, 1989) in which they were first told, "We are interested in the things that you typically or characteristically are trying to do in your everyday behavior. Think about the objectives that you are typically trying to accomplish or attain. We call these personal strivings." Participants were given examples of strivings and were then asked to list eight personal strivings of their own.

Next, we asked participants to rate the extent to which they pursue each striving for external, introjected, identified, and intrinsic reasons, using a Likert-type scale from 1 (*not at all for this reason*) to 7 (*completely for this reason*; Ryan & Connell, 1989; Sheldon & Elliot, 1999, 2000; Sheldon & Houser-Marko, 2001; Sheldon & Kasser, 1995, 1998). Again, the former two reasons are conceptualized as nonconcordant forms of motivation, and the latter two reasons are conceptualized as self-concordant forms of motivation (see Table 1 for the specific item wordings). As in prior research, we computed an aggregate self-concordance score for each participant by summing the eight identified and the eight intrinsic ratings and then subtracting the eight external and the eight introjected ratings. Cronbach's alpha coefficients for this 32-item variable ranged between .70 and .80 across the four samples. Below, we present data for this composite as well as for the four individual motivation dimensions.

In addition, participants were asked to rate the extent to which their goals were self-focused versus other-focused. The following wording was used:

> Goals can be adopted primarily to serve the needs and preferences of the *self* ("self-focused" goals), or to serve the needs and preferences of *social groups*, such as family, team, club, or friends ("group-focused"

TABLE 1
Item Wordings for the Four Motivation Dimensions

Wording	*Dimension*
External (nonconcordant)	You are pursuing this striving because somebody else wants you to or because your situation seems to demand it. Stated differently, you probably wouldn't have this striving if you didn't get some kind of reward, praise, or approval for it (or avoid some kind of punishment, criticism, or disapproval). For example, you might try to "go to church more regularly" because others might criticize you if you didn't, or because you need to be seen at church for your job.
Introjected (nonconcordant)	You are pursuing this striving because you would feel ashamed, guilty, or anxious if you didn't. Rather than having this striving just because someone else thinks you should, you feel that you "ought" to strive for that something. For example, you might try to "go to church more regularly" because you would feel bad about yourself if you didn't.
Identified (concordant)	You are pursuing this striving because you really believe that its an important goal to have. Although others may have urged you to pursue this striving in the past, now you endorse it freely and value it for personal reasons. For example, you might try to "go to church more regularly" because you genuinely feel this is the right thing to do, even if you don't really enjoy it.
Intrinsic (concordant)	You are pursuing this striving because of the fun and enjoyment which the striving provides you. While there may be many good reasons for the striving, the primary "reason" is simply your interest in the experience itself. For example, you might try to "go to church more regularly" because being at church is inherently interesting and enjoyable to you.

goals). For example, one might pursue the goal "get very high grades" because this is what one wants for oneself or because this is what one's family deems important. As another example, one might pursue the goal "get into good physical condition" because this is what one wants for oneself or because this is what one's sports team needs. Of course, a goal may also represent both at the same time. Please rate the extent to which each goal represents your own needs and preferences or the needs/preferences of important social groups.

A Likert-type scale was used in which 1 = *primarily group needs*, 3 = *represents both equally*, and 5 = *primarily personal needs*. Cronbach's alpha coefficients for the self-focus variable ranged between .50 and .66 across the four samples. These coefficients are rather low, suggesting that participants viewed their eight goals as varying considerably on their degree of self versus group focus.

Subjective well-being. In addition, all participants rated the 20 mood adjectives of the Positive Affect Negative Affect Schedule (Watson, Tellegen, & Clark, 1988), indicating how much they have felt each emotion "in the past month or so." A Likert-type scale from 1 (*very slightly or not all*) to 5 (*extremely*) was employed, and positive affect and negative affect scores were derived by averaging the appropriate items. Participants also completed the five items of the Satisfaction With Life Scale (Diener, Emmons, Larsen, & Griffin, 1985), also with reference to the past month or so, using a Likert-type scale from 1 (*strongly disagree*) to 5 (*strongly agree*). These items were averaged to create a life-satisfaction score. Alpha coeffi-

cients ranged between .60 and .82 across the four samples for positive affect, between .63 and .83 for negative affect, and between .75 and .81 for life satisfaction. As in other recent studies (Bettencourt & Sheldon, 2001; Elliot, Sheldon, & Church, 1997; Sheldon & Elliot, 1999), we also computed an aggregate measure of SWB by first standardizing all scores and then subtracting negative affect from the sum of positive affect and life satisfaction (Diener, 1994).

Demographics. At the end of the questionnaire participants rated their family income, using a 5-point Likert-type scale adjusted to each nation's currency and range of income levels. In addition, they rated their mother's level of education and their father's level of education from 1 (*some high school or less*) to 5 (*postgraduate degree*). We intended to control for these variables to ensure that they could not account for the primary results.

RESULTS

SAMPLE-WIDE MEANS IN SWB AND SELF-CONCORDANCE

Table 2 presents the overall sample mean for the SWB and motivation variables. The mean for aggregate self-concordance was positive, indicating that on the whole, participants felt that their personal goals were more internally than externally caused. Also, participants seemed generally happy, with means on life satisfaction and positive affect above the mid-point of the scale and the negative affect mean falling below the mid-point (Myers, 2000).

TABLE 2

Variable Means for the Entire Sample and for Each Subsample

	Sample				
Variables	*Total Sample*	*United States*	*South Korea*	*Taiwan*	*China*
Aggregate SWB	3.51	4.73_a	3.16_b	2.78_c	3.41_b
Positive affect	3.12	3.49_a	2.99_b	2.90_b	3.29_a
Negative affect	2.44	2.10_a	2.56_b	2.56_b	2.64_b
Life satisfaction	2.82	3.34_a	2.73_b	2.44_b	2.77_b
Self-concordance	3.04	3.57_a	3.43_a	2.39_b	3.41_a
External motivation	2.93	2.88	2.82	3.03	3.17
Introjected motivation	3.86	3.82_a	3.39_b	4.35_c	4.22_{ac}
Identified motivation	5.35	5.61_a	5.31_b	5.20_b	5.19_{ab}
Intrinsic motivation	4.59	4.66_a	4.34_a	4.57_a	5.60_b

NOTE: SWB = subjective well-being. Subsample means not sharing subscripts are significantly different from each other at the .01 level.

MEAN DIFFERENCES BETWEEN CULTURES IN SWB AND SELF-CONCORDANCE

Table 2 also presents means for the 10 variables and separately for each sample. We conducted one-way ANOVAs on each of the 10 variables, with cultural group as a four-level factor. Significant omnibus effects emerged in nine cases (Fs ranging from 6.02 to 193.1, all $ps < .01$; external motivation was the exception). For these nine variables, we then conducted a series of t tests to compare each sample to each other sample. Because so many tests were conducted, we employed a .01 alpha level. Table 2 contains the results.

Consistent with earlier studies of national well-being (i.e., Diener, Diener, & Diener, 1995), the U.S. sample evidenced significantly higher levels of all three first-order SWB measures, the only exception being that Chinese participants did not report lower positive affect than the U.S. sample. Also consistent with past results, the U.S. participants evidenced significantly higher aggregate SWB than the other three samples. In addition, the South Korean and Chinese samples evidenced significantly more SWB than the Taiwanese sample.

Next, we turned to the self-concordance variable. One-sample t tests revealed that self-concordance was significantly greater than zero in every sample (all $ps < .01$). This indicates that in every cultural group, people felt more I-PLOC than E-PLOC with respect to their personal goals. There were no significant differences in self-concordance between cultures, with the exception that the Taiwanese sample was lower than the other three samples. Considering the four individual motivation dimensions, no significant differences emerged for external motivation. The South Korean sample reported the least introjected motivation, and the Taiwanese and Chinese samples reported the most, with the U.S. sample in the middle. The U.S. sample reported the most identified motivation, with the other three samples reporting lower levels of identified motivation.

Finally, the Chinese sample reported the most intrinsic motivation for goals, with the U.S., South Korean, and Taiwanese samples reporting less intrinsic motivation.

SAMPLE-WIDE ASSOCIATIONS OF SELF-CONCORDANCE WITH SWB

Turning to our primary hypotheses, we next examined the associations between the motivation measures and the SWB measures. Table 3 presents these correlations collapsed across the four samples ($N = 551$; all measures were standardized within sample prior to this analysis). Consistent with prior findings (Sheldon, 2002), aggregate self-concordance was significantly positively correlated with positive affect, life-satisfaction, and aggregate SWB, and it was significantly negatively correlated with negative affect. Table 3 also provides the correlations between the individual motivation dimensions and SWB. As expected, external and introjected motivation correlated negatively with aggregate SWB, and identified and intrinsic motivation correlated positively with aggregate SWB. The same basic pattern emerged for the four motivation variables in relation to the three first-order SWB variables, although not all of the correlations reached significance.

Next, we turned to the control variables—namely, family income, mother's education, father's education, and self-focused goals. Would the association of self-concordance and SWB in the Asian samples be reducible to the effect of these variables? This was a possibility, given that self-concordance correlated positively with both father's and mother's education ($rs = .16$ and $.14$, respectively, $ps < .05$) and with self-focused goals ($r = .07$, $p < .10$); SWB also correlated positively with father's and mother's education ($rs = .11$ and $.15$, respectively, both $ps < .01$) and with self-focused goals ($r = -.25$, $p < .01$).

To ensure that self-concordance has effects on SWB that are independent of these associations, we conducted a hierarchical regression in which the control variables were entered at the

TABLE 3

Correlations of Goal-Motivation Measures With SWB Measures, Collapsed Across Cultures (N = 551)

	SWB Measures			
Predictors	Positive Affect	Negative Affect	Life-Satisfaction	Aggregate SWB
Self-concordance	.20***	−.31***	.18***	.33***
External	−.15***	.26***	−.11***	−.24***
Introjected	−.06	.21***	−.06	−.16***
Identified	.05	−.09**	.02	.08**
Intrinsic	.16***	−.09**	.18***	.21***

NOTE: SWB = subjective well-being.
**$p < .05$. ***$p < .01$.

first step and self-concordance was entered at the second step. At Step 1, income and mother's education were both significant predictors of SWB (βs = .12 and .13, both $ps < .05$). At Step 2, self-concordance accounted for significant incremental variance (R^2 change = .104, $p < .01$; β = .33). In short, it appears the associations of self-concordance with SWB represent more than the effects of family education, family income, or individualist goal contents.

VARIATIONS IN THE SELF-CONCORDANCE TO SWB ASSOCIATION ACROSS SAMPLES

Table 4 presents the correlation of aggregate self-concordance with each SWB measure, split by sample. As can be seen, self-concordance correlated significantly and positively with aggregate SWB in every sample and, as expected, was significantly associated with the first-order well-being variables in 9 out of 12 cases. Also as expected, external and introjected motivation were negatively correlated with aggregate SWB in every sample, and intrinsic and identified motivation were positively correlated with SWB in every sample (although 7 of the 16 correlations involving individual motivation dimensions did not reach significance). Notably, none of the 80 correlations presented in Table 4 were significant in the direction opposite from that predicted.

Next, we conducted a hierarchical regression analysis to examine a further question; that is, does self-concordance interact with the sample to predict SWB? To simplify the presentation, we analyzed only the aggregate SWB variable, regressing it on self-concordance at Step 1, three dummy variables representing the three Asian samples at Step 2, and three Dummy × Self-Concordance product terms at Step 3 to represent the interactions between sample and self-concordance. At Step 1, self-concordance was significant (R^2 change = .114, $p < .01$; β = .33); at Step 2, the three dummy variables were significant as a set (R^2 change = .204, $p < .01$), and each was significant individually (βs = −.46, −.50, and −.21 for Korea, Taiwan, and China, respectively; all three $ps < .01$). At Step 3, the three product terms were nonsignificant as a set (R^2 change = .002, $p > .50$), and none were significant individually (βs = −.07, .00, and −.06, respectively; all three $ps > .30$). The lack of interactions further supports the hypothesis that self-concordance may have universal benefits.

DISCUSSION

SUMMARY OF RESULTS

In this research, we tried to compare members of an individualist and three collectivist cultures in their levels of goal self-concordance and SWB. We wished to examine both the cultural mean differences in self-concordance and SWB and the cultural differences in patterns of association between self-concordance and SWB. We reasoned that if self-concordance was correlated with SWB in every sample, this would provide important new support for our assumption that self-concordance is beneficial regardless of one's cultural membership.

Analyses of mean differences revealed that Asian participants were much lower than U.S. participants in SWB, a finding that is consistent with earlier work (Diener et al., 1995; Diener & Suh, 1999). However, there was no strong tendency for the Asians to report less concordant motivation than the U.S. participants. For example, there were no cultural differences in external motivation. Also, the South Korean sample reported less introjected motivation than the U.S. participants, and the Chinese sample reported more intrinsic motivation than the U.S. participants. On the other hand, all three Asian samples reported lesser identification with their strivings compared to the U.S. sample. Perhaps most importantly, Asians experienced equal levels of aggregate self-concordance in their personal goals (except in the Taiwanese sample, discussed below). Furthermore, mean levels of self-concordance were positive in every sample, indicating that people feel more autonomous than controlled in every culture. Finally, self-concordance correlated only weakly with demographic variables and with a measure of the self-focused (versus group-focused) content of individuals' goals. Taken together, these findings suggest that it is possible for people to "own their goals" everywhere, regardless of their cultural membership, their income, family education, and the concrete focus of the goals.

Directly supporting our primary SWB-related hypotheses, self-concordance was predictive of every measure of SWB in the aggregate sample and was also predictive of SWB separately within every cultural sample by itself. In no culture did

TABLE 4

Correlations of Goal-Motivation Measures with SWB Measures

Culture	SWB Measures			
	Positive Affect	*Negative Affect*	*Life-Satisfaction*	*Aggregate SWB*
United States				
Self-concordance	.26***	−.42***	.12	.33***
External	−.29***	.43***	−.21***	−.39***
Introjected	−.04	.17**	.02	−.07
Identified	.07	−.15*	−.01	.08
Intrinsic	.20**	−.17**	.09	.19**
South Korea				
Self-concordance	.14**	−.20***	.22***	.27***
External	−.09	.11	−.11	−.14**
Introjected	−.04	.27***	−.17**	−.23***
Identified	.06	−.01	.04	.05
Intrinsic	.11	−.01	.15**	.13*
Taiwan				
Self-concordance	.19**	−.35***	.21***	.40***
External	−.10	.29***	−.10	−.27***
Introjected	−.12	.19**	−.04	−.18**
Identified	.00	−.11	.00	.06
Intrinsic	.13*	−.06	.28***	.25***
China				
Self-concordance	.24	−.30**	.05	.33**
External	−.15	.18	.16	−.07
Introjected	.01	.13	.05	−.04
Identified	.18	−.16	.12	.26
Intrinsic	.31**	−.27*	.23	.46***

NOTE: SWB = subjective well-being.

$*p < .10$. $**p < .05$. $***p < .01$.

self-concordance correlate negatively with SWB as a cultural relativist perspective might predict based on the assumption that self-possessed individuals do not "fit" within collectivist societies. Furthermore, the associations of self-concordance with SWB remained significant when the effects of selffocused goals were partialed out and also remained significant when the effects of demographic characteristics were controlled.

One less consistent finding concerned the Taiwanese sample. Although self-concordance correlated positively with SWB in this sample as in the other samples, Taiwanese participants reported significantly less self-concordance than the other samples as well as reporting significantly less SWB than the other samples. We believe this difference may have emerged because the Taiwanese University (National Sun Yat-Sen) and its city of lo-

cation (Kaohsiung) are fairly traditional and perhaps more collectivistic. In contrast, the other Asian universities in the sample (Hanyang and Guangdon) are located in more Westernized or cosmopolitan cities (Seoul and Guangzhou). However, future research will be required to establish whether Taiwanese samples from less traditional settings might evidence equal self-concordance as South Korean or Chinese samples and, conversely, whether Korean or Chinese students from less urbanized parts of these countries might evidence lower self-concordance.

Overall, these findings are quite consistent with our hypothesis that self-concordant goal pursuit is important in all cultures. Returning to the ongoing example, students (piano or otherwise) in every culture may benefit more when they strive because they enjoy and identify with the process of learning, rather than because they feel they must or should. In other words, when one goes along with strong social forces, it is likely better to reach a state of agreement with them than to resist or resent them. Indeed, this conclusion is consistent with humanistic, existential, organismic, psychosocial, and psychodynamic perspectives regarding optimal human functioning (Ryff & Singer, 1998; Sheldon & Kasser, 2001), which stress the importance of individuals' ability to assimilate and accommodate sociocultural norms, expectations, and constraints.

One positive feature of the current work is that it examined several non-Western cultures rather than just one, as occurs in many cross-cultural studies. Also, several different exemplars of collectivist culture were examined, varying on dimensions such as modern/traditional and democratic/socialist. As noted earlier, the fact that we found the same basic pattern of results across these different cultural contexts lends added confidence to our study conclusions. Yet another innovation of this research is that it employed a mixed idiographicnomothetic methodology, which allowed participants to voice their unique concerns while allowing us to directly compare participants based on their ratings of those concerns (Elliot, Chirkov, Kim, & Sheldon, 2001; Emmons, 1989). This may be especially desirable in cross-cultural studies where the content of people's goals and activities may vary more than the underlying meanings and purposes they represent.

LIMITATIONS AND UNANSWERED QUESTIONS

Limitations of this study include the fact that only college student samples were employed. It will be important to replicate the findings using older adults as college students may represent the most Westernized segment of many traditional cultures. Also, only self-report data were collected. It will also be important to perhaps eliminate method variance confounds by soliciting observer- as well as self-reports regarding participants' apparent self-concordance and/or SWB. In addition, it will be important to measure and control for stable trait variables such as neuroticism or extraversion as these might account for the selfconcordance to SWB effects (but see Elliot & Sheldon, 1998, for evidence that self-concordance effects are not reducible to neuroticism or behavioral inhibition). Future cross-cultural goal research should also examine longitudinal changes in SWB as a function of participants' level of goal attainment during the period of study as such studies might yield different results than those reported here (Oishi & Diener, 2001). Finally, future research should also study self-concordance and SWB in other cultures besides U.S. and Asian cultures as there are many types and styles of collectivism and individualism.

CONCLUSION

At the broadest level, the results of this study suggest a need for greater differentiation and phenomenological specificity in characterizations of autonomy, individualism, and agency. In particular, our results support a view in which humans function more optimally and have more positive experiences when they do what they enjoy and believe in, no matter what their cultural membership. Indeed, one might question the health or sustainability of a culture that did not tolerate this basic expression of human rights (Diener & Suh, 1999).

NOTES

1. Notably, some might view personal goals as an inherently individualistic construct, given that goals, by definition, concern people's proactive personal initiatives (Markus & Kitayama. 1994). However, along with other contemporary goal theorists, we assert that goals are actually among the most important means by which individuals adapt to social contexts and enhance their connectivity with others (Cantor & Sanderson, 1999; Salmela-Aro & Nurmi, 1996). That is, rather than being inherently self-centered, many goals, instead, concern the external world, especially the world of social roles and interpersonal concerns (Ryff & Singer. 1998; Salmela-Aro, Pennanen, & Nurmi, 2001; Sheldon & Elliot, 2000). The fact that many personal goals address social tasks is only logical, given that perhaps the primary adaptive environment for Homo sapiens throughout history has been the social environment (Caporael, 1997).

2. Data from the South Korean sample were used earlier to examine a different set of research questions (Elliot, Chirkov, Kim, & Sheldon, 2001; Sheldon, Elliot, Kim, & Kassel; 2001).

3. One hundred and sixty-one Chinese participants completed questionnaires. Unfortunately, we were able to match up subjective well-being (SWB) data and goal-data for only 41 of these respondents because of an error of questionnaire administration. Providing some assurance that this subsample was equivalent to the main sample, we found no differences between the 41 final participants and the 120 excluded participants on any of the four SWB measures (all $ps > .50$). Thus, we decided to include the Chinese data in this article.

REFERENCES

Bettencourt, B., & Sheldon, K. M. (2001). Social roles as vehicles for psychological need satisfaction within groups. *Journal of Personality and Social Psychology, 81*, 1131-1143.

Cantor, N., & Sanderson, C. (1999). Life-task participation and well-being: The importance of taking part in daily life. In D. Kahneman, E. Diener, & N. Schwarz (Eds.), *Well-being: The foundations of hedonic psychology* (pp. 230-243). New York: Russell Sage Foundation.

Caporael, L. R. (1997). The evolution of truly social cognition: The core configurations model. *Personality and Social Psychology Review, 1*, 276-298.

Chirkov, V. I., Ryan, R. M., Kim, Y., & Kaplan, R. (2003). Differentiating autonomy from individualism and independence: A self-determination theory perspective on internalization of cultural orientations and well-being. *Journal of Personality and Social Psychology, 84*, 97-109.

Deci, E. L., & Ryan, R. M. (1985). *Intrinsic motivation and self-determination in human behavior.* New York: Plenum.

Deci, E. L., & Ryan, R. M. (2000). The "what" and "why" of goal pursuits: Human needs and the self-determination of behavior. *Psychological Inquiry, 4*, 227-268.

Deci, E. L., Ryan, R. M., Gagne, M., Leone, D. R., Usunov, J., & Kornazheva, B. P. (2001). Need satisfaction, motivation, and well-being in the work organizations of a former Eastern Bloc country. *Personality and Social Psychology Bulletin, 27*, 930-942.

Diener, E. (1994). Assessing subjective well-being: Progress and opportunities. *Social Indicators Research, 31*, 103-157.

Diener, E., Diener, M., & Diener, C. (1995). Factors predicting the subjective well-being of nations. *Journal of Personality and Social Psychology, 69*, 851-864.

Diener, E., Emmons, R., Larsen, R., & Griffin, S. (1985). The Satisfaction with Life Scale. *Journal of Personality Assessment, 47*, 1105-1117.

Diener, E., & Suh, E. M. (1999). National differences in subjective well-being. In D. Kahneman, E. Diener, & N. Schwarz (Eds.), *Well-being: The foundations of hedonic psychology* (pp. 434-452). New York: Russell Sage Foundation.

Elliot, A. J., Chirkov, V., Kim, Y., & Sheldon, K. M. (2001). A cross-cultural analysis of avoidance (relative to approach) personal goals. *Psychological Science, 12*, 505-510.

Elliot, A. J., & Sheldon, K. M. (1998). Avoidance personal goals and the personality-illness relationship. *Journal of Personality and Social Psychology, 75*, 1282-1299.

Elliot, A. J., Sheldon, K. M., & Church, M. (1997). Avoidance personals goals and subjective well-being. *Personality and Social Psychology Bulletin, 23*, 915-927.

Emmons, R. A. (1989). The personal strivings approach to personality. In L. A. Pervin (Ed), *Goal concepts in personality and social psychology*. Hillsdale, NJ: Lawrence Erlbaum.

Hayarnizu, T. (1997). Between intrinsic and extrinsic motivation: Examination of reasons for academic study based on the theory of internalization. *Japanese Psychological Research, 39*, 98-108.

Iyengar, S. S., & Lepper, M. R. (1999). Rethinking the value of choice: A cultural perspective on intrinsic motivation. *Journal of Personality and Social Psychology, 76*, 349-366.

Markus, H., Kitayama, S., & Heiman, R. (1996). Culture and basic psychological principles. In E. T. Higgins & W. Kruglanski (Eds.), *Social psychology: Handbook of basic principles* (pp. 857-913). New York: Guilford.

Markus, H. R., & Kitayama, S. (1994). The cultural construction of self and emotion: Implications for social behavior. In S. Kitayama & H. R. Markus (Eds.), *Emotion and culture: Empirical studies of mutual influence* (pp. 89-130). Washington, DC: American Psychological Association.

Myers, D. (2000). The funds, friends, and faith of happy people. *American Psychologist, 55*, 56-67.

Oishi, S. (2000). Goals as cornerstones of subjective well-being: linking individuals and cultures. In E. Diener & E. Suh (Eds), *Culture and subjective well-being* (pp. 87-112). Cambridge, MA: MIT Press.

Oishi, S., & Diener, E. (2001). Goals, culture, and subjective well-being. Personality and Social Psychology Bulletin, 27, 1674-1682.

Ryan, R. M., & Connell, J. P. (1989). Perceived locus of causality and internalization: Examining reasons for acting in two domains. *Journal of Personality and Social Psychology, 57*, 749-761.

Ryff, C. D., & Singer, B. (1998). The role of purpose in life and personal growth in positive human health. In P. T. P. Wong & P. S. Fry (Eds.), *The human quest for meaning: A handbook of psychological research and clinical applications* (pp. 213-235). Mahwah, NJ: Lawrence Erlbaum.

Salmela-Am, K., & Nurmi, J. (1996). Uncertainty and confidence in interpersonal projects: Consequences for social relationships and well-being. *Journal of Social and Personal Relationships, 13*, 109-122.

Salmela-Am, K., Pennanen, R., & Nurmi, J. (2001). Self-focused goals: What they are, how they function, and how they relate to well-being. In P. Schmuck & K. Sheldon (Eds.), *Life goals and well-being: Towards a positive psychology of human striving* (pp. 148-166). London: Hogrefe.

Sheldon, K. M. (2002). The self-concordance model of healthy goal-striving: When personal goals correctly represent the person. In E. L. Deci & R. M. Ryan (Eds.), *Handbook of self-determination research* (pp. 65-86). Rochester, NY: University of Rochester Press.

Sheldon, K. M., & Elliot, A. J. (1999). Goal striving, need satisfaction, and longitudinal well-being: The Self-Concordance Model. *Journal of Personality and Social Psychology, 76*, 546-557.

Sheldon, K. M., & Elliot, A. J. (2000). Personal goals in social roles: Divergences and convergences across roles and levels of analysis. *Journal of Personality, 68*, 51-84.

Sheldon, K. M., Elliot, A. J., Kim, Y., & Kasser, T. (2001). What's satisfying about satisfying events? Comparing ten candidate psychological needs. *Journal of Personality and Social Psychology, 80*, 325-339.

Sheldon, K. M., & Houser-Marko, L. (2001). Self-concordance, goal-attainment, and the pursuit of happiness: Can there be an upward spiral? *Journal of Personality and Social Psychology, 80*, 152-165.

Sheldon, K. M., & Kasser, T. (1995). Coherence and congruence: Two aspects of personality integration. *Journal of Personality and Social Psychology, 68*, 531-543.

Sheldon. K. M., & Kasser, T. (1998). Pursuing personal goals: Skills enable progress but not all progress is beneficial. *Personality and Social Psychology Bulletin, 24*, 1319-1331.

Triandis, H. C. (1997). Cross-cultural perspectives on personality. In R. Hogan, J. Johnson, & S. Briggs (Eds.), *Handbook of personality psychology* (pp. 439-464). San Diego, CA: Academic Press.

Watson, D., Tellegen, A., & Clark, L. (1988). Development and validation of brief measures of positive and negative affect: The PANAS scales. *Journal of Personality and Social Psychology, 54*, 1063-1070.

Yamauchi, H., & Thnaka, K. (1998). Relations of autonomy, self-referenced beliefs and self-regulated learning among Japanese children. *Psychological Reports, 82*, 803-816.

Kennon M. Sheldon received his Ph.D. in social-personality psychology from the University of California at Davis in 1992. He is an associate professor of psychology at the University of Missouri. He studies goals, motivation, and psychological well-being. Much of his work is summarized in his 2003 book with Williams and Joiner, *Self-Determination Theory in the Clinic: Motivating Physical and Mental Health (Yale University Press).*

Andrew J. Elliot is a professor of psychology at the University of Rochester. He received his Ph.D. from the University of Wisconsin–Madison. His research focuses on approach-avoidance motivation and personality—in particular, within the achievement domain.

Richard M. Ryan is a professor of psychology and psychiatry at the University of Rochester, where he has been on the faculty since 1981. As a researcher, he is best known for his work on human motivation, particularly his investigations of intrinsic motivation and internalization processes. He is the author of numerous research articles in both theoretical and applied areas, including the topics of motivation in health care, the development of self-regulation, psychopathology, education, work, sport and exercise, and parenting, among other foci.

Valery Chirkov received a Ph.D. in industrial psychology from Leningrad State University in Russia and came to the United States in 1995 for further training. He received his Ph.D. in social psychology at the University of Rochester in 2001 and is currently an assistant professor of psychology at the University of Saskatchewan. His research focuses on the problem of the internalization of cultural practices and values, the role of parents and teachers in the transmission of cultural values, and the psychological aspects of immigration, acculturation, and cultural adjustment.

Youngmee Kim, Ph.D., is a director of family studies at the Behavioral Research Center at the National Home Office of the American Cancer Society. She received her B.A. and M.A. from Yonsei University and her M.A. and Ph.D. in social and personality psychology from the University of Rochester. Her research focuses on the physical and psychological effect of cancer in the family.

Cindy Wu is an assistant professor in the Hankamer School of Business at Baylor University. She received her Ph.D. from the University of Illinois at Urbana-Champaign. Her research focuses on employee motivation, training, leadership, and cross-cultural management.

Meliksah Demir got his B.A. from the Middle East Technical University, Ankara, Turkey. He is currently a Ph.D. student at Wayne State University, Detroit, Michigan. His research interests are friendship and subjective well-being.

Zhigang Sun is the director of the Center for Advanced Social Research of the University of Missouri's School of Journalism. His research interests include the effects of mass communication on social capital and civic norms, health communication, political communication, and the application of research design and methodology in social attitudinal and behavioral studies.

Making Sense of Self-Esteem

Mark R. Leary[1]
Department of Psychology, Wake Forest University, Winston-Salem, North Carolina

Abstract
Sociometer theory proposes that the self-esteem system evolved as a monitor of social acceptance, and that the so-called self-esteem motive functions not to maintain self-esteem per se but rather to avoid social devaluation and rejection. Cues indicating that the individual is not adequately valued and accepted by other people lower self-esteem and motivate behaviors that enhance relational evaluation. Empirical evidence regarding the self-esteem motive, the antecedents of self-esteem, the relation between low self-esteem and psychological problems, and the consequences of enhancing self-esteem is consistent with the theory.
Keywords
self-esteem; self; self-regard; rejection

Self-esteem has been regarded as an important construct since the earliest days of psychology. In the first psychology textbook, William James (1890) suggested that the tendency to strive to feel good about oneself is a fundamental aspect of human nature, thereby fueling a fascination—some observers would say obsession—with self-esteem that has spanned more than a century. During that time, developmental psychologists have studied the antecedents of self-esteem and its role in human development, social psychologists have devoted attention to behaviors that appear intended to maintain self-esteem, personality psychologists have examined individual differences in the trait of self-esteem, and theorists of a variety of orientations have discussed the importance of self-regard to psychological adjust-ment. In the past couple of decades, practicing psychologists and social engineers have suggested that high self-esteem is a remedy for many psychological and social problems.

Yet, despite more than 100 years of attention and thousands of published studies, fundamental issues regarding self-esteem remain poorly understood. Why is self-esteem important? Do people really have a need for self-esteem? Why is self-esteem so strongly determined by how people believe they are evaluated by others? Is low self-esteem associated with psychological difficulties and, if so, why? Do efforts to enhance self-esteem reduce personal and social problems as proponents of the self-esteem movement claim?

PERSPECTIVES ON THE FUNCTION OF SELF-ESTEEM

Many writers have assumed that people seek to maintain their self-esteem because they possess an inherent "need" to feel good about themselves. However, given the apparent importance of self-esteem to psychological functioning, we must ask why self-esteem is so important and what function it might serve. Humanistic psychologists have traced high self-esteem to a congruency between a person's real and ideal selves and suggested that self-esteem signals people as to when they are behaving in self-determined, autonomous ways. Other writers have proposed that people seek high self-esteem because it facilitates goal achievement. For example, Bednar, Wells, and Peterson (1989) proposed that self-esteem is subjective feedback about the adequacy of the self. This feedback—self-esteem—is positive when the individual copes well with circumstances but negative when he or she avoids threats. In turn, self-esteem affects subsequent goal achievement; high self-esteem increases coping, and low self-esteem leads to further avoidance.

The ethological perspective (Barkow, 1980) suggests that self-esteem is an adaptation that evolved in the service of maintaining dominance in social relationships. According to this theory, human beings evolved mechanisms for monitoring dominance because dominance facilitated the acquisition of mates and other reproduction-enhancing resources. Because attention and favorable reactions from others were associated with being dominant, feelings of self-esteem became tied to social approval and deference. From this perspective, the motive to evaluate oneself positively reduces, in evolutionary terms, to the motive to enhance one's relative dominance.

One of the more controversial explanations of self-esteem is provided by terror management theory, which suggests that the function of self-esteem is to buffer people against the existential terror they experience at the prospect of their own death and annihilation (Solomon, Greenberg, & Pyszczynski, 1991). Several experiments have supported aspects of the theory, but not the strong argument that the function of the self-esteem system is to provide an emotional buffer specifically against death-related anxiety.

All of these perspectives offer insights into the nature of self-esteem, but each has conceptual and empirical difficulties (for critiques, see Leary, 1999; Leary & Baumeister, in press). In the past few years, a novel perspective—sociometer theory—has cast self-esteem in a somewhat different light as it attempts to address lingering questions about the nature of self-esteem.

SOCIOMETER THEORY

According to sociometer theory, self-esteem is essentially a psychological meter, or gauge, that monitors the quality of people's relationships with others (Leary, 1999; Leary & Baumeister, in press; Leary & Downs, 1995). The theory is based on the assumption that human beings possess a pervasive drive to maintain significant interpersonal relationships, a drive that evolved because early human beings who belonged to social groups were more likely to survive and reproduce than those who did not (Baumeister & Leary, 1995). Given the disastrous implications of being ostracized in the ancestral environment in which human evolution occurred, early human beings may have developed a mechanism for monitoring the degree to which other people valued and accepted them. This psychological mechanism—the *sociometer*—continuously monitors the social environment for cues regarding the degree to which the individual is being accepted versus rejected by other people.

The sociometer appears to be particularly sensitive to changes in relational evaluation—the degree to which others regard their relationship with the individual as valuable, important, or close. When evidence of low relational evaluation (particularly, a decrement in relational evaluation) is detected, the sociometer attracts the person's conscious attention to the potential threat to social acceptance and motivates him or her to deal with it. The affectively laden self-appraisals that constitute the "output" of the sociometer are what we typically call self-esteem.

Self-esteem researchers distinguish between *state self-esteem*—momentary fluctuations in a person's feelings about him- or herself—and *trait self-esteem*—the person's general appraisal of his or her value; both are aspects of the sociometer. Feelings of state self-esteem fluctuate as a function of the degree to which the person perceives others currently value their relationships with him or her. Cues that connote high relational evaluation raise state self-esteem, whereas cues that connote low relational evaluation lower state self-esteem. Trait self-esteem, in contrast, reflects the person's general sense that he or she is the sort of person who is valued and accepted by other people. Trait self-esteem may be regarded as the resting state of

the sociometer in the absence of incoming information relevant to relational evaluation.

SELF-ESTEEM AND ITS RELATIONSHIP TO BEHAVIOR

Sociometer theory provides a parsimonious explanation for much of what we know about self-esteem. Here I examine how sociometer theory answers four fundamental questions about self-esteem raised earlier.

The Self-Esteem Motive

As noted, many psychologists have assumed that people possess a motive or need to maintain self-esteem. According to sociometer theory, the so-called self-esteem motive does not function to maintain self-esteem but rather to minimize the likelihood of rejection (or, more precisely, relational devaluation). When people behave in ways that protect or enhance their self-esteem, they are typically acting in ways that they believe will increase their relational value in others' eyes and, thus, improve their chances of social acceptance.

The sociometer perspective explains why events that are known (or potentially known) by other people have much greater effects on self-esteem than events that are known only by the individual him- or herself. If self-esteem involved only private self-judgments, as many psychologists have assumed, public events should have no greater impact on self-esteem than private ones.

Antecedents of Self-Esteem

Previous writers have puzzled over the fact that self-esteem is so strongly tied to people's beliefs about how they are evaluated by others. If self-esteem is a *self*-evaluation, why do people judge themselves by *other* people's standards? Sociometer theory easily explains why the primary determinants of self-esteem involve the perceived reactions of other people, as well as self-judgments on dimensions that the person thinks are important to significant others. As a monitor of relational evaluation, the self-esteem system is inherently sensitive to real and potential reactions of other people.

Evidence shows that state self-esteem is strongly affected by events

that have implications for the degree to which one is valued and accepted by other people (Leary, Haupt, Strausser, & Chokel, 1998; Leary, Tambor, Terdal, & Downs, 1995). The events that affect self-esteem are precisely the kinds of things that, if known by other people, would affect their evaluation and acceptance of the person (Leary, Tambor, et al., 1995). Most often, self-esteem is lowered by failure, criticism, rejection, and other events that have negative implications for relational evaluation; self-esteem rises when a person succeeds, is praised, or experiences another's love—events that are associated with relational appreciation. Even the mere possibility of rejection can lower self-esteem, a finding that makes sense if the function of the self-esteem system is to warn the person of possible relational devaluation in time to take corrective action.

The attributes on which people's self-esteem is based are precisely the characteristics that determine the degree to which people are valued and accepted by others (Baumeister & Leary, 1995). Specifically, high trait self-esteem is associated with believing that one possesses socially desirable attributes such as competence, personal likability, and physical attractiveness. Furthermore, self-esteem is related most strongly to one's standing on attributes that one believes are valued by significant others, a finding that is also consistent with sociometer theory.

In linking self-esteem to social acceptance, sociometer theory runs counter to the humanistic assumption that self-esteem based on approval from others is false or unhealthy. On the contrary, if the function of self-esteem is to avoid social devaluation and rejection, then the system must be responsive to others' reactions. This system may lead people to do things that are not always beneficial, but it does so to protect their interpersonal relationships rather than their inner integrity.

Low Self-Esteem and Psychological Problems

Research has shown that low self-esteem is related to a variety of psychological difficulties and personal problems, including depression, loneliness, substance abuse, teenage pregnancy, academic failure, and criminal behavior. The evidence in support of the link between low self-esteem and psychological problems has often been overstated; the relationships are weaker and more scattered than typically assumed (Mecca, Smelser, & Vasconcellos, 1989). Moreover, high self-esteem also has notable drawbacks. Even so, low self-esteem tends to be more strongly associated with psychological difficulties than high self-esteem.

From the standpoint of sociometer theory, these problems are caused not by low self-esteem but rather by a history of low relational evaluation, if not outright rejection. As a subjective gauge of relational evaluation, self-esteem may parallel these problems, but it is a coeffect rather than a cause. (In fact, contrary to the popular view that low self-esteem causes these problems, no direct evidence exists to document that self-esteem has any causal role in thought, emotion, or behavior.) Much research shows that interpersonal rejection results in emotional problems, difficulties relating with others, and maladaptive efforts to be accepted (e.g., excessive dependency, membership in deviant groups), precisely the concomitants of low self-esteem (Leary, Schreindorfer, & Haupt, 1995). In addition, many personal problems lower self-esteem because they lead other people to devalue or reject the individual.

Consequences of Enhancing Self-Esteem

The claim that self-esteem does not cause psychological outcomes may appear to fly in the face of evidence showing that interventions that enhance self-esteem do, in fact, lead to positive psychological changes. The explanation for the beneficial effects of programs that enhance self-esteem is that these interventions change people's perceptions of the degree to which they are socially valued individuals. Self-esteem programs always include features that would be expected to increase real or perceived social acceptance; for example, these programs include components aimed at enhancing social skills and interpersonal problem solving, improving physical appearance, and increasing self-control (Leary, 1999).

CONCLUSIONS

Sociometer theory suggests that the emphasis psychologists and the lay public have placed on self-esteem has been somewhat misplaced. Self-esteem is certainly involved in many psychological phenomena, but its role is different than has been supposed. Subjective feelings of self-esteem provide ongoing feedback regarding one's relational value vis-à-vis other people. By focusing on the monitor rather than on what the monitor measures, we have been distracted from the underlying interpersonal processes and the importance of social acceptance to human well-being.

Recommended Reading

Baumeister, R. F. (Ed.). (1993). *Self-esteem: The puzzle of low self-regard*. New York: Plenum Press.
Colvin, C. R., & Block, J. (1994). Do positive illusions foster mental health? An examination of the Taylor and Brown formulation. *Psychological Bulletin, 116*, 3–20.
Leary, M. R. (1999). (See References)
Leary, M. R., & Downs, D. L. (1995). (See References)
Mecca, A. M., Smelser, N. J., & Vasconcellos, J. (Eds.). (1989). (See References)

Note

1. Address correspondence to Mark Leary, Department of Psychology, Wake Forest University, Winston-Salem, NC 27109; e-mail: leary@wfu.edu.

References

Barkow, J. (1980). Prestige and self-esteem: A biosocial interpretation. In D. R. Omark, F. F. Strayer, & D. G. Freedman (Eds.), *Dominance relations: An ethological view of human conflict and social interaction* (pp. 319–332). New York: Garland STPM Press.
Baumeister, R. F., & Leary, M. R. (1995). The need to belong: Desire for interpersonal attachments as a fundamental human motivation. *Psychological Bulletin, 117*, 497–529.
Bednar, R. L., Wells, M. G., & Peterson, S. R. (1989). *Self-esteem: Paradoxes and innovations in clinical theory and practice*. Washington, DC: American Psychological Association.
James, W. (1890). *The principles of psychology* (Vol. 1). New York: Henry Holt.
Leary, M. R. (1999). The social and psychological importance of self-esteem. In R. M. Kowalski & M. R. Leary (Eds.), *The social psychology of emotional and behavioral problems: Interfaces of social and clinical psychology* (pp. 197–221). Washington, DC: American Psychological Association.
Leary, M. R., & Baumeister, R. F. (in press). The nature and function of self-esteem: Sociometer theory. *Advances in Experimental Social Psychology*.
Leary, M. R., & Downs, D. L. (1995). Interpersonal functions of the self-esteem motive: The self-esteem system as a sociometer. In M. H. Kernis (Ed.), *Efficacy, agency, and self-esteem* (pp. 123–144). New York: Plenum Press.
Leary, M. R., Haupt, A. L., Strausser, K. S., & Chokel, J. L. (1998). Calibrating the sociometer: The relationship between interpersonal appraisals and state self-esteem. *Journal of Personality and Social Psychology, 74*, 1290–1299.
Leary, M. R., Schreindorfer, L. S., & Haupt, A. L. (1995). The role of self-esteem in emotional and behavioral problems: Why is low self-esteem dysfunctional? *Journal of Social and Clinical Psychology, 14*, 297–314.
Leary, M. R., Tambor, E. S., Terdal, S. J., & Downs, D. L. (1995). Self-esteem as an interpersonal monitor. The sociometer hypothesis. *Journal of Personality and Social Psychology, 68*, 518–530.
Mecca, A. M., Smelser, N. J., & Vasconcellos, J. (Eds.). (1989). *The social importance of self-esteem*. Berkeley: University of California Press.
Solomon, S., Greenberg, J., & Pyszczynski, T. (1991). A terror management theory of social behavior: The psychological functions of self-esteem and cultural worldviews. *Advances in Experimental Social Psychology, 24*, 93–159.

Why we overestimate our competence

Social psychologists are examining people's pattern of overlooking their own weaknesses.

BY TORI DeANGELIS

We've all seen it: the employee who's convinced she's doing a great job and gets a mediocre performance appraisal, or the student who's sure he's aced an exam and winds up with a D.

The tendency that people have to overrate their abilities fascinates Cornell University social psychologist David Dunning, PhD. "People overestimate themselves," he says, "but more than that, they really seem to believe it. I've been trying to figure out where that certainty of belief comes from."

Dunning is doing that through a series of manipulated studies, mostly with students at Cornell. He's finding that the least competent performers inflate their abilities the most; that the reason for the overinflation seems to be ignorance, not arrogance; and that chronic self-beliefs, however inaccurate, underlie both people's over and underestimations of how well they're doing.

Meanwhile, other researchers are studying the subjective nature of self-assessment from other angles. For example, Steven Heine, PhD, a psychologist at the University of British Columbia, is showing that self-inflation tends to be more of a Western than a universal phenomenon. And psychologist Larry Gruppen, PhD, of the University of Michigan Medical School, is examining inaccurate self-assessments among medical students, where the costs of self-inflation can be particularly high (see related article).

Knowing thyself isn't easy

There are many reasons why it's hard to "know ourselves" in certain domains, Dunning says. In a subjective area like intelligence, for example, people tend to perceive their competence in self-serving ways. A student talented in math, for instance, may emphasize math and analytical skills in her definition of intelligence, while a student gifted in other areas might highlight verbal ability or creativity.

Another problem is that in many areas of life, accurate feedback is rare. People don't like giving negative feed-

back, Dunning says, so it's likely we will fail to hear criticism that would help us improve our performance.

"It's surprising how often feedback is nonexistent or ambiguous," he asserts. "It's a pretty safe assumption that what people say to our face is more positive than what they're saying behind our backs." People also overestimate themselves out of ignorance, Dunning says. Take the ironic example of an elderly man who thinks he's an excellent driver but is a hazard on the road, or the woman who reads a book about the stock market and is ready to compete with a professional stockbroker.

Dunning is addressing some of these self-overestimation issues empirically. In a series of studies reported in the December 1999 *Journal of Personality and Social Psychology* (Vol. 77, No. 6), he and co-author Justin Kruger, PhD, then a Cornell graduate student and now an assistant professor at the University of Illinois at Urbana-Champaign, examined the idea that ignorance is at the root of some self-inflation. Cornell students received short tests in humor, grammar and logic, then assessed how well they thought they did both individually and in relation to other Cornell students. In all three areas, students who performed the worst greatly overestimated their performance compared to those who did well.

In another article in the January issue of the *Journal of Personality and Social Psychology* (Vol. 84, No. 1), Dunning and Cornell doctoral candidate Joyce Ehrlinger describe four studies revealing a potential source of people's errors in self-judgment: their longstanding views of their talents and abilities. Depending on which measure the team looked at, such self-views were equally or more related to performance estimates than to their performance itself, and these self-views often produced errors in their reporting on how well they had just performed.

In one of the studies, for instance, the team tacitly pulled information from Cornell students to see if they thought they had logical ability. After that, the students took a multiple-choice test described as focusing on logical reasoning, then estimated the number of items they had answered correctly. Students who initially ranked themselves high on logical ability believed they were more likely to do well than those who rated themselves low on the ability, even when their performances ended up the same. Similarly in two other studies, the researchers manipulated students' chronic view of a particular talent by asking questions priming them to raise or lower their view of it. Depending on the questions, students became more or less optimistic about how well they did on a test of the talent, even though their performance was equal.

Dunning also has studied people's self-assessments in the moral domain and unearthed what he calls a "holier-than-thou" syndrome. In a series of studies reported in the December 2000 *Journal of Personality and Social Psychology* (Vol. 79, No. 6), he and Nicholas Epley, PhD, then a Cornell graduate student and now an assistant professor at Harvard University, found that undergraduates consistently overrated the likelihood that they would act in generous or selfless ways.

One of the studies, for example, uses a version of the classic "prisoners' dilemma" experiment, in which subjects must choose between self-interest and cooperation. In Dunning's study, 84 percent of the students initially predicted they would cooperate with their partner, but only 61 percent actually did. Furthermore, students' actual performance squared with their estimates of how others would behave, thus demonstrating a propensity to see others more accurately than they see themselves, Dunning comments.

Some critics have faulted Dunning's work for methodological problems, saying that it overstates the degree to which people overestimate their abilities. For example, in a 2002 article in *Personality and Individual Differences* (Vol. 33, No. 4), Georgia Institute of Technology psychologist Phillip Ackerman, PhD, and colleagues assert that Dunning fails to account for "regression to the mean," a statistical phenomenon which finds that if people are on the low end of a distribution, they will naturally rank themselves higher simply because their perceptions of ability aren't correlated with actual ability. In response, Dunning contends that he and Kruger did address the regression problem in their 1999 paper and that, in subsequent work, he has corrected for regression effects and still finds his numbers hold up.

Cross-cultural comparisons

Regardless of how pervasive the phenomenon is, it is clear from Dunning's and others' work that many Americans, at least sometimes and under some conditions, have a tendency to inflate their worth. It is interesting, therefore, to see the phenomenon's mirror opposite in another culture. In research comparing North American and East Asian self-assessments, Heine of the University of British Columbia finds that East Asians tend to underestimate their abilities, with an aim toward improving the self and getting along with others.

These differences are highlighted in a meta-analysis Heine is now completing of 70 studies that examine the degree of self-enhancement or self-criticism in China, Japan and Korea versus the United States and Canada. Sixty-nine of the 70 studies reveal significant differences between the two cultures in the degree to which individuals hold these tendencies, he finds.

In another article in the October 2001 *Journal of Personality and Social Psychology* (Vol. 81, No. 4), Heine's team looks more closely at how this occurs. First, Japanese and American participants performed a task at which they either succeeded or failed. Then they were timed as they worked on another version of the task. "The results made a symmetrical X," says Heine: Americans worked longer if they succeeded at the first task, while Japanese worked longer if they failed.

There are cultural, social and individual motives behind these tendencies, Heine and colleagues observe in a paper in the October 1999 *Psychological Review* (Vol. 106, No. 4). "As Western society becomes more individualistic, a successful life has come to be equated with having high self-esteem," Heine says. "Inflating one's sense of self creates positive emotions and feelings of self-efficacy, but the downside is that people don't really like self-enhancers very much."

Conversely, East Asians' self-improving or self-critical stance helps them maintain their "face," or reputation, and as a result, their interpersonal network. But the cost is they don't feel as good about themselves, he says. Because people in these cultures have different motivations, they make very different choices, Heine adds. If Americans perceive they're not doing well at something, they'll look for something else to do instead. "If you're bad at volleyball, well fine, you won't play volleyball," as Heine puts it. East Asians, though, view a poor performance as an invitation to try harder.

Interestingly, children in many cultures tend to overrate their abilities, perhaps because they lack objective feedback about their performance. For example, until about third grade, German youngsters generally overrate their academic achievement and class standing. This tendency declines as feedback in the form of letter grades begins. But researchers also have shown significant cross-cultural differences in youngsters' performance estimates—American children, it appears, are particularly prone to overestimate their competence. Other cross-cultural differences appear in whether children attribute good performance to ability or to effort, and in strategies used to improve performance. Researchers have linked different teaching strategies to these variations (see *"Further Reading"* and visit www.vcld.org/pages/newsletters/01_02_fall/attribu.htm for references).

Wanted: good feedback

One antidote to inaccurate self-assessment is high-quality feedback, Dunning says. One place such feedback would be particularly useful, for instance, is in the medical arena, where physicians are mandated to identify their own weaknesses and improve on them through education and research. The difficulty is that doctors—and for that matter, people in general—often can't see those weaknesses, he says.

Dunning is now starting a study that will look more closely at the issue of "blind spots." If indeed people avoid improvement because they simply don't see their own failings, the area is ripe for intervention, he believes.

"A little pointed feedback might be the exact motivator people need to work on their shortcomings," says Dunning. "If adolescents don't realize that they really know very little about safe sex, or physicians don't know that medical technology and information has significantly changed, they can't be expected to be motivated to improve their situation."

Tori DeAngelis is a writer in Syracuse, N.Y.

UNIT 3
Social Cognition and Social Perception

Unit Selections

7. **How Social Perception Can Automatically Influence Behavior**, Melissa J. Ferguson and John A. Bargh
8. **Make-Believe Memories**, Elizabeth F. Loftus
9. **How Culture Molds Habits of Thought**, Erica Goode
10. **More Than One Way to Make an Impression: Exploring Profiles of Impression Management**, Mark C. Bolino and William H. Turnley

Key Points to Consider

- Have you ever met a new stranger who immediately reminded you of someone else? How did you respond to the new acquaintance? Did you respond the same way you did to your former acquaintance? Why did you react the way you did?

- What role do you think memory plays in forming impressions of others? What role do you think learning plays in impression formation?

- Are eyewitnesses accurate? Why are some witnesses more credible or more believable than others? Can ideas and memories related to events that never happened really be "planted" in someone's mind? How so? What consequences do eyewitness inaccuracies have for defendants? Are there any methods for overcoming problems associated with eyewitness testimony?

- How does culture mold thoughts? How does culture shape social inferences? What is an attribution? How do citizens of Western and Eastern cultures differ in the ways they make attributions about others?

- What is impression management? Do others really manipulate the way they present themselves to us? Have you ever presented a false or glorified image to anyone else? Why do people do this?

- What role does the situation or environment play in person perception? What is the fundamental attribution error? How can we overcome this error so as to improve our perceptions of others? Can you think of other cognitive biases that color our impressions?

- What is a job interview? Why is it necessary for an interviewer to establish an accurate impression of a job candidate? How can interviewers enhance their "hit" rates, that is, improve their chances of hiring a good person for the job?

 **Links: www.dushkin.com/online/**
These sites are annotated in the World Wide Web pages.

Cognitive and Psychological Sciences on the Internet
http://www-psych.stanford.edu/cogsci/
Nonverbal Behavior and Nonverbal Communication
http://www3.usal.es/~nonverbal/

One neighbor called the police about another neighbor. The first did not know the second, but when she heard slapping sounds and painful grunts emanating from the neighbor's apartment, she thought child or spousal abuse was occurring. During the investigation, the police determined that there was no abuse. Upon further inquiry, the police realized that the first neighbor was highly sensitized to slapping sounds because she herself had been abused as a child. "What" you ask "was the second neighbor doing?" He was watching professional wrestling on television!

How we perceive and interpret others' behaviors, sentiments, and emotions is very important. Without such insights we would not accomplish much in our social interactions. You should remember that others are observing you and scrutinizing your actions in an effort to better understand you. Try to imagine a world where we do not feel competent to predict others' actions or to understand their moods and motives.

In this third unit, we move from self-perception to social cognition and social perception. Most theories of social perception and social cognition assume that we are fairly rational and methodical in our assessments of others. But, is this really the case? Do we instead make snap judgments of others? Research on cognitive misers (lazy perceivers of social information) suggests that we characteristically prefer quick appraisals.

Social *cognition* involves the way people think about others, represent others in memory, and strategize to understand oth-

ers. Processes such as learning and remembering are important to social cognition. And, once again, culture plays an active role in how we proceed to understand others. Besides the story about wrestling, another astonishing example of social cognition gone awry is the inaccuracy of eyewitnesses. Despite the witness's confidence, research demonstrates that most eyewitnesses are inaccurate, including professional witnesses such as the police.

Social *perception* or person perception entails how we form overall impressions of others. Another example is in order. Suppose someone you hardly know steals a valued possession from you. You might jump to the conclusion that this individual is just plain bad. Social psychologists would say that you attribute (ascribe or assign) a description of or form an opinion about this other person on the basis of just one behavior. Your attribution is most probably inaccurate. All humans display both positive and negative qualities. What if later you are attending synagogue and the Rabbi announces that this same person made a sizeable donation for an addition to the building. Would you agree that your appraisal of the individual might merit modification? Would you be willing to adjust your characterization of the person?

Besides misattribution, our impressions of others (and the impressions we in turn leave on others) are muddied by a variety of additional processes that consequently make our interpersonal tasks more difficult. Some individuals actively manipulate the perceptions others form of them. One such individual is known as a *self-monitor* or someone who is chameleon-like. The individual feigns friendliness, likes to attract attention at parties, appears studious and intellectual in class, and at the same time gives the impression of somberness and devotion at church. While all of us are culpable of manipulation from time to time, the self-monitor is the champion impression manager.

Let us further examine some of these issues in two sub-units—the first on social cognition and the other on social perception.

In "How Social Perception Can Automatically Influence Behavior," Ferguson and Bargh, argue that our memories can unintentionally and unknowingly alter our impressions of someone. The memory might even be of a similar person. The authors claim that such reminiscences are automatic and outside of our awareness. In sum, the authors provide yet another reason to question the accuracy of our evaluations of others.

The article that follows details some of the fascinating work on eyewitness memory alluded to above. Leading social psychologist, Elizabeth Loftus, shares her decades of research on the topic with the reader. The overarching conclusion is that many eyewitnesses are indeed mistaken.

The subunit on social cognition would be incomplete without commentary on the role culture plays in fashioning our assumptions about others. Author Erica Goode discusses the notion that Eastern and Western cultures differ in how their members make attributions about another's behavior.

The subunit on social perception commences with an article entitled "More Than One Way to Make an Impression." Bolino and Turnley discuss specific ways to manage impressions we leave on others. Along the way, they introduce information about self-monitors and about gender differences.

A common error in social judgments occurs because of the *fundamental attribution error*. You will recall that "to attribute" generally means to ascribe or assign. Attribution, therefore, signifies that our search is underway to find the cause of another's behavior. For this reason, the fundamental attribution error means that most of us make the basic mistake of ascribing the causes of someone else's behavior to that person's character or traits. The role of the situation is largely forgotten.

How social perception can automatically influence behavior

Melissa J. Ferguson[1] and John A. Bargh[2]

Do we always know the reasons for our actions? Or is our behavior sometimes unknowingly and unintentionally influenced by what we have recently perceived? It has been traditionally assumed that the automatic influence of knowledge in memory is limited to people's interpretation of the world, and stops short of shaping their actual behavior. Researchers in experimental social psychology have begun to challenge this assumption by documenting how people's behaviors can be unknowingly influenced by knowledge that is incidentally activated in memory during social perception. We review findings that suggest that the social knowledge that is incidentally activated while reading words or imagining events subsequently affects participants' behaviors across a range of ostensibly unrelated domains.

Experimental social psychologists have amassed a large body of findings over the past three decades suggesting that social knowledge is automatically activated in memory during the natural course of perception. That is, while people are seeing and listening to the world around them, social knowledge that corresponds to perceived stimuli is spontaneously and immediately activated in memory without people's awareness or intention. This research has also shown that automatically activated information then shapes and guides people's impressions, judgments, feelings and intentions without people being aware that such influence is occurring.[1,2,3]

Although there is now a general consensus that people's understanding of the world is automatically shaped by previous experiences and knowledge, many people assume that complex behaviors are untainted by such influences. Instead, behaviors are often presumed to result solely from conscious, intentional thought. Recent research in social psychology has placed this long-standing assumption under scrutiny by showing that complex behaviors can also be automatically initiated and guided. This represents a significant shift in the kind of effects automatic social knowledge activation has, from subjective impressions of the world to actual behaviors in the world. Such a shift is crucial for developing theories, not only

about how behavioral information is represented in memory, but also about the determinants of everyday behaviors. Just as previous research has informed us that our impressions of the world are inevitably shaped by factors outside of our awareness, the current work suggests that we might not always be aware of how we are behaving—or perhaps more importantly, why. This article first briefly describes the research on how incidental knowledge activation influences judgments and impressions, and then reviews recent findings concerning automatic effects on social behavior.

Perception automatically activates social knowledge

Social psychological research about how social knowledge is automatically activated during perception was inspired by research in cognitive psychology a quarter of a century ago.[4,5] Cognitive psychologists showed that the perception of a stimulus in the environment (e.g. a bird) activates in memory a vast array of semantically and lexically related information (e.g. robin, wings, trees, etc.). This was discovered using priming paradigms, which demonstrated that people inevitably 'go beyond the information given', inferring more information from a perceived stimulus than is physically present.[6] Furthermore, this work showed that the activation of such knowledge does not require the perceiver's intention.[4,5]

Inspired by these findings, social psychologists demonstrated that *social* information is also activated in an automatic fashion (see Box 1).[1,2,3] Using a variety of priming methodologies, researchers established that when a per-

[1]Department of Psychology, Cornell University, Ithaca, NY 14853, USA
[2]Department of Psychology, Yale University, New Haven, CT 06520, USA

Box 1. Automaticity in contemporary social psychology

What constitutes an automatic effect of knowledge activation on judgment or behavior? Historically, efficient processes that occur without the person's awareness, intention or control have been considered automatic[3,4,5,56,57,58]. Research that addresses whether a given process meets these criteria for automaticity, as well as speculation about how the concept of automaticity should be conceptualized, is prevalent within social psychology [1,2,3,56,57,59,60,61,62,63,64]. Much contemporary work on automatic processes, however, has focused on the criterion of awareness (although see research on efficient social processes [10,11]). In particular, given the well-established finding that people are unaware of the vast amount of social knowledge that becomes activated during social perception, researchers have tested the degree to which people's judgments and behavior are unknowingly influenced by such incidental knowledge activation. If participants are unaware that their behavior has been influenced by recently perceived information, they necessarily did not intend such an influence, nor could they have controlled the influence. Although this kind of operationalization of automaticity is regularly being scrutinized and refined, it does effectively capture the unintentional and nonconscious aspects of many social behaviors, the determinants of which have traditionally been assumed to be completely conscious and deliberate.

How do researchers ensure that participants are unaware of the impact of a priming episode on their judgment or behavior? The critical requirement is that participants do not suspect any influence of the priming on their subsequent behavior [65], and this can be accomplished even when participants are consciously processing the priming stimuli, as long as the cover story obscures the relation between the two. Accordingly, many researchers present priming stimuli in tasks that are ostensibly unrelated to subsequent dependent measures[66]. One common method is to use a scrambled sentence task in which prime words are embedded in sentences that participants have to unscramble as part of a 'linguistic task'[67].

At the end of an experiment, researchers carefully assess participants' suspicion by administering a 'funnel debriefing'[66]. This procedure consists of increasingly specific questions aimed at probing participants' awareness and suspicion. For example, the first question asks participants to speculate in general about the purpose of the experiment, whereas the later questions ask whether they noticed any connection between certain words in the first part of the experiment, and their answers or behaviors in the latter part of the experiment[66]. Although this type of measure might not capture those participants who were actually suspicious but do not want to admit to 'spoiling' the experimenter's plans[68], it could encourage those participants who actually were not suspicious to report nevertheless their awareness to avoid appearing gullible. Because there are possible ways in which a funnel debriefing might be either a conservative or liberal proxy of awareness, researchers are continually striving for more sensitive ways to measure the degree to which behavioral effects occur non-consciously.

themselves also leads to the activation of social knowledge. When people read about an actor performing a behavior, trait knowledge that corresponds to that behavior is spontaneously and unintentionally activated.[10,11,12] Taken together, this research suggests that the perception of any social stimulus will inevitably activate in memory a diverse array of related knowledge.

Incidentally activated knowledge affects social judgment

Knowledge that is incidentally activated during perception can influence people's judgments because it can guide the categorization of judgment-relevant stimuli. Social stimuli are often inherently ambiguous in that they are multiply categorizable.[13] For instance, people can be judged according to their membership in any of numerous groups (e.g. race, sex, age, etc.), and social behaviors can usually be interpreted in multiple ways (e.g. is he acting in a conceited or shy manner?). Because there are always many categories into which a person or event can be placed, the ultimate classification of a stimulus will depend on the relative accessibility of the relevant categories[14].

This is when incidentally activated knowledge can determine the categorization of a stimulus, and therefore influence later judgments and interpretations. A particular category can become accessible because of the recent perception of an event, and then capture a subsequently encountered stimulus, even if the only relation between the perceived event and the subsequent stimulus is a semantic one. For instance, a particular social category, such as African-Americans, might become activated naturally and incidentally when perceiving a member of that group in the street (or on television or in a newspaper); but that category will remain activated ('primed') for some time thereafter, even after the original stimulus is no longer present in the environment. During the time it remains active and accessible, it can influence the categorization of other, race-ambiguous people. But perhaps more importantly, because any categorization carries with it a unique set of social stereotypes, attitudes and knowledge, all of this associated knowledge (e.g. stereotypic traits, such as hostility) also remains accessible and likely to be used in the interpretation of other people's behavior. This well-established research suggests that people are not only unaware of the information that is activated during the normal course of perception, but also of the way in which such information guides their judgments and impressions of the world around them.

Incidentally activated knowledge affects behavior

Until recently, it has been largely assumed that although judgments and feelings can be shaped by factors outside of people's awareness, complex social behavior is determined by people's conscious and deliberately made choices. This assumption is part of a rich tradition of rational-choice theories of behavior as well as the humanis-

son perceives a member of a social group, such as an elderly person, information about that group is instantly activated, including attitudes, exemplars (i.e. memories of individual group members), and social stereotypes (beliefs and expectancies about the group; *e.g. elderly people are slow and forgetful*).[7,8,9] The perception of behaviors tic tradition within psychology, both of which assume that people more or less carefully and intentionally weigh their behavioral options and then choose the optimal one.[1,2]

In contrast to this assumption, researchers in social psychology have begun to demonstrate that complex behavior is also automatically shaped and guided by the knowledge that is incidentally activated during perception. Their argument builds on previous theory and research suggesting that behavioral representations can be automatically activated in memory during perception, and, once activated, can guide actual behavior.

Perception activates behavioral representations
Numerous theorists have argued that behavior is mentally represented in a similar way to other social information such as judgments and attitudes. In particular, theorists have asserted that behavioral and perceptual representations are closely interconnected in memory [15,16,17,18,19,20,21,22,23,24], and recent research supports this claim. For instance, researchers have found, in both Macaque monkeys[25] and humans[26], that the same area of the premotor cortex is active both when monkeys and humans perceive an action and when they perform that action themselves.

On the assumption that behavioral responses are mentally represented and associated with perceptual representations, behavioral responses might be among the forms of knowledge that are automatically activated in response to perceiving a social stimulus. For instance, just as a stereotype presumably becomes associated with a group after repeated group-stereotype pairings, a behavior that a person repeatedly performs in a particular situation, or in response to a particular other person, might become associated in memory with the features of that situation or person. In both cases, the mere perception of the group member, or situation, might automatically activate the respective stereotype or behavior.

Activated behavioral information affects behavior
Assuming that behavioral responses are represented mentally and can be automatically activated during the normal course of perception, can they influence how a person behaves? There is a long history of theories arguing for this very possibility. For example, William Carpenter in the 1860s developed the principle of 'ideomotor action', in which simply thinking about an action is sufficient to lead to the performance of that action[27,28]. William James elaborated on this notion in the 1890s by asserting that the occurrence of thoughts about actions leads to the performance of those actions unless the person consciously intervenes to prevent it[29].

Much contemporary work on human mimicry suggests that in fact the perception of certain actions can lead to the performance of those actions. There is abundant evidence that people exhibit imitative behavior from an early age onwards, mimicking everything from facial expressions to the speech of their conversation partners[30,31,32,33]. This research suggests that the knowledge that is activated in response to perceiving a given action can also lead to the performance of that same action, at least for simple behaviors such as facial expressions and the use of syntax.

Recent research on automatic social behavior
Social psychologists have recently explored whether more complex social behavior is influenced by incidental knowledge activation. For example, although research has suggested that people will adopt the accent of a conversation partner [32], will a person act more aggressively if she or he perceives the trait *hostility*? As an initial attempt to test this possibility, Bargh, Chen and Burrows [16] covertly primed participants with trait knowledge about *rudeness* (Study 1), stereotypes of the elderly (and thus the trait *slowness*; Study 2), and stereotypes of African-Americans (and thus the trait *hostility*; Study 3).

Those participants primed with trait information were significantly more likely than non-primed participants to show behavior relevant to the primed trait: specifically, to interrupt another person (Study 1), walk slowly down the hallway (Study 2), or express hostility after being provoked (Study 3). Crucially, none of the participants reported any awareness of a connection between the priming episode and their behavior (see Box 1). Thus, when participants faced a situation that could be responded to with either rudeness or politeness, slow or fast walking, hostility or calmness, they acted in accordance with trait information covertly primed only minutes before in an unrelated context.

This first set of studies laid the groundwork for research that has since examined how various behaviors can be automatically guided by information that is incidentally activated from the environment. The studies over the past five years differ in terms of the source of social knowledge activation (e.g. traits, stereotypes, behavior, contexts) as well as the nature of the behavioral effects (e.g. simple, complex).

Trait knowledge influences behavior
Dijksterhuis and van Knippenberg [21] addressed whether social behavior that is more complex than walking speed or hostility can be primed. They subtly primed participants with the trait 'intelligence' or 'stupidity', and then asked them to complete an ostensibly unrelated knowledge test that included questions such as 'Who painted *La Guernica*?' (a. Dali, b. Miro, c. Picasso, d. Velasquez), and 'What is the capital of Bangladesh?' (a. Dhaka, b. Hanoi, c. Yangon, d. Bangkok).

Dijksterhuis and van Knippenberg expected that priming participants with intelligence or stupidity would lead to the increased accessibility of related knowledge, including behavioral responses associated with the corresponding concept. This activated knowledge would then affect their performance on the test, relative to non-primed participants. As expected, those primed with '*intelligence*' significantly outperformed non-primed participants whereas those primed with '*stupidity*' significantly underperformed non-primed participants. None of the participants reported any awareness of a connection between the priming episode and the test. These results suggest that incidentally activated knowledge can influence even complex behavior, such as performance on a knowledge test.

Behavioral information influences behavior

Researchers have also explored whether knowledge other than trait information might influence people's behavior in an automatic fashion. Given the evidence that people tend to adopt the tone and speech of their conversation partners, researchers have examined whether people might also unknowingly mimic the actions of their conversation partners.[34,35,36,37,38] Several recent articles provide support for this hypothesis, and show, for example, that people are significantly more likely to shake their foot or rub their face unconsciously if their conversation partner is doing so than if their partner is not.[19] In all of these studies, participants were carefully questioned after the experiment to assess their awareness of their own and their partner's behaviors. Participants did not report any awareness of their own behavior, their partner's behavior, or any relation between the two. This research suggests that the mere perception of actions automatically increases the likelihood of the performance of those same actions, without the person's intention or awareness.

Recent work has expanded upon this topic by showing that the perception of behaviors does not always increase the likelihood of performing those same behaviors. Tiedens and Fragale[39] hypothesized that the perception of behaviors that connote high or low status might non-consciously lead to the adoption of the opposite (i.e. low or high status, respectively) behaviors. The findings suggest that when participants interacted with a partner whose posture suggested dominance (i.e. an expansive posture), the participants themselves non-consciously adopted submissive postures (i.e. restricted). A sensitive probing process at the end of these experiments indicated that participants were not aware of their own posture, their partner's posture, or any connection between the two. Thus, the perception of another's behavior can unintentionally and unknowingly lead to the performance of either that same behavior, or one that is diametrically opposed in terms of the socially relevant dimension of status.

Goal-relevant information influences behavior

In addition to investigating the kinds of information that can influence social behavior, researchers have also explored the type of behavior that can result from such an influence[40,41,42,43]. Recent research by Bargh *et al.*[42] suggests that incidental social perception also activates goal knowledge that can automatically influence actual goal-pursuit—that is, behavior that is directed towards an objective, persists over time, and resumes after an interruption.

Across several studies, participants were covertly primed with words related to *achievement*, and then completed a series of word-search puzzles. Not only did primed participants perform significantly better than non-primed participants during the same time period, they were more likely than non-primed participants to maximize their performance by disobeying experimenter instructions to stop working on the task. Primed participants were also significantly more likely than non-primed participants to choose to continue working on the puzzles after an interruption rather than begin a cartoon-assessment task that had been rated in another study as more enjoyable. As in other experiments in this area of research, none of the participants in any of the studies reported any awareness of a connection between the priming tasks and the dependent measures. This type of research can potentially extend the effects of incidental knowledge activation on behavior from relatively static displays of a trait-consistent action, to complex, feedback-dependent sequences of behaviors.

Context information influences behavior

Researchers have also investigated whether the perception of social settings might also influence behavior in a similar fashion. Aarts and Dijksterhuis[44] used as priming stimuli locations that were associated with situational norms (i.e. prescriptions for acceptable behavior within a certain situation). For example, some participants were primed with stimuli related to libraries, a location for which the norm is quiet behavior. Those who were primed with the location and who had the goal to visit the location later behaved in ways that were consistent with the norm for that location. For instance, those primed with library subsequently recited a text passage in a significantly softer voice than non-primed participants. Again, none of the participants reported any awareness of a connection between the priming procedure and the subsequent dependent measures.

As another example of research that shows how context information inadvertently influences behavior, researchers have examined whether participants who are primed with crowded group-settings display different amounts of helping behavior compared with non-primed participants. Given the well-established finding in social psychology that people in a crowd exhibit less helping behavior than people who are alone,[45] Garcia *et al.*[46] tested whether the incidental activation of knowledge about being in a large group might automatically influence later, ostensibly unrelated helping behavior. They asked participants either to imagine themselves in a group, or alone (e.g. in a crowded or empty movie theater) and then measured their willingness in a variety of helping behaviors, such as donating money to charity.

Those who imagined themselves in a group context later exhibited significantly less helping behavior than control participants. Great care was taken across five studies to ensure that participants did not suspect any connection between the priming task and the helping measure, and indeed, none of the participants reported any suspicion. These studies suggest that behavioral information can be activated from the mere perception of social settings or contexts (such as a library, or a crowded movie theater) and subsequently influence actual behavior in the absence of people's intentions and awareness.

Parameters of the effect of social perception on behavior

A crucial question concerns the mechanisms that might underlie such automatic effects on behavior, and researchers have identified both some boundary conditions as well as some potential mechanisms[15,47,48,49,50]. For example, Dijksterhuis and colleagues[49,50] have explored how the concreteness of the priming stimuli influences the nature of the effect, by priming participants with trait information either via social groups (e.g. the group *professors* activates the trait *intelligence*) or via exemplars of those social groups (e.g. *Albert Einstein* also primes the trait *intelligence*). In line with findings from the social judgment literature[51,52,53], those participants primed with a social group (i.e. abstract information) exhibited behavior in line with traits associated with the group (i.e. assimilative effects), but those primed with exemplars from the group (i.e. relatively more concrete information) exhibited behavior in contrast with the associated trait (i.e. contrast effects; see Figure 1).

Researchers have argued that whereas the perception of an abstract prime activates an interpretive frame that is used to interpret subsequent stimuli, the perception of concrete exemplars invokes comparative processes whereby the exemplar anchors the dimension of judgment along which subsequent stimuli are judged. When the exemplars are extreme, most subsequently perceived (or in this case, performed) behaviors will be positioned away from the exemplar. Dijksterhuis and colleagues[49] argued that contrast effects emerge in behavior because participants implicitly compare themselves with the primed exemplar and then act accordingly.

As one might expect, the magnitude of the priming effect on behavior has been found to depend upon the strength of association in memory between the prime material (e.g. the social group, context, trait, stereotype) and the particular behavior. Dijksterhuis and colleagues[54] predicted that the effect of priming participants with 'elderly people' on later memory performance would be contingent on how much contact participants previously had with the elderly. As expected, those participants with lots of previous contact with the elderly performed significantly worse on a memory test after being covertly primed with the group (this was expected because poor memory is part of the elderly stereotype). However, those

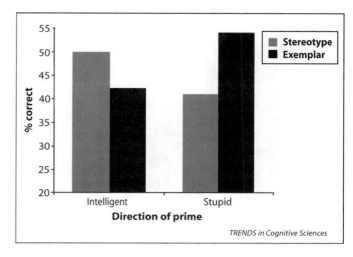

Figure 1. Percentage correct on a general knowledge test as a function of the type (stereotype or exemplar) and direction (intelligence or stupidity) of the primes. Participants were covertly primed with a stereotype indicating intelligence (*professors*) versus stupidity (*supermodels*), or an exemplar indicating intelligence (Albert Einstein) versus stupidity (*Claudia Schiffer*). A significant interaction between the type and direction of primes on percentage correct emerged, such that whereas stereotype primes led to assimilation effects (participants' behavior was in accord with the direction of the prime), exemplar primes led to contrast effects (participants' behavior was in contrast with the direction of the prime). In other words, whereas those primed with professors significantly outperformed those primed with supermodels, those primed with Albert Einstein significantly underperformed those primed with Claudia Schiffer. Adapted from.[50]

with little previous contact did not show any priming effect, suggesting that the degree to which incidental knowledge activation increases the likelihood of performing an associated behavior depends on the presence and strength of that association in memory. Presumably, the belief about the elderly having poor memory was reinforced in those who interacted frequently with members of the group.

Researchers have also recently examined whether the effect on later behavior of being primed with a social group is mediated by the activation of traits associated with that group. Kawakami et al.[55] tested whether the effect of being primed with *elderly* on response speed in a lexical-decision task depended on the activation of the trait *slow* (see Figure 2). The findings showed a priming effect on behavior, as primed participants exhibited a significantly slower response speed overall compared with non-primed participants. In addition, primed participants responded significantly faster to stereotype-consistent (e.g. *slow*) than to inconsistent traits, compared with non-primed participants, who showed no difference, suggesting that the stereotyped traits were activated in memory, as expected. Most importantly, however, the effect of priming on behavior (overall slowness of responses) was independent of the effect of priming on stereotype trait activation. This suggests that the perception of a stimulus activates a diverse array of knowledge (e.g. behaviors, traits, exemplars), and that types of knowledge can have independent effects on subsequent behavior.

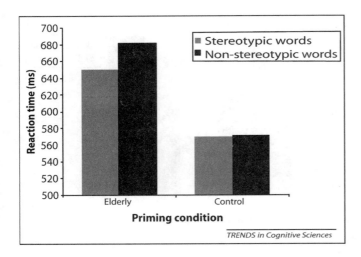

Figure 2. Reaction time to words in a lexical-decision task as a function of priming condition (elderly vs. non-primed control) and type of target words (stereotypic of the elderly vs. non-stereotypic of the elderly). The results suggest a priming effect on behavior such that primed participants responded significantly more slowly overall than non-primed participants. They also suggest a priming effect on stereotype activation such that primed participants responded significantly faster to stereotypic than to non-stereotypic words, whereas non-primed participants showed no difference. Importantly, a mediational analysis demonstrated that the effect of priming on overall response speed was independent of the effect on stereotype activation, suggesting that behavioral effects are not necessarily mediated by the activation of group-relevant traits. Adapted from.55

Conclusions

Over the past five years, researchers in experimental social psychology have demonstrated not only that people's judgments and attitudes are sometimes automatically influenced by factors outside of their awareness, but that their actual behaviors are as well. Given the inherent ambiguity in social stimuli and situations, and thus the range of behavioral responses that might be appropriate for any given situation, it seems likely that people's behavior is often shaped and guided in part by knowledge that has become accessible through incidental means, such as unrelated recent experiences. This suggests that, in contrast to the assumption that we always consciously decide how to behave, we might routinely be unaware of some or even many of the determinants of our behavior.

Future research in this area will increasingly focus on the mechanisms that underlie the apparent potential independence of conscious intention and actual behavior (see Box 2). Not only will this research identify boundary conditions and mediators of such effects, it is likely to uncover a variety of neural substrates that underlie or enable the effects. For example, there is emerging evidence from cognitive neuroscience that points to fundamental dissociations in the human brain between those structures that are responsible for guiding complex motor behavior, and those that afford conscious access to our current intentions and purposes [15]. As researchers gather more information about the nature of these non-con-

Box 2. Questions for future research

- What types of activated knowledge mediate effects on behavior? For example, assuming that the mere perception of a stimulus activates trait, context, goal, affective and behavioral information, which types of knowledge mediate the variety of effects shown in this recent research?
- To what degree do priming effects on complex behavior meet the traditional four criteria for automaticity? For example, to what extent does participant suspicion of a relation between the priming episode and the dependent measures qualify as an 'automatic' priming effect on behavior? What cognitive capacity is required for these effects to occur?
- What are the necessary preconditions for incidental acts of social perception to influence relatively static displays of behavior (e.g. walking slowly), and how do these differ (if at all) from the conditions needed to influence more complex and feedback-dependent sequences of behavior (e.g. the attempt to achieve across multiple tasks and interruptions)?
- What is the magnitude and duration of these types of priming effects, and what factors moderate these variables?
- What sources of knowledge affect behavior in an automatic fashion, beyond those that have been studied so far?
- To what extent do priming effects on various sorts of complex behavior occur in real-life situations (i.e. outside the laboratory)?

scious effects, we may begin to understand more fully the phenomenon of behavior without intention.

References

1. J.A. Bargh and T. Chartrand, The unbearable automaticity of being. *Am. Psychol.* 54 (1999), pp. 462-479.
2. J.A. Bargh and M.J. Ferguson, Beyond behaviorism: on the automaticity of higher mental processes. *Psychol. Bull.* 126 (2000), pp. 925-945.
3. M.S. Gazzaniga and T.F. Heatherton, *The Psychological Science: Mind, Brain, and Behavior,* W.W. Norton (2003).
4. J.H. Neely, Semantic priming and retrieval from lexical memory: rules of inhibitionless spreading activation and limited-capacity attention. *J. Exp. Psychol. Gen.* 106 (1977), pp. 226-254.
5. M.I. Posner and C.R.R. Snyder, Attention and cognitive control. In: R.L. Solso, Editor, *Information Processing and Cognition: The Loyola Symposium,* Erlbaum (1975).
6. J.S. Bruner, On perceptual readiness. *Psychol. Rev.* 64 (1957), pp. 123-152.
7. R.H. Fazio et al., Variability in automatic activation as an unobtrusive measure of racial attitudes: a *bona fide* pipeline?. *J. Pers. Soc. Psychol.* 69 (1995), pp. 1013-1027.

8. E.R. Smith and M.A. Zarate, Exemplar-based model of social judgment. *Psychol. Rev.* 99 (1992), pp. 3-21.
9. I. Blair and M. Banaji, Automatic and controlled processes in stereotype priming. *J. Pers. Soc. Psychol.* 70 (1996), pp. 1142-1163.
10. A. Todorov, and J.S. Uleman, The automaticity of binding spontaneous trait inferences to actors' faces. *J. Exp. Soc. Psychol.* (in press).
11. A. Todorov and J.S. Uleman, Spontaneous trait inferences are bound to actors' faces: evidence from a false recognition paradigm. *J. Pers. Soc. Psychol.* 83 (2002), pp. 1051-1065.
12. J.S. Uleman, Spontaneous versus intentional inferences in impression formation. In: S. Chaiken and Y. Trope, Editors, *Dual-Process Theories in Social Psychology,* Guilford Press (1999), pp. 141-160.
13. G.V. Bodenhausen and C.N. Macrae, Stereotype activation and inhibition. In: R.S. Wyer, Editor, *Advances in Social Cognition* Vol. 11, Erlbaum (1998), pp. 1-52.
14. E.T. Higgins, Knowledge activation: accessibility, applicability, and salience. In: E.T. Higgins and A.W. Kruglanski, Editors, *Social Psychology: Handbook of Basic Principles,* Guilford Press (1996), pp. 133-168.
15. Bargh, J.A. (2003) Bypassing the will: towards demystifying the nonconscious control of social behavior. In *The New Unconscious* (Hassin, R. et al., eds), pp. 111-222, Oxford University Press (in press).
16. J.A. Bargh et al., Automaticity of social behavior: direct effects of trait construct and stereotype priming on action. *J. Pers. Soc. Psychol.* 71 (1996), pp. 230-244.
17. L. Berkowitz, Some effects of thoughts on anti- and prosocial influences of media events: A cognitive-neoassociation analysis. *Psychol. Bull.* 95 (1984), pp. 410-427.
18. L. Berkowitz, Some thoughts extending Bargh's argument. In: R.S. Wyer, Editor, *Advances in Social Cognition* Vol. 10, Erlbaum (1997), pp. 83-94.
19. T.L. Chartrand and J.A. Bargh, The chameleon effect: the perception-behavior link and social interaction. *J. Pers. Soc. Psychol.* 76 (1999), pp. 893-910.
20. A. Dijksterhuis and J.A. Bargh, The perception-behavior expressway: automatic effects of social perception on social behavior. In: M.P. Zanna, Editor, Advances in Experimental Social Psychology Vol. 33, Academic Press (2001), pp. 1-40.
21. A. Dijksterhuis and A. van Knippenberg, Automatic social behavior or how to win a game of trivial pursuit. *J. Pers. Soc. Psychol.* 74 (1998), pp. 865-877.
22. W. Prinz, A common coding approach to perception and action. In: O. Neumann and W. Prinz, Editors, *Relationships Between Perception and Action,* Springer-Verlag (1990), pp. 167-201.
23. R.R. Vallacher, Mental calibration: forging a working relationship between mind and action. In: D.M. Wegner and J.W. Pennebaker, Editors, *Handbook of Mental Control,* Englewood Cliffs, Prentice Hall (1993), pp. 443-472.
24. E. Woody and P. Sadler, On reintegrating dissociated theories: comment on Kirsch and Lynn (1998). *Psychol. Bull.* 123 (1998), pp. 192-197.
25. G. Rizzolatti and M.A. Arbib, Language within our grasp. *Trends Neurosci.* 21 (1998), pp. 188-194.
26. G. Buccino et al., Action observation activates premotor and parietal areas in somatotopic manner: an fMRI study. *Eur. J. Neurosci.* 13 (2001), pp. 400-404.
27. Carpenter, W.B. (1888) *Principles of Mental Physiology,* Appleton.
28. Wegner, D.M. (2002) *The Illusion of Conscious Will,* MIT Press.
29. James, W. (1890) *The Principles of Psychology* (Vol. 2), Holt.
30. J.K. Bock, Syntactic persistence in language production. *Cogn. Psychol.* 18 (1986), pp. 355-387.
31. J.K. Bock, Closed-class immanence in sentence production. *Cognition* 31 (1989), pp. 163-186.
32. G.S. Dell, A spreading activation theory of retrieval in sentence production. *Psychol. Rev.* 93 (1986), pp. 283-321.
33. J.B.J. Smeets and E. Brenner, Perception and action are based on the same visual information: distinction between position and velocity. *J. Exp. Psychol. Hum. Percept. Perform.* 21 (1995), pp. 19-31.
34. Chartrand, T.L. et al. (2003) Beyond the perception-behavior link: the ubiquitous utility and motivational moderators of nonconscious mimicry. In *Unintended Thought II: The New Unconscious,* (Hassin, R. et al., eds), Oxford University Press (in press).
35. Cheng, C.M. and Chartrand, T.L. Self-monitoring without awareness: using mimicry as a nonconscious affiliation strategy. *J. Pers. Soc. Psychol.* (in press).
36. van Baaren, R.B. et al. Mimicry for money: behavioral consequences of imitation. *J. Exp. Soc. Psychol.* (in press).
37. van Baaren, R.B. et al. Mimicry and pro-social behavior. *Psychol. Sci.* (in press).
38. van Baaren, R. et al. The forest, the trees, and the chameleon: context dependency and nonconscious mimicry. *J. Pers. Soc. Psychol.* (in press).
39. L.Z. Tiedens and A.R. Fragale, Power moves: complementarity in dominant and submissive noverbal behavior. *J. Pers. Soc. Psychol.* 84 (2003), pp. 558-568.
40. H. Aarts and A. Dijksterhuis, Habits as knowledge structures: automaticity in goal-directed behavior. *J. Pers. Soc. Psychol.* 78 (2000), pp. 53-63.
41. J.A. Bargh, Auto-motives: preconscious determinants of social thought and behavior. In: E.T. Higgins and R.M. Sorrentino, Editors, *Handbook of Motivation and Cognition* Vol. 2, Guilford Press (1990), pp. 93-130.
42. J.A. Bargh et al., The automated will: nonconscious activation and pursuit of behavioral goals. *J. Pers. Soc. Psychol.* 81 (2001), pp. 1014-1027.
43. G.M. Fitzsimons and J.A. Bargh, Thinking of you: nonconscious pursuit of interpersonal goals associated with relationship partners. *J. Pers. Soc. Psychol.* 84 (2003), pp. 148-163.
44. H. Aarts and A. Dijksterhuis, The silence of the library: environment, situational norm, and social behavior. *J. Pers. Soc. Psychol.* 84 (2003), pp. 18-28.
45. B. Latane and J.M. Darley, Group inhibition of bystander intervention. *J. Pers. Soc. Psychol.* 10 (1968), pp. 215-221.
46. S.M. Garcia et al., Crowded minds: the implicit bystander effect. *J. Pers. Soc. Psychol.* 83 (2002), pp. 843-853.
47. A. Dijksterhuis et al., Of men and mackerels: attention, subjective experience, and automatic social behavior. In: H. Bless and J.P. Forgas, Editors, The *Message Within: The Role of Subjective Experience in Social Cognition and Behavior,* Psychology Press (2000), pp. 37-51.
48. A. Dijksterhuis and J.A. Bargh, The perception-behavior expressway: automatic effects of social perception on social behavior. In: M. Zanna, Editor, *Advances in Experimental Social Psychology* Vol. 33, Academic Press (2001), pp. 1-40.
49. A. Dijksterhuis et al., Seeing one thing and doing another: contrast effects in automatic behavior. *J. Pers. Soc. Psychol.* 75 (1999), pp. 862-871.
50. A. Dijksterhuis et al., Reflecting and deflecting stereotypes: assimilation and contrast in impression formation and automatic behavior. *J. Exp. Soc. Psychol.* 37 (2001), pp. 286-299.
51. G.B. Moskowitz and I.W. Skurnik, Contrast effects as determined by the type of prime: trait versus exemplar primes initiate processing strategies that differ in how accessible constructs are used. *J. Pers. Soc. Psychol.* 76 (1999), pp. 911-927.

52. D.A. Stapel and W. Koomen, The impact of interpretation versus comparison mindsets on knowledge accessibility effects. *J. Exp. Soc. Psychol.* 37 (2001), pp. 134-149.

53. D.A. Stapel and W. Koomen, How far do we go beyond the information given? The impact of knowledge activation on interpretation and inference. *J. Pers. Soc. Psychol.* 78 (2000), pp. 19-37.

54. A. Dijksterhuis *et al.*, On the relation between associative strength and automatic behavior. *J. Exp. Soc. Psychol.* 36 (2000), pp. 531-544.

55. K. Kawakami *et al.*, Automatic stereotyping: category, trait, and behavioral activations. *Pers. Soc. Psychol. Bull.* 28 (2002), pp. 3-15.

56. J.A. Bargh, Conditional automaticity: varieties of automatic influence in social perception and cognition. In: J.S. Uleman and J.A. Bargh, Editors, *Unintended Thought*, Guilford Press (1989), pp. 3-51.

57. J.A. Bargh, The four horsemen of automaticity: awareness, intention, efficiency, and control in social cognition. In: R.S. Wyer and T.K. Srull, Editors, *Handbook of Social Cognition* Vol. 1, Erlbaum (1994), pp. 1-40.

58. L.W. Barsalou, Cognitive Psychology: *An Overview for Cognitive Scientists*, Erlbaum (1992).

59. J.A. Bargh, Automaticity in social psychology. In: E.T. Higgins and A.W. Kruglanski, Editors, *Social Psychology: Handbook of Basic Principles*, Guilford Press (1996), pp. 169-183.

60. J.A. Bargh, The automaticity of everyday life. In: R.S. Wyer, Editor, *Advances in Social Cognition* Vol. 10, Erlbaum (1997), pp. 1-61.

61. S. Chaiken and Y. Trope, *Dual-Process Theories in Social Psychology*, Guilford Press (1999).

62. Hassin, R. *et al. The New Unconscious*, Oxford University Press (in press).

63. D. Wegner and J.A. Bargh, Control and automaticity in social life. In: D.T. Gilbert and S.T. Fiske, Editors, *The Handbook of Social Psychology* Vol. 1, McGraw-Hill (1998), pp. 446-496.

64. D.M. Wegner, Ironic processes of mental control. *Psychol. Rev.* 101 (1994), pp. 34-52.

65. J.A. Bargh, Does subliminality matter to social psychology? Awareness of the stimulus versus awareness of its influence. In: R.F. Bornstein and T.S. Pittman, Editors, *Perception Without Awareness: Cognitive, Clinical, and Social Perspectives*, Guilford Press (1992), pp. 236-255.

66. J.A. Bargh and T.L. Chartrand, The mind in the middle: a practical guide to priming and automaticity research. In: H.T. Reis and C.M. Judd, Editors, *Handbook of Research Methods in Social and Personality Psychology*, Cambridge University Press (2000), pp. 253-285.

67. T.K. Srull and R.S. Wyer, Jr, The role of category accessibility in the interpretation of information about persons: some determinants and implications. *J. Pers. Soc. Psychol.* 37 (1979), pp. 1660-1672.

68. M.T. Orne, On the social psychology of the psychological experiment: with particular reference to demand characteristics and their implications. *Am. Psychol.* 17 (1962), pp. 776-783.

Make-Believe Memories

Research on memory distortion has shown that postevent suggestion can contaminate what a person remembers. Moreover, suggestion can lead to false memories being injected outright into the minds of people. These findings have implications for police investigation, clinical practice, and other settings in which memory reports are solicited.

Elizabeth F. Loftus

In the spring of 2003, Alan Alda visited the University of California, Irvine (UC Irvine), to film segments for an upcoming series as part of his *Scientific American Frontiers* program. Many know him from his role as Hawkeye Pierce in the classic TV series *M*A*S*H*. Alda wrote and directed many of the *M*A*S*H* episodes, and during his 11 years with the show, he won the Emmy Award five times. What you may not realize that he is a lifelong science buff and loves hosting *Scientific American Frontiers* in part because he gets to travel the globe in the name of science and in part because he gets the chance to meet scientists everywhere. On this particular day in April, Alan Alda visited a number of memory scientists at UC Irvine, and we all had a chance to demonstrate our research paradigms.

A week earlier, Alan had filled out some questionnaires ostensibly designed to gather information about his lifelong history with foods and his personality. He thought my students and I were interested in the relationship between eating behavior and personality. Once in the lab, we tried to convince him that when he was a child he had gotten sick eating too many hard-boiled eggs. We explained that a sophisticated computer program had analyzed all of his data and discovered several facts to be true about him, including the "gotten sick" fact. An hour or so later, he had a picnic in the park with students, postdocs, and other members of my lab. There were many foods from which to choose: sandwiches, pickles, shrimp cocktail, hard-boiled eggs, deviled eggs, and more. He refused to eat the eggs.

Alan Alda's reluctance to eat a hard-boiled egg at that particular picnic could be due to many causes, of course. But his avoidance on that day was filmed and, through *Scientific American Frontiers*, will be shown to millions. When this happens, it will constitute a unique opportunity to illustrate some new discoveries about human memory. I will get to these later, but first some background.

Eyewitness Memory

For more than three decades, I have been studying memory and the ways it can go awry. My first studies of eyewitness testimony addressed several key questions: When someone sees a crime or accident, how accurate is his or her memory? What happens when this person is questioned by police officers, and what if those questions are leading in some way? While others in the field of memory were studying memory for words or nonsense syllables, or sometimes sentences, I began showing people films of traffic accidents and questioning them in various ways. The question "Did you *see* the broken headlight?" led to more false reports of a broken headlight than the same question asked with the verb *hit*. "How fast were the cars going when they *smashed* into each other?" led to higher estimates of speed than a more neutral question that used the verb *hit*. Moreover, the "smashed" question led more people to later falsely claim that they had seen broken glass when there was none. My early papers concluded that leading questions could contaminate or distort a witness's memory (see Loftus, 1979/1996, for a summary of this early research).

In fact, leading questions are only one way to distort memory. Related studies showed that memory could become skewed with various techniques that fed misinformation to unsuspecting individuals. The studies used a simple procedure. Participants first see a complex event, such as a simulated automobile accident. Next, half of the participants receive misleading information about the accident, whereas the other half receive no misinformation. Finally, all of the participants try to remember the original accident. In one actual study using this paradigm, participants saw an accident, and later some of them received misinformation about the traffic sign used to control the intersection. The misled participants got the false suggestion that the stop sign that they had actually seen was a yield sign. When asked later what kind of traffic sign they personally remembered seeing at the intersection, those who had been given the false suggestion tended to adopt it as their memory and now claimed that they had seen a yield sign. Those who had not received the phony information had much more accurate memories.

Today, hundreds of studies have been published documenting memory distortion induced by exposure to misinformation. In these studies, not only have people recalled stop signs as yield signs but they have also recalled nonexistent broken glass and tape recorders, a blue vehicle used in a crime scene as white, Minnie Mouse when they really saw Mickey Mouse, and, most recently, wounded animals (that were not there) near the scene of a tragic terrorist bombing that actually had occurred in Russia a few years earlier (Nourkova, Bernstein, & Loftus, 2003). Taken together, these studies show that misinformation can change an individual's recollection in predictable, and sometimes very powerful, ways.

Misinformation can influence people's memories when they are interrogated in a suggestive fashion or when they talk to other people who give their version of the events. Misinformation can sway people when they see biased media coverage about some event that they may have experienced themselves. This phenomenon would ultimately be called the *misinformation effect* (Loftus & Hoffman, 1989).

It might be tempting to suggest that memory distortion observed in the safety and pallid world of a laboratory setting would not generalize to the outside world or real events (as Yuille & Cutshall, 1986, have suggested). Indeed there are differences in the active/ passive role, in the opportunity to observe, in the degree of emotional arousal, and more. To explore this issue, a Norwegian research group recently exposed participants to a "live" crime and compared their memory performance with those who watched a video of the same crime (Ihlebaek, Love, Eilertsen, & Magnussen, 2003). The "live" group were participants in a course designed to teach them to cope with dangerous and violent armed-robbery situations and to cope with the psychological effects of experiencing such traumas. Robberies were staged, and participants experienced them live. Videotapes of those same robberies were shown to comparable participants. The results showed that participants who watched the videos reported more details and with higher accuracy than those who saw the live events, suggesting that laboratory experiments may actually overestimate memory performance.

After more than two decades exploring the misinformation effect, many psychological scientists have contributed to the knowledge, and collectively we have learned a great deal about the conditions of its power. One group showed that postevent information can even affect the memories of three-month-old infants (Rovee-Collier, Borza, Adler, & Boller, 1993). Another group showed that one can even get the misinformation effect with pigeons (Harper & Garry, 2000). Fortunately, we have also learned that warning people about misinfor-

mation effects can sometimes enable them to successfully resist those effects (Highhouse & Bottrill, 1995). Many highly sophisticated models have been developed that specify when memory impairments will and will not be expected (Metcalfe, 1990).

The misinformation research tradition continues today. For example, one group showed that people who thought they were drinking alcohol, but actually drank plain tonic water, were more swayed by misinformation than those who were not under the influence of an alcohol placebo (Assefi & Garry, 2002). Another research group recently examined the relative suggestive power of misinformation versus hypnosis (Scoboria, Mazzoni, Kirsch, & Milling, 2002). Participants heard a story and were later asked either neutral or misleading questions, either in or out of hypnosis. When tested later, the use of hypnosis increased memory errors, but the misleading questions produced even more errors. Moreover, the combination of the two (hypnosis and misleading questions) produced more errors than either method by itself. The particular kind of error made by those who were asked misleading questions was to shift from reporting not knowing an answer to questions to reporting false information about the past. From this example, it becomes evident that researchers are learning a great deal about the precise way in which misinformation has immediate and persisting deleterious effects on memory. That misleading questions might have more pernicious effects than prior exposure to hypnosis led Scoboria et al. (2002) to question existing legal practices concerning the circumstances under which witness testimony is admitted or excluded in court cases.

Planting False Memories

It is one thing to change a stop sign into a yield sign, to turn Mickey into Minnie, or to add a detail to a memory report for something that actually did happen. But could one create an entire memory for an event that never happened? My first attempt to do this used a procedure whereby participants were given short narrative descriptions of childhood events and encouraged to try to remember those events. While participants believed that all of the descriptions were true and had been provided by family members, one was actually a pseudoevent that had not occurred. In this study, approximately 25% of participants were led to believe, wholly or partially, that at age 5 or 6 they had been lost in a shopping mall for an extended time, were highly upset, and were ultimately rescued by an elderly person and reunited with their family (Loftus & Pickrell, 1995). Many added embellishing details to their accounts.

The method of using family members to help plant false memories has been dubbed the *familial informant false narrative procedure* (Lindsay, Hagen, Read, Wade, & Garry, in press), but it is probably easier to call it simply the *lost-in-the-mall* technique. Many investigators have used the lost-in-the-mall technique to plant false memories of events that would have been far more unusual, bizarre, painful, or even traumatic had they actually occurred. Participants have been led to believe that they had been hospitalized overnight or that they had an accident at a family wedding (Hyman, Husband, & Billings, 1995; Hyman & Pentland, 1996). They have been convinced that they had nearly drowned and had to be rescued by a lifeguard (Heaps & Nash, 2001). They have fallen sway to the suggestion that they were once the victims of a vicious animal attack (Porter, Yuille, & Lehman, 1999). Most studies find that a significant minority of participants will develop partial or complete false memories. In a set of studies reviewed by Lindsay et al. (in press), the average false-memory rate was 31%, but in individual studies, of course, the figures can vary. Sometimes people have been resistant to suggestions, as they were when investigators tried to plant false memories of having received a rectal enema (Pezdek, Finger, & Hodge, 1997). Conversely, sometimes false memories have been planted in the minds of more than 50% of exposed individuals, as they were when investigators tried to plant false memories of having gone up in a hot-air balloon ride (Wade, Garry, Read, & Lindsay, 2002). Particularly striking are the complete false memories, or what might be termed *rich false memories*, which are experiences about which a person can feel confident, provide details, even express emotion about made-up events that never happened (Loftus & Bernstein, in press).

Rich False Memories

One interpretative issue that recurs in this memory distortion research is whether we are truly planting a false memory. Perhaps the suggestive manipulation is leading people to discover a true memory rather than leading them to embrace a false one. To investigate this issue, researchers have adopted several methods, including one that attempts to create a false memory for a recent event (e.g., "What you did on a particular day?"). If you as a researcher know precisely what happened that day and you lead the participant to "remember" doing something else, you have fairly good evidence that you have created a false report. This strategy was first adopted by Goff and Roediger (1998) and later modified by my colleague and me (Thomas & Loftus, 2002). In one study, participants sat in front of a large table filled with numerous objects. They heard a series of statements (e.g., "flip the coin") and then had to perform or imagine performing the called-for actions. The next time they came to the lab, there were no objects in front of them, but they simply imagined that they performed various actions. In a final session, their memory for what they did that first day was tested. After a few imaginations, participants occasionally remembered performing actions that they had not performed. They falsely claimed that they did things that would have been common (e.g., roll the

dice), but they also claimed that they did things that would have been rather bizarre or unusual, such as "rub the chalk on your head" or "kiss a plastic frog" (Thomas, Bulevich, & Loftus, in press; Thomas & Loftus, 2002).

Imagination can not only make people believe they have done simple things that they have not done but can also lead people to believe that they have experienced more complex events. In one study, participants watched a video clip of a drunk-driving incident. Later, some participants imagined a scene that was not part of the presented scenario. They imagined seeing a policeman stop the car and ask the driver to step out but the driver refused. Later, 15% of "imagine" participants mentioned seeing the false details when tested with free recall, and an astonishing 41% claimed to have seen these false details when tested with recognition-type memory items (Wright, Loftus, & Hall, 2001).

Another method for assessing whether the suggestive manipulations are planting false memories is to try to plant memories for things that would be implausible or even impossible. For instance, it has been possible to plant beliefs or false memories of witnessing demonic possession as a child (Mazzoni, Loftus, & Kirsch, 2001). And it has been even easier to plant a false memory of meeting Bugs Bunny at a Disney Resort (Braun, Ellis, & Loftus, 2002). The latter was accomplished by presenting participants with fake ads for Disney that featured Bugs Bunny.

In one study, exposure to the fake ad led 16% of participants to later claim that they had personally met Bugs at Disneyland. This could not have occurred because Bugs Bunny is a Warner Brothers character and would not be found at Disneyland. This impossibility was far more colorfully put by Andrew Malcolm in his unsigned (voice of the paper) editorial in the *Los Angeles Times*: "the wascally Warner Bros. Wabbit would be awwested on sight" at Disney ("You Must Remember This," 2003, p. 10). Follow-up studies showed that even more individuals (25% in one study; 36% in another) fell sway to the suggestion about meeting Bugs after multiple exposures to fake ads featuring Bugs Bunny (Grinley, 2002). What do people remember about their encounter with this character whom they could not have met? Of those recalling a personal encounter with Bugs, 62% said they shook his hand, and 46% remembered hugging him. Others remembered touching his ear or tail, or even hearing him speak ("What's up, Doc?"). These false memories, thus, were imbued with sensory detail, just the kind of sensory detail that people use as a cue to decide whether a memory is true or false.

Alan Alda looked at our fake ads for Disney. He closely examined the one featuring Bugs and compared it with our generic ad for Disney that did not mention the cartoon character. He explained that he preferred the generic ad, mostly because of its colors. Later, while picnicking in the park, he was asked about his own childhood trip to Disney and which characters he met there. When asked specifically about Bugs Bunny, he said, "No way, he's a Warner Brothers character." Thus, he resisted the suggestion in the fake ad, as did most of our real experimental participants. But, as I explain later, his resistance did not appear to be operating when it came to the hard-boiled egg.

False Memories Matter

True memories seem to have consequences for people. If you remember that someone insulted you in the past, you might avoid encounters with that unpleasant individual in the future. But what if you had a false memory of being insulted? Would you similarly avoid that person later? It seems like this would be the case, but virtually all of the false-memory research stops when the affected individual accepts the scenario. Occasionally, there have been efforts to find out if the person has merely a belief that the event happened with no accompanying feelings of recollection. Sometimes that is all there is to the experience, simply a false belief. But sometimes the person has the subjective sense of recollection, replete with sensory details. It is this experience that is more akin to what has been called a rich false memory. In the typical study, debriefing of participants occurs after probing for a memory report, and the study is soon over. Now, what if debriefing could be delayed so that one could see whether the false memory affects the thoughts or behaviors of the person down the road? One might then be able to show that false memories have consequences, that they do matter.

Another way to think about this issue is to realize that suggestions can render an individual willing to make a new, possibly false memory report. This has been amply demonstrated. But are there memory correlates? Are there other mental processes or behaviors that also are affected in the process of exposure to suggestive influences? If so, one might be seeing an even deeper effect of those influences.

This was the rationale behind one study designed to see if planting the suggestion about meeting Bugs Bunny at Disney would affect the recipient's thought processes (Grinley, 2002). In this study, participants were first convinced that they had met Bugs Bunny at a Disney resort. Later, they were given a new test: They saw the names of pairs of cartoon characters, such as Mickey Mouse and Donald Duck, and had to indicate how related the characters were to one another. Some pairs were highly related, like Mickey and Minnie Mouse. Some pairs were not particularly related, like Donald Duck and Sleeping Beauty. After being exposed to the fake Disney ads featuring Bugs Bunny, people rated the pair Mickey Mouse and Bugs Bunny to be more closely related. For a time, then, the thought processes or semantic structures of ad-exposed individuals were influenced.

A further investigation of the consequences of false beliefs or memories involves a recent ongoing collaboration with postdoctoral fellow Daniel Bernstein and two graduate students, Cara Laney and Erin Morris. We induced participants to believe that when they were children they got sick eating hard-boiled eggs (or, for other participants, that they got sick eating dill pickles). We accomplished this mental feat by gathering data from the participants and plying them with false feedback. We told them that a sophisticated computer program had analyzed their data and determined that they had had one of these "sick" experiences as a child. We found that those given the "dill pickle" feedback became more confident that they had had the experience as a child and those given the "hard-boiled egg" feedback became more confident of that experience.

But would the increase in belief translate into subsequent behavior change? Would they, for example, avoid these foods when given the opportunity to eat them? To find out, we gave participants a "Party Behavior" questionnaire. They imagined themselves at a large barbeque and had to indicate which foods they would like to eat. Those who were seduced by the dill pickle feedback reported being less likely to want to eat pickles, whereas those who fell for the egg feedback reported being less likely to want to eat eggs.

When we demonstrated our methodology for Alan Alda during his visit to UC Irvine, he showed increased confidence that he had gotten sick eating hard-boiled eggs as a child. When later offered hard-boiled eggs and deviled eggs at a picnic in the park, Alda declined to eat them. Our findings in the "food" study constitute the beginning of a method for studying false memories and their consequences. But they also hint at unexpected applications: what a potentially easy way to make people avoid certain foods.

In *The Tragedy of King Richard the Second*, Shakespeare asked a simple question: "Who can . . . cloy the hungry edge of appetite by bare imagination of a feast?" We cannot do this, he suggested, any more than we can easily walk "naked in December snow by thinking on fantastic summer's heat." Thinking about the good, Shakespeare noted, makes us feel worse. Our results would give Shakespeare food for thought (excuse the pun). It is not a feast that one should imagine but getting sick on that feast.

More generally, our results are showing that changing a belief or memory can have important consequences for subsequent thoughts or behaviors. When you change memory, it changes you.

True Versus False Memories

In the ideal world, people would have a means of distinguishing true and false memories. Statistically, one occasionally can do this. In an effort to plant false memories of being lost in a shopping mall, we showed that true memories were held with more confidence than the false ones (Loftus & Pickrell, 1995). Other researchers have also found group differences. Wade et al. (2002), who planted false memories of taking a hot-air balloon ride as a child by showing participants doctored photographs, also showed that the true events they asked about were recalled with greater confidence than the false one. Porter et al. (1999), who planted false memories of being victimized by a serious animal attack as a child, found that the planted memories were rated as less coherent than real memories.

There have also been promising efforts to use neurophysiological measures to distinguish true and false memories. Some differences have been reported using human lateralized brain potentials (Fabiana, Stadler, & Wessels, 2000), using the P300 component of event-related potentials (Miller, Baratta, Wynveen, & Rosenfeld, 2000), and using neuroimaging techniques (Schacter, Buckner, Koutstaal, Dale, & Rosen, 1997). By necessity, these studies have been done with true and false memories of words heard in a word list rather than with the eyewitness details or rich false memories. While promising, these preliminary efforts are still a long way from allowing researchers to take one individual memory and reliably classify it as being true or false.

Theoretical and Practical Implications

Collectively, researchers have learned a great deal about how false memories develop and are almost at the point of being able to write a recipe. First, the individual gets convinced that the false event is plausible. Even events that start out being rather implausible can be made to seem more plausible by simple suggestion. Next, the individual gets convinced that the false event was personally experienced. Plying the person with false feedback is a particularly effective way to accomplish this. At this point, the individual might merely believe that the event is true but have no sense of recollection. But with guided imagination, with visualization of the stories of others, and with suggestive feedback and other sorts of manipulations, a rich false memory can develop.

The research on false beliefs and memories has enormous relevance to everyday life. Analyses of the growing number of wrongful convictions, proven wrong by DNA evidence, have taught us that faulty eyewitness memory is the major cause (Technical Working Group for Eyewitness Evidence, 1999). This revelation has led to numerous recommendations for the legal system to protect the fact-finding process from the tragedies of mistaken memory, both in the United States and Canada (Yarmey, 2003). Analyses of the hundreds of cases in which patients were led to believe falsely that they were molested for years in satanic rituals or that they were abducted by aliens and taken up in spaceships have taught us that suggestion is a key factor leading to these beliefs (McNally, 2003). Moreover, once they take hold, these "memories" can be expressed with great confidence, detail, and emotion. In one study, individuals who believed they had been abducted by aliens were as emotionally aroused by thinking of their terrifying abductions as they were about other stressful experiences, or as "nonabducted" individuals were when they recalled personal traumas (McNally, 2003). Two take-home lessons flow from this research: (a) Suggestion can lead to rich false memories, and (b) just because a memory report is expressed with confidence, detail, and emotion does not necessarily mean the underlying event actually happened. McNally (2003) expressed his faith in the value of cognitive psychology to help resolve some of the controversies in this area. It is with the methods of cognitive psychology, he argued, that scientists will be able to test their hypotheses not only about how people may forget traumatic events but also about how people "come to believe they have been traumatized when, in fact, they have not" (McNally, 2003, p. 274).

My efforts to write about the power of suggestion to create false memories have been with the hope of encouraging changes in procedures and practices (Loftus, 2002, 2003; Loftus & Ketcham, 1991, 1994). Aggressive efforts to unearth presumably recalcitrant trauma memories can lead to false-memory reports. Uncritical acceptance of every trauma memory report can harm the false victims and, also sadly, trivialize the experiences of the true victims.

Outside the world of litigation or psychotherapy, the findings about memory distortion have implications for ordinary life. Take the reading of autobiographies and memoirs. The pioneering physicist Edward Teller recently wrote one (Teller, 2001) and was resoundingly criticized for his "notorious" selective memory, and specifically for "vividly remembering events that never happened." A more charitable analysis of Teller's work might involve appreciating it not as a deliberately self-serving untruthful chronicle but for its possible insights into normal memory-distortion processes. Untruths are not necessarily lies. As for the "memoir" of Benjamin Wilkomirski in *Fragments*—the false account of a small child's ordeal in the Holocaust—was it a deliberate lie, or did he somehow come to convince himself it was true? (See Eskin, 2002.) A different area of psychological science is needed to distinguish the deliberate lie from the "honest" lie. But sometimes what starts as a deliberate lie becomes the person's "truth." The story creates a memory rather than the other way around.

It has been said that we are sum of our memories, that all that we have ever experienced goes into that end product. But after three decades of my research on memory in general and memory distortion in particular, it makes sense to consider the reverse of this statement. People's memories are not only the sum of all that they have done, but there is more to them: The memories are also the sum of what they have thought, what they have been told, what they believe. Who we are may be shaped by our memories, but our memories are shaped by who we are and what we have been led to believe. Or as the psychiatrist Sally Satel (2003) said, "We are always angling the prism of memory" (p. 31). We seem to reinvent our memories, and in doing so, we become the person of our own imagination.

Editor's Note

Elizabeth F. Loftus received the Award for Distinguished Scientific Applications of Psychology. Award winners are invited to deliver an award address at the APA's annual convention. A version of this award address was delivered at the 111th annual meeting, held August 7–10, 2003, in Toronto , Ontario, Canada. Articles based on award addresses are reviewed, but they differ from unsolicited articles in that they are expressions of the winner's reflections on their work and their views of the field.

Author's Note

Correspondence concerning this article should be addressed to Elizabeth F. Loftus, Department of Psychology and Social Behavior and Department of Criminology, Law and Society, University of California, Irvine, CA 92697-7085. E-mail: eloftus@uci.edu

References

Assefi, S. L., & Garry, M. (2002). Absolute memory distortions: Alcohol placebos influence the misinformation effect. *Psychological Science, 14*, 77–80.

Braun, K. A., Ellis, R., & Loftus, E. F. (2002). Make my memory: How advertising can change our memories of the past. *Psychology and Marketing, 19*, 1–23.

Eskin, B. (2002). *A life in pieces: The making and unmaking of Binjamin Wilkomirski.* New York: Norton.

Fabiana, M., Stadler, M. A., & Wessels, P. M. (2000). True but not false memories produce a sensory signature in human lateralized brain potentials. *Journal of Cognitive Neuroscience, 12*, 941–949.

Goff, L. M., & Roediger, H. L., III. (1998). Imagination inflation for action events: Repeated imaginings lead to illusory recollections. *Memory & Cognition, 26*, 20–33.

Grinley, M. J. (2002). *Effects of advertising on semantic and episodic memory.* Unpublished master's thesis, University of Washington.

Harper, D. N., & Garry, M. (2000). Postevent cues bias recognition performance in pigeons. *Animal Learning and Behavior, 28*, 59–67.

Heaps, C. M., & Nash, M. (2001). Comparing recollective experience in true and false autobiographical memories. *Journal of Experimental Psychology: Learning, Memory, and Cognition, 27*, 920–930.

Highhouse, S., & Bottrill, K. V. (1995). The influence of social (mis)information on memory for behavior in an employment interview. *Organizational Behavior and Human Decision Processes, 62*, 200–229.

Hyman, I. E., Jr., Husband, T. H., & Billings, F. J. (1995). False memories of childhood experiences. *Applied Cognitive Psychology, 9*, 181–197.

Hyman, I. E., Jr., & Pentland, J. (1996). The role of mental imagery in the creation of false childhood memories. *Journal of Memory and Language, 35*, 101–117.

Ihlebaek, C., Love, T., Eilertsen, D. E., & Magnussen, S. (2003). Memory for a staged criminal event witnessed live and on video. *Memory, 11*, 319–327.

Lindsay, D. S., Hagen, L., Read, J. D., Wade, K. A., & Garry, M. (in press). True photographs and false memories. *Psychological Science.*

Loftus, E. F. (1996). *Eyewitness testimony.* Cambridge, MA: Harvard University Press. (Original work published 1979)

Loftus, E. F. (2002). Memory faults and fixes. *Issues in Science and Technology, 18*(4), 41–50.

Loftus, E. F. (2003). Our changeable memories: Legal and practical implications. *Nature Reviews: Neuroscience, 4*, 231–234.

Loftus, E. F., & Bernstein, D. M. (in press). Rich false memories: The royal road to success. In A. Healy (Ed.), *Experimental cognitive psychology and its applications: Festschrift in honor of Lyle Bourne, Walter Kintsch, and Thomas Landauer.* Washington DC: American Psychological Association.

Loftus, E. F., & Hoffman, H. G. (1989). Misinformation and memory: The creation of memory. *Journal of Experimental Psychology: General, 118*, 100–104.

Loftus, E. F., & Ketcham, K. (1991). *Witness for the defense.* New York: St. Martin's Press.

Loftus, E. F., & Ketcham, K. (1994). *The myth of repressed memory.* New York: St. Martin's Press.

Loftus, E. F., & Pickrell, J. E. (1995). The formation of false memories. *Psychiatric Annals, 25*, 720–725.

Mazzoni, G. A. L., Loftus, E. F., & Kirsch, I. (2001). Changing beliefs about implausible autobiographical events: A little plausibility goes a long way. *Journal of Experimental Psychology: Applied, 7*, 51–59.

McNally, R. J. (2003). *Remembering trauma.* Cambridge, MA: Harvard University Press.

Metcalfe, J. (1990). Composite holographic associative recall model (CHARM) and blended memories in eyewitness testimony. *Journal of Experimental Psychology: General, 119*, 145–160.

Miller, A. R., Baratta, C., Wynveen, C., & Rosenfeld, J. P. (2001). P300 latency, but not amplitude or topography, distinguishes between true and false recognition. *Journal of Experimental Psychology: Learning, Memory, and Cognition, 27*, 354–361.

Nourkova, V., Bernstein, D. M., & Loftus, E. F. (2003). *Altering traumatic memory.* Manuscript submitted for publication.

Pezdek, K., Finger, K., & Hodge, D. (1997). Planting false childhood memories: The role of event plausibility. *Psychological Science, 8*, 437–441.

Porter, S., Yuille, J. C., & Lehman, D. R. (1999). The nature of real, implanted, and fabricated memories for emotional childhood events: Implications for the recovered memory debate. *Law and Human Behavior, 23*, 517–537.

Rovee-Collier, C., Borza, M. A., Adler, S. A., & Boller, K. (1993). Infants' eyewitness testimony: Effects of postevent information on a prior memory representation. *Memory & Cognition, 21*, 267–279.

Satel, S. (2003, May 19). The trauma society. *New Republic, 228*, 29–36.

Schacter, D. L., Buckner, R. L., Koutstaal, W., Dale, A. M., & Rosen, B. R. (1997). Late onset of anterior prefrontal activity during true and false recognition: An event related fMRI study. *Neuroimage, 6*, 259–269.

Scoboria, A., Mazzoni, G., Kirsch, I., & Milling, L. S. (2002). Immediate and persisting effects of misleading questions and hypnosis on memory reports. *Journal of Experimental Psychology: Applied, 8*, 26–32.

Technical Working Group for Eyewitness Evidence. (1999). *Eyewitness evidence: A guide for law enforcement.* Washington, DC: U.S. Department of Justice, Office of Justice Programs.

Teller, E. (with Schoolery, J.). (2001). *Memoirs: A 20th century journey in science and politics.* Cambridge, MA: Perseus.

Thomas, A. K., Bulevich, J. B., & Loftus, E. F. (in press). Exploring the role of repetition and sensory elaboration in the imagination inflation effect. *Memory & Cognition.*

Thomas, A. K., & Loftus, E. F. (2002). Creating bizarre false memories through imagination, *Memory & Cognition, 30*, 423–431.

Wade, K. A., Garry, M., Read, J. D., & Lindsay, D. S. (2002). A picture is worth a thousand lies. *Psychonomic Bulletin and Review, 9*, 597–603.

Wright, D. B., Loftus, E. F., & Hall, M. (2001). Now you see it, now you don't: Inhibiting recall and recognition of scenes. *Applied Cognitive Psychology, 15*, 471–482.

Yarmey, A. D. (2003). Eyewitness identification: Guidelines and recommendations for identification procedures in the United States and Canada. *Canadian Psychology, 44*, 181–189.

You must remember this [Editorial]. (2003, February 24). *Los Angeles Times*, p. 10, Part 2.

Yuille, J. C., & Cutshall, J. L. (1986). A case study of eyewitness memory of a crime. *Journal of Applied Psychology, 71*, 291–301.

How Culture Molds Habits of Thought

By ERICA GOODE

For more than a century, Western philosophers and psychologists have based their discussions of mental life on a cardinal assumption: that the same basic processes underlie all human thought, whether in the mountains of Tibet or the grasslands of the Serengeti.

Cultural differences might dictate what people thought about. Teenage boys in Botswana, for example, might discuss cows with the same passion that New York teenagers reserved for sports cars.

But the habits of thought—the strategies people adopted in processing information and making sense of the world around them—were, Western scholars assumed, the same for everyone, exemplified by, among other things, a devotion to logical reasoning, a penchant for categorization and an urge to understand situations and events in linear terms of cause and effect.

Recent work by a social psychologist at the University of Michigan, however, is turning this long-held view of mental functioning upside down.

In a series of studies comparing European Americans to East Asians, Dr. Richard Nisbett and his colleagues have found that people who grow up in different cultures do not just think about different things: they think differently.

"We used to think that everybody uses categories in the same way, that logic plays the same kind of role for everyone in the understanding of everyday life, that memory, perception, rule application and so on are the same," Dr. Nisbett said. "But we're now arguing that cognitive processes themselves are just far more malleable than mainstream psychology assumed."

A summary of the research will be published next winter in the journal Psychological Review, and Dr. Nisbett discussed the findings Sunday at the annual meetings of the American Psychological Association in Washington.

In many respects, the cultural disparities the researchers describe mirror those described by anthropologists, and may seem less than surprising to Americans who have lived in Asia. And Dr. Nisbett and his colleagues are not the first psychological researchers to propose that thought may be embedded in cultural assumptions: Soviet psychologists of the 1930's posed logic problems to Uzbek peasants, arguing that intellectual tools were influenced by pragmatic circumstances.

But the new work is stirring interest in academic circles because it tries to define and elaborate on cultural differences through a series of tightly controlled laboratory experiments. And the theory underlying the research challenges much of what has been considered gospel in cognitive psychology for the last 40 years.

"If it's true, it turns on its head a great deal of the science that many of us have been doing, and so it's sort of scary and thrilling at the same time," said Dr. Susan Andersen, a professor of psychology at New York University and an associate editor at Psychological Review.

In the broadest sense, the studies—carried out in the United States, Japan, China and Korea—document a familiar division. Easterners, the researchers find, appear to think more "holistically," paying greater attention to context and relationship, relying more on experience-based knowledge than abstract logic and showing more tolerance for contradiction. Westerners are more "analytic" in their thinking, tending to detach objects from their context, to avoid contradictions and to rely more heavily on formal logic.

In one study, for example, by Dr. Nisbett and Takahiko Masuda, a graduate student at Michigan, students from Japan and the United States were shown an animated underwater scene, in which one larger "focal" fish swam among smaller fishes and other aquatic life.

Asked to describe what they saw, the Japanese subjects were much more likely to begin by setting the scene, saying for example, "There was a lake or pond" or "The bottom was rocky," or "The water was green." Americans, in contrast, tended to begin their descriptions with the largest fish, making statements like "There was what looked like a trout swimming to the right."

What Americans notice: the biggest, fastest and shiniest.

Over all, Japanese subjects in the study made 70 percent more statements about aspects of the background environment than Americans, and twice as many statements about the relationships between animate and inanimate objects. A Japanese subject might note, for example, that "The big fish swam past the gray seaweed."

"Americans were much more likely to zero in on the biggest fish, the brightest object, the fish moving the fastest," Dr. Nisbett said. "That's where the money is as far as they're concerned."

But the greater attention paid by East Asians to context and relationship was more than just superficial, the researchers found. Shown the same larger fish swimming against a different, novel background, Japanese participants had more difficulty recognizing it than Americans, indicating that their perception was intimately bound with their perception of the background scene.

When it came to interpreting events in the social world, the Asians seemed similarly sensitive to context, and quicker than the Americans to detect when people's behavior was determined by situational pressures.

Psychologists have long documented what they call the fundamental attribution error, the tendency for people to explain human behavior in terms of the traits of individual actors, even when powerful situational forces are at work. Told that a man has been instructed to give a speech endorsing a particular presidential candidate, for example, most people will still believe that the speaker believes what he is saying.

Yet Asians, according to Dr. Nisbett and his colleagues, may in some situations be less susceptible to such errors, indicating that they do not describe a universal way of thinking, but merely the way that Americans think.

In one study, by Dr. Nisbett and Dr. Incheol Choi, of Seoul National University in Korea, the Korean and American subjects were asked to read an essay either in favor of or opposed to the French conducting atomic tests in the Pacific. The subjects were told that the essay writer had been given "no choice" about what to write. But subjects from both cultures still showed a tendency to "err," judging that the essay writers believed in the position endorsed in the essays.

When the Korean subjects were first required to undergo a similar experience themselves, writing an essay according to instructions, they quickly adjusted their estimates of how strongly the original essay writers believed what they wrote. But Americans clung to the notion that the essay writers were expressing sincere beliefs.

One of the most striking dissimilarities found by the researchers emerged in the way East Asians and Americans in the studies responded to contradiction. Presented with weaker arguments running contrary to their own, Americans were likely to solidify their opinions, Dr. Nisbett said, "clobbering the weaker arguments," and resolving the threatened contradiction in their own minds. Asians, however, were more likely to modify their own position, acknowledging that even the weaker arguments had some merit.

In one study, for example, Asian and American subjects were presented with strong arguments in favor of financing a research project on adoption. A second group was presented both with strong arguments in support of the project and weaker arguments opposing it.

Both Asian and American subjects in the first group expressed strong support for the research. But while Asian subjects in the second group responded to the weaker opposing arguments by decreasing their support, American subjects increased their endorsement of the project in response to the opposing arguments.

In a series of studies, Dr. Nisbett and Dr. Kaiping Peng of the University of California at Berkeley found that Chinese subjects were less eager to resolve contradictions in a variety of situations than American subjects. Asked to analyze a conflict between mothers and daughters, American subjects quickly came down in favor of one side or the other. Chinese subjects were more likely to see merit on both sides, commenting, for example, that, "Both the mothers and the daughters have failed to understand each other."

Given a choice between two different types of philosophical argument, one based on analytical logic, devoted to resolving contradiction, the other on a dialectical approach, accepting of contradiction, Chinese subjects preferred the dialectical approach, while Americans favored the logical arguments. And Chinese subjects expressed more liking than Americans for proverbs containing a contradiction, like the Chinese saying "Too modest is half boastful." American subjects, Dr. Nisbett said, found such contradictions "rather irritating."

Dr. Nisbett and Dr. Ara Norenzayan of the University of Illinois have also found indications that when logic and experiential knowledge are in conflict, Americans are more likely than Asians to adhere to the rules of formal logic, in keeping with a tradition that in Western societies began with the Ancient Greeks.

For example, presented with a logical sequence like, "All animals with fur hibernate. Rabbits have fur. Therefore rabbits hibernate," the Americans, the researchers found, were more likely to accept the validity of the argument, separating its formal structure, that of a syllogism, from its content, which might or might not be plausible. Asians, in contrast, more frequently judged such syllogisms as invalid based on their implausibility—not all animals with fur do in fact hibernate.

While the cultural disparities traced in the researchers' work are substantial, their origins are much less clear. Historical evidence suggests that a divide between Eastern and Occidental thinking has existed at least since ancient times, a tradition of adversarial debate, formal logical argument and analytic deduction flowering in Greece, while in China an appreciation for context and complexity, dialectical argument and a tolerance for the "yin and yang" of life flourished.

How much of this East-West difference is a result of differing social and religious practices, different languages or even different geography is anyone's guess. But both styles, Dr. Nisbett said, have advantages, and both have limitations. And neither approach is written into the genes: many Asian-Americans, born in the United States, are indistinguishable in their modes of thought from European-Americans.

Dr. Alan Fiske, an associate professor of anthropology at the University of California at Los Angeles, said that experimental research like Dr. Nisbett's "complements a lot of ethnographic work that has been done."

"Anthropologists have been describing these cultures and this can tell you a lot about everyday life and the ways people talk and interact," Dr. Fiske said. "But it's always difficult to know how to make sense of these qualitative judgments, and they aren't controlled in the same way that an experiment is controlled."

Yet not everyone agrees that all the dissimilarities described by Dr.

Nisbett and his colleagues reflect fundamental differences in psychological process.

Dr. Patricia Cheng, for example, a professor of psychology at the University of California at Los Angeles, said that many of the researchers' findings meshed with her own experience. "Having grown up in a traditional Chinese family and also being in Western culture myself," she said, "I do see some entrenched habits of interpretation of the world that are different across the cultures, and they do lead to pervasive differences."

But Dr. Cheng says she thinks that some differences—the Asian tolerance for contradiction, for example—are purely social. "There is not a difference in logical tolerance," she said.

Still, to the extent that the studies reflect real differences in thinking and perception, psychologists may have to radically revise their ideas about what is universal and what is not, and to develop new models of mental process that take cultural influences into account.

More Than One Way to Make an Impression

Exploring Profiles of Impression Management

This research explores the use of impression management tactics in combination. Two studies were conducted to identify three profiles of impression management use and to examine how three individual difference variables are related to these patterns. The results suggest that women are less aggressive than men in using impression management, that high self-monitors favor positive impression management strategies, and that high Machs use impression management tactics rather indiscriminately. The findings also suggest that individuals who either avoid using impression management or who use only positive tactics are seen more favorably than those who use relatively high levels of all types of impression management. Some implications and directions for future research are discussed as well.

Mark C. Bolino and William H. Turnley

A growing body of research indicates that individuals in organizations often engage in impression management behaviors that are designed to influence the way in which they are perceived by others (e.g., Bozeman and Kacmar, 1997; Leary & Kowalski, 1990; Rosenfeld, Giacalone & Riordan, 1995). To date, most empirical work on impression management has focused either on how situational or individual factors affect the use of specific impression management behaviors or how certain impression management tactics influence outcomes such as promotions, performance appraisal ratings, and career success. For example, Wayne and Ferris (1990) found that the use of ingratiation by employees was positively associated with supervisor liking and performance ratings. Also, Judge and Bretz (1994) found that individuals using ingratiation achieved higher levels of career success, while individuals using self-promotion experienced lower levels of career success.

A similar, but conceptually distinct, stream of research investigates the use of influence tactics in organizations. While impression management refers to behaviors that individuals use to control the images that others have of them (Rosenfeld et al., 1995), the term influence tactics is used to describe the ways in which individuals use bargaining, reasoning, friendliness, assertiveness, coalitions, and other strategies to influence the decisions or behaviors of their colleagues, superiors, or subordinates (Kipnis & Schmidt, 1988). In comparison to the research on impression management behavior, though, research examining influence tactics has more often focused on the ways that such tactics are used in combination (e.g., Farmer & Maslyn, 1999; Farmer, Maslyn, Fedor & Goodman, 1997; Kipnis and Schmidt, 1983, 1988). For example, Kipnis and Schmidt (1983) identified three styles of influence: a *shotgun* approach, in which individuals use relatively high levels of influence and emphasize the tactics of assertiveness and bargaining; a *tactician* approach, in which individuals use only an average amount of influence and emphasize the tactic of reason; and a *bystander* approach, in which individuals use relatively low levels of influence tactics. Furthermore, Farmer and Maslyn's (1999) study supported the validity of these three distinct influence styles.

Thus, while the use of various patterns of influence tactics has received significant research attention, comparable work with regard to the use of differing patterns of impression management is lacking. Likewise, research has not examined the impact that different combinations of impression management might have on others' impressions. This research, then, seeks to further our understanding of impression management by exploring the use of impression management tactics in combination. In doing so, this study has three goals.

First, the research seeks to identify clusters (or groups) of individuals who use different impression management tactics in similar ways. Specifically, cluster analysis is used to examine how students working in teams tend to use various combinations of five impression management tactics—namely, ingratiation, self-promotion, exemplification, supplication, and intimidation (Jones & Pittman 1982). Then, the research seeks to replicate the patterns of impression management use found in the first sample of participants in a second, independent sample of participants. Second, the research explores the ways in which three individual difference variables—gender, self-monitoring, and Machiavellianism—are related to these patterns or styles of impression management. Third and finally, the research explores the relationship between different patterns or styles of impression management and how individuals are perceived by their peers.

A Profile Model of Impression Management

Researchers have proposed several different theoretical frameworks of impression management (e.g., Bozeman & Kacmar, 1987; Jones & Pittman, 1982; and Tedeschi & Melburg, 1984). Empirically-derived models of impression management have been introduced as well (e.g., Wayne & Ferris. 1990). In this paper, we use the Jones and Pittman (1982) model to examine the use of impression management tactics in combination. Their framework is especially well suited to this research for three reasons. First, while several theoretical and empirical frameworks have been proposed, the Jones and Pittman (1982) taxonomy is the only theoretical model that has been validated empirically (Bolino & Turnley, 1999). Second, this framework proposes five different tactics that encompass a wide variety of behaviors that are likely to occur in the context of work groups, making it ideal for studying the use of impression management behaviors in combination. Third, Bolino & Turnley (1999) have already developed items to measure these five tactics in organizational settings. Their existing scales, then, could be used to develop measures of these behaviors in a sample of student work groups.

According to Jones and Pittman (1982), individuals typically use five impression management tactics: (1) *Ingratiation*, whereby individuals seek to be viewed as likable by flattering others or doing favors for them; (2) *Self-promotion*, whereby individuals seek to be viewed as competent by touting their abilities and accomplishments; (3) *Exemplification*, whereby individuals seek to be viewed as dedicated by going above and beyond the call of duty; (4) *Supplication*, whereby individuals seek to be viewed as needy by showing their weaknesses or broadcasting their limitations; and (5) *Intimidation*, whereby individuals seek to be viewed as intimidating by threatening or bullying others.

Clearly, Jones and Pittman (1982) and other researchers (e.g., Tedeschi & Melburg, 1984; Wayne & Ferris, 1990) posit that impression management is a multidimensional construct. However, as Law, Wong, and Mobley (1998) point out, there are many multidimensional constructs in which the overall construct's relations with its specific dimensions are not explicitly detailed. Such is the case with the construct of impression management.

The taxonomy proposed by Law et al. (1998) suggests three ways in which multidimensional constructs can be conceptualized. First, the label *latent model* describes multidimensional constructs that exist at deeper levels than their individual dimensions. Second, the label *aggregate model* denotes multidimensional constructs that are formed based on algebraic functions of their dimensions. Third, the label *profile model* designates multidimensional constructs formed as different profiles of their dimensions.

Law et at. (1998) suggest that the interrelations between a construct and its dimensions can be defined under all three models of multidimensional constructs. For example, using the latent model, individuals would have to engage in relatively high levels of all five impression management tactics in order to be described as actively managing impressions. Under the aggregate model, impression management would be defined as the simple sum (or an alternative mathematical combination) of an individual's impression management behaviors across the five tactics. Finally, using the profile model, one's impression management style can be examined by looking at patterns comprised of varying levels of the five impression management strategies or dimensions. Most of the extant research on impression management, however, has not addressed the relationships between specific impression management dimensions. Rather, in prior research, individuals have been considered to be managing impressions when they engage in one or more of the specific impression management tactics. Thus, in order to advance our understanding of this construct, it might be useful to examine the relationships that exist among various impression management tactics more thoroughly.

Using the Law et al. (1998) taxonomy, the latent model seems relatively inappropriate for defining impression management behavior. That is, it appears somewhat tenuous to assert that individuals do not engage in impression management unless they utilize each and every form of impression management proposed by any given multidimensional conceptualization. Likewise, the aggregate model does not seem very well suited for defining impression management behavior. Although there may be a tendency for individuals to generally manage impressions (or to generally avoid such behavior), certain forms of impression management are likely to be moderately correlated (such as self-promotion and exemplification) while others are likely to be much less correlated (such as self-promotion and supplication). By simply aggregating scores across tactics, then, we may be oversimplifying the use of impression management by combining scores across tactics that are distinct in meaningful ways.

Examining impression management using the profile method, though, could potentially help clarify some of the fundamental characteristics of this construct. For example, some individuals may not use any of the impression management strategies, while others may use all of them. Likewise, other individuals may use high levels of particular tactics like ingratiation and supplication and low levels of other tactics such as self-promotion, exemplification, and intimidation. The first goal of this study, then, is to use cluster analysis to identify different patterns, or profiles, of impression management use.

Study 1

Although previous theory indicates that individuals are likely to use different types of impression management (Jones, 1990; Jones & Pittman, 1982), there has been little theoretical work outlining the various ways in which these tactics might be employed together as a set. Based on previous research on influence styles, though, we expect at least three different patterns of impression management to emerge. As described earlier, one of the principal findings of the literature on the use of influence tactics in combination has been that some individuals seem to have an all or nothing approach to using these tactics (Farmer & Maslyn, 1999; Kipnis & Schmidt, 1988). In other words, some individuals use relatively high levels of multiple influence tactics (i.e., the shotgun approach), while others use relatively low levels of influence tactics (i.e., the bystander). It is expected that two similar patterns will emerge here. That is, it is anticipated that some individuals will tend to engage in relatively high levels of all types of impression management. In contrast, it is expected that others will engage in relatively low levels of impression management across the five different tactics.

In addition, prior research suggests that some impression management tactics seem to have more in common than others (Turney & Bolino, 2001). Specifically, ingratiation, self-promotion, and exemplification are all tactics utilized by individuals attempting to make a positive impression on others. However, supplication and intimidation are tactics for which even the "desired" images (i.e., of being seen as "needy" and "intimidating") are likely to have negative repercussions. Thus, although employees may gain assistance from others by appearing needy or achieve their own ends through intimidation, they may also be seen less favorably as a result of this kind of behavior. The third pattern of impression management that is expected, then, is one in which individuals use relatively high levels of ingratiation, self-promotion, and exemplification, coupled with relatively low levels of supplication and intimidation.

It is possible that a pattern could also emerge in which individuals use relatively high levels of supplication and intimidation in conjunction with relatively low levels of ingratiation, self-promotion, and exemplification. However, previous research suggests that this combination is somewhat improbable because supplication and intimidation tactics are used very infrequently (Becker & Martin, 1995; Bolino & Turnley, 1999). Thus, while such a pattern is theoretically plausible, it seems unlikely to occur in practice.

Method

Sample

Participants in this study were junior and senior level students in organizational behavior courses at a university in the Midwestern United States. The students were assigned to work in mixed-gender, four- or five-person groups on a semester-long research project, The students were assigned to groups in such a way as to ensure that each group had at least two members of each gender. However, within each gender, students were assigned randomly to the groups. For the project, the students had to do background research on a topic, identify an organization in which to study this topic, collect data from members of the organization, analyze the data, and provide both a written and oral report of their findings. While participation in the class project was mandatory, participation in this study was voluntary. Eighty-six of 89 students participated in this research, providing a response rate of 97%. Fifty-six percent of the participants were male.

Measures

Students reported the extent to which they engaged in impression management behaviors during the course of the project. Respondents were informed that their anonymity was guaranteed with respect to the instructor. Jones and Pittman's (1982) five impression management tactics were measured using a modified version of Bolino and Turnley's (1999) impression management scale. This measure taps the extent to which individuals in organizational settings engage in ingratiation, self-promotion, exemplification, supplication, and intimidation. In this study, some of the items were reworded and a few additional items were added to each of the subscales in order to better capture the nature of impression management in the context of student workgroups. The measure asked how accurate each of 32 statements was in describing the individual's behavior during the group project. Responses were made on a scale ranging from (1) Very Inaccurate to (5) Very Accurate.

A sample item from the ingratiation subscale is: "Do personal favors for members of the group to show them that you are friendly." A sample item from the self-promotion subscale is: "Make other group members aware of your unique skills and abilities." A sample item from the exemplification subscale is: "Let others know that you have been putting in a lot of time on the project." A sample item from the supplication subscale is: "Act like you need assistance on your part of the project so that other group members will help you." A sample item from the intimidation subscale is: "Be intimidating with other group members when it is necessary for the good of the project."

A confirmatory factor analysis (CFA) using maximum likelihood estimation and randomly created item parcels (as outlined by Floyd and Widaman (1995)) supported the 5-factor structure ($\chi^2 = 79.97$, df = 67). The key fit indices for the 5-factor model were as follows: GFI = .88, AGFI = .82, RMSEA = .048, CFI = .97, and TLI = .96. The fit of this 5-factor model was also compared with the fit of six alternative models (i.e., a 1-factor model, a 2-factor model, and four different 4-factor models). In every instance, the fit of the 5-factor model was significantly better than the fit of any alternative model. Finally, an unparcelled CFA model indicated that each of the impression management items loaded significantly on its specified factor. Cronbach's alpha for the five impression management dimensions were as follows: Ingratiation (.82), Self-Promotion (.82), Exemplification (.76), Supplication (.88), and Intimidation (.82).

Results

The goal of Study 1 was to examine the various ways in which individuals utilize the five impression management strategies proposed by Jones and Pittman (1982). Cluster analysis was employed to identify specific patterns of impression management used by the participants in the study. Hierarchical clustering techniques do not require *a priori* knowledge of the number of clusters and, thus, are ideal for determining the number of clusters in a data set. In contrast, nonhierarchical clustering techniques require knowledge about the number of clusters, but typically yield better cluster solutions than hierarchical methods. Therefore, as recommended by Sharma (1996), hierarchical cluster analysis (using the centroid method) was used first to determine the appropriate number of clusters. We plotted the root-mean-square standard deviation versus the distance between the clusters, as well as the semi-partial R-squared versus the R-squared, in order to evaluate possible cluster solutions. Both plots indicated that a three-cluster solution was most appropriate. That is, these analyses suggested three patterns (or clusters) of ways in which individuals employ the five impression management tactics. Then, as outlined by Sharma (1996), nonhierarchical clustering (i.e., k-means cluster analysis) was used to obtain the final, three-cluster solution.

Cluster 1 consisted of 38 individuals who had the highest use of those impression management tactics aimed at achieving positive-only images (i.e., ingratiation, self-promotion, and exemplification); these individuals used supplication and intimidation relatively less frequently. For this reason, the individuals comprising this cluster were labeled the "positives." The second cluster was made up of 38 individuals who used relatively high levels of all five impression management tactics. Thus, the individuals in Cluster 2 were described as the "aggressives." Finally, Cluster 3 consisted of 10 individuals who used relatively low levels of all five impression management tactics. The individuals in this cluster were labeled the "passives."

The results of Study 1 suggest that the individuals in this study used combinations of impression management tactics in three different ways. While some individuals tended to use only the positive tactics (i.e., the positives), others tended to use either all of the tactics (i.e., the aggressives) or relatively few of the tactics (i.e., the passives). However, in order to demonstrate the validity of a cluster solution it must be replicated in another sample and be shown to relate in logical ways to other variables within its nomological network (Sharma, 1996). Moreover, the sample size used in Study 1 was rather small. Thus, one could have more confidence in the cluster solution that emerged if data had been collected from a larger number of respondents. For these reasons, then, a second study was conducted in which additional data were collected from a larger sample in order to confirm the impression management profiles identified in Study 1 and to determine whether these patterns are useful for further understanding the antecedents and consequences of impression management.

Study 2

As described above, for the profiles generated in Study 1 to be of practical value, it is necessary to link the patterns of impression management with other variables within the relevant nomological network (i.e., variables which are thought to predict or be an outcome of impression management). Thus, Study 2 has three objectives: (1) to replicate the profiles of impression management identified in Study 1 using another group of participants; (2) to examine some potential antecedents of these profiles of impression management by looking at variables that have been linked with impression management behavior in previous research; and (3) to relate these patterns of impression management to the focal outcome of impression management—namely, the image or perception that others have of the person using impression management tactics.

Antecedents of Impression Management Profiles

Previous research suggests that a variety of situational factors and individual differences are related to the use of impression management behaviors (Bozeman & Kacmar, 1997; Gardner & Martinko, 1988; Leary & Kowalski, 1990). However, because the context for this study is student work teams, it seemed unlikely that the situational factors that have been examined in previous research would be relevant here. For example, because the parameters of the research project were well defined by the instructor, factors such as situational ambiguity or uncertainty were likely to be relatively constant across groups. In addition, due to the homogeneity of the sample in terms of age, race, and educational level, it was not possible to examine the effects of these variables on the use of impression management. However, the relationship between gender and patterns of impression management could be assessed in this study. Moreover, the relevance of the two dispositional variables that have received the most attention in previous studies of impression management—self-monitoring and Machiavellianism—were examined, too. Thus, in this second study, we examine how gender, self-monitoring, and Machiavellianism are related to profiles of impression management.

Gender

Research on impression management suggests that men and women often seek to manage impressions in different ways (Gardner & Martinko, 1988; Judge & Bretz, 1994). Indeed, according to Eagly's (1987) role theory of gender differences in social behavior, individuals tend to engage in behaviors that are consistent with their socially-prescribed gender roles. Since the female gender role typically discourages aggressive or assertive behavior (Eagly, Makhijani & Klonsky, 1992), it is expected that women will be less likely than men to use an aggressive approach to managing impressions and will be more likely to use a passive approach. In contrast, the male gender role typically encourages and rewards assertiveness (Eagly et at., 1932). For this reason, it is expected that men will be more likely than women to actively manage impressions and to do so in an aggressive fashion. Therefore, relative to men, it is expected that women will be more likely to be passives and less likely to be aggressives.

Finally, although there is a theoretical basis for expecting gender-related differences with regard to the passives and aggressives clusters, it is unclear whether those using a positive strategy will be more likely to be men or to be women. That is, men and women alike may believe that the best means of creating a favorable image is to emphasize the more positive impression management strategies. It is expected, then, that men and women will be equally likely to use a positive strategy.

Hypothesis 1. Relative to men, women are more likely to be passives and less likely to be aggressives.

Self-monitoring

Another individual difference variable likely to influence how individuals utilize impression management behaviors is self-monitoring. Self-monitoring refers to one's ability to control one's expressive behavior (Snyder, 1974). High self-monitors are sensitive to the appropriateness of the image they are projecting and have the ability to change their behaviors to suit different situations. In prior research, self-monitoring has been positively associated with the extent of impression management use (Fandt & Ferris, 1990; and Rosenfeld et al., 1995). However, Turnley and Bolino (2001) suggest that, relative to low self-monitors, high self-monitors may also be more selective in their use of impression management tactics. In particular, high self-monitors may be especially wary of using those tactics that are likely to lead to less favorable images (i.e., supplication and intimidation). Overall, then, while high self-monitors will tend to use impression management (i.e., they are unlikely to be passives), they should also tend to be more selective in their use of impression management compared with low self-monitors (i.e., high self-monitors are unlikely to be aggressives).

Hypothesis 2. Relative to low self-monitors, high self-monitors are more likely to be positives and less likely to be aggressives or passives.

Machiavellianism

Finally, an individual's level of Machiavellianism is likely to affect how he or she uses different types of impression management. Machiavellianism describes the extent to which individuals behave manipulatively, hold cynical views of human nature, and have a generally low regard for conventional standards of morality (Christie & Geis, 1970). Research suggests that Machiavellianism is likely to be positively correlated with the use of impression management (Christie & Geis, 1970). However, whereas high self-monitors often use impression management to please others, research suggests that Machiavellians may use impression management behaviors that more immediately benefit themselves (Ickes, Reidhead & Patterson, 1986). It is expected, then, that high Machs will be more likely to use a wide array of impression management tactics, including those which may be viewed as less socially acceptable (i.e., supplication and intimidation). Thus, high Machs will be more likely than low Machs to be either aggressives or positives. Low Machs, in contrast, should be less likely to use impression management altogether (i.e., low Machs are more likely than high Machs to be passives).

Hypothesis 3. Relative to low Machs, high Machs are more likely to be aggressives or positives and less likely to be passives.

Profiles of Impression Management and One's Image

The general goal of most impression management behavior is to be viewed by others in a desirable light and to avoid being viewed in an undesirable light (Gardner & Marcinko, 1988; Leary & Kowalski, 1990). In this context, it is reasonable to expect that most individuals would like their peers to consider them as desirable colleagues with whom to work. Clearly, there is evidence that some forms of impression management are effective in eliciting desirable images (e.g., Judge & Bretz, 1994 Wayne & Ferris, 1990). Logically, then, individuals who tend to be rather passive in their use of impression management (i.e., the passives) should be less likely to be seen favorably by others than those who use impression management to at least some degree. On the other hand, researchers also suggest that attempts to manage impressions sometimes backfire (e.g., Crant, 1996), thereby resulting in unfavorable images. Thus, individuals who are somewhat careless, or less judicious, in their use of impression management (i.e., the aggressives) may be seen more negatively, too. For these reasons, it seems reasonable to expect that the most favorable images will accrue to those individuals who are more selective in their use of impression management and tend to emphasize more positive impression management behaviors (i.e., the positives).

Hypothesis 4. Positives are more likely to be seen as a desirable workgroup colleague than aggressives or passives.

Method

Sample

The participants in Study 2 were completely independent of those participating in Study 1. However, as with the participants of the first study, they were also business students enrolled in organizational behavior courses at a university in the Midwestern United States. Like the participants in Study 1, all of students were at the junior or senior level in their undergraduate program and were assigned to work in mixed-gender, four- or five-person groups on a semester-long research project in such a way as to ensure that each group had at least two members of each gender. Within each gender, though, students were assigned randomly to the groups. Again, participation in the class project was mandatory, but participation in the study was voluntary. One hundred seventy-three of 188 students participated in this research, providing a response rate of 92%. Fifty-five percent of the participants were male.

Procedure

Students used the first three letters of their mother's name and the month of her birth to create a code name for themselves. The students shared their code name with the other members of their group, but it was not provided to the course instructor. Thus, the respondent's anonymity could be maintained (with respect to the instructor). Participants completed the Machiavellianism and self-monitoring scales at the beginning of the project. At the conclusion of the project, participants indicated the extent to which they had engaged in each of the impression management tactics. Approximately 1 week later, participants provided their perceptions of each of their group members. All of this information was collected before students received their grade on the project.

Measures

Self-monitoring Self-monitoring was measured using the 18-item revised version of the Self-monitoring Scale (Snyder & Gangestad, 1986). As recommended by Briggs and Cheek (1986), a 5-point scale, ranging from (1) Strongly Disagree to (5) Strongly Agree, was used rather than the True–False format. Sample items include: "I find it hard to imitate the behavior of other people" (reverse scored) and "I am not always the person I appear to be." Cronbach's alpha for the scale was .80.

Machiavellianism. Machiavellianism was measured with the 20-item scale developed by Christie and Geis (1970). Responses were made on a 6-point scale ranging from (1) Strongly Disagree to (6) Strongly Agree. Sample items include: "The best way to handle people is to tell them what they want to hear" and "Never tell anyone the real reason you did something unless it is useful to do so." Cronbach's alpha for the scale was .76.

Impression management tactics. The same 32-item scale used in Study 1 was used in this study. Again, a CFA using maximum likelihood estimation and randomly created item parcels (as outlined by Floyd & Widaman. 1995) supported the 5-factor structure ($\chi^2 = 107.71$, df = 67). The key fit indices for the 5-factor model were as follows: GFI = .92, AGFI = .88, RMSEA = .060, CFI = .96, and TLI = .95. As in the first study, the fit of this 5-factor model was also compared with the fit of six alternative models (i.e., a 1-factor model, a 2-factor model, and four different 4-factor models). In every instance, the fit of the 5-factor model was significantly better than the fit of any alternative model. Moreover, an unparcelled CFA model indicated that each of the impression management items loaded significantly on to its specified factor. Cronbach's alpha for the five impression management dimensions were as follows: Ingratiation (.80), Self-Promotion (.84), Exemplification (.66), Supplication (.85), and Intimidation (.82).

Impression outcome. A scale was created to tap the general impression that individuals had of each of the other members of their group. Items assessed whether or not the person was generally perceived as a desirable group member. The scale was comprised of 12 adjectives (e.g., likable, cooperative, hard-working, conscientious, bossy (reverse scored), lazy (reverse scored)). Responses were made on a 5-point scale ranging from (1) Strongly Disagree to (5) Strongly Agree. Responses were averaged across the group members in order to determine each individual's score on the impression outcome measure. Cronbach's alpha for the impression outcome scale was .90.

A correlation matrix of all the variables used in this study is provided in Table 1 The means and standard deviations for the scales are also provided in Table 1.

Results

The first goal of Study 2 was to replicate the profiles of impression management identified in Study 1. Again, cluster analysis was used to identify the patterns of impression management tactics used by the respondents. Based on the results of Study 1, three clusters were expected. For this reason, nonhierarchical cluster analysis was used here. The results of the cluster analysis confirm the profiles of impression management found in the first study. In other words, the results obtained in Study 2 were very similar to those found in Study 1. Specifically, the first cluster consisted of 86 positives—individuals who used relatively high levels of ingratiation, self-promotion, and exemplification, but used supplication and intimidation relatively less frequently. The second cluster was comprised of 49 aggressives—individuals using relatively high levels of all five impression management tactics. Lastly, the third cluster consisted of 38 passives—individuals who used relatively low levels of each tactic.

The second goal of Study 2 was to determine how individual difference variables relate to the profiles of impression management identified in this research. Specifically, this study exam-

Table 1. Correlation matrix of variables for Study 2

	Mean	S.D.	1	2	3	4	5	6	7	8
1. Gender	.55	.50								
2. Self-monitoring	2.99	.55	.20**							
3. Machiavellianism	3.05	.57	.19*	.21**						
4. Ingratiation	3.12	.75	.06	.10	−.12					
5. Self-promotion	2.98	.79	.25**	.25**	−.05	.48***				
6. Exemplification	2.84	.72	.24**	.21**	.02	.44***	.59***			
7. Supplication	1.93	.69	.19*	.03	.28***	.28***	.20**	.25***		
8. Intimidation	2.28	.75	.31***	.10	.17*	.24**	.37**	.38***	.50***	
9. Impression	4.11	.48	−.04	−.01	−.05	.11	−.03	.05	−.24**	−.14

Gender was coded such that female = 0 and male = 1.
* $p < .05$ ** $p < .01$ ***$p < .001$

Table 2. Logistic regression analyses

	Dependent variable: impression management cluster (positive, aggressive, passive)	
	Parameter estimate	S.E.
Intercept 1	-1.27	1.12
Intercept 2	.21	1.12
Gender	.71*	.32
Self-monitoring	1.13**	.32
Machiavellianism	-1.04**	.30
Overall model fit		
Likelihood ratio		
Chi-square = 26.34**		
df = 3		
R-square = .15		
Maximum-rescales		
R-square = .17		

* $p < .05$
** $p < .001$

ined whether gender, self-monitoring, and Machiavellianism are associated with an individual's membership in the "positive," "aggressive," or "passive" cluster. Because cluster membership is a categorical dependent variable, logistic regression was used to test the first three hypotheses. The three independent variables included in the logistic regression model were gender, self-monitoring, and Machiavellianism; the dependent variable was cluster. The results of the logistic regression analysis appear in Table 2. As shown here, the overall model was significant (the likelihood-ratio test statistic had a χ^2 value of 26.34, df = 3, $p < .001$). Moreover, there were also significant effects for gender ($p < .03$), self-monitoring ($p < .001$), and Machiavellianism ($p < .001$).

A frequency table was developed in order to determine the nature of the relationship between gender and impression management cluster. As expected, the most striking gender differences were with regard to the passive and aggressive clusters. Among women, 35% were passives and 21% were aggressives. In contrast, among men, only 11% were passives while 34% were aggressives. Thus, in comparison to men, women were more likely to report using low levels of all impression management tactics. Males, though, were more likely than their female counterparts to be aggressive. There were fewer gender differences with regard to the positive strategy (the most popular strategy overall, regardless of gender). Specifically, 55% of men tended to utilize this strategy, while 44% of women favored this approach. These results suggest that there are significant differences in the way men and women use impression management. In general, men in this sample tended to be more aggressive in their use of impression management than women. Compared to men, women were more passive and engaged in fewer impression management behaviors across the board. The differences between men and women with regard to the use of

a positive strategy, though, were less dramatic. Therefore, Hypothesis 1 was supported.

An examination of the relationship between self-monitoring and impression management cluster revealed a notable contrast in impression management styles among low and high self-monitors. (In order to develop a frequency table to further examine these results, respondents were classified as either low self-monitors or high self-monitors using a median split.) Specifically, high self-monitors were more likely to be positives (63% of high self-monitors were positives) than were low self-monitors (42% of low self-monitors were positives). That is, high self-monitors, who are sensitive to how they are seen by others, tend to emphasize the more positive strategies of impression management. In contrast, low self-monitors were more likely than high self-monitors to be either aggressives (low self-monitors made up 60% of the aggressives cluster) or passives (low self-monitors made up 60% of the passives cluster). Thus, high self-monitors did not necessarily engage in more impression management across the board; rather, they tended to emphasize those behaviors that sought to obtain favorable attributions. Hypothesis 2, then, was supported.

Finally, there were also manifest differences in the patterns of impression management tactics employed by high Machs and low Machs. (In order to further examine these results, a frequency table was developed by classifying individuals as either low Machs or high Machs using a median split.) As expected, the aggressive group tended to be made up largely of high Machs (55%). However, somewhat unexpectedly, high Machs also comprised the majority (54%) of the passives cluster. In contrast, low Machs made up 56% of the positives. Thus, compared to low Machs, high Machs tended to be either aggressive or passive in their use of the five impression management tactics whereas low Machs tended to emphasize the more positive impression management behaviors.

On the surface these findings may seem somewhat surprising. That is, it was expected that low Machs would engage in fewer impression management behaviors than high Machs (i.e., low Machs were expected to make up the majority of the passives cluster). In hindsight, though, this finding actually provides some support for the idea that Machiavellianism is not necessarily related to the amount of impression management used by individuals, but instead to individuals' willingness to engage in more risky, and perhaps more deceptive, forms of impression management. That is, relative to low Machs, high Machs seem to have an all or nothing approach to managing impressions. Thus, in many ways, these results are consistent with other research on Machiavellianism which suggests that high Machs are not necessarily concerned with using their impression management to please others; rather, they tend to use impression management only in ways which satisfy their own ends (e.g., Ickes et al., 1986). Overall, then, Hypothesis 3 was only partially supported.

The final research question sought to determine whether passives, positives, and aggressives were viewed differently by their workgroup colleagues. Specifically, the study examined whether the patterns of impression management tactics differentially influenced whether the individuals were perceived as desirable workgroup colleagues. ANOVA was used to answer

Table 3. Analysis of variance results

	Dependent variable: impression outcome (desirable colleague)	
	Mean	S.D.
Independent variable: IM cluster		
Passives	4.19 (a)	.45
Aggressives	3.93 (b)	.54
Positives	4.19 (a)	.41
Overall model		
$F = 4.96*$		
df = 2159		
R-square = .06		

Means with the same letter are not significantly different.
*$p < .01$

this final research question. The results of the ANOVA are displayed in Table 3.

The ANOVA results indicate that there were significant differences in how passives, positives, and aggressives are viewed by their colleagues. A Tukey pair-wise comparison test revealed that aggressives were significantly less likely to be seen as desirable workgroup colleagues than either the passives or the positives. However, group members did not have significantly different perceptions of positives and passives. Thus, individuals in this sample responded more favorably when their group members used either a combination of positive impression management tactics or when they used fairly low levels of impression management across all types of tactics. When individuals used relatively high levels of all of the impression management tactics, however, they were less likely to be seen as a desirable workgroup colleague. Thus, Hypothesis 4 was only partially supported.

Discussion

The present research examined how individuals attempt to influence the image others hold of them by using impression management tactics in combination. The results of the study support the idea that not only do individuals differ in how they use specific impression management tactics, but also in the ways they employ such strategies in combination. In these two studies, one group favored the use of the positive impression management tactics of ingratiation, self-promotion, and exemplification. A second group tended to engage in impression management aggressively, using the tactics somewhat indiscriminately. Finally, a third group was more reserved or passive in their use of all the impression management tactics.

Individual differences significantly predicted the patterns of impression management employed, with women tending to take a passive stance in their use of impression management relative to men and men opting for a more aggressive approach relative to women. Also, as expected, high self-monitors emphasized positive impression management tactics. However, high Machs tended to fall into either the aggressives or passives categories, while low Machs were more likely to be positives. Finally, the ways in which individuals used impression management tactics

in combination significantly affected how they were perceived by their workgroup colleagues. Specifically, compared to the aggressives, positives and passives were more likely to be viewed as desirable workgroup colleagues.

Taken together, these studies provide some evidence for the argument advanced by Law et al. (1998). That is, using a profile model to examine the multidimensional construct of impression management helps to further our understanding of the construct and its dimensions. For example, the conclusions regarding the impact of self-monitoring on impression management are different when using a profile model than when using the more typical approach of examining the specific impression management dimensions in isolation. An examination of the correlation matrix (cf. Table 1) suggests that self-monitors simply use more self-promotion and exemplification. However, the cluster analysis and logistic regression results reveal that high self-monitors are most likely to use high levels of ingratiation, self-promotion, and exemplification combined with relatively low levels of supplication and intimidation. Viewing impression management tactics in isolation, then, does not give a full picture regarding the use of impression management tactics in combination.

This research also provides some direction for future theoretical and empirical work on impression management. The results of the cluster analyses suggest that participants in both studies used the same three patterns of impression management. However, in other contexts, different impression management profiles might emerge. For example, in groups that are more hierarchical, supervisors may be more willing than subordinates to use combinations of impression management that include the tactic of intimidation. Likewise, a passive approach to impression management may be more evident in short-term groups than in groups that are established for longer-term projects. More theoretical work, then, is needed to develop taxonomies describing the ways individuals use impression management tactics together. In addition, more theoretical attention should be given to factors that might affect individuals' use of impression management tactics in combination and the images that are likely to accrue to those individuals using particular patterns of impression management.

A logical starting point for research along these lines is to revisit the basic motives thought to underlie different impression management strategies. For example, ingratiation is used in an attempt to be seen as likable, while supplication is used in order to appear needy. Researchers could attempt to formulate theory that specifies the circumstances under which individuals in organizations might be more or less likely to engage in certain forms of impression management at relatively high, low, or equivalent levels. In this way, it may ultimately be possible to build theoretical models that explain when individuals will use relatively high levels of intimidation, self-promotion, and exemplification coupled with relatively low levels of ingratiation and supplication. While certain combinations of tactics seem rather improbable (something which could also be articulated using a theoretical model), future research may be able to make more informed predictions about which combinations are more or less likely to occur in certain situations or to be employed by certain individuals.

In addition to theory exploring the patterns themselves, more attention should also be given to the contextual factors that shape the use of combinations of impression management tactics, especially within team settings. Specifically, the relational demography of the team could influence the ways in which impression management tactics are utilized. For example, different patterns of impression management may be used within demographically heterogeneous and homogeneous groups. Moreover, individuals may seek to manage one impression with some group members and attempt to manage a different impression with other members. In other words, because there are multiple targets within group settings, individuals may be forced to manage multiple impressions at the same time. Achieving one's image goals, then, may be more complicated in the context of work teams than it is in the context of dyadic relationships.

In this study, the impressions of group members were aggregated to form an overall impression outcome measure. However, even when the same impression management tactics are targeted toward members of the same group, it is possible that some members may respond favorably to such behaviors while others respond less favorably. For example, an individual's impression management tactics may lead him or her to be seen as highly competent by some members of the group and highly conceited by others. Accordingly, there may ultimately be some meaning or significance to the distribution of impressions within a group. In other words, there might be practical differences between someone who is seen as moderately likeable by everyone in the group, versus someone who is seen as very liked by some and very disliked by others. Thus, additional research is needed to better understand how the outcomes of impression management are best conceptualized and measured in the context of groups.

Similarly, impression formation is a cyclical and dynamic process (Jones, 1990). Unfortunately, though, most impression management research examines it as if it were a fairly static process. In particular, the members of a work team are not only managing impressions, but also forming impressions of their teammates at the same time. It is possible, then, that different norms about the ways in which impression management is utilized and interpreted may develop within different work groups. More studies that utilize longitudinal research designs and seek to explain the influence of contextual factors and group dynamics upon impression management processes would contribute to our understanding of this phenomenon.

Additional work is needed, too, that examines both the positive and negative outcomes associated with combinations of impression management tactics. For instance, previous research suggests that self-promotion can often be risky (e.g., Wayne & Ferris. 1990). This tactic may be especially hard to successfully pull off when it is coupled with other impression management tactics, such as intimidation; however, it may be more likely to succeed when coupled with tactics such as exemplification and ingratiation. Similarly, previous research suggests that observer attributions often play an important role in determining whether attempts to manage impressions ultimately succeed or fail (Jones & Pittman, 1982). In particular, if observers feel they are being manipulated, they typically react negatively to impression management behavior. Unfortunately, here, we do not have data concerning the attributions that observers made with regard to the impression management behavior of their peers. For this reason, more work is needed which explores the variables that might moderate the relationship between the use of combinations of impression management tactics and their associated outcomes.

Finally, future studies should also address how researchers can best conceptualize and study the multidimensional construct of impression management more generally. The theory proffered by Law et at. (1998) could serve as a useful starting point in this regard. For example, while it may make sense to use the profile model to examine some research questions, in other contexts the aggregate or latent approach might be more appropriate. Likewise, more work is needed to integrate the various taxonomies and typologies of impression management that have been developed in the literature. For example, Wayne and Ferris' (1990) typology classifies impression management behaviors based on their focus—job, supervisor, or self. Thus, it is possible that (similar to the results obtained here) certain combinations of these tactics may be more effective than others. Also, there may be meaningful predictors of the ways in which individuals focus these different combinations of impression management behaviors as well.

Although this study improves our understanding of impression management, it is not without limitations. First, the research described here is somewhat exploratory. Additional studies that build upon the theoretical base provided in this research and in past studies would be especially useful. In addition, future studies that successfully replicate the profiles of impression management identified in these studies would strengthen the confidence that one can have in the results obtained here. Second, like many other studies of impression management, the sample used here consisted of undergraduate students. Moreover, the sample size for the first study was fairly small. While the sample size for Study 2 was larger, ideally, these profiles should be extended to an organizational setting. Accordingly, it is unclear how generalizable these results may be to other contexts. Indeed, there may be a different set of strategies used in corporate settings than the positives-aggressives-passives pattern that was found here. This point reinforces the idea that more theoretical work is needed to gain a better understanding of how individuals use combinations of impression management tactics in different settings. Third and finally, this research focused on only a relatively small set of predictor variables and a single criterion variable. Therefore, additional studies are also needed to examine other important antecedents and outcomes associated with the use of various impression management profiles. Furthermore, future research should also examine contextual factors and potential moderators so that a more complete picture of the impression management process can be developed.

Nevertheless, as a starting point for the investigation of impression management profiles, this research has some notable strengths. First, whereas previous studies have generally focused on one or two tactics of impression management, the present research examined five different impression management strategies based on Jones and Pittman's (1982) taxonomy. Also, the results suggest real differences in how individuals utilize the various impression management behaviors in combination, and the patterns of impression management usage were consistent across two independent samples. Furthermore, although these samples were comprised of students working in project teams, it is reasonable to expect that many of the same impression management processes at work in these groups are likely to occur in organizational work teams. In particular, the groups used in these studies are similar to autonomous work teams in which group members have fairly equal status. (However, the use of student teams did preclude the examination of many contextual variables that might be relevant in organizational settings, such as team structures that are more hierarchical.) In addition, the findings suggest that individual differences predicted the different patterns of impression management use and that the different profiles of impression management use predicted how the individuals were viewed by their workgroup colleagues. Moreover, the data examined here were collected both longitudinally and using multiple sources.

Finally, there are potential practical implications of this research. In particular, prior research has sometimes offered guidelines on the best ways to use impression management (Jones 1990; Judge & Bretz, 1994; Wayne & Ferris). By and large, this advice speaks mainly to the use of impression management tactics in isolation. Clearly, though, the results of this study demonstrate that individuals use a variety of tactics to shape the images that others have of them. Therefore, it is possible that some of the practical recommendations that have been made in the past may require reexamination in order to address instances in which impression management tactics are used together. In other words, this research suggests that using a variety of impression management tactics in combination may be substantively different than using each of these tactics in isolation. Accordingly, practicing mangers seeking to create favorable impressions at work should strive to find the combination of tactics that enable them to achieve their impression management goals.

Mark C. Bolino Department of Mangement, Mendoza College of Business, University of Notre Dame, Norte Dame, IN 46556, USA
William H. Turnley Department of Management, College of Business Administration, Kansas State University, Manhattan, KS 66506, USA

References

T.E. Becker and S.L. Martin, Trying to look bad at work: Methods and motives for managing poor impressions in organizations. *Academy of Management Journal* 38 (1995), pp. 174–199.

M.C. Bolino and W.H. Turnley, Measuring impression management in organizations: A scale development based on the Jones and Pittman taxonomy. *Organizational Research Methods* 2 (1999), pp. 187–206.

D.P. Bozeman and K.M. Kacmar, A cybernetic model of impression management processes in organizations. *Organizational Behavior and Human Decision Processes* 69 (1997), pp. 9–30.

S. Briggs and J. Cheek, The role of factor analysis in the development and evaluation of personality scales. *Journal of Personality* 54 (1986), pp. 106–148.

Christie, R., & Geis, F. 1970. *Studies in Machiavellianism*. New York: Academic Press.

J.M. Crant, Doing more harm than good: When is impression management likely to evoke a negative response? *Journal of Applied Social Psychology* 26 (1996), pp. 1454–1471.

Eagly, A. H. 1987. *Sex differences in social behavior: A social-role interpretation*. Hillsdale, NJ: Lawrence Erlbaum.

A.H. Eagly, M.G. Makhijani and B.G. Klonsky, Gender and the evaluation of leaders: A meta-analysis. *Psychological Bulletin* 111 (1992), pp. 3–22.

P.M. Fandt and G.R. Ferris, The management of information and impressions: When employees behave opportunistically. *Organizational Behavior and Human Decision Processes* 45 (1990), pp. 140–158.

S.M. Farmer and J.M. Maslyn, Why are styles of upward influence neglected? Making the case for a configurational approach to influences. *Journal of Management* 25 (1999), pp. 653–682.

S.M. Farmer, J.M. Maslyn, D.H. Fedor and J.S. Goodman, Putting upward influence strategies in context. *Journal of Organizational Behavior* 18 (1997), pp. 17–42.

F.J. Floyd and K.F. Widaman, Factor analysis in the development and refinement of clinical assessment instruments. *Psychological Assessment* 7 (1995), pp. 286–299.

W.L. Gardner and M.J. Martinko, Impression management in organizations. *Journal of Management* 14 (1988), pp. 321–338.

W. Ickes, S. Reidhead and M. Patterson, Machiavellianism and self-monitoring: As different as "me" and "you". *Social Cognition* 4 (1986), pp. 58–74.

Jones, E. E. 1990. *Interpersonal perception*. New York: W.H. Freeman.

Jones, E. E., & Pittman, T. S. 1982. Toward a general theory of strategic self-presentation. In J. Suls (Ed.), *Psychological perspectives on the self*. Vol. 1, 231–262. Hillsdale, NJ: Lawrence Erlbaum.

T.A. Judge and R.D. Bretz, Political influence behavior and career success. *Journal of Management* 20 (1994), pp. 43–65.

Kipnis & Schmidt, 1983. Kipnis, D., & Schmidt, S. M. 1983. An influence perspective on bargaining. In M. Bazerman & R Lewicki (Eds.), *Negotiating in organizations*: 303–319. Beverly Hills, CA: Sage.

D. Kipnis and S.M. Schmidt, Upward-influence styles: Relationship with performance evaluations, salary, and stress. *Administrative Science Quarterly* 33 (1988), pp. 528–542.

K.S. Law, C. Wong and W.H. Mobley, Toward a taxonomy of multidimensional constructs. *Academy of Management Review* 23 (1998), pp. 741–755.

M.R Leary and R.M. Kowalski, Impression management: A literature review and two component model. *Psychological Bulletin* 107 (1990), pp. 34–47.

Rosenfeld, P.R, Giacalone, R.A., & Riordan, C.A. 1995. *Impression management in organizations: Theory, measurement, and practice*. New York: Routledge.

Sharma, S. 1996. *Applied multivariate techniques*. New York: Wiley.

M. Snyder, Self-monitoring of expressive behavior. *Journal of Personality and Social Psychology* 30 (1974), pp. 526–537.

M. Snyder and S. Gangestad, On the nature of self-monitoring: Matters of assessment, matters of validity. *Journal of Personality and Social Psychology* 51 (1986), pp. 125–139.

Tedeschi, J.T., & Melburg, V. 1984. Impression management and influence in the organization. In S.B. Bacharach & E.J. Lawler (Eds.), *Research in the sociology of organizations:* Vol. 3, 31–58. Greenwich, CT: JAI Press.

W.H. Turnley and M.C. Bolino, Achieving desired images while avoiding undesired images: Exploring the role of self-monitoring in impression management. *Journal of Applied Psychology* 86 (2001), pp. 351–360.

S.J. Wayne and G.R. Ferris, Influence tactics, affect, and exchange quality in supervisor-subordinate interactions: A laboratory experiment and field study. *Journal of Applied Psychology* 75 (1990), pp. 487–499.

UNIT 4
Attitudes

Unit Selections

11. **Sources of Implicit Attitudes**, Current Directions in Psychological Science
12. **The Science and Practice of Persuasion**, Robert B. Cialdini and Noah J. Goldstein
13. **Overcoming Terror**, Philip Zimbardo and Bruce Kluger

Key Points to Consider

- What attitudes do you hold? Do you think you are unaware of certain attitudes and beliefs that influence you anyway? How did you develop your attitudes? What makes you think your attitudes are "correct"? How do your attitudes differ from those of other people, e.g. are you in the majority or the minority on some issues?

- What are implicit attitudes? What are explicit attitudes? How do they differ? Which type of attitudes do you think are more important and why? Which type of attitude influences you the most? How can researchers investigate implicit attitudes if the holder is unaware of them?

- Why is attitude change so formidable? How do psychologists study attitude change? Why is knowledge of persuasion so important? What applications does this subfield of social psychology have for daily life?

- What are some tried and true persuasion techniques? Can you provide an example of each, perhaps from advertising you have recently viewed? What other persuasion methods can you think of? Would any of these techniques have an effect on you? To which would you be most resistant? How do you feel when you know your attitude is being manipulated?

- What are the main components of any attitude change message? Can you provide a sample message (e.g. a newspaper editorial or a media advertisement) and detail its various parts?

- How is threat best utilized in a persuasive message? Can you think of other themes attitudes messages might contain? Do these strategies work or not? Why are terrorist alerts ineffective, according to social psychologists? How can terror alert messages be improved?

- Can you piece together an actual attitude change message that demonstrates your understanding of persuasion? Have you ever thought about a career in marketing or politics? In what other occupations would knowledge about attitudes and persuasion be useful?

 **Links: www.dushkin.com/online/**
These sites are annotated in the World Wide Web pages.

Propaganda and Psychological Warfare Research Resource
http://ww2.lafayette.edu/~mcglonem/prop.html

The Psychology of Cyberspace
http://www.rider.edu/users/suler/psycyber/psycyber.html

Several new college graduates formed a company on the basis of a single idea. What was the idea? The idea was a small circular refrigerator that could be used as an end table. The shelves inside rotated so that the consumer wouldn't have to arise to reach refreshments in the back. The refrigerator would make cold refreshments available in offices, for television viewers, and in employee break rooms. The young women and men who established the company believed their idea was "a quick sell," "a sure thing," something that would make them millionaires. After considerable marketing research, the company began making and selling the small refrigerators disguised as furniture. Appliance and furniture stores were the company's main targets, but sales in college bookstores were also pursued. In no time, the meager savings of the graduates were exhausted; large loans were called in by banks, and bankruptcy was filed. What went wrong?

Despite the best-laid plans and hard work of most manufactures, most new products fail. Why? In the case of the circular refrigerator-end table, the young entrepreneurs forgot that most homes already contain a refrigerator not too far from the television, and many businesses already offer some form of refrigeration in employee break rooms. Frankly, there was little need for this stubby, superfluous appliance. Consumers had never developed a need for the refrigerator, so they held the opinion that it was an unnecessary expense.

This case is fictional but helps to highlight the importance of attitudes. *Attitudes* are learned tendencies to evaluate something as positive or negative. Apparently, consumers held negative attitudes (e.g. it just isn't necessary) toward the little refrigerator.

Social psychologists are extremely interested in how attitudes are formed, why they are so staunchly maintained, and how to persuade individuals to change attitudes. Attitudes appear to be formed by interaction with others. Generally speaking, many attitudes are learned from significant others, such as our parents. Other attitudes are acquired as a result of being exposed to certain environments, such as educational institutions.

Research in social psychology indicates that a specific attitude is not held by an individual in a vacuum. That is, one attitude is typically connected to another which is connected to still another. Thus, an attitudinal network is formed. For example, suppose you assume that the moon is made of bleu cheese, you hate bleu cheese and therefore would never, ever want to go to the moon. Moreover, you might also maintain that the moon is too close to the sun, the sun causes skin cancer, your family is prone to skin cancer, and, again, there is little reason for you to go to the moon.

This tongue-in-cheek example of an attitudinal network also demonstrates how attitudes and behaviors usually are connected. Many people act on their attitudes. And some social psychologists suggest that our behaviors help in turn to establish our attitudes.

Once attitudes become intertwined, they are hard to change. Most theoreticians assume that people prefer consistency among their various attitudes. People feel uncomfortable or experience dissonance when attitudes are inconsistent or when attitudes and behaviors are disparate.

Some attitudes, however, are not always expressed—either verbally or behaviorally. A few business owners, for instance, harbor strong negative prejudices (a type of attitude) against certain groups. They know that by law they cannot act on their prejudices; they cannot keep the groups out of their place of business.

Research on the attitudinal network also suggests that attitude change is difficult. Persuasion has long been a fertile area for social psychological research. There are many important applications of attitude change research; here are but a few: advertisements, presentations to juries, editorials in the newspaper, psychotherapy, and international diplomacy.

Social psychologists have broken attitudinal messages into three major research areas. One area involves the *content of the message,* for example the use of threat (e.g. "If you don't brush your teeth with new White-Bright, your teeth will rot"). Another heavily researched aspect is the *role of the messenger,* for instance a celebrity endorser who claims to use White-Bright. *The audience* is another vital ingredient in any attempt to change attitudes. Some audiences are initially hostile to the message (e.g. "My teeth are too sensitive for regular toothpastes"), others are open-minded (e.g. "Gee, I could try that if there were a coupon"), while yet others are neutral to the communication ("Was that a toothpaste ad?"). Finally, *the situation* surrounding the persuasive message is important. Whether the message is accompanied by music and on what medium (e.g. television, radio, or newspaper) also influence persuasive efforts.

In this unit we will explore several aspects of attitudes and attitude change. The first article, "Sources of Implicit Attitudes," reveals that some are *explicit attitudes* in that we are aware of them. Other attitudes influence us but we remain ignorant of their influence; these are *implicit attitudes.* Why these two types of attitudes exist and how each functions provide the crux of the information in this summary of the literature.

The second article is authored by Robert Cialdini, a leading social psychologist who is ready to "give psychology away" to the public. In this article, Cialdini with coauthor Noah Goldstein offer six tried and true strategies to enhance persuasiveness.

The final selection of this unit presents a timely issue—terrorism and the government's response to it, especially efforts to warn citizens. Philip Zimbardo, noted scientist and social psychologist, provides an incisive critique of what the United States government is doing wrong, especially in terms of what we know about attitude change.

Sources of Implicit Attitudes

Laurie A. Rudman

Response latency measures have yielded an explosion of interest in implicit attitudes. Less forthcoming have been theoretical explanations for why they often differ from explicit (self-reported) attitudes. Theorized differences in the sources of implicit and explicit attitudes are discussed, and evidence consistent with each theory is presented. The hypothesized causal influences on attitudes include early (even preverbal) experiences, affective experiences, cultural biases, and cognitive consistency principles. Each may influence implicit attitudes more than explicit attitudes, underscoring their conceptual distinction.

Attitude researchers have long been wary of taking people's reports of their own attitudes at face value, particularly when the topics being considered impinge on people's morality. Prejudice and attitudes toward immoral (e.g., cheating) or illegal (e.g., substance abuse) behaviors are but a few examples of such topics. Response latency measures, which yield evaluations that are unlikely to be controlled, have been heralded because they override the obvious problem of distortion. This is because they are taken from reaction time tasks that measure people's attitudes or beliefs indirectly (i.e., without asking people how they feel or think). That is, people's attention is focused not on the attitude object, but on performing an objective task, and attitudes are then inferred from systematic variations in task performance. For example, in the Implicit Association Test, automatic pro-White bias is indicated when people show faster performance categorizing pleasant words and Whites (and unpleasant words and Blacks) together, compared with categorizing unpleasant words and Whites (and pleasant words and Blacks) together. Thus, implicit attitudes can be characterized as the automatic association people have between an object and evaluation (whether it is good or bad). By contrast, explicit attitudes may reflect more thoughtful or deliberative responding.

More substantively, response latency measures have also led to increased interest in potential theoretical differences between implicit and explicit attitudes. Although there have been no formal frameworks (cf. Fazio & Olson, 2003), there have been a few attempts to conceptually distinguish what is being measured when people report their attitudes from what is measured by response latency. In this review, I discuss four factors that have been theorized to influence implicit more than explicit attitudes. Although preliminary, the evidence suggests that automatic and controlled evaluations stem from different sources and, therefore, should be conceptualized as distinct constructs.

EARLY EXPERIENCES

A prominent conception is that implicit attitudes stem from past (and largely forgotten) experiences, whereas explicit attitudes reflect more recent or accessible events (Greenwald & Banaji, 1995). In a study supporting this hypothesis (Rudman & Heppen, 2001), smokers' implicit attitudes toward their habit covaried with their earliest experiences with smoking, which were mainly unpleasant (e.g., aversion to tobacco smoke and nausea from their first cigarettes). Thus, automatic attitudes were negative if early experiences were unpleasant. By contrast, smokers' explicit attitudes covaried with their recent experiences toward smoking, which were mainly positive (e.g., drinking coffee and smoking with friends). Thus, self-reported attitudes were negative if recent experiences were unpleasant. Differences in the underlying sources of smokers' implicit and explicit attitudes helps to explain why they were only weakly related.

A logical extension of Greenwald and Banaji's (1995) argument is that developmental events may inform implicit more than explicit attitudes. Much of what is learned early in life is preverbal and taught indirectly. These lessons form the foundation on which later learning is built and may also serve as a nonconscious source for related evaluations and actions. Goodwin and I obtained results consistent with this possibility when we investigated whether early (even preverbal) attachment to maternal caregivers was associated with people's gender-related attitudes (Rudman & Goodwin, 2003). First, people raised primarily by their mothers implicitly preferred women to men.

Second, people implicitly favored women if they automatically preferred their mothers to their fathers. By contrast, explicit attitudes toward parents and gender were not related.

Finally, in three experiments (Rudman & Heppen, 2003), women who possessed an automatic association between romantic partners and chivalric roles (e.g., White Knight, Prince Charming) reported less interest in personal power, including economic and educational achievement, than woman who did not have this automatic association. By contrast, explicit romantic fantasies did not covary with explicit power-related variables. Because women are socialized early and often to view men as their heroes and rescuers (e.g., through romantic fairy tales), these findings indirectly support the hypothesis that developmental events can inform automatic mental habits.

AFFECTIVE EXPERIENCES

It is also possible that implicit attitudes are more sensitive to affective experiences than are explicit attitudes. For example, Phelps et al. (2000) found that estimates of implicit (but not explicit) prejudice positively covaried with activation in a brain structure called the amygdala in Whites exposed to photos of Blacks. Because the amygdala is implicated in the control of affective responses, these results suggest that implicit attitudes may stem from automatic emotional reactions to stimuli, whereas explicit attitudes may be "cooler" (more cognitively controlled).

In addition, my colleagues and I found that Whites who volunteered for diversity education showed reduced anti-Black attitudes, both implicit and explicit, at the end of the course. However, changes in the two kinds of attitudes were only weakly associated. Further examination revealed that reductions in implicit attitudes were linked to emotion-based predictors, including reduced fear of Blacks, increased friendships with Blacks, and liking for the African American professor who taught the course. By contrast, reductions in explicit attitudes covaried with students' increased awareness of bias and their desire to overcome their own prejudice (i.e., "trying hard" to change). These findings suggest that changes in implicit attitudes may depend on emotional reconditioning, whereas changes in explicit attitudes may depend on more cognitive and motivational factors (Rudman, Ashmore, & Gary, 2001).

Finally, the sensitivity of implicit attitudes to priming effects (i.e., to the influence of contextual factors) has now been well established (Blair, 2002). Because priming manipulation are recent events, at first blush such findings appear to conflict with the hypothesis that early experiences impact implicit more than explicit attitudes. However, the two views can be reconciled if affect comes into play during the priming manipulation. Learning about admired Blacks and criminal Whites, mentally imagining heroic women, and listening to rap music have all been shown to modify implicit associations. It is possible that these effects were due, at least in part, to the feelings aroused by the stimuli. Likewise, it is conceivable that the studies that found past events influenced implicit attitudes more than explicit attitudes obtained these results precisely because the events were emotional (e.g., aversive experiences with smoking, maternal bonding, and romantic fantasies). Although speculative, the possibility that affect accounts for the influence of both recent and past experiences on implicit attitudes seems worthy of pursuit.

CULTURAL BIASES

The third possibility is that implicit attitudes are more influenced by one's cultural milieu than explicit attitudes are (Devine, 1989). For example, Greenwald, McGhee, and Schwartz (1998, Experiment 2) found that Korean and Japanese American students showed greater automatic in-group bias to the extent they were immersed in their ancestors' culture (e.g., spoke the language). The linkage between attitudes and culture was less evident using a self-report measure of attitudes.

Further, it has been shown repeatedly that Blacks and Whites alike possess more anti-Black bias on implicit measures, compared with self-reports (e.g., Nosek, Banaji, & Greenwald, 2002). Although the pattern for Blacks is provocative, it is consistent with system justification theory's argument that minorities nonconsciously rationalize their lower status by internalizing society's negative view of their group (Jost & Banaji, 1994). My colleagues and I (Rudman, Feinberg, & Fairchild, 2002) tested this hypothesis using minority groups whose relative status (based on explicit ratings from an independent sample) ranged from low (poor, overweight) to high (Asians, Jews). The results supported system-justification theory. First, the lower their cultural status, the more minorities implicitly favored the dominant out-group. In fact, poor and overweight participants showed significant preference for rich and slim out-group members, respectively. Second, participants were asked to report their group's relative status, and these ratings also covaried with their implicit attitudes. For example, Jews who ranked Christians as higher in status than Jews tended to automatically associate Christians with positive attributes and Jews with negative attributes. In contrast to these results, minorities showed robust explicit in-group bias, which was unrelated to their status.

More dramatically, Livingston (2002) found that social standing had opposite influences on Blacks' automatic and self-reported in-group bias. Specifically, Blacks who perceived that Whites disliked their group showed stronger automatic pro-White bias, but at the same time, stronger pro-Black bias in their self-reports, compared with Blacks who perceived that Whites liked their group. When the same variable pulls implicit attitudes in one direction and explicit attitudes in another, their conceptual distinction is strongly supported.

Finally, high-status groups (e.g., Whites, Christians, slim people, rich people) routinely show stronger implicit in-group bias than do low-status groups, but again, this is a function of their relative status (whereas explicit in-group bias is not; Rudman et al., 2002). Thus, for members of dominant and minority groups alike, societal evaluations appear to have an assimilative effect on automatic (but not controlled) attitudes, suggesting that cultural biases inform implicit attitudes more than explicit attitudes. Because learning about one's place in the world is likely to occur early (and often) in life, and is likely to be emotionally charged, the influence of cultural biases on implicit attitudes may be reconcilable with the influence of early and affective experiences.

COGNITIVE CONSISTENCY PRINCIPLES

A venerable principle in social psychology is that people prefer consonant (as opposed to dissonant) evaluations of related attitude objects. For example, according to this principle, if I like myself and I am female, then I should also like women. This prediction means that cognitive consistency should be observed among the variables of self-esteem, gender identity, and gender attitude. In a compelling demonstration suggesting that automatic and controlled evaluations stem from different causes, implicit attitudes, identity, self-esteem, stereotypes, and self-concept conformed to cognitive consistency principles, whereas self-reports of these same constructs did not (an observation that led the development of the unified theory of implicit social cognition; Greenwald et al., 2002). The general pattern of results the unified theory predicts for implicit measures can be characterized as "If I am Y and I am X, then X is also Y," where Y represents evaluation and X represents group membership. In five experiments, this pattern of results was obtained using the Implicit Association Test. For example, Whites who showed high self-esteem and who identified with their ethnicity also preferred Whites to Blacks. Thus, the logic underlying implicit attitudes was "If I am good and I am X, then X is also good." A similar pattern emerged when implicit stereotypes and self-concept were measured, rather than attitudes and self-esteem. For example, men and women who associated themselves with warmth (or power) also associated warmth (or power) with their own gender, provided they identified with their gender; self-report measures did not conform to this pattern. Identical findings were found using an academic (math-arts) gender stereotype, but again, only with implicit estimates of self-concept, stereotypes, and gender identity. By uncovering cognitive balance at the automatic level, research that supports the unified theory underscores important differences in the sources of implicit and explicit constructs.

The unified theory may be reconciled with other theories that distinguish sources of implicit and explicit attitudes. First, the theory converges with the hypothesis that cultural milieu biases implicit attitudes. Societal evaluations clearly influence implicit in-group appraisal, which contributes to self-appraisal when in-group identification is strong. Second, affect may inform the unified model by means of evaluative links that involve the self. Given that people likely do not view themselves impartially, emotional self-appraisals may spill over into automatic (more than self-reported) evaluations. For example, early and affective lessons learned about the self may shape one's implicit appraisals of other objects that are (or are not) connected to the self. Interestingly, the resulting implicit structure can be counterstereotypical (e.g., "If I am warm and I am male, then men are warmer than women"). In this way, automatic self-appraisals may counter the influence of culture on implicit associations.

FUTURE DIRECTIONS

In sum, the preliminary evidence indicates that early and affective experiences may influence automatic evaluations more than explicit attitudes. In addition, there is growing evidence that systemic, culturally held appraisals can bias people's automatic evaluations irrespective of their personal opinion. Finally, only implicit (not explicit) evaluations appear to be sensitive to cognitive consistency principles. By better understanding disparities in the underlying causes of implicit and explicit attitudes, psychologists can begin to formulate more sophisticated frameworks for conceptualizing them. At the very least, the observation that they stem from different sources suggests they should be viewed as theoretically distinct.

The argument that implicit and explicit attitudes are conceptually distinct can help to explain why the two types of attitudes are often dissociated, and why response latency measures (sometimes) predict behaviors better than self-reports. Although the untrustworthiness of self-reports is often blamed for these findings, the picture is more complex than that. For one thing, implicit and explicit attitudes sometimes correlate well. This is particularly true when attitude objects are controversial (e.g., politicians, academic subjects, and vegetarianism), but even measures of implicit and explicit prejudice sometimes converge. Moreover, implicit and explicit attitudes can be dissociated even for noncontroversial objects (e.g., flowers, insects, apples, candy bars). Thus, a challenge for future research is to uncover the variables that determine when implicit and explicit attitude converge. To meet this challenge, researchers should go beyond the controllability of self-reports as an explanation for the weak convergence between implicit and explicit attitudes because this explanation assumes that the underlying evaluation is the same for both types of attitudes (and people are either unable or unwilling to report their "true" attitude). If automatic and controlled evaluations stem from different sources, their underlying valence may dramatically differ. That is, implicit attitudes may be unfavorable despite favorable explicit attitudes, and vice versa. Attending to source differences provides a rationale for deeming both kinds of evaluations as genuine, albeit limited in their ability to encompass the range of human responses to attitude objects.

Future work should also focus on the conditions under which implicit attitudes predict behavior better than explicit attitudes. It has been proposed that automatic and controlled evaluations best predict spontaneous and deliberative actions, respectively. Although there is some evidence that implicit attitudes are linked to involuntary behaviors (e.g., eye blinking), the larger picture is more complicated. First, implicit attitudes often influence deliberative actions, including choosing which consumer products to purchase, volunteering for leadership roles, using condoms, and discriminating against job applicants who are minority-group members. Second, there is substantial evidence, some of it presented here, that controlled responses covary with implicit attitudes (e.g., reports of early experiences covaried with implicit attitudes toward smoking, explicit predictions of status predicted implicit in-group bias, and self-reported interest in power correlated with implicit romantic fantasies). And finally, as already noted, implicit and explicit attitudes sometimes converge. Thus, although implicit attitudes might be the best predictor of spontaneous actions, they are also capable of predicting a large array of controlled behaviors. As opposed to taking a purely "process-matching" approach to predicting behavior, researchers should consider additional factors, including the extent to which the situation increases the salience of implicit attitudes and their relevance to the behavior or judgment at hand (see also Fazio & Olson, 2003).

Focusing on the automatic versus controlled nature of implicit and explicit attitudes has been fruitful, but may mask other ways in which they differ, including their underlying causes. I have presented four factors known to influence implicit attitudes more than explicit attitudes, and suggested how they might overlap. Attending to differences in sources should promote integrative theoretical frameworks that differentiate the two kinds of attitudes. It should also aid in identifying factors that modify each, variables that determine when implicit and explicit attitudes converge, and conditions that promote their utility in predicting behavior.

The Science and Practice of Persuasion

From business owners to busboys, the ability to harness
the power of persuasion is often an essential component of success
in the hospitality industry.

Robert B. Cialdini; Noah J. Goldstein

Research reveals that there are six basic principles that govern how one person might influence another. Those principles can be labeled as: liking, reciprocation, consistency, scarcity, social validation, and authority.[1] In the pages that follow we elaborate on each of those six principles and highlight some of their applications in the hospitality industry—for instance, how a restaurant manager might reduce the reservation no-show rate by two-thirds; how to influence the size of the gratuity patrons leave for their servers; how to encourage customers to order additional food when they do not really want it; and how to get customers to comply with employees' reasonable requests.

Simply put, in general people are inclined to favor and to comply with those whom they like. A good illustration of this fundamental principle of influence in action is the Tupperware party, in which salespeople invite their friends and neighbors to their homes to pitch useful household plastic products. A study done by Frenzen and Davis confirmed what the Tupperware Corporation knew all along: guests' liking for their hostess was twice as important as was their opinion of the products in influencing their purchase decisions.[2]

In the case of the Tupperware party, the seller is not just a likeable person, but is probably a friend and respected community member as well. The power of the "liking" principle is so pervasive, however, that even perfect strangers can recognize whether there is any affinity between them within a relatively short time. Researchers have identified four primary determinants of our fondness for another person: physical attractiveness, similarity, cooperation, and the extent to which we feel the person likes us.

Looking good. Most of us acknowledge that those who are physically attractive have a social advantage held by few others, but evidence suggests that we have grossly underestimated the degree to which that is true. For example, good-looking candidates received more than two-and-a-halftimes as many votes as did unattractive candidates in the 1974 Canadian federal elections,

despite the fact that most voters adamantly denied that attractiveness had any influence on their decisions.[3]

One possible explanation for such findings is that we tend to view attractive individuals as possessing numerous other positive qualities that would be considered relevant to our liking them—such as talent, kindness, honesty, and intelligence.[4] One practical (and unfortunate) result of the "attractiveness" principle is that less-attractive individuals who rely heavily on tips for income may have to work especially hard to gain customers' affection, approval, and cash.[5]

The social and monetary rewards that beautiful people garner extend far beyond those benefits; they are also more successful at eliciting compliance with their requests. Reingen and Kernen found that an attractive fundraiser for the American Heart Association collected almost twice as many donations as did less-attractive individuals.[6] That finding suggests that training programs in the hospitality industry could increase the effectiveness of trainees by including, for instance, grooming tips.

Simpatico. Similarity is another important factor that affects our liking for others. The effects of similarity—however superficial—can be quite astounding because of the instant bond that similarity can create between two people. Consider that in one study a fundraiser on a college campus more than doubled the contributions received by simply adding the phrase "I'm a student, too" to the request.[7] Just as salespeople are trained to find or even manufacture links between themselves and their prospective clients, individuals whose livelihoods depend on quick-forming rapport with their customers—such as food servers or valets—may enhance their earnings simply by pointing out a connection between themselves and their guests. "Hold the mayonnaise? Yeah, I don't eat it very often myself," and "Wow, you're from Chicago? My wife is from just south of there. She sure doesn't miss the winters" are examples of commonplace attempts to create such a bond.

Similarities need not be overtly called to the other individual's attention to obtain the desired compliance. Researchers found that a person was significantly more likely to receive a requested dime from a stranger when the two were dressed similarly than when they were not.[8] Since the majority of workers in the restaurant and hospitality industry wear uniforms, this subtle form of persuasion may be rare. As a notable exception, however, many waiters and waitresses at one popular restaurant chain wear a myriad of buttons pertaining to their interests on their uniforms, at least some of which are likely to match the backgrounds and interests of their guests.

Allies. Cooperation has also been shown to engender feelings of liking, even between parties that previously exhibited mutual animosity. Muzafer Sherif and his colleagues found that preexisting disdain between two groups of children at a camp was transformed into affection after they worked together to accomplish a necessary, mutual goal.[9] Wane would hope that food servers would start off on a better footing with their guests than the children in Sherifs study had with one another, so an air of cooperation should already exist. However, just as car salespeople "go to war" with their managers on behalf of their clients, some food servers benefit by making themselves seem particularly cooperative with their guests: "You want more chips and salsa, sir? Well, the manager normally asks us to charge extra for that, but I'll see whether I can get you some at no charge."

Our fondness for another person also depends on the extent to which we believe the other person likes us. Just ask Joe Girard, the world's greatest car salesman for 12 years in a row (according to the Guinness Book of World Records). One secret to his success may lie in a simple greeting card that he sent to all 13,000 of his former customers every single month. Although the holiday theme of each month's card differed, the text never varied. Other than his name, the only words written on the card were, "I like you."[10]

As a general rule we tend to like and to be more willing to comply with the requests of those who show they are partial to us.[11] Interestingly, one study revealed that a flatterer's laudatory comments engendered just as much liking for the sweet-talker when the remarks were false as when they were correct.[12] Thus, praise is one way for food servers to show their fondness for their clientele— and thereby to increase their tips. Having pointed that out, however, servers would be wise to proceed with caution—or better yet, with honesty—because the "praise" tactic runs the risk of backfiring if guests perceive servers' comments to be a duplicitous attempt to manipulate them.

Researchers have established that there are a number of fairly basic strategies servers can use to increase the average gratuity they receive by at least 20 percent. Many of those strategies use the simplicity of the liking principle. Squatting, smiling, and occasional touching, for example, help to build a friendly rapport, while writing "thank you" and drawing a happy face on the bill are presumably signals to patrons that they are liked and that their waiter or waitress was especially happy to serve them.[13]

It is important to note that these techniques are not necessarily additive and that the appropriateness of each strategy varies depending on a number of factors, including the type of eating establishment, the disposition of each guest, and even the gender of the food server.[14] For example, waitresses who drew smiling faces on their customers' checks significantly increased average tip size by 18 percent.[15] No significant difference was found for their male counterparts, however. If anything, the smiley-face strategy actually backfired when used by waiters. Due to perceived violations of gender-based expectations, it appears that for males, drawing a smiling face on the check may very well draw out a frowning face from the guests.

Reciprocation

A Chinese proverb states, "Favors from others should be remembered for a thousand years." The maxim succinctly emphasizes the importance of the norm of reciprocity— that we are obligated to repay others for what we have received from them—in all human societies. The norm pushes us toward fairness and equity in our everyday social interactions, our business dealings, and our close relationships, while it helps us build trust with others. At the same time, however, it also leaves us susceptible to the manipulations of those who wish to exploit our tendencies to achieve inequitable personal gains.

An informative study of the reciprocity principle and its potential to be exploited was conducted by Dennis Regan in 1971.[16] In the experiment, individuals who received a small, unsolicited favor from a stranger ("Joe") in the form of a can of Coca-Cola purchased twice as many raffle tickets from Joe as those who received no favor at all. This occurred even though the favor and the request took place one-half hour apart, and that Joe made neither implicit nor explicit reference to the original favor when he made his pitch about the raffle tickets. Interestingly, despite all that we have stated about the strong association between liking and compliance, Regan found that individuals who received a Coke from Joe made their purchase decisions completely irrespective of the extent to which they liked him. That is, those who didn't like Joe purchased just as many raffle tickets as those who did like him if they were the recipients of the gift earlier on. Thus, we see that the feelings of indebtedness caused by the power of the reciprocity manipulation are capable of trumping the effects of the liking principle.

While we have so far established that the norm of reciprocity is powerful, the principle's true power comes from its ability to create situations in which unequal exchanges rake place. Regan found that on average, the Coke-bearing stranger had a 500-percent return on his investment, hardly an equal exchange at all!

Corporations and fundraisers alike have been aware of the power of reciprocity for many years, and have attempted to use those principles with the public. The Disabled American Veterans organization, a charitable group that seeks donations via fundraising letters, for example, increased its average response rate from 18 percent to 35 percent simply by enclosing a small gift in the envelope.[17] The new addition—a set of personalized address labels—caused the recipients to feel an immediate sense of obligation to repay the organization, despite the fact that the gift was inexpensive to produce and the recipients never asked for it in the first place.

Individuals in the hospitality, travel, and tourism industries are also in an appropriate position to harness the power of the reciprocity principle. After all, tipping in the U.S. service industry is supposed to be based on a reciprocity-related quid pro quo system, in which it is tacitly acknowledged that the consumer will make a more generous payment in exchange for better-than-average service. Although the strength of the actual relationship between service and tipping has been challenged,[18] it is clear that food-service workers and others who rely heavily on tips stand to benefit substantially by providing better overall service; specifically, the server should make "additional" efforts that at least slightly exceed customer expectations. For example, Lynn and Gregor showed that a bellman nearly doubled his tip earnings by adding three simple and seemingly inconsequential steps to his standard duties: He showed the guests how to operate the television and thermostat, opened the drapes to expose the room's view, and offered to bring the guests ice from the machine down the hall.[19]

Tip Tips.

The above example illustrates the success of an individual who essentially made a low-risk investment that often paid big dividends. Food servers can take advantage of the reciprocity principle, too.[20] In one study it was shown that tips were higher when the servers allowed each guest to select a fancy piece of chocolate at the end of the meal than when no offer was made. Given that finding, we can see that the proprietor of the first dine-in Chinese restaurant to serve fortune cookies at the end of the meal made a clever and profitable decision. Unfortunately for the wait staff in Chinese restaurants today, patrons have come to see a fortune cookie at the end of a meal as part of the experience—that is, as more of a right than a privilege or extra treat.

A second study by the same researchers showed that allowing the guests to select two relatively inexpensive pieces of chocolate proved even more fruitful than when the server offered just one.[21] More revealing, the server who offered two pieces was most successful when she first offered each guest one piece of candy, gestured as if she was about to leave the table, and then let each guest choose one more piece of chocolate, as opposed to when she simply allowed the guests to choose both pieces at once. It seems likely that the guests in the "1 + 1" condi-

tion assumed that the waitress was making an extra effort beyond what was normally required of her by the managers, possibly because she liked these diners more than she did most of her guests. These findings suggest that hotel housekeepers who leave mints on pillows may be the recipients of larger tips than those who do not, but that they may be even more successful by placing several extra mints on top of a personal thank you note the day before their guests check out.

Hotel managers might find the use of the reciprocity norm especially helpful when appealing to guests to reuse towels and linens in an effort to conserve energy and resources. Currently, most pleas rake approaches that either educate the guests regarding the total amount of energy necessary to clean those items daily for a year, or invoke the guests' sense of social responsibility. Some hotels emphasize the benefit to themselves in their appeals; few guests, however, will be motivated to give up their clean sheets in exchange for a clean getaway by the hotel owner with the profits gained from such compliance. Perhaps in addition to one of the other two appeals mentioned, hotel managers may achieve a higher rate of participation by extending a reciprocation-based approach in the form of a promise to donate a portion of the money saved to an environmental-conservation organization or any other cause deemed worthy. For example, the Windows of Hope Family Relief Fund, an organization that provides aid to the families of those in the food-service profession who were victims of the World Trade Center tragedy, successfully used this principle in an event dubbed DineOut, which took place on the day exactly one month after the attack. More than 4,000 restaurants throughout the world participated and agreed to donate at least 10 percent of that evening's sales to the fund, which both raised millions of dollars for the charity and dramatically increased many of the participating restaurants' business for that night and potential beyond.

Bargaining.

While the rule of reciprocity most often takes the form of gifts or favors, a specific application of the principle is frequently used in the negotiation process, which involves reciprocal concessions. That is, if Person A rebuffs a large request from Person B, and Person B then concedes by making a smaller request, Person A will feel obligated to reciprocate this concession with a concession of his or her own by agreeing to this lesser plea.

The first author and his colleagues conducted a study to examine this phenomenon in the mid-1970s.[22] Half of the students in the experiment were approached on a college campus walkway and asked if they would agree to chaperone juvenile-detention-center inmates on a day trip to the local zoo; relatively few (17 percent) responded in the affirmative. The other half of the students were asked a different question first; a plea was made for them to volunteer as a counselor for these inmates for two hours per week for the next two years. Not surprisingly, everyone who heard this appeal refused to participate. But when this same group was then asked if they would agree to chaperone the inmates at the onetime-only day trip to the zoo, the compliance rate for this smaller request was nearly triple that of the half who were never approached with the larger plea.

Some hotel managers make use of this approach when negotiating deals for conventions and banquets by holding back in their initial offer so that they can later appear to concede to the client a number of amenities nor present in the original proposal. The assumption in this case is that the client will feel the need to reciprocate this concession by accepting the deal without making any more demands. Similarly, many managers start off the bargaining process with higher-than-desired price quotes in anticipation of having to shave off from the total charge during negotiations.

Consistency

Prior to 1998, Gordon Sinclair, the owner of a prominent Chicago eatery; was too often the victim of a common occurrence in the restaurant business: the dreaded reservation no-show. On average, approximately 30 percent of all would-be patrons who called for reservations failed to appear and never bothered to notify the restaurant with a statement of cancellation. One day, Sinclair thought of a way that might minimize the problem, so he asked his receptionists to make a few slight modifications in the reservation-taking procedure. Instead of ending their phone calls with "Please call if you have to change your plans," Sinclair instructed the receptionists to ask, "Will you please call if you have a change to your plans?" and then to pause for a moment to allow the caller to respond. Once the new strategy was implemented, the no-show-no-call rate dropped from 30 to 10 percent.

Sinclair's technique was successful because it took advantage of a fundamental human tendency to be and to appear consistent with ones actions, statements, and beliefs. This principle was illustrated in a study that found that residents who accepted and agreed to wear a small lapel pin supporting a local charity were significantly more likely to make donations to that charity during a fundraiser at a later date than those who had not been approached before the donation drive took place.[23] Those who had previously been induced to make public commitments to that charity felt compelled to act consistently with these commitments and to support it later on. Similarly, those who called for reservations and made a public commitment regarding their future actions felt obligated to be consistent with their statements and to live up to their pledges.

Dessert first.

Some shrewd servers benefit from their keen understanding of this principle by drawing out commitments from their guests regarding potential dessert purchases when the patrons (and their stomachs) are at their most vulnerable. At one restaurant in particular, immediately following the introduction, some food servers enthusiastically ask, "Who here is getting cheesecake tonight?" After each person gives an affirmative response—an action that originates not from the brain, but the belly—the server then goes through the standard procedures. Once everyone at the table is feeling full and bloated after completing the main course, their server comes back, reminds the guests of their earlier commitments in a non-threatening, jovial manner, and begins to make dessert suggestions. In the end, despite initial urges to decline—tendencies that now originate from a full belly, the brain, and the wallet—many patrons still feel obligated to say yes.

Scarcity

In the early 1970s Stephen West discovered that undergraduates' ratings of a University of Wisconsin campus cafeteria rose significantly within a nine-day span of time.[24] Surprisingly, the difference in opinion had nothing to do with a change in the quality of the eatery's food or service, but rather with its availability. Before the second set of ratings were assessed, students learned that due to a fire they would not be able to eat there for the next two weeks.

Whether it's an unavailable eating establishment, the last piece of apple pie, the only remaining convertible in a rental company's lot, the last lobster in the tank, the only hotel room with a balcony that's still vacant, or the final unclaimed blanket on an airplane, items and opportunities that are in short supply or unavailable tend to be more desirable to us than those that are plentiful and more accessible.[25] This often adaptive mental shortcut is one that naturally develops, since we learn early on in our lives that things existing in limited quantities are hard to get, and that things that are hard to get are typically better than those that are easy to get.[26]

Act now! Marketing strategists and compliance practitioners take advantage of the scarcity principle by emphasizing that their products are in limited supply, available for a limited time only, or are one-of-a-kind—often without regard to the veracity of those claims. Although assertions regarding availability status are in many cases spurious, businesses frequently employ scarcity-based marketing strategies legitimately in a genuine effort to make their offers more attractive. Lower rates for plane flights, hotel rooms, cruises, tours, and vacation packages are especially likely to be justifiably advertised as "limited time only" and "in limited supply" because such offers tend to be made for the small pockets of time when business would otherwise be slower.

Proprietors of nightclubs and restaurants can also make use of those principles by artificially limiting the availability of space. Nightclub owners, for example, commonly restrict the number of people allowed inside even though there is plenty of space for more, not due to concerns regarding maximum occupancy laws, but because the apparent inaccessibility of the clubs makes these establishments seem more desirable. Similarly, some restaurant managers limit the actual number of seats available to use the power of scarcity.

The domains in which the scarcity principle operates are not just limited to products and opportunities, but to information, as well. Research has shown that information that is exclusive is seen as more valuable and more persuasive. For instance, a former doctoral student of the first author showed that wholesale beef buyers more than doubled their orders when they were informed that a shortage of Australian beef was likely due to weather conditions overseas.[27] When those purchasers were told that the information came from an exclusive source at the Australian National Weather Service, however, they increased their orders by an astounding 600 percent. In this case the information regarding the upcoming shortages was true, but one can imagine the potential for abuse of this principle, given its dramatic effectiveness. Thus, we should question any situation in which an individual claims that he or she is supplying us—and only us—with a certain piece of information.

Up to this point we have explained the scarcity principle in terms of the mental shortcut it provides between something's availability and its quality. There is another factor at work here as well, and it is related to the idea that as opportunities become less available, we lose freedoms. According to Jack Brehm's well-supported theory of psychological reactance, whenever our freedoms are threatened or restricted, we vigorously attempt to reassert our free choice, with a specific focus on retaining or regaining exactly what was being limited in the first place.[28]

A study conducted by Reich and Robertson suggests that a sign posted next to the hotel pool that reads, "Don't You Dare Litter" or even just "Don't Litter" is likely to backfire, especially with regard to young, unsupervised children. Instead, a less-strongly phrased message that emphasizes the social norm, such as "Keeping the Pool Clean Depends on You," stands the greatest chance of success.[29] Similar results were found in another study that showed that high-threat anti-graffiti placards placed in restroom stalls were defaced to a greater extent than were the low-threat placards,[30] Thus, some proprietors of bars—whose restrooms are particularly susceptible to such vandalism—stand to benefit by replacing messages that may be perceived as hostile or threatening with more moderate pleas.

Social Validation

Earlier we described how some nightclub owners make their businesses appear more desirable by restricting the number of individuals allowed in at anyone time. The secret of the success of this policy lies not only in its manip-

ulation of scarcity, but also in its use of the principle of social validation, which asserts that we frequently look to others for cues on how to think, feel, and behave, particularly when we are in a state of uncertainty.

Before returning to the example of a nightclub, an examination of a study done by Peter Reingen should prove informative.[31] In the experiment, a group of researchers posing as fundraisers went door-to-door to solicit donations for a local charity. As part of their request, the purported fundraisers showed homeowners a list of neighbors who had already agreed to donate to that particular cause. The experiment revealed that the likelihood of donation was positively correlated with the length of the list of names.

Just as many of those in the Reingen study decided how they would act based on the number of people they thought were engaging in the same behavior, individuals selecting where they would like to spend their time and money for an evening often use the number of others participating in a particular activity to gauge the popularity—and thus, the worthiness of that activity. Since club operators limit the rate at which the inbound traffic moves, a figurative gridlock occurs, producing long lines of people waiting for their turn to move forward and into the club. As a result, passersby view the large crowd of individuals waiting to get in as evidence of the club's value. In this case, quantity is believed to be a true indicator of quality: If that many people are willing to endure the wait to get in, it must really be worth it.

In like manner, bartenders and live entertainers sometimes seed their tip jars with a number of bills in an attempt to manipulate patrons' perceptions of the ripping norm. Consider the difference in the messages conveyed by a jar filled three-fourths of the way to the top with one- and five-dollar bills, versus a jar completely devoid of anything, except a nickel and seven pennies, a ticket stub from the movie Ishtar, and an East German Deutschmark. The former indicates that tipping—specifically, with bills—is the norm and creates a pressure for others to be consistent with this rule, while the latter suggests that tipping hasn't been the norm since the fall of the Berlin Wall.

Most companies have long understood the ability of social validation to sway our opinions and our wallets in their direction, which is why marketers spend much of their time thinking of ways to spin their products as the leading, the largest-selling, or the most popular ones out there. A common strategy is to make nebulous, lawsuit-proof claims to convey the product's popularity among the public such as, "We're the number-one cruise line in North America," even if not true by any reasonable statistical standard. Still others attempt to quantify their success, such as the McDonald's Corporation, which claims "Billions and Billions Served."

The outcomes of social validation at work are often the result of deliberate planning by businesses to harness this principle's power, but sometimes the effects of the principle fortuitously appear in unplanned and unintended domains. For example, some restaurants that are located inside malls (and airports) give pagers to their patrons and encourage them to walk around while they wait for a table to become available. Since the pagers are in most cases too large to place in one's pocket, the guests usually hold them in their hands as they stroll around the complex. Although clearly not intended to work in such a fashion, the beepers—which are being carried around by a multitude of individuals—act as a signal to others that the restaurant is a popular and worthwhile place to eat a meal. This suggests that if a mall contains more than one eating establishment with this policy, then each restaurant would make the greatest use of the principle of social validation if its pagers were both large and distinctive enough in colors, patterns, or design so that a potential customer could easily identify the restaurant to which it belonged.

Supplying individuals with specific descriptive norms—essentially, information about what other people are doing[32]—to elicit comparable behavior has proven to be successful in a number of different domains, including neighborhood household recycling.[33] Similarly, another way that hotel managers may attain greater results with their pleas for resource conservation is to inform their guests that a large number of people have already participated in the program since its inception.

Authority

On the bitterly cold afternoon of January 13, 1982, Air Florida Flight 90 sat on the tarmac of National Airport in Washington, D.C. Following a series of delays, the plane was finally cleared to take off. As the captain and the first officer were completing their last round of pre-flight checks, the following exchange took place regarding one of the systems:

First officer: God, look at that thing. That don't seem right, does it? Uh, that's not right.
Captain: Yes it is, there's eighty
First officer: Naw, I don't think that's right. Ah, maybe it is.[34]

Shortly after this conversation transpired, the plane took off. Less than one minute later. Flight 90 crashed into the icy waters of the Potomac River.

This tragedy is an example of a troubling and all-too-pervasive problem in aviation that officials in the airline industry have referred to as "Captainitis."[35] This occurs when crew members fail to correct an obvious error made by the plane's captain, resulting in a crash. In this case—and many others like it—the copilot made the calamitous decision to defer to the captain's authority. This is a clear example of the power of the principle of authority; that is, we tend to defer to the counsel of authority figures and experts to help us decide how to behave, especially when we are feeling ambivalent about a decision or when we are in an ambiguous situation. Experts also have a hand in helping us decide what we should think. For example, one study found that when an acknowledged expert's opinion on an issue was aired just once on national television, public opinion shifted in the direction of the expert's view by as much as 4 percent.[36]

Although we have seen how the principle of authority has the potential to steer us wrong, more often than not experts provide reliable information that we use as shortcuts to make good decisions. In an increasingly complex world, deferring to individuals with highly specialized knowledge in their fields is often an essential part of smart decision making.

Some research shows that we are more swayed by experts who seem impartial than those who have something to gain by convincing us.[37] For instance, we tend to believe a laminated copy of a restaurant review from a local newspaper posted in that particular restaurant's front window or entryway because we have reason to believe that food critics have no vested interest in the outcome. Our confidence in a particular expert wanes, however, when we believe that he or she is biased in some way. Although many people see a "Chefs Choice" label next to an entree listed on the menu as more appetizing because it is coming from a credible authority on the restaurant's food—the one who cooks it—a number of others would be less convinced. After all, a label like this might be subject to the biases and motivations of the restaurant managers, who could be trying to boost the sales of a less-popular choice or increase net earnings by choosing dishes with high profit margins.

Food Experts.

Some crafty servers are careful to keep these principles in mind when taking their guests orders. Their general approach is as follows: A guest asks about or orders a particular dish from the menu, to which the food server replies, as if it were a secret, "I'm afraid that is not as good [or fresh] tonight as it normally is. May I recommend instead [the names of two slightly less-expensive dishes]?" Notice that the food server accomplishes two important objectives. First, the server establishes him- or herself as an authority regarding the quality of the restaurant's food. Second, by suggesting two less-expensive entrees, the server seems to be making recommendations against the restaurant's and his or her own interests, since it could theoretically lead to a smaller bill and, subsequently, to a smaller tip. The server knows that, in actuality, the tip will probably be larger because the guests will like the server more and want to reciprocate the favor by leaving a generous gratuity. In addition, because the server now appears to be a trustworthy authority on the restaurant's food, the guests are more likely to take any other advice offered throughout the course of the meal, such as suggestions to order expensive desserts and wine that they would not have ordered otherwise.

Car-rental agencies may use a derivative of this approach, even inadvertently, when their employees offer customers extra insurance options. In many cases a customer won't be completely aware of his or her own insurance policy's car-rental coverage, so the rental agent makes some recommendations. The staff member, who is seen as the authority on car-rental insurance, says something like, "Well, you are going to have the car for only two days, so you'd probably be wasting your money with personal-accident insurance, the personal-effects coverage, or the supplemental liability insurance. However, I would recommend that you get the partial damage waiver, which is what most people go for." (Notice the additional use of social validation.)

Knowledge of the power of the tactic used in the above two examples goes back many centuries. Francois Duc de La Rochefoucauld, a seventeenth-century French writer and moralist, wrote, "We only confess our little faults to persuade people that we have no big ones." Many companies today have implemented such a strategy in marketing. By mentioning a shortcoming of their product, they hope to appear more honest and trustworthy to their potential customers, meaning that prospective consumers will assume that the product is likely to be of high quality in all other respects. For instance, one well-known company slogan is "Avis: We're number two, but we try harder."

We have thus far examined the role of impartiality and trust in how we perceive experts and the advice they dispense. In all of the examples above, those serving their customers could be considered—at least to some degree—legitimate authorities. To what extent can people be led astray by someone who is no more an authority than they are? A study sought to answer this question by examining the connection between perceived authority and the way an individual is dressed. [38] The researchers had a 31-year-old man illegally cross the street on a number of different occasions, while they surreptitiously observed the number of pedestrians who followed him across each time. Three times more people followed the jaywalking man into traffic and across the street when he wore formal business attire than when he was dressed in a more casual work outfit. Clearly, there are dangers of various kinds inherent in allowing non-authority figures to make decisions for us—some of which could be potentially hazardous.

Some Final Considerations

It is important to emphasize that although we discussed each of the six tendencies separately for the sake of clarity, these principles often work in conjunction with one another to produce a more potent persuasive effect. For example, we mentioned earlier how some sly waiters and waitresses use their authority to gain larger tips by preventing their patrons from making an ostensibly poor entree choice. Since most customers would view this action as a favor done for them by an amicable individual, the

servers also commission the power of the liking and reciprocation principles.

Be Honest.

We also feel that it is imperative to stress that knowledge of the fundamental principles of social influence does not carry with it the right to use this information unscrupulously. In trying to persuade others, one can ethically point to genuine expertise, accurate social validation, real similarities, truly useful favors, legitimate scarcity, and existing commitments. Those who do attempt to dupe or to trap others into compliance are setting themselves up for a double-barreled whammy—by breaking the code of ethics and by risking getting caught—that can produce the disagreeable consequences of diminished self-concept and diminished future profit.

References

1. See also: Harsha E. Chacko, "Upward Influence: How Administrators Get Their Way," *Cornell Hotel and Restaurant Administration Quarterly*, Vol. 29, No. 2 (August 1988). pp. 48-50.
2. Jonathan K. Frenzen and Harry L. Davis, "Purchasing Behavior in Embedded Markets," *Journal of Consumer Research*, Vol. 17 (1990), pp. 1-12.
3. M.G. Efran and E.W.J. Patterson, "The Politics of Appearance," unpublished paper, University of Toronto, 1976.
4. For a review, see: Alice H. Eagly, Wendy Wood, and Shelly Chaiken, "Causal Inferences about Communicators and Their Effect on Opinion Change," *Journal of Personality and Social Psychology*, Vol. 36 (1978), pp. 424-435.
5. For evidence of the pervasiveness of this discrepancy in the salaries of North Americans, see Daniel S. Hammermesh and Jeff E. Biddle, "Beauty and the Labor Market," *The American Economic Review*. Vol. 84 (1994), pp. 1174-1194.
6. Peter H. Reingen and Jerome B. Kernen, "Social Perception and Interpersonal Influence: Some Consequences of the Physical Attractiveness Stereotype in a Personal Selling Setting," *Journal of Consumer Psychology*, Vol. 2, No. 1 (1993), pp. 25-38.
7. Kelly R. Aune and Michael D. Basil, "A Relational Obligations Approach to the Foot-in-the-mouth Effect," *Journal of Applied Social Psychology*, Vol. 24, No. 6 (1994), pp. 546-556.
8. Tim Emswiller, Kay Deaux, and Jerry B. Willits, "Similarity, Sex, and Requests for Small Favors," *Journal of Applied Social Psychology*. Vol. 1 (1971), pp. 284-291.
9. Muzafer Sherif, O.J. Harvey, B.J. White, W.R. Hood, and C.W. Sherif, Intergroup Conflict and Cooperation: The Robbers' Cave Experiment (Norman, OK: University of Oklahoma Institute of Intergroup Relations, 1961).
10. Robert B. Cialdini, *Influence: Science and Practice,* fourth edition (Boston, MA: Allyn & Bacon, 2001).
11. Ellen Berscheid and Elaine Hatfield Walster, *Interpersonal Attraction* (Reading, MA: Addison Wesley, 1978).
12. See: David Drachman, Andre deCarufel, and Chester A. Insko, "The Extra-credit Effect in Interpersonal Attraction," *Journal of Experimental Social Psychology*, Vol. 14 (1978), pp. 458-467; and Donn Byrne, Lois Rasche, and Kathryn Kelley, "When 'I Like You' Indicates Disagreement," *Journal of Research in Personality*, Vol. 8 (1974), pp. 207-217.
13. For a review, see Michael Lynn, "Seven Ways to Increase Servers' Tips," *Cornell Hotel and Restaurant Administration Quarterly*, Vol. 37, No. 3 (1996), pp. 24-29.

14. Ibid.

15. Bruce Rind and Prashant Bordia, "Effect of Restaurant Tipping of Male and Female Servers Drawing a Happy, Smiling Face on the Backs of Customers' Checks," *Journal of Applied Social Psychology* Vol. 26, No. 3 (1996), pp. 218-225.

16. Dennis T. Regan, "Effects of a Favor and Liking on Compliance," *Journal of Experimental Social Psychology.* Vol. 7 (1971), pp. 627-639.

17. Jill Smolowe, "Read This!!!!!!!!," *Time,* Vol. 136, No. 23 (November 26, 1990), pp. 62-70.

18. See: Michael Lynn, "Restaurant Tipping and Service Quality: A Tenuous Relationship," *Cornell Hotel and Restaurant Administration Quarterly.* Vol. 42, No. 1 (February 2001), pp. 14-20.

19. Michael Lynn and Robert Gregor, "Tipping and Service: The Case of the Hotel Bellman," *Hospitality Management,* Vol. 20 (2001), pp. 299-303.

20. David B. Strohmetz, Bruce Rind, Reed Fisher, and Michael Lynn, "Sweetening the Till—The Use of Candy to Increase Restaurant Tipping," *Journal of Applied Social Psychology,* Vol. 32, No. 2 (2002), pp. 300-309.

21. Ibid.

22. Robert B. Cialdini, Joyce E. Vincent, Stephen K. Lewis, Jose Catalan, Diane Wheeler, and Betty Lee Darby, "Reciprocal Concessions Procedure for Inducing Compliance: The Door-in-the-Face Technique," *Journal of Personality and Social Psychology* Vol. 31 (1975), pp. 206-215.

23. Patricia Pliner, Heather Hart, Joanne Kohl, and Dory Saari, "Compliance without Pressure—Some Further Data on the Foot-in-the-door Technique," *Journal of Experimental Social Psychology* Vol. 10 (1974), PP. 17-22.

24. Stephen G. West, "Increasing the Attractiveness of College Cafeteria Food: A Reactance Theory Perspective," *Journal of Applied Psychology,* Vol. 60 (1975), pp. 656-658.

25. Michael Lynn, "Scarcity Effects on Value," *Psychology and Marketing,* Vol. 8 (1991), pp. 43-57.

26. Michael Lynn, "Scarcity Effect on Value: Mediated by Assumed Expensiveness," *Journal of Economic Psychology,* Vol. 10 (1989), pp. 257-274.

27. Amram Knishinsky, "The Effects of Scarcity of Material and Exclusivity of Information on Industrial Buyer-perceived Risk in Provoking a Purchase Decision," Ph.D. dissertation, Arizona State University, 1982.

28. Jack W. Brehm, *A Theory of Psychological Reactance* (New York: Academic Press, 1966).

29. John W. Reich and Jerie L. Robertson, "Reactance and Norm Appeal in Anti-littering Messages," *Journal of Applied Social Psychology.* Vol. 9, No. 1 (1979), pp. 91-101.

30. James W. Pennebaker and Deborah Y. Sanders, "American Graffiti: Effects of Authority and Reactance Arousal," *Personality and Social Psychology Bulletin,* Vol. 2, No. 3 (1976), pp. 264-267.

31. Peter H. Reingen, "Test of a List Procedure for Inducing Compliance with a Request to Donate Money," *Journal of Applied Psychology.* Vol. 67 (1982), pp. 110-118.

32. Robert B. Cialdini, Raymond R Reno, and Carl A. Kallgrem, "A Focus Theory of Normative Conduct: A Theoretical Refmement and Reevaluation of the Role of Norms in Human Behavior," *Advances in Experimental Social Psychology,* Vol. 21 (1990), pp. 201-234.

33. P. Wesley Schultz, "Changing Behavior with Normative Feedback Interventions: A Field Experiment on Curbside Recycling," *Basic and Applied Social Psychology,* Vol. 21, No. 1 (1999), pp. 25-36.

34. www.avweb.com/articles/boguspr/cvr.html. (as viewed on May 9, 2002).

35. Clayton M. Foushee, "Dyads at 35,000 Feet: Factors Affecting Group Processes and Aircraft Performance," American Psychologist, Vol. 39 (1984), pp. 885-893.

36. Benjamin Page, Robert Y. Shapiro, and Glenn R. Dempsey,

Overcoming Terror

Is Washington terrorizing us more than Al Qaeda?

By Philip Zimbardo with Bruce Kluger

Log on to the Department of Homeland Security's Web site, ready.gov, and click on "nuclear blast."

Thanks to the recently formed agency, ordinary citizens can now get a crash course in emergency preparedness in the event that a big bomb is dropped on their block.

Step one, says the terse tip sheet, is to "take cover." Step two: "Assess the situation." Step three? "Limit your exposure to radiation."

While the well-meaning 300-word document goes on to reveal a few other curious dos and don'ts for a doomsday scenario (e.g., ingesting potassium iodide is definitely a bad idea when radioactive iodine is coursing through the atmosphere), what's missing from the text is an acknowledgment of the psychological damage that such cursorily assembled, blithely disseminated information can wreak on the public. Presumably intended as a mental health balm in this time of unprecedented global stress, these simplistic big-blast CliffsNotes merely skate atop the frozen pond of the nuclear nightmare, ultimately leaving the befuddled citizen to wonder—and often panic—about the real and present danger that lurks just beneath the ice.

Unfortunately, the Department of Homeland Security's site is just one example of a national warning system that in the end stirs up more anxiety than it quells. Loaded with scientific terminology, yet woefully bereft of any tangible data, the U.S.' early-warning mechanism has transformed us into a nation of worriers, not warriors. Forcing citizens to ride an emotional roller coaster without providing any clear instructions on how to soothe their jitters, the current security system has had a profoundly negative impact on our individual and collective mental health. I call this a "pre-traumatic stress syndrome," and its effect on our day-to-day lives is debilitating.

Established in March 2002, the U.S. terrorism warning system is broken down into the now-famous color-coded levels of alert—green, blue, yellow, orange and red. The degree of risk changes from level to level, even though the specificity of the threat need not. Beginning with a "low risk" green, the threat levels then graduate to "general," "increased and predictable," "likely" (the notorious Code Orange) and culminate with the red-hot "imminent."

Since September 11, 2001, the state of domestic alert has randomly seesawed through the color spectrum, rising as high as "orange" on at least eight occasions. Each time the color has changed, a public official has stepped before the cameras with explanations that alternate between vague and indecipherable. Goose-bump-inducing terms such as "dirty bombs" and "shelter-in-place" are nonchalantly tossed out, but never are Americans given a soup-to-nuts explanation of exactly what is going on. This exercise in ambiguity doesn't serve to calm people as intended. Instead, it scares the bejesus out of them. After all, terrorism is not about war in the traditional sense of the word. It is about psychology—about frightening ordinary people, making them feel confused and vulnerable. And, regrettably, the government is unwittingly engaging in this activity as effectively as Al Qaeda.

Like a car alarm that sounds not when a vehicle is broken into, but instead, whenever it passes through a bad neighborhood, the nation's early-warning system has effectively rendered Americans paralyzed behind the wheel, unable—or unwilling—to step on the gas.

Contemporary clinical data—and my own extended research in this area—prove time and again that to be optimally effective, safety alarms must include four basic components: (1) a credible, trustworthy source communicating the alarm; (2) a disclosure of the specific and anticipated event that has elicited the warning; (3) an effort to reassure those being alerted about the value of unified efforts; and finally, (4) a clearly defined set of actions that citizens can take in order to escape a calamity.

And yet, since September 11, each of these basic principles has been systematically violated in the design and delivery of terrorist alarms issued by the government.

In the first six warnings after the 2001 attacks, different communicators—from Attorney General John Ashcroft to Homeland Security Director Tom Ridge—appeared before the press, alleging that they possessed "reliable" information from "credible" sources that an attack was "imminent." In most cases, the perpetrators were described as anonymous terrorists; their attack would take place sometime in the immediate future; and their target was any number of unnamed locations in the U.S. (or anywhere else in the world, for that matter). As if this fuzzy description of impending doom wasn't sufficiently stultifying, officials then stopped short of offering any specific action that citizens might take in response to the supposed terrorist attacks, other than to remain on alert and to keep their eyes open.

Eventually, these widely disseminated, narrowly defined warnings created greater levels of fear, which over time morphed into general anxiety.

The psychological situation worsened when the administration delivered—in the same breath as its warnings—a collateral message to "go about your business as normal." Rather than give Americans a hook on which to hang their heebie-jeebies (providing facts, for example, that elucidated the wheres and whens of the threats), this unexpected "hey, don't worry" footnote induced a cognitive and emotional disconnect. After all, how was it possible not to fret after being told that our personal safety and security were now at stake? Naturally, the resulting sense of confusion spilled over into feelings of helplessness.

While the first six post-9/11 warnings seemed, at worst, insensitive to the nation's emotional state, the seventh, issued in early February 2003, was downright reckless. After downgrading the level of alert to "unlikely" (from the previous week's "increased likelihood"), Ridge leapfrogged from the precautionary to the preposterous, recommending ways in which citizens could prepare for an attack by the still-unnamed phantom menace. Among these suggestions was sealing ourselves into our homes using plastic sheeting and duct tape. Americans stormed Home Depot. Jay Leno had a field day.

The fact is, not a single terrorist attack occurred on American soil in the 18 months after 9/11. While this was obviously good news for American security, it wreaked havoc on the nation's psyche. Where were the thousands of terrorists allegedly comprising mysterious cells throughout our country? Where was the debriefing by authorities to explain why, after all the hand-wringing, nothing ever materialized? The high alerts silently evaporated as quickly as they arose, but the high anxiety remained—and remains—at full throttle.

All of which raises the question: Is it possible for a government to keep its citizens braced for attack without incapacitating them with fear? It is not only possible—it is a historical fact: On the night of April 18, 1775, patriot Paul Revere rode his horse through the countryside from Boston Harbor toward Lexington, warning local Colonial leaders that the British army was fast approaching. Throughout the evening, Revere faithfully adhered to my four-point theory for successful dissemination of public alarms (something of a miracle, I should add, in that I wouldn't be born for another 158 years). In retrospect, Revere was the perfect messenger delivering the perfect message: (1) He was known to be a highly credible communicator, both expert and trustworthy; (2) his alarm was focused on a specific anticipated event; (3) the alert was designed to motivate citizens to act as a group; and (4) the warning called for a concrete set of actions—namely, fighting back.

As American history books tell you, the day after Revere took his midnight gallop, the Colonial militia trounced the redcoats at Concord. Not a shred of duct tape was needed.

UNIT 5
Social Influence

Unit Selections

Key Points to Consider

- Can you provide some examples of each of the three types of social influence? Which form of influence do you think prevails in American society? Can you think of other forms of social influence not described in the introduction to this unit? Do you have a favorite (often-used) influence technique? When and why do you use it? What methods that others use on you seem to alter your behavior?

- Have you observed others using these techniques? How do you feel when you know that you are the target of these appeals? Do you feel more resistant? Does it matter who the influencer is?

- Have you heard about the mock prison studies? What factor do you think most affected the outcomes? What are the various explanations for the results? If you were a guard, do you think you would become brutal toward prisoners? Have you ever visited a prison or jail? Have you seen any of the same cruel behaviors exhibited by the guards? Where else have you observed them?

- What is compliance? With whose requests are we most likely to comply? When you see advertisements designed to sell a product, how do you react? Are you more or less likely to acquire it? What advice would you give Bob in order to increase his sales?

- What is the foot-in-the door technique for compliance? Do you find this method particularly manipulative? Do you believe alternatively that making a larger request first and then retreating to a smaller request also would be effective?

 **Links: www.dushkin.com/online/**
These sites are annotated in the World Wide Web pages.

AFF Cult Group Information
http://www.csj.org
Center for Leadership Studies
http://www.situational.com
Social Influence Website
http://www.influenceatwork.com/

Bob obtained an associates degree in business and achieved high honors at his community college. Upon graduation, he was immediately hired by a life insurance company. Bob's job was to sell insurance policies to clients. The policies supposedly accrued value as the client matured, leaving the buyer or beneficiary with a tidy sum of money upon the death of the insured person.

Bob considered himself very lucky; he came from a large extended family and had made many friends at the college. He even considered some of the faculty and staff at the college to be more than mere acquaintances. As Bob began his new life as a salesman, he was quite sure that he "had it made in the shade," as he told his brother, because there were so many potential customers already available.

Bob soon discovered that selling anything to friends and family is difficult. In fact, his initial sales were so low that he had to call strangers and go door-to-door in an attempt to sell more policies. "What's going wrong?," Bob wondered. "I thought this would be so easy."

In the previous unit (Unit 4. Attitudes), you learned that for a myriad of reasons persuasion is very difficult. Related to the issue of persuasion is the topic of social influence. *Social influence* is like social pressure—obvious or subtle—to make others submit to our wishes. There are three major types of social influence studied by social psychologists: conformity, compliance, and obedience in respective order of their degree of directness, from least to most direct.

Conformity, the subtlest type of social influence, was one of the first social influence phenomena studied by social psychologists. Conformity is the result of subtle pressure to do or think like others. Solomon Asch in the 1940s and 1950s examined the effects of group pressure on an individual. In the prototype of his research, participants were asked to judge which line—A, B, or

C—was closest in length to comparison line D. Unbeknownst to the real subject, other participants were allies of the researcher. After giving several appropriate answers, the confederates started providing the wrong answers. Asch waited to see what the real participant would do: submit to group pressure and give the wrong answer or stick to the correct answer in the face of perceived coercion. Asch discovered that many Americans are conformists, something that the average American probably might vehemently deny.

A second type of social influence is compliance, in which someone makes a direct request for you to do something. When Bob tried to sell his insurance policies to friends, he was really making a request that apparently his friends did not feel compelled to fulfill. There are many compliance techniques which are well-known by salespeople like Bob. Social psychologists, via their research, have also noted that public compliance sometimes occurs in the absence of private acceptance.

A third form of social influence is *obedience*. Obedience takes place when one person responds to a direct order by a second person who is usually an authority figure. Obedience is an issue that permeates many settings, including military life, laws and public policies, prisoner behaviors, and other real world phenomena. Some of the classic studies in social psychology have demonstrated all too well that many individuals follow orders without much thought. In fact, some individuals when asked to harm someone else will do so just because a powerful person asked them.

Social influence is a very important issue in the fabric of community life. We will explore it with three different articles. The first article, "Abu Ghraib Brings a Cruel Reawakening," Clive Cookson examines the issue and causes of the torture of Iraqi prisoners by American soldiers.

Rebecca Clay, for *Monitor on Psychology,* examines compliance, a more restrained form of social influence than obedience. Remember, compliance is a response to a direct request from another. Robert Cialdini, in "Liking the Friendly Thief," discusses how and why pressure to comply is especially high when we admire the requester. Evidently, Bob was liked by his friends, but they still did not comply with his request to purchase life insurance from him.

The final article in this unit by Michael Lovaglia describes one specific social influence technique known as the foot-in-the-door effect. Using this method, the requester first issues a small request, followed by a larger (and more desired request). This technique is remarkably effective.

Abu Ghraib Brings a Cruel Reawakening

The recent revelations of abuse at the Iraqi jail have had far-reaching effects on the victims of past violence, says Clive Cookson.

CLIVE COOKSON

The shocking pictures from Abu Ghraib prison in Baghdad have come as a double blow to the doctors and therapists working with torture survivors in 170 rehabilitation centres around the world. On top of their dismay that US forces could treat prisoners so cruelly, staff have been overwhelmed with requests for help over the past few weeks, as the images and descriptions reawaken horrific memories in people who have been tortured.

"The events at Abu Ghraib have had a profound effect on the people we care for," says Allen Keller, director of the Bellevue/New York University Program for Survivors of Torture. "The pictures have been very disturbing and retraumatising for many of our patients, who have been suffering a recurrence of nightmares and other sleeping problems."

Gill Hinshelwood, senior examining doctor at the Medical Foundation for the Care of Victims of Torture in London, reports a similar surge in symptoms. "Some of my Iraqi clients (who suffered under Saddam Hussein's regime) have had a resurgence of nightmares; others are coming back with aches and pains," she says. "Many are obsessed with what is going on."

Yet staff at rehabilitation centres say some good will come out of the horror of Abu Ghraib, if it increases awareness of how to diagnose and treat torture. At present the medical community pays insufficient attention to what Prof Keller calls a global public health problem. "Around 400,000 torture survivors have come to live in the US alone," he says.

Richard Mollica, director of the Harvard Program in Refugee Trauma, agrees. "Despite routine exposure to the suffering of victims of human brutality, healthcare professionals tend to shy away from confronting this reality," he says. "Clinicians avoid addressing torture-related symptoms of illness because they are afraid of opening a Pandora's box: they believe they won't have the tools or time to help torture survivors once they've elicited their history."

Even the damage caused by physical brutality may be hard for a general practitioner to spot. For instance, falanga, in which the soles of the feet are beaten with

rods, may leave no outward sign of damage even though internal damage to nerves and tendons can make walking excruciatingly painful.

Diagnosing and treating the psychological legacy of torture is even more difficult. All the attention given by psychology researchers to post-traumatic stress disorder has not necessarily helped those working with torture victims.

"This emphasis on PTSD has obscured the reality that the most common mental illness diagnosed in torture survivors is depression—often a serious and socially debilitating condition associated with serious medical consequences," says Prof Mollica. The depression caused by torture and extreme violence can be distinguished from other forms of depression by the intense and repetitive nightmares that accompany it.

Dr. Hinshelwood says this depression is best described as "a deep and long-term sense of passivity and pessimism". She adds: "People—and men in particular—are even more depressed if their torture includes rape or sexual abuse."

Sexual abuse was, of course, a prominent feature of the American mistreatment of prisoners at Abu Ghraib. Although there has been some debate about whether this amounted to torture, organisations working with torture victims, such the Medical Foundation in London, state unequivocally that it did. And they say that US interrogators have used an unacceptably harsh sort of coercion—sometimes called "stress and duress" or "torture lite"—systematically, not only in Iraq, but also at Guantanamo Bay in Cuba and Bagram air base in Afghanistan.

In response to the shock of many Americans, who asked why "seemingly normal" US soldiers could behave so sadistically in Iraq, the American Psychological Association put the professional view that "most of us could behave this way under similar circumstances".

Two famous experiments proved the point more than 30 years ago. First Stanley Milgram at Yale University showed that most normal volunteers would follow the instructions of an authority figure—a scientist in a white coat—and give other people a series of increasingly powerful electric shocks, even though they elicited agonising screams.

Then Philip Zimbardo set up a simulated prison at Stanford University, in which students were randomly selected to play the roles of prisoners and guards. Prof Zimbardo believes his experiment has striking similarities with Abu Ghraib: "I have exact, parallel pictures of naked prisoners with bags over their heads, who are being sexually humiliated by the prison guards, from the 1971 study."

According to the APA, these two classic experiments—and other psychological studies in the laboratory and in the field—go a long way to explaining what went wrong at Abu Ghraib. Any prison is an environment in which the balance of power is so unequal that normal people can become brutal and abusive, unless the institution has strong leadership and transparent oversight to prevent the abuse of power.

Abu Ghraib not only lacked such leadership, but also had another ingredient for abuse: an ethnic, cultural, linguistic and religious gulf between guards and prisoners. Robert Jay Lifton, psychiatry professor at Harvard Medical School, says people are naturally predisposed to distrust or even attack others whom they categorise as outsiders.

The Abu Ghraib guards allegedly thought they were following orders from intelligence officers. However, this sort of mistreatment is counterproductive even from the narrow viewpoint of intelligence gathering, says Vince Iacopino, research director of the Massachusetts-based group Physicians for Human Rights.

"Unfortunately, some may assume that physical and psychological coercion techniques serve to 'soften up' detainees for interrogation," says Dr Iacopino. "In our experience it is clear that physical and psychological forms of coercion or ill treatment or torture do not provide accurate and reliable information. On the contrary, by inflicting physical and/or emotional pain, perpetrators reduce their victims to a point that precludes obtaining reliable 'information'—and victims frequently falsely confess to whatever they think interrogators want to hear."

Prof Mollica points out that perpetrators can also be psychologically damaged by their experience and requests to treat them can put doctors in a difficult position.

"In medicine we have the controversial concept of 'medical neutrality', which holds that the doctor has an obligation to treat someone regardless of political situation or the circumstances that made them ill," he says. "But if a perpetrator of torture comes to you for therapy, what do you do?"

There are clearly far more victims than perpetrators of torture—and most are more seriously damaged. But there is hope, as psychologists around the world gain experience in helping torture victims to recover their mental health, first through proper diagnosis and then through a mixture of therapy and, if appropriate, treatment with antidepressants or other drugs.

"Twenty years ago there was a widespread impression that survivors of extreme violence could never really recover from the experience," says Prof Mollica. "Now we are much more optimistic."

While many of the world's torture victims suffer renewed torment through the images of Abu Ghraib, their long-term prospects may be becoming slightly brighter.

Liking: The Friendly Thief

Robert B. Cialdini

The main work of a trial attorney is to make a jury like his client.

Few of us would be surprised to learn that, as a rule, we most prefer to say yes to the requests of people we know and like. What might be startling to note, however, is that this simple rule is used in hundreds of ways by total strangers to get us to comply with *their* requests.

The clearest illustration I know of the professional exploitation of the liking rule is the Tupperware party, which I consider a classic compliance setting. Anybody familiar with the workings of a Tupperware party will recognize the use of the various weapons of influence:

Reciprocity. To start, games are played and prizes won by the party goers; anyone who doesn't win a prize gets to choose one from a grab bag so that everyone has received a gift before the buying begins.

Commitment. Participants are urged to describe publicly the uses and benefits they have found for the Tupperware they already own.

Social proof. Once the buying begins, each purchase builds the idea that other, similar people want the products; therefore, it must be good.

All the weapons of influence are present to help things along, but the real power of the Tupperware party comes from a particular arrangement that trades on the liking rule. Despite the entertaining and persuasive selling skills of the Tupperware demonstrator, the true request to purchase the product does not come from this stranger; it comes from a friend to every person in the room. Oh, the Tupperware representative may physically ask for each party goer's order, all right; but the more psychologically compelling requester is sitting off to the side, smiling, chatting, and serving refreshments. She is the party hostess, who has called her friends together for the demonstration in her home and who, everyone knows, makes a profit from each piece sold at the party.

By providing the hostess with a percentage of the take, the Tupperware Home Parties Corporation arranges for its customers to buy from and for a friend rather than from an unknown salesperson. In this way, the attraction, the warmth, the security, and the obligation of friendship are brought to bear on the sales setting (Taylor, 1978). In fact, consumer researchers who have examined the social ties between the hostess and the party goers in home

party sales settings have affirmed the power of the company's approach: The strength of that social bond is twice as likely to determine product purchase as is preference for the product itself (Frenzen & Davis, 1990). The results have been remarkable. It was recently estimated that Tupperware sales now exceed 2.5 million dollars a day! Indeed, Tupperware's success has spread around the world to societies in Europe, Latin America, and Asia, where one's place in a network of friends and family is more socially significant than in the United States (Markus & Kitayama, 1991; Triandis, 1995). As a result, now less than a quarter of Tupperware sales take place in North America.

What is interesting is that the customers appear to be fully aware of the liking and friendship pressures embodied in the Tupperware party. Some don't seem to mind; others do, but don't seem to know how to avoid these pressures. One woman I spoke with described her reactions with more than a bit of frustration in her voice.

> *It's gotten to the point now where I hate to be invited to Tupperware parties. I've got all the containers I need; and if I wanted any more, I could buy another brand cheaper in the store. But when a friend calls up, I feel like I have to go. And when I get there, I feel like I have to buy something. What can I do? It's for one of my friends.*

With so irresistible an ally as friendship, it is little wonder that the Tupperware Corporation has abandoned retail sales outlets and is pushing the home party concept. Statistics reveal that a Tupperware party now starts somewhere every 2.7 seconds. Of course, all sorts of other compliance professionals recognize the pressure to say yes to someone we know and like. Take, for instance, the growing number of charity organizations that recruit volunteers to canvass for donations close to their own homes. They understand perfectly how much more difficult it is for us to turn down a charity request when it comes from a friend or neighbor.

Other compliance professionals have found that the friend doesn't even have to be present to be effective; often, just the mention of the friends' name is enough. The

Shaklee Corporation, which specializes in door-to-door sales of various home-related products, advises its salespeople to use the "endless chain" method for finding new customers. Once a customer admits that he or she likes a product, that customer can be pressed for the names of friends who would also appreciate learning about it. The individuals on that list can then be approached for sales *and* a list of their friends, who can serve as sources for still other potential customers, and so on in an endless chain.

The key to the success of this method is that each new prospect is visited by a salesperson armed with the name of a friend "who suggested I call on you." Turning the salesperson away under those circumstances is difficult; it's almost like rejecting the friend. The Shaklee sales manual insists that employees use this system: "It would be impossible to overestimate its value. Phoning or calling on a prospect and being able to say that Mr. So-and-so, a friend of his, felt he would benefit by giving you a few moments of his time is virtually as good as a sale 50 percent made before you enter."

MAKING FRIENDS TO INFLUENCE PEOPLE

Compliance practitioners' widespread use of the liking bond between friends tells us much about the power of the liking rule to produce assent. In fact, we find that such professionals seek to benefit from the rule even when already formed friendships are not present for them to employ. Under these circumstances, the professionals still make use of the liking bond by employing a compliance strategy that is quite direct: They first get us to like *them*.

There is a man in Detroit, Joe Girard, who specialized in using the liking rule to sell Chevrolets. He became wealthy in the process, making over $200,000 a year. With such a salary, we might guess that he was a high-level GM executive or perhaps the owner of a Chevrolet dealership. But no. He made his money as a salesman on the showroom floor. He was phenomenal at what he did. For twelve years straight, he won the title of "Number One Car Salesman"; he averaged more than five cars and trucks sold every day he worked; and he has been called the world's "greatest car salesman" by the *Guinness Book of World Records*.

For all his success, the formula he employed was surprisingly simple. It consisted of offering people just two things: a fair price and someone they liked to buy from. "And that's it," he claimed in an interview. "Finding the salesman you like, plus the price. Put them both together, and you get a deal."

Fine. The Joe Girard formula tells us how vital the liking rule is to his business, but it doesn't tell us nearly enough. For one thing, it doesn't tell us why customers liked him more than some other salesperson who offered a fair price. There is a crucial—and fascinating—general question that Joe's formula leaves unanswered. What are the factors that cause one person to like another? If we

knew *that* answer, we would be a long way toward understanding how people such as Joe can so successfully arrange to have us like them and, conversely, how we might successfully arrange to have others like us. Fortunately, social scientists have been asking this question for decades. Their accumulated evidence has allowed them to identify a number of factors that reliably cause liking. As we will see, each is cleverly used by compliance professionals to urge us along the road to "yes."

WHY DO I LIKE YOU?
LET ME LIST THE REASONS

Physical Attractiveness

Although it is generally acknowledged that good-looking people have an advantage in social interaction, recent findings indicate that we may have sorely underestimated the size and reach of that advantage. There seems to be a *click, whirr* response to attractive people. Like all *click, whirr* reactions, it happens automatically, without forethought. The response itself falls into a category that social scientists call *halo effects*. A halo effect occurs when one positive characteristic of a person dominates the way that person is viewed by others. The evidence is now clear that physical attractiveness is often such a characteristic.

Research has shown that we automatically assign to good-looking individuals such favorable traits as talent, kindness, honesty, and intelligence (for a review of this evidence, see Eagly, Ashmore, Makhijani, & Longo, 1991). Furthermore, we make these judgments without being aware that physical attractiveness plays a role in the process. Some consequences of this unconscious assumption that "good-looking equals good" scare me. For example, a study of the 1974 Canadian federal elections found that attractive candidates received more than two and a half times as many votes as unattractive candidates (Efran & Patterson, 1976). Despite such evidence of favoritism toward handsome politicians, follow-up research demonstrated that voters did not realize their bias. In fact, 73 percent of Canadian voters surveyed denied in the strongest possible terms that their votes had been influenced by physical appearance; only 14 percent even allowed for the possibility of such influence (Efran & Patterson, 1976). Voters can deny the impact of attractiveness on electability all they want, but evidence has continued to confirm its troubling presence (Budesheim & DePaola, 1994).

A similar effect has been found in hiring situations. In one study, good grooming of applicants in a simulated employment interview accounted for more favorable hiring decisions than did job qualifications—this, even though the interviewers claimed that appearance played a small role in their choices (Mack & Rainey, 1990). The advantage given to attractive workers extends past hiring day to payday. Economists examining U.S. and Canadian samples have found that attractive individuals get paid

READER'S REPORT 5.1

From a Chicago Man

Although I've never been to a Tupperware Party, I recognized the same kind of friendship pressures recently when I got a call from a long distance phone company saleswoman. She told me that one of my buddies had placed my name on something called the "MCI Friends and Family Calling Circle."

This friend of mine, Brad, is a guy I grew up with but who moved to New Jersey last year for a job. He still calls me pretty regularly to get the news on the guys we used to hang out with. The saleswoman told me that he could save 20 percent on all the calls he made to the people on his Calling-Circle list, provided they are MCI phone company subscribers. Then she asked me if I wanted to switch to MCI to get all the blah, blah, blah benefits of MCI services, and so that Brad could save 20 percent on his calls to me.

Well, I couldn't have cared less about the benefits of MCI service; I was perfectly happy with the long distance company I had. But the part about wanting to save Brad money on our calls really got to me. For me to say that I didn't want to be in his Calling Circle and didn't care about saving him money would have sounded like a real affront to our friendship when he heard about it. So, to avoid insulting him, I told her to switch me to MCI.

I used to wonder why women would go to a Tupperware Party just because a friend was holding it, and then buy stuff they didn't want once they were there. I don't wonder anymore.

Author's note: *This reader is not alone in being able to testify to the power of the pressures embodied in MCI's Calling Circle idea. When* Consumer Reports *magazine inquired into the practice, the MCI salesperson they interviewed was quite succinct: "It works 9 out of 10 times," he said.*

on average of 12–14 percent more than their unattractive coworkers (Hammermesh & Biddle, 1994).

Equally unsettling research indicates that our judicial process is similarly susceptible to the influences of body dimensions and bone structure. It now appears that good-looking people are likely to receive highly favorable treatment in the legal system (see Castellow, Wuensch, & Moore, 1991; and Downs & Lyons, 1990, for reviews). For example, in a Pennsylvania study (Stewart, 1980), researchers rated the physical attractiveness of 74 separate male defendants at the start of their criminal trials. When, much later, the researchers checked court records for the results of these cases, they found that the handsome men had received significantly lighter sentences. In fact, attractive defendants were twice as likely to avoid jail as unattractive defendants.[1] In another study—this one on

the damages awarded in a staged negligence trial—a defendant who was better looking than his victim was assessed an average amount of $5,623; but when the victim was more attractive of the two, the average compensation was $10,051. What's more, both male and female jurors exhibited the attractiveness-based favoritism (Kulha & Kessler, 1978).

Other experiments have demonstrated that attractive people are more likely to obtain help when in need (Benson, Karabenic, & Lerner, 1976) and are more persuasive in changing the opinions of an audience (Chaiken, 1979). Here, too, both sexes respond in the same way. In the Benson et al. study on helping, for instance, the better-looking men and women received aid more often, even from members of their own sex. A major exception to this rule might be expected to occur, of course, if the attractive person is viewed as a direct competitor, especially a romantic rival. Short of this qualification, though, it is apparent that good-looking people enjoy an enormous social advantage in our culture. They are better liked, more persuasive, more frequently helped, and seen as possessing more desirable personality traits and greater intellectual capacities. It appears that the social benefits of good looks begin to accumulate quite early. Research on elementary school children shows that adults view aggressive acts as less naughty when performed by an attractive child (Dion, 1972) and that teachers presume good-looking children to be more intelligent than their less attractive classmates (Ritts, Patterson, & Tubbs, 1992).

It is hardly any wonder, then, that the halo of physical attractiveness is regularly exploited by compliance professionals. Because we like attractive people, and because we tend to comply with those we like, it makes sense that sales training programs include grooming hints, fashionable clothiers select their floor staffs from among the good-looking candidates, and con men and women are attractive.[2]

Similarity

What if physical appearance is not much at issue? After all, most people possess average looks. Are there other factors that can be used to produce liking? As both researchers and compliance professionals know, there are several, and one of the most influential is similarity.

We like people who are similar to us (Byrne, 1971). This fact seems to hold true whether the similarity is in the area of opinions, personality traits, background, or lifestyle. Consequently, those who want us to like them so that we will comply with them can accomplish that purpose by appearing similar to us in a wide variety of ways.

Dress is a good example. Several studies have demonstrated that we are more likely to help those who dress like us. In one study, done in the early 1970s when young people tended to dress in either "hippie" or "straight" fashion, experimenters donned hippie or straight attire and asked college students on campus for a dime to make a phone call. When the experimenter was dressed in the same way as the student, the request was granted in more than two-thirds of the instances; when the student and requester were dissimilarly dressed, the dime was provided less than half the time (Emswiller, Deaux, & Willits, 1971). Another experiment showed how automatic our positive response to similar others can be. Marchers in an antiwar demonstration were found to be more likely to sign the petition of a similarly dressed requester *and* to do so without bothering to read it first (Suedfeld, Bochner, & Matas, 1971). *Click, whirr.*

Another way requesters can manipulate similarity to increase liking and compliance is to claim that they have backgrounds and interests similar to ours. Car salespeople, for example, are trained to look for evidence of such things while examining a customer's trade-in. If there is camping gear in the trunk, the salespeople might mention, later on, how they love to get away from the city whenever they can; if there are golf balls on the back seat, they might remark that they hope the rain will hold off until they can play the eighteen holes they scheduled for later in the day; if they notice that the car was purchased out of state, they might ask where a customer is from and report—with surprise—that they (or their spouse) were born there, too.

As trivial as these similarities may seem, they appear to work (Brewer, 1979; Tajfel, 1981). One researcher who examined the sales records of insurance companies found that customers were more likely to buy insurance when a salesperson was like them in age, religion, politics, and cigarette-smoking habits (Evans, 1963). Another researcher was able to significantly increase the percentage of people who responded to a mailed survey by changing one small feature of the request: On a cover letter, he modified the name of the survey-taker to be similar to that of the survey recipient. Thus, Robert Greer received the survey from a survey center official named Bob Gregar while Cynthia Johnston received hers from a survey center official named Cindy Johanson. In two separate studies, adding this little bit of similarity to the exchange nearly doubled survey compliance (Garner, 1999). These seemingly minor commonalties can affect decisions that go well beyond whose insurance to purchase or whose survey to complete. They can affect the decision of whose life to save. When asked to rank-order a waiting list of patients suffering from kidney disorder as to their deservingness for the next available treatment, people chose those whose political party preference matched their own (Furnham, 1996).

Because even small similarities can be effective in producing a positive response to another and because a veneer of similarity can be so easily manufactured, I would advise special caution in the presence of requesters who claim to be "just like you."[3] Indeed, it would be wise these days to be careful around salespeople who just *seem* to be just like you. Many sales training programs now urge trainees to "mirror and match" the customer's body posture, mood, and verbal style, as similarities along each of these dimensions have been shown to lead to positive results (Chartrand & Bargh, 1999; Locke & Horowitz, 1990; Woodside & Davenport, 1974).

Compliments

Actor McLean Stevenson once described how his wife tricked him into marriage: "She said she liked me." Although designed for a laugh, the remark is as instructive as it is humorous. The information that someone fancies us can be a bewitchingly effective device for producing return liking and willing compliance (Berscheid & Walster, 1978; Howard, Gengler, & Jain, 1995, 1997). So, often when people flatter us or claim affinity for us, they want something from us.

Remember Joe Girard, the world's "greatest car salesman," who says the secret of his success was getting customers to like him? He did something that, on the face of it, seems foolish and costly. Each month he sent every one of his more than 13,000 former customers a holiday greeting card containing a printed message. The holiday greeting card changed from month to month (Happy New Year, Happy Valentine's Day, Happy Thanksgiving, and so on), but the message printed on the face of the card never varied. It read, "I like you." As Joe explained it, "There's nothing else on the card, nothin' but my name. I'm just telling 'em that I like 'em."

"I like you." It came in the mail every year, 12 times a year, like clockwork. "I like you," on a printed card that went to 13,000 other people, too. Could a statement of liking so impersonal, obviously designed to sell cars, really work: Joe Girard thought so, and a man as successful as he was at what he did deserves our attention. Joe understood an important fact about human nature: we are phenomenal suckers for flattery. Although there are limits to our gullibility—especially when we can be sure that the flatterer is trying to manipulate us (Jones & Wortman, 1973)—we tend, as a rule, to believe praise and to like those who provide it, often when it is probably untrue (Byrne, Rasche, & Kelley, 1974).

An experiment done on a group of men in North Carolina shows how helpless we can be in the face of praise. The men in the study received comments about themselves from another person who needed a favor from them. Some of the men got only positive comments, some got only negative comments, and some got a mixture of good and bad. There were three interesting findings. First, the evaluator who provided only praise was liked best by the men. Second, this tendency held true even when the men fully realized that the flatterer stood to gain from their liking him. Finally, unlike the other types of comments, pure praise did not have to be accurate to work. Positive comments produced just as much liking for the flatterer when they were untrue as when they were true (Drachman, deCarufel, & Insko, 1978).

Apparently we have such an automatically positive reaction to compliments that we can fall victim to someone who uses them in an obvious attempt to win our favor.

Click, whirr. When seen in this light, the expense of printing and mailing well over 150,000 "I like you" cards each year seems neither as foolish nor as costly as before....

Notes

1. This finding—that attractive defendants, even when they are found guilty, are less likely to be sentenced to prison—helps explain one fascinating experiment in criminology (Kurtzburg, Safar, & Cavior, 1968). Some New York City jail inmates with facial disfigurements underwent plastic surgery while incarcerated; other inmates with similar disfigurements did not. Furthermore, some members of each group received services (such as counseling, training, etc.) designed to rehabilitate them to society. One year after the inmates had been released from jail, a check of the records revealed that (except for heroin addicts) criminals given the cosmetic surgery were significantly less likely to have returned to jail. The most interesting feature of this finding was that it was equally true for those inmates who had not received the traditional rehabilitative services and for those who had. Apparently, some criminologists then argued that when it comes to ugly inmates, prisons would be better off to abandon the costly rehabilitation services they typically provide and offer plastic surgery instead; the surgery seems to be at least as effective and decidedly less expensive. The importance of the Pennsylvania data (Stewart, 1980) is that it suggests that the argument for surgery as a means of rehabilitation may be faulty. Making ugly criminals more attractive may not reduce the chances that they will commit another crime; it may only reduce their chances of being sent to jail for it.

2. Have you ever noticed that despite their good looks, many attractive people don't seem to share the positive impressions of their personalities and abilities that observers have? Research has not only confirmed the tenuous and inconsistent relationship between attractiveness and self-esteem (see Adams, 1977), it has also offered a possible explanation. One set of authors has produced evidence suggesting that good-looking people are aware that other people's positive evaluations of them are not based on their actual traits and abilities but are often caused by an attractiveness "halo" (Major, Carrington, & Carnevale, 1984). Consequently, many attractive people who are exposed to this confusing information may be left with an uncertain self-concept.

3. Additional work suggests yet another reason for caution when dealing with similar requesters: we typically underestimate the degree to which similarity affects our liking for another (Gonzales, Davis, Loney, Lukens, & Junghans, 1983).

Persuasion: What Will It Take to Convince You?

Michael J. Lovaglia

University of Iowa

PERSUASION BY INCHES

Have you noticed that big building projects always seem to cost much more than was originally estimated? No matter how high the original estimate, the project almost always ends up costing millions, sometimes billions of dollars more. It is not that accurate estimates are too difficult to make. If accuracy were the problem, then the original estimate would be too high only about half the time and too low the rest. The error here is too one-sided to be accidental. Taxpayers, certainly, do not like having to pay additional billions of dollars for a new highway. Yet contractors continue to give low estimates then ask for increases along the way. No matter how annoyed people get, the practice continues. Social psychology explains why.

An initially low estimate is a powerful persuasive tool, whether you are buying a car or the government is buying a highway. When people are shopping for a car, they are often strongly attracted to one more expensive than they can easily afford. The salesperson's job is to persuade them to buy a car that will strain but not break their financial resources. Suppose you are shopping for a car. You have made a firm resolution to spend no more than $12,000. At one dealership, however, you are attracted to one that costs $16,000. You realize this is out of your price range and start to move on. At that point, salespeople are taught to ask, "Would you be interested if I could get the price of this car down to $10,900?"

There are two reasons for the salesperson's question. First, notice that it is a leading question. He did not say that he could get the price reduced by $5,000. He only asked if you would be interested. How-ever, by asking the leading question, he implied that a price of $10,900 was at least possible. Second, you would probably answer yes to the question. (A good salesperson would already have found out that it was in your price range.) Once you agree that you are interested in that car at that price, you have made a commitment. We are all taught to keep our commitments. It is difficult for people to stop and reverse themselves once they have started something. By agreeing that you would be interested, you committed yourself in a small way to buying that car. If the salesperson is good at his job, then you will buy that car and be happy with it, but the price you pay will be closer to $16,000 than it will be to $10,900. Had the salesperson accurately estimated that you might be able to buy the car for $14,900, you would not have been interested. To the salesperson's credit, you probably like your new car more than any you could have found for less than $12,000. On the other hand, your financial situation may be shaky for a while because of it.

Cialdini, Cacioppo, Bassett, and Miller (1978) investigated why giving a very low initial cost estimate is such a persuasive technique. Researchers called people on the phone to ask them to participate in a psychology study. Half of the people were told immediately that the study would take place at 7 A.M. The early hour made it unlikely that many people would agree to participate. The rest of the people were told about the study and that it would take place at a variety of times during the day. Then all of the people in the study were asked if they would like to participate first. Only after people said that they were interested in participating were they told that they would be needed at the 7 A.M. session of the study. Researchers wanted to know if getting people to agree that they were interested in the study first, before they knew how early they would have to arrive, would increase the number who eventually showed up for a 7 A.M. study.

Cialdini and colleagues (1978) showed that giving a low initial cost estimate effectively persuaded people to participate in their study. When researchers told subjects up front that the study would take place at 7 A.M., less than a third (31 percent) agreed to participate. However, when researchers got people to agree that they were interested in participating before telling them what time the study would take place, more than half (56 percent) agreed to participate. But would more people really show up for the study after having had a chance to consider their decision? Saying yes on the phone is one thing. But if people actually get out of bed in the morning to come to a study, then they really must have been persuaded. Cialdini and colleagues found that giving a low initial cost estimate was even more effective when it came to changing people's actual behavior. When researchers forthrightly told people about the 7 A.M. study time, less than a quarter (only 24 percent) actually showed up for the study. However, when researchers got people to agree that they were interested before telling them about the early starting time, more than half (53 percent) showed up on time. Almost all of those who agreed to participate actually appeared. Once we commit in even a small way to participating in a project, we are unlikely to drop out, even if the cost of continuing increases dramatically along the way.

MENTIONING A LITTLE TO GET A LOT

Charitable organizations that solicit contributions face an interesting dilemma. If they ask for large amounts of money from people, then more people will say no. However, if solicitors ask for small amounts, more people will say yes, but rarely will large amounts be given. How can solicitors convince as many people as possible to contribute without decreasing the average amount that each person gives?

Cialdini and Schroeder (1976) found a solution to the problem faced by charitable organizations that required adding only five words to the end of a request for a contribution: "Even a penny will help." In their study, research assistants solicited funds for the American Cancer Society. All used a standard request for funds: "Would you be willing to help by giving a donation?" However, half the research assistants added the sentence "Even a penny will help." Almost twice as many people contributed when they were told that even a penny would help. More surprisingly, their contributions were no smaller than the contributions given by those who were not told that a penny would help. Researchers concluded that mentioning the penny legitimized a small donation, making it more difficult for people to say no. However, because the amount suggested—a penny—was so small, people did not use it to estimate the size of a reasonable donation.

WHO WILL HELP YOU?

Most people realize that if you want people to help you, it is good to help them. The practice of giving and receiving gifts is universal in human culture. From a very young age, we learn to give things to people in the hope that we will get something else in return. We have no guarantee that the people we give gifts to will give us gifts in return, or give us gifts of equal value. However, we are all taught that giving gifts is a good thing and that we should not keep too close an account of who gives us what in return. The idea is that by giving gifts we start to form lasting relationships with people. For example, in my large extended family, it would not be practical for everyone to give everyone else a Christmas present. We would all be broke and spend the whole year shopping. Instead, we draw names and everyone gives one other person a gift. I give my aunt a scarf. My nephew gives me a sweater. Almost no one gets a gift from the person to whom she or he gave one. Nonetheless, gift giving works

to maintain good relationships among people. Although I do not see my relatives often, I feel comfortable asking for help from my aunt or nephew when I need it. A good way to persuade people to help you is to start by giving them a gift, doing them a favor, providing some small service.

Salespeople and charitable organizations know something more surprising about giving gifts and doing favors. Another good way to persuade people to help you in the future is to get them to do you a small favor first. This is the opposite of how we are taught the social world works. We grow up thinking that we can expect about as much help from other people as we are willing to give in return. If someone does us a favor, then that person should be less likely to do us another favor right away. It is as if we have withdrawn some of our credit in the goodwill bank account. We will not be eligible for another favor until we make a deposit by helping someone else. But there are good social psychological reasons to continue helping someone we have already helped.

Recall from a previous section that once people commit to a project, they are likely to continue with it although the cost involved inches steadily upward. We feel the same way about people, but to a greater degree. It is important to us to keep and maintain our personal relationships. So once we have committed to helping a person, we are likely to agree to help the next time we are asked. We will continue to help even though the second favor requested of us is bigger than the first. Have you noticed that if you send a small donation to a charitable organization, they will send you requests for more money every couple of months? The more money that you give, the bigger and more frequent are the requests that follow. Aren't charities worried that they will wear out donors with repeated, escalating requests for money? Apparently not.

Freedman and Fraser (1966) showed that by getting a person to do you a small favor first, you increase the chance that she will do you a bigger favor later. To test this surprising idea, researchers contacted people by telephone. Researchers wanted to find out how many people would agree to a big favor that researchers would ask of them. Researchers requested that they be allowed to enter people's homes and for several hours catalog their personal belongings. Most people would be hesitant to grant such a request over the phone. Half the people contacted were first asked for a small favor. Researchers asked people

merely to answer a few questions for a consumer survey. Then, three days later, researchers called back with the big request. The rest of the people in the survey were only asked if they would agree to the big favor, allowing researchers to come to their homes and make a list of their possessions. Would more people agree to let researchers come into their houses after they had first agreed to the small favor of answering a few survey questions?

Getting people to agree to doing a small favor first had a major effect (Freedman and Fraser 1966). When people were first asked to answer a few survey questions, more than half (53 percent) later agreed to let researchers come into their homes. (Imagine how successful you would be if you called strangers and asked if you could come over and go through their stuff for a couple of hours!) In contrast, when only the large request was made, just 28 percent, a little more than a quarter, agreed to let researchers come into their homes. By asking for a small favor first, researchers nearly doubled the percentage of people who would agree to grant their major request.

The lesson is clear. If you will need someone's help in the future, get that person to help you in small ways now, thus increasing the likelihood of agreement to an important request later. Note that as with the low initial bid technique of the previous section, getting people to do you a small favor requires no pressure. Persuasion starts to occur before a request is ever made. The more people help you, the more people will want to continue helping you. They become committed to your success.

The technique of gaining people's commitment by getting them to do you a favor can work for customers as well as salespeople. The one time in my life where it seemed that I got an especially good deal on a used car is an example. I had moved back to California from Idaho. I was working, selling furniture, but I no longer needed the truck that I had used to deliver waterbeds and hot tubs. I had decided to go back to school and needed a reliable car. A few blocks from the furniture store where I worked was a car lot where a national car rental company sold the rental cars to the public after they were a couple of years old. One day, as I drove by the lot, a Mustang convertible caught my eye. What better car to drive to college in California? After driving by that car several days in a row, I wanted it badly. I stopped by the lot after work to find out more about the car. With tax and license, the total price would be a little over $9,000. The salesperson told me that I would have to get my own financing. Also, the company had a strict "one-price" policy. Car prices were not negotiable. The best price for each car was plainly marked on it. No haggling. While this seems a fair way to sell cars, it leaves the dealer firmly in control of the ultimate price that customers pay. I decided to try a little social psychology to get the price down.

I returned to the car lot prepared to buy the car. Nonetheless, I let the salesperson go through his entire sales routine. I drove the car a second time. I let him tell me at length about the company's one-price policy that was such a benefit for customers because it relieved them of the anxiety of negotiating. We practiced putting the convertible top up and down. I asked him to show me how to operate everything on the car. I asked him to help me make sure that everything worked. In social psychological terms, I was gaining his commitment to sell me that car. Every time I asked him to help me with something, to show me something, he became a little more committed to completing the sale. The only thing salespeople have to work with is their time. While he was spending time with me, he could not work with anyone else. The more time he spent with me, the more important it was to him that our meeting result in a successful sale.

Eventually he suggested that we go to his desk to "get some information" from me. He was getting impatient. At his desk, we talked about price again. He repeated the company's no-exceptions one-price policy. No negotiating. I told him that I had already arranged a loan and that the price seemed reasonable. However, $9,000 was more than I was prepared to pay. Instead, I gave him a cashier's check for $8,000 and asked him to sell me the car for that amount. He laughed a little nervously at that point. He knew I was serious—$8,000 is a lot of money and a cashier's check has more impact than a personal check. He told me that he could not do it. It was against company policy to lower the price. I paused for what seemed like a long time, then said, "OK, let's go look at the car again." More time commitment from the salesperson.

I had already noticed a small tear in the outer shell of the convertible top, perhaps half an inch long. It seemed minor but might get worse. I pointed it out to the salesperson and asked how much a new convertible top would cost. He said that he did not know. I smiled and said, "Why don't we find out?" Back at his desk, I

went through the yellow pages and asked him to call convertible top repair shops. More commitment; he was doing me a favor. We eventually agreed that a new convertible top would cost about $1,200 dollars. I suggested that we subtract the price of a new top from the price of the car and complete the sale. He said that he couldn't do that. I asked him what he could do. He said he would have to find out. Would he do that for me, please? More commitment. I told him that I was taking my new girlfriend to lunch and would be back in an hour or two.

The salesperson had spent a substantial amount of his working day with me. He had nothing to show for it yet. He was committed. When my girlfriend and I got back from lunch, the salesperson agreed to drop the "nonnegotiable" price by $500. After a little more bargaining, I wrote him a personal check for about $150 to add to the cashier's check of $8,000 that I had already given him. I had saved about $1,000. By getting him to help me repeatedly in small ways, I gained his commitment to help me in a bigger way. When I asked him to help me get the price I wanted, he found it difficult to refuse. As for the tear in the convertible top, a tube of vinyl repair goo fixed it nicely. Many good things got started that day. I drove to college with the top down and made it to graduation. Then I married my girlfriend.

TO PERSUADE THEM, LET THEM PERSUADE YOU

Cialdini, Green, and Rusch (1992) put an interesting twist on the idea that people want to help people who have helped them. Because people feel the need to reciprocate, researchers proposed that if someone has persuaded you to do something in the past, then that person will be easier for you to persuade to do something in the future. Salespeople experience the situation often. When I sold furniture to a person in business, I felt obligated to use their services as well. When a family that owned a dry cleaners brought both dining room and living room furniture from me, I started taking my clothes to their cleaners, although it required driving across town.

Cialdini and colleagues (1992) proposed that a person would be persuaded more easily by someone who had yielded to her arguments on some unrelated topic. That is, once a person has persuaded you of something, that person will feel the need to reciprocate, return the favor, by letting you persuade her on some other issue. Re-

searchers first asked people to give their opinions about the minimum drinking age. For half the people in the study, a research assistant at first disagreed but then admitted to bring convinced by their arguments. For the rest of the people in the study, the research assistant remained unconvinced by their arguments. Then in the second part of the study, the research assistant's opinions about whether to require comprehensive exams in college were given to people. Researchers wanted to find out if people would agree more with the researcher after the researcher had agreed with them about the drinking age issue.

After the research assistant was persuaded by their arguments, people were more likely to be persuaded by the research assistant on a different topic. Cialdini et al. (1992) were correct. Researchers asked people to estimate how much their attitude had changed after listening to the research assistant's arguments. When the research assistant had agreed with people's opinions on the earlier topic, people reported that on average their attitudes had been changed 27 percent by the research assistant. That is, the research assistant's brief statement of her or his opinions had been highly persuasive. However, when the research assistant had been unconvinced by people's opinions on an earlier topic, people reported that on average their attitudes had been changed only 6 percent by the research assistant.

To get people to agree with you, first agree with them. The implications go well beyond any individual negotiations. These research results suggest a personal style that will increase your success in social life. Most arguments people get into are silly because the outcome doesn't matter very much. But those minor disagreements set the stage for major conflict when an important issue does arise. When I was in high school I loved to argue. I practiced and studied ways to construct a sound argument. I believed that logic would prevail. It was important for me to be right and for people to acknowledge that I was right. An implication that I had not considered was that by acknowledging I was right, people would be admitting that they were wrong. People do not like to admit that they are wrong.

For several years I argued every chance I got. It puzzled me, however, that no matter how brilliant my argument, the people I argued with never seemed to be convinced. After a particularly heated argument, I would review it in my mind for days to make sure I had been right. Yet later I would find that the person I had argued with remained unconvinced. My logic was sound enough but my social psychology was weak. I had ignored the importance of reciprocity in human relationships. To convince somebody of something, it helps to let that person convince you of something else first. And because the outcome of most arguments doesn't matter very much, it pays to agree with other people most of the time. Save your arguments for situations where the outcome is truly important to you. Agree with people unless you have a good reason not to. Let them convince you. That was exactly the opposite of the way I had approached my relationships with people. I wanted to show people that I was right. So I argued about everything. But people were not convinced. A better way to approach the people in your life is to agree with them as much as possible. Show them how right they are. Then, when an issue comes up that is very important to you, you will be more likely to convince them that on this rare but important occasion, you might be right.

STATUS AS THE MOST SUBTLE WAY TO PERSUADE

Most of this chapter has described effective, subtle, and sometimes devious techniques that salespeople and organizations use to persuade people. You have seen how you can benefit from using similar techniques when you need to persuade someone to help you.... Some people do not seem to need such techniques to persuade others. The doctor merely tells you that an operation is necessary and you agree to let her remove part of your body. Why doesn't your doctor need the subtle techniques of persuasion commonly used by salespeople?

The answer is *status*. Your status is your standing within a group based on your prestige, the respect that other group members give you. Doctors have high status in our society. They are respected, honored. The magic of high status is that people will try to find out what it is you want them to do, and do it for you, without your ever having to make a request. I noticed myself doing this just last week. By watching my diet and starting to exercise, I recently lost most of the excess weight I had carried around for years. I have more energy and feel healthier. Then last week it occurred to me that I should go to my doctor for the first time in years to get a physical examination. Why should I want to go to the doctor now that I feel great? I usually avoid going when I am sick. What I really wanted was my doctor's approval. I wanted the doctor to tell me what a good job I had done getting rid of that extra body fat. Her approval is important to me because of her high status. My doctor never told me I should lose weight, although she did hint last time that a little exercise would help. However, I thought my doctor would approve if I lost weight. Thus the opinion I expected her to have influenced my behavior without her having to express that opinion directly. When people have high status, their opinions count.

Techniques of persuasion can be highly effective in specific situations, but to wield real influence, a person needs high status....

FURTHER READING

Of General Interest

Bacharach, S. B., Lawler, E. J. (1984). *Bargaining*. San Francisco: Jossey-Bass.

Cialdini, R. B. (1993). *Influence: Science and practice*. New York: HarperCollins.

Damasio, A. R. (1994). *Descarte's error: Emotion, reason, and the human brain*. New York: Grosset/Putnam.

Pfeffer, J. (1992). *Managing with power: Politics and influence in organizations*. Boston: Harvard Business School Press.

Recent and Technical Issues

Axsom, D., Yates, S., & Chaiken, S. (1987). Audience response as a heuristic cue in persuasion. *Journal of Personality and Social Psychology, 53,* 30–40.

Fleming, J. H., Darley, J. M., Hilton, J. L., & Kojetin, B. A. (1990.) Multiple audience problem: A strategic communication perspective on social perception. *Journal of Personality and Social Psychology, 58,* 593–609.

Frey, K. P., & Eagly, A. H. (1993). Vividness can undermine the persuasiveness of messages. *Journal of Personality and Social Psychology, 65,* 32–44.

Gorassini, D. R., Olson, J. M. (1995). Does self-perception change explain the foot-in-the-door effect? *Journal of Personality and Social Psychology, 69,* 91–105.

Kruglanski, A., Webster, D. M., & Klem, A. (1993). Motivated resistance and openness to persuasion in the presence or absence of prior information. *Journal of Personality and Social Psychology, 65,* 861–876.

Petty, R. E., Schumann, D. W., Richman, S. A., & Strathman, A. J. (1993). Positive mood and persuasion: Different roles for affect under high- and low-elaboration conditions. *Journal of Personality and Social Psychology, 64,* 5–20.

Vorauer, J. D., & Miller, D. T. (1997). Failure to recognize the effect of implicit social influence on the presentation of self. *Journal of Personality and Social Psychology, 73,* 281–295.

Zarnoth, P., & Sniezek, J. A. (1997). The social influence of confidence in group decision making. *Journal of Experimental Social Psychology, 33,* 345–366.

UNIT 6
Social Relationships

Unit Selections

Key Points to Consider

- What factors make people first take notice of one another? After initial impressions are formed, what other factors lead people to friendships? Do you think the foundation for all friendships is the same? For example, do you think similarity is the leading factor in friendship formation?

- Why do friendships break up? Does life just lead people on different paths or do you think that conflict is the major source for termination of friendships? Can men be friends with women and vice versa? What types of friendships do you think are best—same-sex or opposite-sex?

- What is shyness? Have you ever felt shy? Under what circumstances do you think most people experience interpersonal anxiety? Does shyness affect only interpersonal behaviors (between two or three individuals) or does it also affect public behaviors? Are there extreme forms of shyness? What is social anxiety disorder? Why is it considered a disorder? Are there any treatments for it?

- How has the Internet changed how friendships and romantic relationships develop? Do you think the internet is the most common place to find new acquaintances? How else do people meet strangers who become friends or lovers? Do you think using the Internet to establish relationships is risky? How so? Have you surfed the Internet in search of friends; what has been your experience?

- What exactly is physical attractiveness? What makes one person more attractive than another? Does attractiveness vary by culture? By gender? Does evolution play a role in what we deem attractive? How and why are attractive people more successful than unattractive people?

- How are committed or romantic relationships such as marriage different from friendships? How are they similar? Why do some marriages end while others thrive? Does marriage or couples counseling work? Would you ever go for couples counseling if your significant other requested you to? Why or why not?

 **Links: www.dushkin.com/online/**
These sites are annotated in the World Wide Web pages.

American Association of University Women
http://www.aauw.org

Coalition for Marriage, Family, and Couples Education
http://www.smartmarriages.com

GLAAD: Gay and Lesbian Alliance Against Defamation
http://www.glaad.org

The Kinsey Institute for Reasearch in Sex, Gender, and Reproduction
http://www.indiana.edu/~kinsey/

Marriage and Family Therapy
http://www.aamft.org/index_nm.asp

The National Organization for Women (NOW) Home Page
http://www.now.org

The Society for the Scientific Study of Sexuality
http://www.ssc.wisc.edu/ssss/

As children, Amanda and Yolanda were attracted to each other because their names rhymed. Not only did they attend the same elementary school, but they soon discovered that their interests were the same. Both girls were tomboys. Amanda loved animals and so, too, did Yolanda.

In high school, although the girls often found themselves in different classes, they still spent much of their free time together—so much that both of their mothers teased them about being twins. The two young women agreed that they ought to attend the same college and be roommates. Other students at the high school could not help but notice their unique bond and soon referred to them as the "Anda" twins.

In their junior year of high school, Yolanda and Amanda became interested in and attracted to the same new student, a young man named Ty. At first, Ty relished in the attention that the women bestowed on him. "And why not?," he mused to himself. "I'm good-looking, smart, and athletic." Ty quickly became one of the most popular boys at the school.

Amanda and Yolanda soon found themselves skirmishing over Ty. Amanda wanted to sit next to him at lunch, but so, too, did Yolanda. Amanda claimed that Ty invited her to watch him play basketball, and Yolanda became jealous and confronted Ty. On the other hand, Yolanda waited in the library for Ty to appear, and they would sit together. Upon discovering them, Amanda would storm out of the library.

The rivalry between the girls became so intense that their grades suffered. Other students began to ridicule them. Ty soon felt the sting of other students' scorn and decided to forego his friendship with Amanda and Yolanda. Of course, Yolanda and Amanda blamed each other for Ty's disinterest. In self-defense, Ty soon started dating an entirely different young woman, Sara, who was not friends with either of the "Anda" twins.

The friendship between Amanda and Yolanda never repaired itself. Each of them applied to and was accepted at different universities so went their separate ways. Years later at their tenth high school reunion, Yolanda and Amanda were still not speaking to one another. And what of Ty? He and Sara attended the reunion as a happily married couple.

How and why do people become friends or lovers? What types of people are attracted to one another whether the same or opposite sex? These questions and others relate to social relationships—the topic of this unit.

The unit contains two subunits—one on interpersonal relationships such as friendships and the second on intimate relationships such as marriage. We will commence with the topic of interpersonal relationships.

In "Beyond Shyness and Stage Fright: Social Anxiety Disorder," details about social anxiety disorder are revealed. Shyness is one thing; social anxiety disorder is another. *Social anxiety disorder* is more than temerity about interacting with others. It can dramatically alter the sufferer's life. Fortunately, the disorder is treatable.

In a companion article, "Linking Up Online," author Rebecca Clay discusses loneliness—a likely companion of shyness. Lonely individuals feel that their need to be with others is unmet. Some social psychologists have suggested that the Internet offers intriguing opportunities to interact with others. Social psychologists are examining communities established solely on the Internet in chat rooms and elsewhere.

Our attention next turns to intimate and romantic relationships such as dating and marriage. Three articles disclose interesting information on close relationships.

The first article is entitled "Isn't She Lovely?" by Brad Lemley. Lemley discusses the power of beauty over observers. Beautiful and handsome people tend to be perceived as superior to everyone else. What makes us perceive someone is attractive or unattractive forms the heart of this article.

As mentioned above, some individuals are using the internet to meet others. The internet has burgeoned with people looking not only for friendship but also for dates and mates. This web-wide universe is changing how people meet, date, and find love, according to Karen Gold, author of the next article.

This unit concludes with one additional article on intimate relationships. Marriage, or at least lifetime commitment to another, is the single most intimate relationship of all. Close relationships like marriage, however, can sour. Romantic attraction can and does elicit strong emotions – both positive and negative. In "The Marriage Savers," Richard Corliss and Sonja Steptoe present information about couples therapy and research on its effectiveness.

Beyond shyness and stage fright:
Social anxiety disorder

Irrational fear of personal rejection constricts and damages lives, but it can be dispelled with treatment.

Nearly half of Americans describe themselves as shy, and most of us can be nervous when we have to face an audience. But for a surprisingly large number of people, these problems are more than an inconvenience. What would otherwise be normal reticence or stage fright becomes a disorder when the resulting symptoms make individuals miserable or seriously interfere with their work, friendships, and family life. This crippling dread of certain personal encounters and social situations is called social anxiety disorder or social phobia, and it's increasingly understood to be a treatable condition.

There are two kinds. Specific social anxiety, often called performance anxiety, arises in only a few situations. It is a serious matter mainly for people whose work requires them to perform in public. Generalized social anxiety occurs in a wide variety of settings and has pervasive effects on a person's life. People with this disorder may drop out of school because they fear being called on in class. They don't get the jobs they deserve because they are afraid of interviews. They may be reluctant to use a public restroom or even eat in a restaurant or write in the presence of others. They hate being introduced to new people or speaking to strangers. They are slow to make friends and are likely to marry and start families late, if at all.

Anxiety usually has physical symptoms that may include a racing heart, a dry mouth, a shaky voice, blushing, trembling, sweating, and nausea. In specific social anxiety, fear that people will notice these symptoms may impair performance, causing embarrassment that justifies avoiding the situation. The pervasive discomfort and embarrassment of generalized social anxiety are often contagious. Others become ill-at-ease, and the expectation of being rejected becomes a self-fulfilling prophecy, justifying further social withdrawal.

In children, social anxiety disorder is distressing or incapacitating shyness that lasts for six months or more. These children fear strangers—other children as well as adults—at an age when it is no longer normal. They may be anxious about reading aloud, writing on a blackboard, starting a conversation, or attending a birthday party. They cling to their parents and may refuse to go to school. Some will talk only to family and a few close friends—a condition known as elective mutism.

Generalized social anxiety resembles the personality disorder called avoidant personality. People with this disorder strike others as painfully shy. They are timid, uneasy, and self-conscious. They misinterpret neutral or friendly reactions as hostile, are easily intimidated by criticism, and constantly fear saying something foolish or inappropriate. They may regard themselves as personally unattractive or inferior.

They need to be sure of being liked before they will get close to anyone, and therefore rarely allow themselves to get close or be liked. Often they try to suppress all feeling and seem outwardly indifferent. They adopt a self-defeating policy of rejecting before they can be rejected—and it works because their defensiveness makes others uncomfortable and impatient.

Some believe that avoidant personality is only another way of describing a particularly severe case of generalized social anxiety. Others think it has a broader scope. Avoidant personalities tend to fear not just social situations but novelty of any kind. They exaggerate the risks of doing anything outside their usual routine.

Prevalence

Social anxiety disorder is common. According to the National Comorbidity Survey, 13% of the adult population is afflicted at some time in their lives, and 8% at any given time—including 10%-20% of those seen in clinics for anxiety disorders. About three quarters of these people are suffering from generalized social anxiety. It's thought to be more common in women, but men are more likely to seek help for it.

People with social anxiety disorder have a high rate of other anxiety disorders, including generalized anxiety disorder (see Harvard Mental Health Letter, January 2003), panic disorder (see Harvard Mental Health Letter, March 2001), and specific phobias. Children with social anxiety disorder have an especially high rate of phobias and separation anxiety and little tolerance for stress of any kind. Adults with the disorder are seven times more likely than average to become depressed, 13 times more likely to attempt suicide, and twice as likely to develop alcohol dependence. About 20% of people treated for alcohol disorders and 30% of those with panic attacks also have social anxiety disorder. Depression, alcoholism, and panic attacks usually appear after social anxiety and may be the result of it.

Symptoms of social anxiety disorder

- You fear being in certain situations that may expose you to embarrassing and humiliating scrutiny and judgment.
- In these situations you are likely to show symptoms of anxiety, which may include freezing, panic, and shrinking back.
- You know (if you are an adult) that your fears are unreasonable and excessive.
- Nevertheless, you avoid these situations or endure them under stress.
- The problem seriously interferes with your work or social life or causes severe distress.
- The social anxiety is not caused by a medication or other drug, and it is not caused by the symptoms of a medical disorder (such as stuttering, Parkinson's disease, or a skin condition).
- The symptoms are not explained by any other psychiatric disorder.

Adapted from the American Psychiatric Association's Diagnostic and Statistical Manual, Fourth Edition.

Roots

Fear of social rejection or disapproval is an evolutionary survival mechanism, as normal as fear of heights or darkness. In a small band of hunter-gatherers, exclusion by the group for any reason could be lethal. It's less clear why this normal wariness and reserve becomes maladaptive.

Inherited temperament is almost certainly a large part of the explanation. The parents of people with social anxiety disorder have a high rate of anxiety disorders, and adoption studies show that this connection is genetic. Psychological experiments show that certain children are biologically vulnerable to anxious apprehension. About 15% of infants and young children are "behaviorally inhibited." As early as four months of age, they show a tendency to cry and shrink back when faced with new situations and people. When strangers approach, their hearts beat faster and their pupils dilate—signs of a stress response.

These responses persist into adulthood, as indicated by a study in which 22-year-olds were given PET (positron emission tomography) scans while they looked at the faces of strangers. In those classified as behaviorally inhibited at age two, the amygdala, a center of fear conditioning, showed much greater activity. In people judged to be extroverted as children, the amygdala remained relatively quiet.

Chronic fearfulness in both monkeys and humans is associated with irregularities in the activity of the neurotransmitters dopamine and serotonin and with high levels of corticotropin releasing factor, a key element of the stress response. A recent study shows that social withdrawal in six-month-old children accompanies high activity on the right side of the prefrontal cortex and high levels of the stress hormone cortisol.

But social anxiety is not all genetic or biological. A study of children who avoided social contact at age two found that only 40% were still fearful at age four. We don't know which environmental influences make a difference, but some believe it depends on the quality of affection a child gets. Mice of a strain genetically designed to be fearful showed less behavioral inhibition when they were licked and groomed often by foster mothers of another, more extroverted strain. The feelings of inadequacy that provoke social anxiety could result from childhood physical and sexual abuse or from subtler deficiencies in parenting. Anxious parents, in particular, may seem both overprotective and insufficiently affectionate—or simply unable to provide the extra encouragement and special coaching needed by a child who is temperamentally inhibited.

As always, though, these situations are subject to interpretation. Memories of upbringing may be distorted. Parents trying desperately to satisfy the needs of highly anxious children may seem alternately smothering and neglectful as they shift between indulgence and exasperation. People who blame their performance anxiety on a traumatically embarrassing experience may be mistaking the first time the symptom appeared for its cause.

Looking for help

Social anxiety disorder received little attention 10 or 20 years ago. Today there are many support groups, and the Anxiety Disorders Association of America lists hundreds of therapists who provide treatment. Still, many people with the disorder get little or no help. They would have to meet new people and confront authority figures—among their greatest fears. And they may irrationally anticipate that their complaints will be regarded as trivial and received with disdain—another form of social rejection.

In one survey, only 5% of people with social anxiety disorder said they had sought mental health services for the problem, and only 20% had sought professional help for any mental health or emotional problem. In another study, only 30% of parents of a child with social anxiety disorder had discussed it with a pediatrician. People are more likely to look for professional help when they develop a related condition, such as depression, alcoholism, or panic attacks—and even then, the underlying social anxiety may not be noticed. But if the problem can be brought to light, controlled studies show that cognitive behavioral therapy and medications are effective.

Psychosocial treatment

According to behavioral theory, anxiety disorders result from stimulus-response associations that do not reflect real threats. Behavioral therapists try to correct these associations and build confidence by exposing the patient to the feared situations until he or she becomes habituated.

Exposure proceeds in small steps, just as in the treatment of phobias. A person with acrophobia accommodates to gradually increasing heights, a person with social anxiety disorder to increasingly more frightening social situations. For example, the patient might start by saying, "Hello," and go on to add the name of the person being addressed. Homework assignments might include commenting on the weather to a stranger in the supermarket, greeting 10 people at an office party, starting a conversation with a person of the opposite sex, eating or drinking in front of others, giving and receiving compliments, revealing personal information, and expressing opinions. Treatment for specific social anxiety may require a performance before a small audience. The whole process—and especially the physical symptoms—can be eased by training in deep breathing and muscle relaxation.

Fear of being humiliated, embarrassed, and rejected does not always go away with simple exposure. Patients may also need to free themselves of unrealistic performance standards and unlearn their catastrophic misinterpretations of social situations. Everyone is not constantly watching and judging them. People don't notice their anxiety and minor mistakes, or don't care. Only one person out of a hundred yawned. That woman did not leave the room because she disliked the person or what he or she was doing or saying; she simply had to go to the bathroom. That man is writing in the back of the room not because he is bored but because he is making a note, perhaps a question or some advice or suggestions. Cognitive therapy helps patients with social anxiety disorder to recognize and resist the many varieties of self-defeating thinking.

While their fears are being relieved and their thoughts corrected, some patients may also need social skills training because they have never learned how close to stand, when to make eye contact, what to talk about and when, and how to handle pauses in conversation. The therapist helps by providing a model and rehearsing with the patient.

Cognitive and behavioral methods can be used in individual therapy, but they are sometimes more effective in groups, which provide a built-in social situation in which members can provide mutual advice and comfort, make friends, and try out new behaviors. The difficulty is getting these patients to leave their fears behind long enough to join a group.

Medications

Several kinds of drugs have been found effective in the treatment of social anxiety. Because of their relatively mild side effects, selective serotonin reuptake inhibitors (SSRIs) are usually the first choice. The FDA has specifically approved paroxetine (Paxil) and sertraline (Zoloft), but others should be effective as well. The most common side effects are nausea, headache, agitation, and sexual problems. SSRIs (and some other antidepressants) are also helpful for the other anxiety disorders and the depression that often accompany social anxiety disorder. Relief from social anxiety may take 2–3 months or more and often requires higher doses than those used for depression.

MAO inhibitors are also highly effective for social anxiety disorder. But these drugs—the most widely used is phenelzine (Nardil)—have more serious side effects, including a possible sudden rise in blood pressure when taken in combination with certain foods. Other possible side effects are weight gain, dizziness, and insomnia (see Harvard Mental Health Letter, September 2003).

The anti-anxiety drugs buspirone (BuSpar), clonazepam (Klonopin), and alprazolam (Xanax) may also be used, either alone or in combination with an SSRI. Because they work immediately, they can serve to reduce anxiety while patient and therapist wait for an antidepressant or cognitive behavioral therapy to take effect. The risks of alprazolam and clonazepam include hangover grogginess, drowsiness, memory problems, and a withdrawal reaction that requires a gradual reduction of the dose. In some recent research the anticonvulsant gabapentin (Neurontin) has been found effective for social anxiety. Its chief side effects are dizziness and dry mouth.

Beta-adrenergic blockers such as propranolol (Inderal) are a popular remedy for performance anxiety. Taken an hour before a public lecture or stage performance, they ease the mind by suppressing the physical symptoms of anxiety. Beta blockers should not be used by people with diabetes, asthma, or a slow heart rate.

For the future

Scientific study of social anxiety disorder has barely begun. Except for the work on behavioral inhibition, little is known about the origins of the disorder, and almost nothing about how to prevent it. More brain imaging and neurotransmitter research may help, especially in distinguishing between the biological characteristics associated with vulnerability to social anxiety disorder and those associated with the symptoms themselves.

We also need to learn much more about treatments. Which approaches are best for specific as opposed to generalized social anxiety? Little is known about the treatment of social anxiety disorder in children and adolescents. Long-term research is rare. Is cognitive behavioral therapy more effective than drugs in the long run? When should drug treatment stop? We have made great progress in understanding that severe social anxiety is not just a fate to be endured, but we have far to go in helping people escape that fate.

References

Ballenger JC, et al. "Consensus Statement on Social Anxiety Disorder from the International Consensus Group on Depression and Anxiety," *Journal of Clinical Psychiatry* (1998): Vol. 59, Suppl. 17, pp. 54–60.

Beidel DC, et al. *Shy Children, Phobic Adults: Nature and Treatment of Social Phobia.* American Psychological Association, 1998.

Rettew DC, "Avoidant Personality Disorder, Generalized Social Phobia, and Shyness: Putting the Personality Back into Personality Disorders," *Harvard Review of Psychiatry* (December 2000): Vol. 8, No. 6, pp. 283–97.

Schmidt LA, et al., eds. *Extreme Fear, Shyness and Social Phobia: Origins, Biological Mechanisms, and Clinical Outcomes.* Oxford University Press, 1999.

Schneier FR, ed. "Social Anxiety Disorder," Psychiatric Clinics of North America (December 2001): Vol. 24, No. 4.

Article 18

Linking up Online

Is the Internet enhancing interpersonal connections or leading to greater social isolation?

REBECCA A. CLAY

Leslie, a graduate student in psychology at a Midwestern university, couldn't find anyone she was interested in dating. Then she placed a personal ad on a Web site for singles. Not long after, she received an e-mail that changed her life. Although she and her correspondent had completely different backgrounds—he didn't have a college degree, for instance—they quickly discovered they shared interests and values.

Today they're in love. "If you looked at how different our backgrounds were, nobody would ever have matched us up," says Leslie. "Even though we lived in the same town, we never would have met except through the Internet." As Leslie's story illustrates, e-mail and other Internet technologies are changing friendship and romance, both online and in the real world. But while Leslie's story has a happy ending, others do not. Some confront disappointment when they come face to face with online correspondents; others use cyber-affairs to avoid working through problems with their real-life partners.

No one knows for sure what the long-term effects of forming and developing Internet relationships will be. Does using this technology ultimately enhance interpersonal connection or lead to greater social isolation? And is online sexuality pathological or healthy?

With the number of Americans online growing every day, these questions have become urgent.

"As we integrate Internet use into our culture, we've got to maximize its potential benefits and mitigate any possible adverse consequences," says Russ Newman, PhD, JD, executive director for professional practice at APA. "If we just proceed blindly down the Internet road, we could find ourselves in 10 or 20 years having radically changed the way people relate to each other and realizing we're stuck with those changes. As experts in behavior and relationships, psychologists have an important role to play in making sure that doesn't happen."

Isolation or connection?

Psychologists are already hard at work studying the Internet's effects. So far, their findings have been mixed.

The first study to specifically examine the Internet's impact on emotional well-being was the widely publicized 1998 study by Robert Kraut, PhD, Sara Kiesler, PhD, and colleagues at Carnegie Mellon University's Human Computer Interaction Institute. Their "HomeNet" project focused on 169 individuals in 93 Pittsburgh families recruited from schools and community groups as they began using the Internet. Logging programs recorded Internet use by individual family members, who assessed their own well-being and social involvement at the project's beginning, one year later and two years later.

To the researchers' surprise, they discovered that greater use of the Internet resulted in small but statistically significant increases in depression and loneliness and decreases in social engagement. Internet users, the researchers hypothesized in their *American Psychologist* report (No. 53, p. 1017–1031), were replacing the intimate, supportive relationships of real life with shallower relationships online.

The findings set off a firestorm. Critics pointed to the study's lack of random selection and a control group, which the researchers say they couldn't afford. Others noted the participants had a high degree of social connectedness to begin with and simply moved closer to the mean. Not so, say the researchers. Such an explanation, they say, doesn't address the fact that individuals with high use experienced greater declines and that those who were depressed or lonely didn't start using the Internet more.

A recent study conducted on behalf of the Stanford Institute for the Quantitative Study of Society seems to corroborate the "HomeNet" findings, although the project focused on the Internet's societal rather than psychological impact.

In the study, a company called Inter-Survey provided Internet access and equipment that allows users to go online via their televisions to a nationally representative sample of 2,689 households containing both Internet users and nonusers. An Internet-based survey revealed that 55 percent of the 4,113 adults in these households used the Internet. Of these, about a third spent more than five hours a week online.

About a quarter of these regular Internet users reported that their time online had reduced the amount of time they spent interacting with family and friends in person and on the phone. Eight percent said they spent less time attending social events.

Like the Carnegie Mellon study, these preliminary results have attracted controversy. Some critics point to research that conflicts with these negative findings. Others note that Internet users may simply find online relationships more rewarding than those available in their offline lives. Even one of the study's authors admits that Internet use had some positive benefits, with the most enthusiastic Internet users also reporting less time watching television and caught in traffic.

"There's a big gap in the research," says Linda A. Jackson, PhD, a psychology professor at Michigan State University in East Lansing.

Although the Carnegie Mellon study is the only one that has systematically tracked Internet use via computer-logging, she says, several surveys and ethnographic studies have suggested that Internet use actually enhances people's well-being and social contacts.

To help answer the question, Jackson is now trying to replicate the HomeNet study. With funding from the National Science Foundation, she is engaged in a pilot study that will use computer-logging to track the psychosocial effects of 18 months of Internet use on 45 African-American families and 45 white families.

Other researchers already have evidence that counters what they call the "apocalyptic" claims the HomeNet study and similar research have aroused.

Research scientist Katelyn Y.A. McKenna, PhD, and professor John A. Bargh, PhD, of New York University's psychology department compare the Internet's bad press to the fear of new technology that once prompted people to resist telephones in the belief that people could eavesdrop on their homes even with the phone on the hook.

McKenna and Bargh have conducted research that provides a very different picture of the Internet's impact on relationships. In a manuscript submitted for publication, they describe a recent study that found people were indeed using the Internet to form close relationships. Using data from 568 surveys from participants in randomly selected news groups, they discovered that the Internet provided a safe way for socially anxious and lonely people to form and maintain relationships. Of critical importance was their ability to express what they considered their real selves online.

These are not just virtual relationships, the researchers emphasize. Fifty-four percent of respondents later met their Internet friends face to face. Sixty-three percent had talked on the phone. And these relationships lasted. A two-year follow-up study revealed that 57 percent of the relationships formed online had not only continued but actually increased in intimacy.

Romantic relationships fared particularly well, says McKenna. Seventy percent of the romantic relationships formed online still existed at the two-year follow-up. Some participants had even married. These results are in marked contrast to the fate of couples who meet in a more traditional manner, says McKenna, pointing to a study that found that more than half of romantic relationships dissolve after two years.

"Online relationships begin on the basis of similar interests and values," says McKenna. "They allow people to bypass physical appearance and other 'gating' mechanisms that might prevent them from even giving the other person the time of day in real life."

Arguing that the Carnegie Mellon team's results held true only for the teen-agers in the group, McKenna and Bargh emphasize the importance of not making blanket statements.

"For some people, the Internet can be a great medium for making connections, widening their social circles and enriching their lives," says McKenna, citing single working mothers and the elderly as examples. "For others, it may be problematic."

For communications expert Judee K. Burgoon, PhD, conflicting findings like these underline the fact that the Internet's effect on relationships isn't inherently good or bad.

"You can't give a simple answer to that question," says Burgoon, a professor of communication and family studies at the University of Arizona in Tucson. "It all depends on how people are using the technology."

Take e-mail, she says. The lack of facial and verbal cues, for instance, can create greater intimacy or lead to misunderstandings. E-mail can facilitate relationships by allowing people to take the time to say what they mean and to communicate without the intrusion of day-to-day tensions and grievances. It can also encourage people to idealize their correspondent and lose sight of the real person behind the e-mail address. Of course, says Burgoon, the people you meet online may not even be who you think they are. In one online game, a computer program posing as "Julia" attracted the intense and persistent attentions of several male participants.

"We're only beginning to study the Internet," says Burgoon. "As the technology changes, we'll come to different conclusions than we had even two years ago."

Obsession or exploration?

That's certainly true when it comes to discussions of online sexuality, says Alvin Cooper, PhD, clinical director of the San Jose Marital and Sexuality Centre in the heart of Silicon Valley.

Cooper used to believe the hype about the dangers of online sexuality. Once he started investigating, however, he found a much more nuanced picture of how the Internet actually affects the 20 percent of users who now go online for sexual purposes. While the Internet can destroy lives, he says, it also provides a powerful tool for enhancing users' sexual relationships.

As Cooper describes in *Professional Psychology* (Vol.30, No. 2, p. 154–164), he developed an extensive questionnaire and put an announcement on an online news site to recruit participants who had used the Internet for sexual pursuits at least once. The 9,177 people who responded revealed that the vast majority used pornography, sexual chat rooms and other online sexual activities the same way they used *Baywatch*—as casual recreation. Only the 8 percent of users who spent more than 11 hours a week on online sexuality reported that these activities caused psychological distress and interfered with other parts of their lives.

The Internet may also pose risks to relationships that wouldn't otherwise have had problems except for what Cooper calls the "triple A"of the Internet: access, affordability and anonymity. A husband having a fight with his wife, for instance, probably won't take the trouble to punish his wife by going out to a bar to pick up a woman. Going into the other room, logging on and acting out sexual scenarios with virtual partners, however, is much easier.

But the "triple A" has plenty of positive effects, Cooper emphasizes. Users can go online to safely explore their fantasies or try new sexual experiences. Sexually disenfranchised groups, such as gays, lesbians and transgendered individuals, can create virtual communities. People with health problems, sexual dysfunction or histories of rape or abuse can find support from others. And many in what Cooper calls our "sexually illiterate" society can benefit from the sex information available online.

"After all, if you want to learn how to bake a cake, you can ask your mother or a neighbor," he says. "If you want to learn about oral sex, who are you going to ask?"

The future

The Internet has already revolutionized sexual relationships, says Cooper, citing cyber-affairs and virtual sex as examples. In just a few years, he predicts, people will use specialized equipment to have real sex over the Internet. Instead of simply masturbating as they type, he says, people will be able to send and receive actual sexual sensations.

Jim Blascovich, PhD, professor of psychology at the University of California at Santa Barbara, is one of the people who may help make such scenarios possible. In the Research Center for Virtual Environments and Behavior he co-founded at the university, he and his colleagues have created an immersive virtual environment that allows people to "be" in the same room no matter where they're located in the real world. Now he's trying to represent people's images three dimensionally.

The technology will have tremendous implications for online relationships, says Blascovich. Instead of talking by phone, for instance, people could come together in a virtual room and be able to see each other's non-verbal reactions.

"I can only speculate at this point, but this technology will have a major impact," says Blascovich, adding that this capability is only a few years away. "Whatever you can do on the Internet, for good or for bad, will be magnified a thousandfold by immersive virtual environments."

Rebecca A. Clay is a writer in Washington, D.C.

Isn't She Lovely?

If you think that physical appeal is strictly a matter of personal taste and cultural bias, think again. Who you find attractive, say psychobiologists, is largely dictated by evolutionary needs and hardwired into your brain

BY BRAD LEMLEY

She's cute, no question. Symmetrical features, flawless skin, looks to be 22 years old—entering any meat-market bar, a woman lucky enough to have this face would turn enough heads to stir a breeze. But when Victor Johnston points and clicks, the face on his computer screen morphs into what a mesmerized physicist might call a discontinuous state of super-heated, crystallized beauty. "You can see it. It's just so extraordinary," says Johnston, a professor of biopsychology at New Mexico State University who sounds a little in love with his creation.

The transformation from pretty woman to knee-weakening babe is all the more amazing because the changes wrought by Johnston's software are, objectively speaking, quite subtle. He created the original face by digitally averaging 16 randomly selected female Caucasian faces. The morphing program then exaggerated the ways in which female faces differ from male faces, creating, in human-beauty-science parlance, a "hyperfemale." The eyes grew a bit larger, the nose narrowed slightly, the lips plumped, and the jaw contracted. These are shifts of just a few millimeters, but experiments in this country and Scotland are suggesting that both males and females find "feminized" versions of averaged faces more beautiful.

Johnston hatched this little movie as part of his ongoing study into why human beings find some people attractive and others homely. He may not have any rock-solid answers yet, but he is far from alone in attempting to apply scientific inquiry to

so ambiguous a subject. Around the world, researchers are marching into territory formerly staked out by poets, painters, fashion mavens, and casting directors, aiming to uncover the underpinnings of human attractiveness.

The research results so far are surprising—and humbling. Numerous studies indicate that human beauty may not be simply in the eye of the beholder or an arbitrary cultural artifact. It may be an ancient, hardwired, universal, and potent behavior-driver, on a par with hunger or pain, wrought through eons of evolution that rewarded reproductive winners and killed off losers. If beauty is not truth, it may be health and fertility: Halle Berry's flawless skin may rivet moviegoers because, at some deep level, it persuades us that she is parasite-free and consequently good mating material. Acquired, individual preferences factor in, but research increasingly indicates that their influence is much smaller than many of us would care to know. While romantic writers blather about the transcendence of beauty, Elizabethan poet Edmund Spenser more than 400 years ago pegged the emerging scientific thesis: "Beauty is the bait which with delight allures man to enlarge his kind."

Implications of human-beauty research range from the practical—providing cosmetic surgeons with pretty-people templates—to the political and philosophical. Landmark studies show that attractive males and females not only garner more attention from the opposite sex, they also get more affection from their mothers, more

money at work, more votes from the electorate, more leniency from judges, and are generally regarded as more kind, competent, healthy, confident, and intelligent than their big-nosed, weak-chinned counterparts. (Beauty is considered such a valuable trait by some that one entrepreneur recently put up a Web site offering to auction off the unfertilized ova of models.)

Human attractiveness research is a relatively young and certainly contentious field—the allure of hyperfemales, for example, is still hotly debated—but those on its front lines agree on one point: We won't conquer "looks-ism" until we understand its source. As psychologist Nancy Etcoff, author of the 1999 book *Survival of the Prettiest*, puts it: "The idea that beauty is unimportant or a cultural construct is the real beauty myth. We have to understand beauty, or we will always be enslaved by it."

THE MODERN ERA OF BEAUTY STUDIES got a big push 20 years ago with an awkward question in a small, airless room at Louisiana State University in Baton Rouge. Psychology graduate student Judith Langlois was defending her doctoral dissertation—a study of how preschool children form and keep friendships—when a professor asked whether she had factored the kids' facial attractiveness into her conclusions. "I thought the question was way off the mark," she recalls. "It might matter for college students, but little kids?" After stammering out a noncommittal answer—and passing the examination—she resolved to dig deeper, aiming to determine the age at which human beings could perceive physical attractiveness.

Langlois, who had joined the faculty at the University of Texas at Austin, devised a series of experiments. In one, she had adults rate photos of human faces on a spectrum from attractive to unattractive. Then she projected pairs of high- and low-rated faces in front of 6-month-old infants. "The result was straightforward and unambiguous," she declares. "The babies looked longer at the attractive faces, regardless of the gender, race, or age of the face." Studies with babies as young as 2 months old yielded similar results. "At 2 months, these babies hadn't been reading *Vogue* magazine," Langlois observes dryly.

Her search for the source of babies' precocious beauty-detection led her all the way back to nineteenth-century research conducted by Sir Francis Galton, an English dilettante scientist and cousin of Charles Darwin. In the late 1870s, Galton created crude, blurry composite faces by melding mug-shot photographs of various social subgroups, aiming to prove that each group had an archetypal face. While that hypothesis fizzled—the average criminal looked rather like the average vegetarian—Galton was shocked to discover that these averaged faces were better looking than nearly all of the individuals they comprised. Langlois replicated Galton's study, using software to form digitally averaged faces that were later judged by 300 people to be more attractive than most of the faces used to create them.

Human beings may be born "cognitive averagers," theorizes Langlois. "Even very young infants have seen thousands of faces and may have already constructed an average from them that they use for comparison."

Racial preferences bolster the idea, say some scientists. History shows that almost universally when one race first comes into contact with another, they mutually regard each other as homely, if not freakish. Etcoff relates that a delegation of Japanese samurai visiting the United States in 1860 observed that Western women had "dogs' eyes," which they found "disheartening." Early Western visitors to Japan thought the natives' epicanthic folds made the eyes appear sleepy and small. In each case, Etcoff surmises, the unfamiliar race most likely veered from the internal, averaged ideal.

But why would cognitive averaging have evolved? Evolutionary biology holds that in any given population, extreme characteristics tend to fall away in favor of average ones. Birds with unusually long or short wings die more often in storms. Human babies who are born larger or smaller than average are less likely to survive. The ability to form an average-mate template would have conveyed a singular survival advantage.

Inclination toward the average is called koinophilia, from the Greek words *koinos*, meaning "usual," and *philos*, meaning "love." To Langlois, humans are clearly koinophiles. The remaining question is whether our good-mate template is acquired or innate. To help solve the mystery, Langlois's doctoral student Lisa Kalakanis has presented babies who are just 15 minutes old with paired images of attractive and homely faces. "We're just starting to evaluate that data," says Langlois.

But koinophilia isn't the only—or even supreme—criterion for beauty that evolution has promoted, other scientists argue. An innate yearning for symmetry is a major boon, contend biologists Anders Moller and Randy Thornhill, as asymmetry can signal malnutrition, disease, or bad genes. The two have found that asymmetrical animals, ranging from barn swallows to lions, have fewer offspring and shorter lives. Evolution would also logically instill an age preference. Human female fertility peaks in the early 20s, and so do assessments of female attractiveness. Between 1953 and 1990, the average age of *Playboy* centerfold models—who are presumably selected solely for sexual appeal—was 21.3 years. Similarly, Johnston has found that the beauty of a Japanese female face is judged to be at its peak when its perceived age is 22.4 years. Because men are fertile throughout most of their adult lives, their attractiveness ratings—while dropping as they age past their late 20s—remain relatively higher as their perceived age increases. As Johnston puts it, "Our feelings of beauty are exceptionally well tuned to the age of maximum fertility."

STILL, A SPECIES CAN STAGNATE WITHOUT some novelty. When competition for mates is intense, some extreme traits might help to rivet a roving eye. "A male peacock is saying, 'Look at me, I have this big tail. I couldn't grow a tail this big if I had parasites,'" says Johnston. "Even if the trait is detrimental to survival, the benefit in additional offspring brought about by attracting females can more than compensate for the decrease in longevity." The concept seems applicable to humans, too, because it helps to resolve a nagging flaw

in average-face studies. In many of them, "there were always a few individual faces in the population that were deemed even prettier than the average," says Etcoff. "If average were always best, how could that be?"

Psychologist David Perrett of the University of St. Andrews in Scotland aimed to find out by creating two averaged faces—one from a group of women rated attractive and another from men so judged. He then compared those faces with averaged faces constructed from a larger, random set of images. The composites of the beautiful people were rated more appealing than those made from the larger, random population. More surprising, when Perrett exaggerated the ways in which the prettiest female composite differed from the average female composite, the resulting face was judged to be even more attractive.

"It turned out that the way an attractive female face differs from an average one is related to femininity," says Perrett. "For example, female eyebrows are more arched than males'. Exaggerating that difference from the average increases femininity," and, in tandem, the attractiveness rating. In the traffic-stopping female face created for this experiment, 200 facial reference points all changed in the direction of hyperfemininity: larger eyes, a smaller nose, plumper lips, a narrower jaw, and a smaller chin.

"All faces go through a metamorphosis at puberty," observes Johnston. "In males, testosterone lengthens the jaw. In females, estrogen makes the hips, breasts, and lips swell." So large lips, breasts, and hips combined with a small jaw "are all telling you that I have an abundant supply of estrogen, so I am a fertile female." Like the peacock, whose huge tail is a mating advantage but a practical hindrance, "a small jaw may not, in fact, be as efficient for eating," Johnston says. But it seems attractive because it emphasizes *la différence;* whatever survival disadvantage comes along with a small jaw is more than made up for by the chance to produce more babies, so the trait succeeds.

Along with his morphing program, Johnston approached the hyperfemale hypothesis through another route. Starting with 16 computer-generated random female Caucasian faces, he had visitors to his Web site rate the attractiveness of each face on a scale of one to nine. A second generation of faces was then computed by selecting, crossing, and mutating the first generation in proportion to beauty ratings.

After 10,000 people from around the world took part in this merciless business, the empirically derived fairest-of-them-all was born. Facial measurements confirm that she is decidedly hyperfemale. While we might say she is beautiful, Johnston more accurately notes that the face displays "maximum fertility cues."

Johnston's findings have set off a ruckus among beauty scientists. In a paper titled "Attractive Faces Really Are Only Average," Langlois and three other researchers blast the notion that a deviation from the average—what they term "facial extremes"—explains attractiveness better than averageness does. The findings of Perrett and his team, she says, are "artifacts of their methodology," because they used a "forced-choice" scenario that prevented subjects from judging faces as equally attractive. "We did the same kind of test, but gave people a rating scale of one to five," says Langlois. "When you do it that way, there is no significant difference—people would tell us that, basically, the two faces looked like twins." Langlois argues that if extremes create beauty, "then people with micro-jaws or hydrocephalic eyes would be seen as the most beautiful, when, in fact, eyes that are too big for a head make that head unattractive."

As the world becomes more egalitarian, beauty becomes more inclusive

---

But for Etcoff, circumstantial evidence for the allure of some degree of hyperfemininity is substantial. "Female makeup is all about exaggerating the feminine. Eye makeup makes the brow thinner, which makes it look farther from the eye," which, she says, is a classic difference between male and female faces. From high hair (which skews facial proportions in a feminine direction, moving up the center of gravity) to collagen in lips to silicone in breasts, women instinctively exaggerate secondary female sex characteristics to increase their allure. "Langlois is simply wrong," declares Johnston. In one of his studies, published last year in *Psychophysiology*, both male and female subjects rated feminized pictures as more attractive. Further, male subjects attached to electrical-brain-activity monitors showed a greater

response in the P3 component, a measure of emotional intensity. "That is, although both sexes know what is attractive, only the males exhibit an emotional response to the feminized picture," Johnston says.

AND WHAT ABOUT MALE ATTRACTIVEness? IT stands to reason that if men salivate for hyperfemales, women should pursue hypermales—that is, men whose features exaggerate the ways in which male faces differ from female ones. Even when adjusted for differing overall body size, the average male face has a more pronounced brow ridge, more sunken eyes, and bushier brows that are set closer to the eyes. The nose and mouth are wider, the lower jaw is wider and longer. Ramp up these features beyond the norm, and you've got a hunk, right?

There's no question that a dose of this classic "maleness" does contribute to what is now called handsome. Actor Brad Pitt, widely regarded as a modern paradigm of male attractiveness, is a wide-jaw guy. Biologically speaking, he subconsciously persuades a female that he could chew more nutrients out of a leafy stalk than the average potential father of her children—a handy trait, in hunter-gatherer days anyway, to pass on to progeny.

But a woman's agenda in seeking a mate is considerably more complex than simply whelping strong-jawed kids. While both men and women desire healthy, fertile mates, a man can—and, to some extent, is biologically driven to—procreate with as many women as possible. Conversely, a woman "thinks about the long haul," notes Etcoff. "Much of mate choice is about finding a helpmate to bring up the baby." In several studies, women presented with the hypermale face (the "Neanderthal type" as Etcoff puts it) judged its owner to be uncaring, aggressive, and unlikely to be a good father.

Female preferences in male faces oscillate in tandem with the menstrual cycle, suggests a study conducted by Perrett and Japanese researchers and published last June in *Nature*. When a woman is ovulating, she tends to prefer men with more masculine features; at less fertile times in her monthly cycle, she favors male faces with a softer, more feminine look. But amid the hoopla that this widely publicized finding generated, a critical fact was often overlooked. Even the "more masculine" face preferred by the ovulating women was 8 percent feminized from the male average (the less masculine face was 15 to 20 percent

feminized). According to Perrett's study, even an averagely masculine face is too male for comfort.

To further complicate the male-appeal picture, research indicates that, across the board in mating species, an ugly guy can make up ground with status and/or wealth. Etcoff notes that female scorpion flies won't even look at a male unless his gift—a tasty bit of insect protein—is at least 16 square millimeters wide. The human situation isn't all that different. Anthropologist John Marshall Townsend showed photos of beautiful and homely people to men and women, and described the people in the photos as being in training for either low-, medium-, or high-paying positions—waiter, teacher, or doctor. "Not surprisingly, women preferred the best-looking man with the most money," Etcoff writes, "but below him, average-looking or even unattractive doctors received the same ratings as very attractive teachers. This was not true when men evaluated women. Unattractive women were not preferred, no matter what their status."

IT'S ALL A BIT BLEAK. TALK TO ENOUGH psychobiologists, and you get the impression that we are all rats—reflexively, unconsciously coupling according to obscure but immutable circuitry. But beauty researchers agree that, along with natural selection and sexual selection, learned behaviors are at least part of the attractiveness radar. In other words, there is room for individuality—perhaps even a smattering of mystery—in this business of attraction between humans.

"Human beauty really has three components," says Johnston. "In order of importance, there's natural selection, which leads to the average face and a limited age range. Then there's sexual selection," which leads men, at least, to be attracted to exaggerated feminine traits like the small lower jaw and the fuller lips. "Finally, there's learning. It's a fine-tuning mechanism that allows you to become even more adapted to your environment and culture. It's why one person can say 'She's beautiful' and another can say, 'She's not quite right for me.'"

The learned component of beauty detection is perhaps most evident in the give-and-take between races. While, at first meeting, different racial groups typically see each other as unattractive, when one race commands economic or political power, members of other races tend to emulate its characteristics: Witness widespread hair straightening by American blacks earlier in this century. Today, black gains in social equity are mirrored by a growing appreciation for the beauty of such characteristically black features as relatively broader noses and tightly curled hair. "Race is a cultural overlay on beauty and it's shifting," says Etcoff.

She adds that human appearance is about more than attracting sex partners. "There was a cartoon in the *New Yorker*. A mother and daughter are in a checkout line. The girl is saying to the cashier, 'Oh, no, I *do* look like my mother, with her *first* nose!' As we make ourselves more beautiful, we take away things like family resemblance, and we may realize that's a mistake. Facial uniqueness can be a wonderful emotional tag. Human beings are always looking for kinship as well as beauty."

Midway between goats and gods, human beings can find some accommodation between the notion that beauty is all and that it is nothing. "Perhaps it's best to enjoy the temporary thrill, to enjoy being a mammal for a few moments, and then do a reality check and move on," writes Etcoff. "Our brains cannot help it, but we can."

If it's easy access that really makes you click, log on here

Stupid Cupid! Karen Gold searches for the e-spot

Karen Gold

From: Gold, Karen

To: Ben-Ze'ev, Aaron—psychologist, philosopher and author of *Love Online: Emotions on the Internet*

Subject: Does cybersex count as cheating on your partner, or is it just an adolescent game sustained by chocolate pixels?

KG: If we were doing this interview face to face, you'd know if I was a 50-year-old man pretending to be a 22-year-old lesbian. We're not, and so you don't. Does that make it impossible for either of us to believe anything the other is saying?

AB: One paradoxical feature of online romantic relationships is that they encourage deception and sincerity. The anonymity of cyberspace and the voluntary nature of online self-presentation allow people to present themselves inaccurately. In one survey, 48 per cent of users said they changed their age "occasionally" and 23 per cent did so "often".

Furthermore, 38 per cent changed their race online, and 5 per cent admitted to changing their sex occasionally.

But online relationships also encourage many people to present a more accurate picture of their true self. People can express themselves more freely because they are more anonymous and hence less vulnerable. Many people present themselves honestly online. This is especially true if the relationship grows.

KG: Are the emotions people feel in online relationships the same as the ones they experience face to face? Is the experience of cybersex comparable to real sex?

AB: The emotions are similar, but the role of imagination online is greater. Many people testify that their online sexual experience has been the most intense and wild sex they have ever had. One 32-year-old woman, married for the second time, claims: "The sexual release

from cybering has been a great experience and the arousal factor is just magnificent."

Emotions in online relationships incorporate more intellectual elements.

The weight of conversation is far greater in online relationships than in offline relationships.

A woman who has participated in cybersex writes: "The best sex, obviously, is with someone literate enough to 'paint a picture' describing activities or thoughts. I suppose that in face-to-face activities, someone stupid could still be extraordinarily sexy. But stupid doesn't work online, at least not for me."

KG: What kind of person seeks love online? What kind of person finds it?

AB: All kinds. Online relationships increase your chances of finding a more suitable and exciting partner because it's easier to identify willing people and cheaper and less risky to conduct the relationship. The computer's ability to sort people by characteristics is much greater than in offline circumstances, so it's easier to find people with attributes you like.

For example, an obese woman who feels insecure approaching new people face to face because of her weight may interact online with people who share her interests. When she reveals that she is overweight, some people may not want to continue the correspondence. But others may find her physical size irrelevant or her other characteristics very attractive.

For such people, who have to break a lot of eggs to make an omelette, cyberspace provides many eggs. Millions of people eagerly wait for you on the net every moment of the day.

KG: You say cyber relationships last a few months on average. Is there a pattern to them?

AB: There are many types of online relationships. It's hard to find a pattern, but I distinguish three major types:

- relationships intended to find an offline sexual or romantic partner
- cyberflirting and cybersex
- profound online-only romantic relationships.

KG: Do women have an advantage in online relationships? They're generally better communicators than men, and you say in your book that they feel less inhibited—raunchy even—online than in person. They're not being judged on how they look, though that might be an advantage for some men, too. What difference does all this make?

AB: Online relationships are advantageous for all people whose communicative and intellectual abilities are better than their looks.

Because external appearance generally has more weight in men's judgement of women than in women's judgement of men, it does benefit women. It lets people get to know each other without the heavy burden of the attractiveness stereotype.

Thus, someone writes about his online girlfriend: "She is not even my type when it comes to physical attraction, but she is now the most beautiful girl I have ever met and will ever meet." The reduced concern about external appearance allows women to enjoy sex more and to be much freer in this respect. As one woman said: "It was great not having to worry about being unattractive."

KG: The way you describe online affairs—more soul-searching, more intense, more fleeting, easy to switch off, easy to replace—makes them sound…well… rather adolescent. Aren't the people engaging in them just avoiding grown-up relationships?

AB: Online interactions might be considered a kind of virtual laboratory in which people can explore each other and experiment. In this sense, they are similar to the games that children play that allow them to develop, in a relatively safe and benign way, social skills for adult life. Indeed, cyberspace has been characterised as an amazing sex toy.

There's nothing wrong with playing the way children do as long as we know the boundaries between the game and reality. In cyberspace, such boundaries are often blurred.

KG: Isn't it dangerous when they are? Fantasy can be addictive. If people confuse fantasy with reality—if they talk about being more profoundly satisfied by virtual sex and virtual relationships than by real sex and real relationships—aren't they losing touch with reality? And where does this leave their real-life partners and spouses?

AB: You're absolutely right. There is such danger. The great seductiveness of cyberspace and the ease of becoming involved in online affairs bring risks. People are easily carried away.

Moreover, cyberspace doesn't merely satisfy needs, it creates new needs that often cannot be met. Thus, the apparent ease of finding true and everlasting love in cyberspace creates the need to have such "perfect" love. Of course, that is far from simple to achieve. Online affairs are like a new toy with which the human race has not yet learnt how to play. People may confuse the toy with reality and ruin their life.

Cybering is similar, in some senses, to taking drugs. Both provide easy access to pleasure that is often based on virtual realities. Whereas drugs artificially stimulate pleasure centres in the brain, online conversations artificially stimulate pleasure centres in the mind. The price can be high for our overall performance and for those close to us in our offline lives.

KG: How widespread do you think cyber relationships will become? Have you ever had one? Will all this be contractualised some day: in marriage perhaps we'll promise to forsake all others, online as well as off?

AB: I know many people who have had online relationships. I haven't. The internet has changed the romantic domain, and this process will accelerate.

It will modify social forms such as marriage and cohabitation, and romantic practices relating to courtship, casual sex, committed romantic relationships and romantic exclusivity.

I think we can expect more relaxation of social and moral norms concerning romantic exclusivity. It will be difficult to avoid the vast amount of tempting alternatives entirely. The notion of "betrayal" will become less common. But I think the values placed on stability and stronger commitment will increase as well.

By the way, are you a 50-year-old man or an attractive 42-year-old woman, as it seems from your questions?

Aaron Ben-Ze'ev is a psychologist, philosopher and rector of the University of Haifa. *Love Online: Emotions on the Internet* is published by Cambridge University Press on February 14, £18.95.

THE MARRIAGE SAVERS

Does couples therapy really work? The divorce rate says no, but a new breed of therapists offers hope

By Richard Corliss and Sonja Steptoe

The cynic Ambrose Bierce defined love as "a temporary insanity, curable by marriage." It's truer to say the first blush of love is a vacation from reality; marriage is the job you return to. You may like your job, even love it. But you have to work to keep it.

In modern America, there's no shortage of professionals ready and willing to pitch in with the task. In fact, over the past 40 years, the couples-counseling business has exploded. In 1966 there were only about 1,800 experts practicing in the field, according to the Department of Health and Human Services. In 2001 the American Association for Marriage and Family Therapy listed 47,111 marriage and family therapists in the U.S. and estimated that they treat 863,700 couples a year.

Yet how many were helped? The growth of the marriage-industrial complex has not done much to slow the national divorce epidemic. In 1965 the divorce rate was 2.5 per 1,000 people; it reached a high in 1979 and 1981, with 5.3 per 1,000. Today the figure hovers at about 4.0, pretty much where it has been for five years. In some quarters, the suspicion has lingered that the therapist's job is to validate a patient's complaints and act as ministers in reverse, putting couples asunder. "The idea of therapist neutrality often came down to support for breaking up," says William Doherty, director of the Marriage and Family Therapy Program at the University of Minnesota. And therapists weren't appreciated for it. In a 1995 *Consumer Reports* poll, couples seeking

therapy gave marriage counselors low grades for competence.

Lately, however, a new breed of therapist and "marriage educator" is shaking up the profession. These therapists reject the passive, old-style therapies that emphasize personal growth over shared commitment and take a more aggressive, hands-around-the-neck approach to saving marriages. "They feel therapists have been too quick in calling an end to relationships and having people move on," says University of Chicago sociology professor Linda Waite. The new breed also advocates premarital skill training and early intervention in problems—learning the ropes before tying the knot. "It's like a vaccination," says Waite, "instead of having to do surgery when something goes wrong."

The new, pro-marriage generation "is young, far more conservative and more religious" than traditional therapists, says Doherty, author of *Take Back Your Marriage*. "This generation has seen the fruits of the divorce revolution. And they don't think they have to be value-neutral about it." They also tend to be pragmatists. Many of them favor short-term, low-cost interventions based on methods with a record of proved success.

These qualities have drawn the support of religious leaders and conservative politicians, including First Husband George W. Bush, who would like to make marriage education for young couples part of welfare reform. "This is a social movement," says Doherty, "that involves government, church, profes-

sional and lay people." How do these therapies and lessons in connection work? A look at some methods of the movement:

• GOING TO "PREP" SCHOOL

PREP, short for prevention and relationship Enhancement Program, aims to be the industry leader in research-based couples education. Its tenets, which emphasize structured communication, are ingredients in a variety of programs for teens, pre-marrieds and long-marrieds.

Rod Grimm Lewis and his wife Victoria paid $400 to attend a two-day PREP seminar in Los Angeles in a final attempt to save their 28-year-old marriage. "I think this will help," says Victoria, the more eager of the two. "I think of it as chemotherapy." Rod figures he's being a good sport. "I came because she asked me to," he says. "I'm about 5% of the problem, and she's 95%." Marc Sadoff, the workshop leader, says, "It's good to hear that you can acknowledge you're 5%. So many people can't see any role in the problem."

Positive communication, like Sadoff's comment, is the backbone of PREP, developed in the 1980s by psychologists Howard Markman and Scott Stanley, co-directors of the Center for Marital and Family Studies at the University of Denver. In developing it, Markham spent years taping couples having arguments and devising ways to break bad habits. The method, which relies partly on videos of other couples using the technique, is continually tweaked in light of new research, says Stanley. "The idea was to build a program for couples that was based on sound research," he says, "rather than armchair clinical speculation."

Sadoff, a clinical social worker trained in PREP, explains the method to the Lewises and a younger couple sharing the session. They are to agree to set aside a time each week to talk over their problems. These discussions must follow certain rules, which can be posted on the refrigerator door. "The word I is allowed," Sadoff says. "You is not." The partners take turns talking, without interruption. The speaker makes brief statements, which the listener must paraphrase to show he understands what was said. There are also time-outs, which allow one partner to leave the room for an emotional break. That's a scary notion for Victoria, who says that since childhood she has never felt she could leave a heated discussion without repercussions. "Where would I go?"

Rod and Victoria give it a try. While Victoria is speaking, Rod interjects to ask a question. That's not allowed, he's told. Later he doesn't correctly paraphrase what she said. Rod tries again. When he gets it right, Victoria smiles and says, "Yes! That's good." For a moment they have connected. But Rod is struggling to remember his role, and Victoria still feels unnatural: "Does anyone really talk like this?'' Sadoff assures her she will get better with practice. He explains that, although artificial, the technique provides a safe way for couples to talk about thorny issues. "We're after progress, not perfection," he says.

Six months after the first session—and despite follow-up therapy with Sadoff—problems linger. "We tried, but the techniques just don't take care of the deeper issues," says Rod, who is thinking of ending the marriage. "The future of our relationship doesn't look good."

But many evaluators award PREP high marks. While two studies did not find it more effective than other methods, two others, involving a total of 210 couples, found that those who take PREP, either before marriage or after, have lower rates of breakup and divorce than couples who took a different training class or did nothing. Also, seven studies involving about 500 couples concluded that PREP

participants had less negative communication for up to five years after the course. Men are particularly partial to the method.

Such results have made PREP popular around the world and in a wide range of settings, including U.S. military bases and churches. Oklahoma has embraced it as part of a $10 million government initiative to reduce divorce. That's how Shelitha and John Coleman Jr. came to PREP in November, in a Christianized version offered free at their church, G.A.P. [God's Apostolic Prophetic] Restoration Tabernacle in Oklahoma City. The Colemans' marriage of nearly two years was doing fine, but John's parents didn't seem to think so and were interfering. "They wanted me to have the same kind of marriage they had, where I'm the man and I run the whole show," explains John, 28. He and Shelitha, 29, needed a way to declare their independence without sounding rebellious.

PREP techniques helped them do that while improving their own communication. John's parents, says Shelitha, "were having trouble letting go. Our talk revealed some things about how they feel about seeing their children grow up and live on their own. Now all four of us are using PREP methods." The religious aspect of the program was important to the couple. "We make the word of God part of the foundation of our marriage," says John. "In terms of communicating, it shows up in principles about being honest with your partner about everything. When a difficult problem comes up, you shouldn't hide."

• LESSONS FROM THE LOVE LAB

Heinrich Heine called marriage "the high sea for which no compass has yet been invented." John Gottman figures he has found the compass. At the Gottman Institute in Seattle, a husband and wife sit in sensor-loaded chairs with wires strapped across their chests, taped to their fingertips, clipped to their earlobes. The wires are connected to an array of computerized measuring devices that will track physiological data about them. As the couple discuss a glitch in their marriage, a technician in the next room monitors the data: heart rate, sweaty

palms, the speed of blood flow. Another technician watches them on a video screen, recording facial expressions, calibrating emotional vital signs of couples during actual marital conflict. *Survivor, Fear Factor*—that's kid stuff. This is true reality TV.

Gottman, a clinical psychologist, has essentially distilled the art of love and war—a.k.a. marriage—into a kind of science. After 30 years of such studies inside his physiology lab, nicknamed the Love Lab, Gottman's group has developed a model that he claims can assess whether a couple are on a path to dysfunction. Now when Gottman wires up therapy clients and videotapes them, "in the first three minutes of the conflict discussion," he says, "we can predict if a couple is going to divorce." He and research partner Robert Levenson of the University of California, Berkeley, found that during arguments, couples in stable relationships have five times as many positive factors present as negative ones. "In relationships that were working, even during conflict, there was a rich climate of positive things, such as love, affection, interest in one another, humor and support. Couples in unstable unions had slightly more negative factors than positive."

Conflict is endemic in a relationship, Gottman says, but adds—with peculiar precision—that "only 31% of conflicts get resolved over the course of a marriage. The other 69% are perpetual, unsolvable problems." His insight: don't bother trying to fix the unfixable. Spend your energy on selecting a mate with whom you can manage those inevitable annoyances, then learn how to manage them. To admit some problems can't be solved is the first step toward finding a larger solution. Says Gottman: "We try to build up the couple's friendship, their ability to repair conflict and to deal with their gridlock."

The Gottman technique usually involves a $495 two-day workshop, followed by nine private therapy sessions costing $1,260, which Gottman recommends as a supplement. These attempt to conquer the four most common, corrosive negative factors in unstable unions: criticism (*You never ... You always ...*), defensiveness (*Who me? I'm not defensive*), contempt (*You're too stupid to realize how defensive you are*) and stonewalling (*I'll just let it blow over*). Gottman says 85% of stonewallers are men.

Gottman fiercely protects the privacy of his patients and does not provide names of couples to be interviewed. He says his five-year follow-up study shows that after one year, about 75% of the treated couples are happier, "[though] we haven't been able to help the other 25% calm down. They stay irritable, cranky and contemptuous."

● LET'S GET SCHNARCHED!

That cranky quarter of the peace-seeking married contingent may find a sympathetic soul in David Schnarch, author of the book *Passionate Marriage* and creator of the Crucible Approach to marital therapy, which upends nearly all the conventional tenets of couples counseling. He says he is the therapist of last resort for many couples who go to his Marriage and Family Health Center in Evergreen, Colo., for an intensive four-day session: "The worse shape your marriage is in, the more this is the approach of choice." Nor does he recommend that a warring couple break up—that's just "one way therapists can bury their errors."

Schnarch argues that the main issue for most troubled couples "isn't their lack of communication skills. If spouses aren't talking to each other, they are still communicating. They each know they don't want to hear what the other has to say. But communication is no virtue if you can't stand the message. We help people to stand the message." He says couples don't get that from conventional therapy, which tends to pathologize relationships rather than work with their strengths. In the Crucible system, "we don't treat people like they're sick. We speak to the best in people, not their weaknesses. We're about developing resilience and standing up for yourself." People in a troubled marriage say they have grown apart. Schnarch says it's the opposite. "They're usually locked together, emotionally fused. More attachment doesn't make people happier, and it kills sex."

Schnarch uses the word crucible in two senses: metallurgical (a strong caul-

dron) and metaphorical (a test or trial). Both definitions can aptly describe the state of marriage. So in his therapy it's out with the elevator-music approach to saving marriages, in with the hard rock and harsh truths. Dare to tear apart the fuzzy, flabby, ego-suppressing dual personality that is your marriage and find your inner you. That effort will create a stronger individual, one who can deal with a partner with more integrity and authenticity.

Ken Wapman, 45, manager at a Bay Area software firm, and Margee, 45, a therapist, had been married 18 years when they signed up for Schnarch's program in 2001. Busy with their jobs and three kids, their marriage was somewhere between O.K. and icky. "The relationship was sustainable but not very satisfying," says Ken. And their sex life, he says, "was like your commute. You could practically do it with your eyes closed"—er, don't a lot of people do it that way?—"but you don't really look forward to it."

The Schnarch approach immediately appealed to Ken. "I liked that he didn't pull any punches," says Ken, who used to disagree with his wife and others just for the sake of it. "I used to use more imperative-type language. Schnarch helped me to think about developing more collaborative alliances." Working with Schnarch after trying other therapists, says Ken, was like "jumping into a Ferrari compared to driving a Toyota Celica."

At first the Crucible was a bit searing for Margee. "He forces you to see things in yourself that you haven't wanted to see. I used to think Ken's job was to take care of me by knowing how I felt. That's an idea embedded in the culture." Now, Margee says, she has learned to take care of herself. "I'm not dumping anything on him; I have worked my side of the issue. There is less unresolved tension. As a result, I feel love and want to move toward him."

The benefits of the weekend (cost: $925) inspired Margee to want to follow up with the Schnarch nine-day retreat ($2,400). Ken, less enthusiastic, offered a counterproposal. "I cut a deal with her. I said I would go with her to the retreat if I could go on a two-week bike trip in the French Alps." Sounds like Schnarchian self-differentiation in action.

● MAKE AN EFT TURN ON RED

Listen to enough marriage plaints, and you may conclude that Tolstoy was wrong: unhappy families really are all alike. They argue over sex, money, the kids, the lack of free time. After five years of marriage, Tom, 39, and Suzanne, 35, sparred with increasing frequency and rancor over the usual "spending" issues. He thought she was spending too much money; she thought he wasn't spending enough time with her and their two children. The counseling they tried didn't help. "It just made the situation artificial," says Suzanne. She's the verbal one; Tom, from a military family, is the strong, silent type. "So when we would argue, he gets sort of blasted out of the water by me, and he shuts down and shuts me out. It escalated to the point where he was, like, 'I'm out of here.'"

Hoping to break the pattern, they went last May to see Douglas Tilley, a Maryland clinical social worker who uses EFT—Emotionally Focused Therapy—a procedure that, in direct opposition to Schnarch's Crucible, focuses on the emotional need for connection and closeness with your spouse. EFT was devised about 20 years ago by Sue Johnson, a professor of psychology at Ottawa University, and Les Greenberg, now a professor at York University in Canada. "In our culture, we have this funny thing where we see maturity as being independent, not needing other people," says Johnson. "But when the Twin Towers came down in New York, what did people around the world do? They held on to the people they were with, they phoned the person they depend upon the most."

Modern life has overloaded marriage, says Johnson. "Our sister no longer lives next door, our mother phones us once a month, we're too busy at work to create lasting bonds there. So we're even more dependent on our spouses than ever before." In a distressed relationship, that bond is fraying. Typically, one person criticizes and complains, while the other falls into a pattern of defending and withdrawing. "The amazingly sad thing," says Johnson, speaking of the typical pattern in couples, "is they love each other. The man loves his wife so desperately that he has put up this huge wall because he's so terrified he's going to hear that she's disappointed in him. Unless they can find a way into a more secure bond, they'll split."

To re-create a sense of connection between the couple, the EFT therapist creates an environment in which both spouses feel safe talking about their feelings, needs and fears. Like Suzanne and Tom, most couples are pleasantly surprised to hear that the feelings behind apparently hostile behavior are not rejection but a need to connect with their partner. Without that emotional security, Johnson says, all the communication skills in the world won't rebuild a relationship. "You can teach people communication skills up the wazoo," she says, "but if they're afraid of losing the person they depend on, they don't use them."

EFT is one of three approaches that the Society of Clinical Psychology, a division of the American Psychological Association, has found to be backed up by empirical research. Yet it hasn't become a mass therapy in the U.S. One reason may be that no one has yet written a best seller about EFT. And Johnson says EFT is not for abusive marriages. She once turned away a couple in which the husband was so verbally abusive that Johnson decided she shouldn't force the wife to reveal her deepest emotions. "I'm not going to encourage one person to do that when the other is standing there with a machine gun in hand," she says.

EFT seems to have disarmed Suzanne and Tom. Suzanne knows little about its theoretical bases—she calls it "EFT, EMF, whatever"—but she likes the results. "Since we have been going to therapy, Tom says a huge burden has been lifted off him. He's never talked about this kind of stuff before in his life." He now spends much more time with Suzanne and the children and less time with his buddies at the sports bar. Twice a month the couple put the children to bed and have a date—either at home, over a delicious dinner, or out at a restaurant. "We're at the point where if we're having hard times," Suzanne says, "it brings us together rather than apart."

• BRING ON THE DIVORCE BUSTERS

In a studio session to record a CD, David Roth, 39, a Chicago-area sculptor turned singer-songwriter, was having trouble with the part-time bass player—his wife Heidi Meredith. Both had grown up in broken homes and hoped to avoid separation. But after more than a decade together, they had devolved into chronic arguers: how to make the bed, how to make music. "We were in this decaying orbit that was going to crash and burn," says Roth. Says Meredith, 39: "It was never a question of our not loving each other. We would just completely butt heads, and then we would analyze it to death. That just got us in deeper."
Roth suggested they get help. Meredith, who in her day job is a psychiatrist, was skeptical. "I can't tell you how many patients I have seen who have also been in marital therapy for a year or more," she says, "and all they do is scream at each other."

They booked sessions with Michele Weiner-Davis, author of *Divorce Busting* and *The Sex-Starved Marriage*, who practices in Woodstock, Ill., outside Chicago. While many marriage therapies last months or years, Weiner-Davis says, her patients were usually out in half a dozen visits. Her technique favors action, not introspection.

Discord is inevitable: "Only 31% of conflicts get resolved over the course of the marriage"

"Traditional approaches ask people to look at the past and figure out why they're stuck," says Weiner-Davis, whose graduate degree is in social work. "But that insight generally leads people only to be experts in why they're having a problem—and novices in what to do about it. People on the brink of divorce do not have the luxury of time to take this journey backward. They need an instant injection of hope." Weiner-Davis encourages a dose of what she calls "real giving"—asking couples to realize what their partner needs in certain situations and provide what he needs regardless of whether the giver understands it. For example, if your spouse prefers to be alone

when he's upset, allow him quiet time, even if you prefer to talk when you're upset.

Weiner-Davis' action-oriented scheme suited Roth and Meredith. "It's really freeing to just focus on the solution and clear out all the muck," says Meredith. Weiner-Davis encourages couples to identify what they want the marriage to look like, then list actions they can take—dinner out once a week, playing tennis or golf together, help with the housework—to achieve those goals. "The concept of real giving is so simple, but it really gets at the heart of how to make a relationship work," says Meredith.

The approach appeals equally to both sexes. If a guy can be convinced that his marriage is like a rusty carburetor or a clogged kitchen sink, he may be stirred to fix it. "I think men are hesitant to go into therapy because they feel they're going to be targeted," Roth says. "Michele's approach is pragmatic and practical. That's refreshing for a lot of men."

Some of Weiner-Davis' recipes earn hoots from others in the fractious fraternity of couples therapists. Of her advice that troubled couples should "just do it!"—have sex to jump-start a passionless marriage—Schnarch retorts, "Telling low-desire spouses to just do something just pisses them off. Most couples seeking help are angry, and angry sex isn't very generous. These people would rather poke each other's eyes out than stroke each other's genitals."

But she has plenty of satisfied customers—the Roth-Merediths, for two. They work (at their marriage) and play (she's now his band's official bass player). And their son, 4, has noticed the difference. When his parents fought, he used to throw things and scream. Now he sees his parents hugging and delights in squishing himself in to share the love. "I think it has improved the quality of his life," says Roth. "There's a lot more laughter in our house."

• CAN GOOD MARRIAGE BE TAUGHT?

What if you could go to school instead of to a shrink? That's the idea behind Marriage Education. "It's less expensive and

Do Gay Couples Have an Edge?

Sallyanne Monti, 42, and Mickey Neill, 52, began seeing a couples therapist soon after their relationship began six years ago, and they have been in counseling on and off ever since, The have gone to hash out the kinds of problems that plague many couples: guilt, anxiety, miscommunication and dealing with teenage kids.

But Monti and Neill are both women, and while gay and heterosexual couples have plenty of issues in common, there are big differences as well. Gay couples have to cope daily with homophobia, says Robert-Jay Green, a psychologist in San Francisco. An even bigger problem is a lack of clarity about commitment. "In research samples, the average length of same-sex-couple relationships tends to be about six years," says Green, "compared to around 18 for heterosexuals."

One reason is that there is usually less social glue—marriage, family expectation, children—holding gay couples together. "There's really no one rooting for them to stick it out through the tough times the way there is for straight couples," says Green. "There's no ceremony that invokes traditions of what it means to be a couple. It produces tremendous insecurity."

Sometimes, however, having similar perspectives can be more of a curse than a blessing, says psychologist Michael Hendrick, who practices at the Washington Psychological Center in Washington: "Expectations about compatibility can be too high."

That's what Monti and Neill discovered. Both had been previously married to men. "We thought that since men are from Mars and women are from Venus or something like that," says Monti, "in a same-sex relationship, communication would be a slam dunk." Instead they found they had the same kind of miscues and hurt feelings that they had faced with their husbands. "Just because we're the same gender," says Neill, "doesn't mean we think the same."

—Michael D. Lemonisk. Reported by Sonja Steptoe/Los Angeles

---

more effective than therapy," says Diane Sollee, 59, who gave up her marriage-therapy career to create the Coalition for Marriage, Family and Couples Education. "The therapy model is 'I'll treat you, and, voila, your marriage will work.' The education model is much more respectful. It assumes there's nothing wrong with you—you're not sick. You just need better information, and it assumes you can apply it to your situation. It's also not a long-term process."

Every system sounds great—until you ask other marriage specialists about it. "To say therapy isn't working is absolutely wrong," Gottman insists. "These psycho-education interventions are powerful; you have to be careful about applying them. Currently, people in the marriage movement aren't being careful. They go ahead with tremendous optimism and convince people that this is key to family stability. I worry that it will all collapse when couples see that it can't be done that way. This *isn't* like driver ed." No, but when experts start comparing claims and stats, you hear the cacophony of rival used-car salesmen.

Is it the therapists who need educating? Or is it the Marriage Ed folks who need therapy? Somewhere there has to be detente between the clinical remoteness of one group and the evangelical salesmanship of the other—a middle ground, perhaps even a common ground. "A lot of therapy is education," says Gottman, "and a lot of education is therapy." At a time when America's marrieds and soon-to-bes are eager for mediation, the bickering of the two sides is unhelpful. Maybe both sides should consider this advice—both priceless and free—from that sage counselor Ogden Nash:

To keep your marriage brimming,
   With love in the loving cup,
   Whenever you're wrong admit
   it; Whenever you're right shut
   up.

UNIT 7
Social Biases

Unit Selections

22. **The Self-Protective Properties of Stigma: Evolution of a Modern Classic**, Jennifer Crocker and Brenda Major
23. **Change of Heart**, Adam Goodheart
24. **Thin Ice: "Stereotype Threat" and Black College Students**, Claude M. Steele

Key Points to Consider

- What is prejudice? How does it differ from discrimination and stereotyping? How are the three interrelated? Have you ever held social biases? If so, which ones and why? Have you ever been the target of social biases? How did you feel when you experienced it?

- What is stigma? How is stigma related to social bias? How is it related to self-esteem, self concept, and behavior? Do you think most people hold stigmas against others? What do you think it is like to be a stigmatized person, for example an individual in a wheelchair?

- What is a stereotype? How and why do you think stereotypes form? Is it only minority and ethnic groups against whom we have stereotypes? How does stereotyping affect people's performance or self-concept, for example students from minority groups?

- Can you think of any methods for reducing social biases in our culture? Can you imagine a society without social biases? What might it be like? Would you want to live in such a society?

 **Links: www.dushkin.com/online/**
These sites are annotated in the World Wide Web pages.

NAACP Online: National Association for the Advancement of Colored People
   http://www.naacp.org
National Civil Rights Museum
   http://www.civilrightsmuseum.org
United States Holocaust Memorial Museum
   http://www.ushmm.org
Yahoo—Social Psychology
   http://www.yahoo.com/Social_Science/Psychology/disciplines/social_psychology/

The man warned Danny not to tell anyone or he would kill Danny's dog. Danny was terrified. The man drove Danny back to the neighborhood, dropped him off, and sped off. When Danny's parents came home, at first they did not notice how dejected he was. After he revealed the story about the man to his mother, his parents phoned the police who quickly came to their home. The boy was so shattered by what had happened to him and so worried about what to tell the police that he became mute. Danny's mother and father retold the story as best they could.

While Danny and his parents were being interviewed by the police, Danny's father revealed something quite incredible. His father stated to the officers that the man who had molested Danny was an African-American. Danny never told his father this, because *it was not true.* This piece of information led the investigating detectives in the wrong direction. When the man was eventually apprehended, he was White. The story is true, but the names and a few details have been changed.

You should be asking yourself, "Why would Danny's parents say the assailant was Black?" Was it an innocent or intentional mistake? Or did they just assume that when bad things happen to Whites, African-Americans must be responsible. You should also ask yourself if minority groups perceive Whites as the root cause of their troubles.

The interrelated issues of *prejudice, discrimination* and *stereotyping* are the topics of the present unit. To relate these terms to the story about Danny, you should know that his parents were very bigoted and simply assumed that someone outside of their own group *must* have committed the crime. Understand that social biases can be both positive (favorable) and negative (harmful). It is the harmful ones, such as the racial prejudice held by Danny's parents, that most concern social psychologists.

Now, let us define the above terms as they relate to social biases. *Prejudice* can be defined as an attitude toward another person or group that is based solely on group membership. An example would be that a middle-aged woman lives near your campus and believes that all college students are wild and drunk. She has little to no respect or liking for them. If you are a college student you *must* be wild and drunk in her opinion, no matter how sober and studious you really are.

Discrimination is a companion to prejudice in that it is the behavioral manifestation of prejudice. In other words, *discrimination* is an action taken against (or occasionally in favor of) a certain individual because of his or her group membership. Continuing the example of the middle-aged woman, suppose she has an apartment to rent, and several interested individuals visit to preview the home and discuss the monthly rental and lease. The woman briskly cuts short any college student's appointment. She absolutely refuses to rent to any of them much less be courteous. When a middle-aged, recently widowed woman inspects the space, the landlord immediately suggests that she is the perfect tenant and leases it to her.

Not all bigots act on their biases. The presence of prejudice does not mean that discrimination always occurs. One significant reason is that federal and state laws now prohibit discrimination against certain protected groups. Recognize, though, that

A young boy named Danny sat quietly, very quietly at the dinner table. Danny was typically chatty and eager to share the day's events with his mother and father. This particular evening, however, Danny was neither talkative nor happy. His parents soon noted the change in his demeanor and asked him what was wrong. Danny kept telling them that everything was fine, but his parents persisted. The change in Danny was too noticeable to ignore. After dinner, Danny's mother went to his room and found him crying. She comforted her child and prodded him to share with her the events of the day.

Danny told the following story. In the morning, he got on the school bus, rode to school, and eagerly finished the school day. In the afternoon, he readied himself for the ride home. The bus ride was uneventful until he stepped off the bus. In a nearby car, a man called and motioned to him to approach. At first the man seemed friendly and told Danny that in the car were some toys specially made for boys Danny's age. Although Danny had been warned by his parents not to talk to strangers, Danny finally acquiesced to the man's seemingly well-meaning entreaties. When Danny got in the man's car, the car sped off to a remote location where the man sexually molested Danny.

attitudes and beliefs are more difficult to legislate than actions. Some people retain their stereotypes and prejudices but do not actively discriminate against others. In fact, social psychological research has documented that both prejudice and discrimination still exist but have become more subtle and covert than in the past—at least in the United States.

The third term related to social bias is stereotypes. *Stereotypes* are widespread generalizations about certain groups of people that have little if any basis in fact. The middle-aged landlord's stereotype of college students as drunk and wild may have been based solely on her experience one night when a handful of students poured onto her street from a nearby bar and caused boisterous commotions that kept her awake—and angry. Because this event stood out in her mind, she stereotyped all college students the same way: rowdy, disorderly, and inebriated.

Unit 7 contains three articles, one each on prejudice, discrimination, and stereotypes. Jennifer Crocker and Brenda Major, two of the leading social psychologists on stigma and biases, describe their intensive research program. The two scientists explain research on how stigma is related to self-esteem. Interestingly, some of their studies have shown that stigma is not always detrimental. Instead, Crocker and Major have found that stigmatized people often use their own groups for social comparison rather than compare themselves to the majority.

The article, "Change of Heart," by Adam Goodheart, discusses discrimination. Despite public policy, discrimination in the U.S. still occurs in housing, employment, and education. The author shares with us the results of two recent public opinion surveys that show discrimination is decreasing over time.

The final article is "Thin Ice: "Stereotype Threat" and Black College Students." Claude Steele writes that negative stereotypes can have powerful effects on minority students' motivation and self-concepts.

The Self-Protective Properties of Stigma: Evolution of a Modern Classic

Jennifer Crocker
Department of Psychology
University of Michigan

Brenda Major
Department of Psychology
University of California at Santa Barbara

We thank Trish Devine for nominating our work as a modern classic and Ralph Erber and Lenny Martin for giving us this opportunity to reflect on how these ideas originated and evolved over time and how others have used them. Our original idea about the self-protective functions of social stigma germinated for a long time, and there are people who directly and indirectly shaped our ideas, some of whom probably have no idea how they influenced us.

The origins of this work, at least in the mind of one of us (Jennifer Crocker) can be traced to a 1982 invitation to attend a summer institute on Stigma and Interpersonal Relations at the Center for Advanced Study in the Behavioral Sciences at Stanford University. Crocker applied to the summer institute because a secretary put the flyer in her mailbox, and it sounded interesting. She had been studying cognitive processes in stereotyping so thought her work was possibly relevant to stigma, although frankly she wasn't sure.

The summer institute was directed by Dale Miller and Bob Scott; included an interdisciplinary group of psychologists, sociologists, education researchers, anthropologists, and historians; and was a truly exciting intellectual experience. Each morning the stigma scholars met as a group to discuss readings that someone in the group had identified as important or interesting. Among those readings was Porter and Washington's *Annual Review of Sociology* chapter on Black identity and self-esteem, which argued that contrary to popular wisdom and a lot of psychological theorizing, Blacks do not always suffer from low self-esteem (Porter & Washington, 1979). At the time, it was a puzzling finding to Crocker, but not particularly relevant to her work on subtyping and stereotype change, and she didn't think further about it.

Over the next few years at Northwestern University, Crocker's research evolved to include more emotional processes, and she began to study the relations among self-esteem, threats to the self, and prejudice. Established wisdom suggested that people who are low in self-esteem are more prejudiced, but her research indicated that when threatened, high self-esteem people are more likely to derogate out-groups or think their group is superior to out-groups (Crocker & Luhtanen, 1990; Crocker, Thompson, McGraw, & Ingerman, 1987).

In 1985, Crocker left Northwestern (their choice, not hers) and joined the faculty at the State University of New York at Buffalo. Her second semester there, she gave a lecture on stereotyping and prejudice in her Introduction to Social Psychology course. After the class, an African American student approached her, observing that she sometimes wondered whether people were prejudiced against her. For example, she said, she drove a new red car, and recently a White man in a pickup truck almost hit her. She wondered if it could have happened because he was prejudiced against her. Although Crocker couldn't give her an answer, the conversation connected in Crocker's mind with the Porter and Washington (1979) article on race and self-esteem. She thought that the uncertainty, or attributional ambiguity that this student had experienced about whether she was the target of prejudice might account for high self-esteem in African Americans.

As Crocker thought about this, she realized that her colleague, Brenda Major, had a research paradigm that might be really useful for studying this phenomenon of attributional ambiguity. Major was interested in why highly attractive women did not have higher self-esteem than those who were less attractive and had done a study showing that attractive women were less likely to think they had written a good essay when the man who praised their essay could see them, because the blinds were up on a one-way mirror, than when the man couldn't see them because the blinds were down (Major, Carrington, & Carnevale, 1984). When the blinds were up, the women suspected he had ulterior motives for praising their essay, and they were less likely to believe they had written a really good essay. Less attractive women did not show this effect.

Crocker scurried to Major's office to talk about this idea and the connection with her previous research. Major was intrigued by Crocker's idea about attributional ambiguity as an explanation for the lack of self-esteem differences between members of stigmatized and nonstigmatized groups. Major also saw connections and implications that had escaped Crocker and broadened the scope of the idea. Attributional ambiguity, she suggested, might not be the only reason that Blacks do not show the low self-esteem predicted by many theories. She suggested that the tendency to make in-group social comparisons and the tendency to devalue certain domains that one's group doesn't tend to succeed in might also protect self-esteem. Major had been studying the phenomenon of "paradoxical contentment" among working women, who are underpaid relative to men yet just as satisfied with their pay. Her research showed that women's tendency to compare their pay with that of other women, instead of comparing it with that of men, could help to explain this paradoxical contentment—women often didn't realize that they were discriminated against, because they didn't know that men made more than them (Major, 1987). Another explanation that had been offered for this effect was that women simply don't care about money as much as men do. Major argued that this might be so because women held a dim view of their prospects of making money. That is, women devalued money as a self-protective device, because they knew that as women they were unlikely to earn a lot. Major had also just finished writing an article with Kay Deaux exploring how targets' self-beliefs and goals interact with perceivers' stereotypical expectations to influence gender-linked behavior (Deaux & Major, 1987). The connection between Major's ideas and research interests and those of Crocker was clear was compelling, and a collaboration was born.

We decided to write a grant proposal to fund some research. Our graduate students (including Bruce Blaine, Wayne Bylsma, Cathy Cozzarelli, Riia Luhtanen, Oscar Romero, Monica Schneider, and Maria Testa) worked with us on designing some studies, and we submitted the proposal. In the meantime, we thought the ideas themselves were compelling enough that we should write them up. Over the next few months, we began conducting studies and wrote a draft of "The Self-Protective Properties of Stigma" (Crocker & Major, 1989).

We knew from the outset that our ideas could be misinterpreted. We were careful not to say that stigmatized people are motivated to perceive prejudice against them. Rather, we said that when those who are stigmatized explain negative outcomes as being due to discrimination rather than as being due to "internal, stable, and global causes" (Crocker & Major, 1989, p. 613) it can have the consequence of protecting self-esteem. And we were worried that people would interpret our article as claiming that stigma, or prejudice, has no harmful consequences, which we were not claiming.

From the beginning, we also realized that stigma was not always self-protective. Our article (Crocker & Major, 1989) included a section on moderating factors, including the time since the acquisition, concealability, internalization of negative attitudes, responsibility for the condition, and centrality of the stigma in the self-concept. And we also recognized and outlined in our article the potential costs of attributional ambiguity, in-group social comparisons, and devaluation for motivation.

Initial Tests of Our Ideas and Where They Led Us

Our initial attempts to test our ideas in the laboratory met with some frustration. We needed to manipulate positive and negative outcomes in ways that were realistic enough to potentially affect self-esteem, to examine whether attributions to stigma, in-group comparisons, or devaluation could protect self-esteem. Creating believable and ethical manipulations that would have an impact became a challenge. Also, we found that the introduction to psychology pool of research participants included few African American students who could participate in our research, so it would take many semesters to recruit enough participants to fill out the design of a study. That was the original impetus for conducting the studies on women who feel overweight. We also naively assumed that we could use a trait measure of self-esteem as a dependent variable in our studies. Although we sometimes were able to find effects on measures of trait self-esteem, in other studies the effects were only significant for depressed affect. Eventually, we realized we needed to measure state self-esteem. We created a state version of the Rosenberg (1965) self-esteem scale and devised an early implicit measure of state self-esteem for this purpose (Bylsma, Tomaka, Luhtanen, Crocker, & Major, 1992).

Our early attempts to study attributional ambiguity underscored the importance of considering the perceived legitimacy of stigmatization from the target's perspective. Although women and African Americans showed some self-protective consequences of attributing negative evaluations to prejudice (Crocker, Voelkl, Testa, & Major, 1991), overweight women who thought they were rejected because of their weight showed drops in self-esteem (Crocker, Cornwell, & Major, 1993). Early on, we began thinking about the idea that some stigmatized people, especially those who feel responsible for their condition, might feel less deserving of positive outcomes and more deserving of negative outcomes. Hence, they might not attribute negative outcomes to prejudice and, even if they do, they might not be protected by such attributions (Crocker & Major, 1994; Major, 1994). These ideas led to another grant proposal and related research (e.g., Major, Gramzow, et al., 2002; Quinn & Crocker, 1999).

Our early studies also taught us that the self-protective strategies we proposed were more complicated than we initially presumed. For example, one of our first devaluing experiments examined whether men and women would personally devalue a trait if they learned that the other gender group scored higher on it than their own gender group. Men devalued the trait, as we had predicted, but women tended not to (Schmader & Major, 1999). In another study we found that African American college students valued school just as much as did European American students, even though the former recognized that their ethnic group did not do as well in school as the latter group. African American students were more likely than European American students, however, to say that their self-esteem did not depend on their performance in school. These studies led us to recognize the difference between devaluing a domain and disengaging one's self-esteem from that domain (Schmader, Major, & Gramzow, 2001).

Our initial studies also led to the insight that attributionally ambiguous positive outcomes can have negative effects on self-esteem and affect. African American students who were favorably evaluated by a European American peer showed a drop in self-esteem (relative to their initial levels) if the evaluator knew their race. This did not occur if the evaluator did not know their race (Crocker et al., 1991). Our attempts to understand this surprising finding led us to consider the conditions under which those who are stigmatized might distrust positive feedback or believe that it does not reflect their true level of deserving (Major & Crocker, 1993). This finding also led to another grant proposal and to explorations of the affective implications of ostensibly positive acts, such as being the beneficiary of assumptive help (Schneider, Major, Luhtanen, & Crocker, 1996), pity (Blaine, Crocker, & Major, 1995), or preferential selection procedures (Major, Feinstein, & Crocker, 1994).

What Others Have Done With Our Ideas

One of the first people to find our work useful was Claude Steele. Steele was just beginning his work on stigma and the underperformance of African American students—work on the phenomenon that has since been called stereotype threat (Steele, 1992; Steele, 1997). His idea that African American students may disidentify with school as a way of maintaining self-esteem shared our perspective on self-esteem protection and devaluation processes among members of stigmatized groups.

Our work led other scholars to reexamine differences in personal self-esteem between members of stigmatized and nonstigmatized groups. Meta-analyses revealed that although African Americans do have higher self-esteem than European Americans (Gray-Little & Hafdahl, 2000; Twenge & Crocker, 2002), other stigmatized groups, such as the overweight (Miller & Downey, 1999), and other ethnic groups, such as Asian Americans, Hispanic Americans, and Native Americans (Twenge & Crocker, 2002), on average have lower self-esteem than those who are not stigmatized. Other researchers found that people with concealable stigmas had lower self-esteem than those who were not stigmatized, whereas those with nonconcealable stigmas did not (Frable, Platt, & Hoey, 1998). These findings raise interesting and still unresolved questions about why some stigmatized groups have high self-esteem and others do not.

Other researchers, assuming that we had claimed that those who are stigmatized are motivated to perceive prejudice against them, tested whether members of stigmatized groups minimize or maximize their likelihood of being a target of prejudice. In a widely cited study, Ruggiero and Taylor (Ruggiero & Taylor, 1995) reported that those who are stigmatized do not attribute their negative outcomes to discrimination unless discrimination is virtually certain in the situation. This finding cast doubt on the hypothesis that those who are stigmatized might attribute at-

tributionally ambiguous negative outcomes to discrimination. Subsequent work by other researchers, however, failed to replicate this finding (e.g., Inman, in press; Kaiser & Miller, 2001a), and other studies purportedly showing it were later retracted (Ruggiero & Marx, 2001). Other researchers explored how attributions to discrimination are affected by individual-differences factors, such as race-rejection sensitivity (Mendoza-Denton, Downey, Purdie, Davis, & Pietrzak, 2002) and stigma consciousness (Pinel, 1999), and situational factors, such as the attitudes of the evaluator and the clarity of prejudice cues (Operario & Fiske, 2001).

Our hypothesis that attributing outcomes to prejudice can protect the self-esteem of those who are stigmatized proved most generative, as well as most controversial. Nyla Branscombe and her colleagues, for example, argued that because group membership is an aspect of self, attributions to prejudice against the group implicate the self and hence are damaging to personal self-esteem. They showed that chronically perceiving oneself or one's group as a victim of pervasive prejudice is negatively correlated with self-esteem and well-being among members of stigmatized groups such as African Americans (Branscombe, Schmitt, & Harvey, 1999). These findings contradicted our speculation that "People who believe that they personally are frequent victims of discrimination … may have high self-esteem" (Crocker & Major, 1989, p. 621). Other researchers, however, found that once the positive correlation between individuals' perceptions that they are targets of racial discrimination and their chronic sensitivity to rejection in interpersonal relationships is controlled, the negative correlation between perceptions of racial discrimination and personal self-esteem is no longer significant (Mendoza-Denton et al., 2002). In retrospect, it is perhaps not surprising that a chronic perception that one has been a victim of discrimination is negatively related to self-esteem, given that this perception is likely to reflect not only attributional processes but also the frequency and severity of discrimination to which an individual has been exposed, as well as personal dispositions to perceive rejection. The implications of perceived prejudice for psychological well-being continue to be a topic of considerable interest to researchers. We urge researchers to be more precise in their use of terms and measurement of constructs, as well as to resist inferring causation from correlation.

Researchers also followed up on our ideas by exploring the conditions under which attributions to discrimination are and are not psychologically beneficial. For example, although attributing negative outcomes to discrimination results in less depressed affect than does attributing them to an internal, stable, global cause such as a lack of ability (Major, Kaiser, & McCoy, 2003), it does not result in less negative affect compared with attributing negative outcomes to a purely external cause, such as another person's being a jerk (Schmidt & Branscombe, 2002). Researchers also demonstrated that attributing negative outcomes to discrimination could be socially costly. African American targets who blame a negative outcome on discrimination are disliked and seen as troublemakers by European American students, regardless of the probability that discrimination was actually the cause of their outcome (Kaiser & Miller, 2001b).

Researchers have also explored alternative ways in which those who are stigmatized may cope with prejudice and discrimination. Drawing on social identity theory (Tajfel & Turner, 1979), Branscombe and her colleagues hypothesized that those who are stigmatized may cope with perceived discrimination by identifying more strongly with their in-group. This increased group identification, in turn, is hypothesized to lead to higher personal and collective self-esteem (e.g., Branscombe et al., 1999).

What We Have Done With Our Ideas

In the years since the publication of our article (Crocker & Major, 1989), Crocker's work has wandered far afield from the original questions that drove us. A serendipitous finding in another line of research led her to think of the issue of stigma and self-esteem in a different way. Specifically, in a study of collective, or group-based, self-esteem (Crocker, Luhtanen, Blaine, & Broadnax, 1994), she found that for White and Asian students, private and public collective self-esteem were highly correlated, whereas for African American students, they were uncorrelated. In other words, how White students view their social groups is strongly linked to how they think others view their groups, whereas for Black students, their view of their groups was disconnected from how they think others view them. This suggested to Crocker that Blacks and Whites might have different sources of self-esteem, with Whites' self-esteem being more based in others' regard and approval (following Cooley, 1902/1956, and Mead's, 1934, suggestions), whereas Blacks' self-esteem was more disconnected from others' approval. Subsequent research has supported this view (Crocker & Blanton, 1999). This line of thinking took Crocker in an entirely new direction, in which the focus of her work became contingencies of self-worth (Crocker & Wolfe, 2001). Although the impetus for this work was her interest in stigma and self-esteem, in her current work this is a side interest. Things have a way of cycling back, however, and Crocker's current interest in the costs of pursuing self-esteem has implications for the experience of prejudice and stigma that may bring her back to this topic.

Major continues to study responses to stigmatization, from a perspective that integrates justice theories with self-esteem theories. She argues that among those who are stigmatized, motives to protect personal and social identity often conflict with motives to justify existing status arrangements (Major & Schmader, 2001). Her current work examines how beliefs about the legitimacy of group status differences affect the use of self-protective strategies among members of disadvantaged and advantaged groups. She finds that members of lower status groups who believe their lower group status is legitimate are unlikely to devalue an attribute or domain in which higher status groups excel. However, if they are led to question the legitimacy of status differences, they do show the devaluing pattern we had predicted (Schmader, Major, Eccleston, & McCoy, 2001). Status legitimacy beliefs also affect the likelihood of attributing negative outcomes to discrimination. The more members of

lower status groups (e.g., Hispanic Americans, women) endorse ideologies that legitimize their lower status (such as the belief in individual mobility), the less likely they are to attribute rejection by a member of a higher status group to discrimination. Just the opposite relationship is observed when members of higher status groups (European Americans, men) are rejected by a member of a lower status group (Major, Gramzow, et al., 2002). These findings are reminiscent of her earlier research on "paradoxical contentment" among members of disadvantaged groups and illustrate that things really do have a way of cycling back! Major also continues to study the nature and antecedents, as well as psychological and behavioral consequences, of believing that one is a target of discrimination. Indeed, the contradictory findings and controversies that plague research in this area impelled her recently to undertake a review and revision of our original attributional ambiguity perspective (Major, McCoy, & Quinton, 2002).

We continue to be fascinated by the question of how people cope with threatened or devalued identities and, in particular, how it is that some people manage to maintain a sense of self-respect and dignity in the face of people, circumstances, and institutions that devalue them. We are honored that our collaboration has inspired the work of others, and we are delighted that after so many years of concentrating on the "perpetrators" of prejudice, our field has begun to give more attention to the psychological predicaments experienced by the targets of prejudice.

Note

Jennifer Crocker, Department of Psychology, University of Michigan, Ann Arbor, MI 48109-1109. E-mail: jcrocker@umich.edu

References

Blaine, B., Crocker, J., & Major, B. (1995). The unintended negative consequences of sympathy for the stigmatized. *Journal of Applied Social Psychology, 25,* 889-905.

Branscombe, N. R., Schmitt, M. T., & Harvey, R. D. (1999). Perceiving pervasive discrimination among African Americans: Implications for group identification and well-being. *Journal of Personality and Social Psychology, 77,* 135-149.

Bylsma, W. H., Tomaka, J., Luhtanen, R., Crocker, J., & Major, B. (1992). Response latency as an index of temporary self-evaluation. *Personality and Social Psychology Bulletin, 18,* 60-67.

Cooley, C. H. (1956). *Human nature and the social order.* New York: Schocken. (Original work published 1902)

Crocker, J., & Blanton, H. (1999). Social inequality and self-esteem: The moderating effects of social comparison, legitimacy, and contingencies of self-esteem. In T. R. Tyler, R. Kramer, & O. John (Eds.), *The social self* (pp. 171-191). Mahwah, NJ: Lawrence Erlbaum Associates, Inc.

Crocker, J., Cornwell, B., & Major, B. M. (1993). The stigma of overweight: Affective consequences of attributional ambiguity. *Journal of Personality and Social Psychology, 64,* 60-70.

Crocker, J., & Luhtanen, R. K. (1990). Collective self-esteem and ingroup bias. *Journal of Personality and Social Psychology, 58,* 60-67.

Crocker, J., Luhtanen, R., Blaine, B., & Broadnax, S. (1994). Collective self-esteem and psychological well-being among White, Black, and Asian college students. *Personality and Social Psychology Bulletin, 20,* 502-513.

Crocker, J., & Major, B. (1989). Social stigma and self-esteem: The self-protective properties of stigma. *Psychological Review, 96,* 608-630.

Crocker, J., & Major, B. (1994). Reactions to stigma: The moderating role of justifications. In M. P. Zanna & J. M. Olson (Eds.), *The psychology of prejudice: The Ontario symposium* (Vol. 7, pp. 289-314). Hillsdale, NJ: Lawrence Erlbaum Associates, Inc.

Crocker, J., Thompson, L., McGraw, K., & Ingerman, C. (1987). Downward comparison, prejudice, and evaluation of others: Effects of self-esteem and threat. *Journal of Personality and Social Psychology, 52,* 907-916.

Crocker, J., Voelkl, K., Testa, M., & Major, B. M. (1991). Social stigma: Affective consequences of attributional ambiguity. *Journal of Personality and Social Psychology, 60,* 218-228.

Crocker, J., & Wolfe, C. T. (2001). Contingencies of self-worth. *Psychological Review, 108,* 593-623.

Deaux, K., & Major, B. (1987). Putting gender into context: An integrative model of gender-related behavior. *Psychological Review, 94,* 369-389.

Frable, D. E. S., Platt, L., & Hoey, S. (1998). Concealable stigmas and positive self-perceptions: Feeling better around similar others. *Journal of Personality and Social Psychology, 74,* 909-922.

Gray-Little, B., & Hafdahl, A. R. (2000). Factors influencing racial comparisons of self-esteem: A quantitative review. *Psychological Bulletin, 126,* 26-54.

Inman, M. L. (in press). Do you see what I see?: Similarities and differences in victims' and observers' perceptions of discrimination. *Social Cognition.*

Kaiser, C. R., & Miller, C. T. (2001a). Reacting to impending discrimination: Compensation for prejudice and attributions to discrimination. *Personality and Social Psychology Bulletin, 27,* 1357-1367.

Kaiser, C. R., & Miller, C. T. (2001b). Stop complaining! The social costs of making attributions to discrimination. *Personality and Social Psychology Bulletin, 27,* 254-263.

Major, B. (1987). Gender, justice, and the psychology of entitlement. In P. Shaver & C. Hendrick (Eds.), *Review of personality and social psychology* (Vol. 7, pp. 124-148). Beverly Hills, CA: Sage.

Major, B. (1994). From social inequality to personal entitlement: The role of social comparisons, legitimacy appraisals, and group membership. In M. P. Zanna (Ed.), *Advances in experimental and social psychology* (Vol. 26, pp. 293-355). San Diego: Academic.

Major, B., Carrington, P. I., & Carnevale, P. (1984). Physical attractiveness and self-esteem: Attributions of praise from an other-sex evaluator. *Personality and Social Psychology Bulletin, 10,* 43-50.

Major, B., & Crocker, J. (1993). Social stigma: The affective consequences of attributional ambiguity. In D. Mackie & D.L. Hamilton (Eds.), *Affect, cognition and stereotyping: Interactive processes in group perception* (pp. 345-370). San Diego, CA: Academic.

Major, B., Feinstein, J., & Crocker, J. (1994). Attributional ambiguity of affirmative action. *Basic and Applied Social Psychology, 15,* 113-141.

Major, B., Gramzow, R., McCoy, S., Levin, S., Schmader, T., & Sidanius, J. (2002).

Attributions to discrimination: The role of group status and legitimizing ideology. *Journal of Personality and Social Psychology, 82,* 269-282.

Major, B., Kaiser, C. R., & McCoy, S. K. (2003). It's not my fault: When and why attributions to prejudice protect self-esteem. *Personality and Social Psychology Bulletin, 29,* 772-781.

Major, B., McCoy, S. K., & Quinton, W. (2002). Antecedents and consequences of attributions to discrimination: Theoretical and empirical advances. In M. P. Zanna (Ed.), *Advances in Experimental Social Psychology* (Vol. 34, pp. 251-349). San Diego: Academic.

Major, B., & Schmader, T. (2001). Legitimacy and the construal of social disadvantage. In J. Jost & B. Major (Eds.), *The psychology of legitimacy: Emerging perspectives on ideology, power, and intergroup relations* (pp. 176-204). New York: Cambridge University Press.

Mead, G. H. (1934). *Mind, self, and society.* Chicago: University of Chicago Press.

Mendoza-Denton, R., Downey, G., Purdie, V. J., Davis, A., & Pietrzak, J. (2002). Sensitivity to race-based rejection: Implications for African-American students' college experience. *Journal of Personality and Social Psychology, 83,* 896-918.

Miller, C. T., & Downey, K. T. (1999). A meta-analysis of heavyweight and self-esteem. *Personality and Social Psychology Review, 3,* 68-84.

Operario, D., & Fiske, S. T. (2001). Ethnic identity moderates perceptions of prejudice: Judgments of personal versus group discrimination and subtle versus blatant bias. *Personality and Social Psychology Bulletin, 27,* 550-561.

Pinel, E. C. (1999). Stigma consciousness: The psychological legacy of social stereotypes. *Journal of Personality and Social Psychology, 76,* 114-128.

Porter, J. R., & Washington, R. E. (1979). Black identity and self-esteem: A few studies of Black self-concept, 1968-1978. *Annual Review of Sociology, 5,* 53-74.

Quinn, D. M., & Crocker, J. (1999). When ideology hurts: Effects of feeling fat and the Protestant ethic on the psychological well-being of women. *Journal of Personality and Social Psychology, 77,* 402-414.

Rosenberg, M. (1965). *Society and the adolescent self-image.* Princeton, NJ: Princeton University Press.

Ruggiero, K. M., & Marx, D. M. (2001). Retraction. "Less pain and more to gain: Why high-status group members blame their failure on discrimination." *Journal of Personality and Social Psychology, 81,* 178.

Ruggiero, K. M., & Taylor, D. M. (1995). Coping with discrimination: How disadvantaged group members perceive the discrimination that confronts them. *Journal of Personality and Social Psychology, 68,* 826-838.

Schmader, T., & Major, B. (1999). The impact of ingroup vs. outgroup performance on personal values. *Journal of Experimental Social Psychology, 35,* 47-67.

Schmader, T., Major, B., Eccleston, C., & McCoy, S. (2001). Devaluing domains in response to threatening intergroup comparisons: Perceiving legitimacy and the status-value asymmetry. *Journal of Personality and Social Psychology, 80,* 736-753.

Schmader, T., Major, B., & Gramzow, R. (2001). Coping with ethnic stereotypes in the academic domain: Perceived injustice and psychological disengagement. *Journal of Social Issues, 57,* 93-112.

Schmidt, M. T., & Branscombe, N. R. (2002). The internal and external causal loci of attributions to prejudice. *Personality and Social Psychology Bulletin, 28,* 620-628.

Schneider, M. E., Major, B., Luhtanen, R., & Crocker, J. (1996). When help hurts: Social stigma and the costs of assumptive help. *Personality and Social Psychology Bulletin, 22,* 201-209.

Steele, C. M. (1992, April). Race and the schooling of Black Americans. *Atlantic, 269,* 68-78.

Steele, C. M. (1997). A threat in the air: How stereotypes shape intellectual identity and performance. *American Psychologist, 52,* 613-629.

Tajfel, H., & Turner, J. C. (1979). An integrative theory of intergroup conflict. In S. Worchel & W. Austin (Eds.), *Psychology of intergroup relations* (Vol. 2, pp. 7-24). Chicago: Nelson-Hall.

Twenge, J., & Crocker, J. (2002). Race, ethnicity, and self-esteem: Meta-analyses comparing Whites, Blacks, Hispanics, Asians, and Native Americans, including a commentary on Gray-Little and Hafdahl (2000). *Psychological Bulletin, 128,* 371-408.

From *Psychological Inquiry,* Vol. 14, No. 3&4, 2003, pp. 232-237. Copyright © 2003 by Lawrence Erlbaum Associates. Reprinted by permission.

Change of Heart

A landmark survey reveals that most Americans are open to sharing their life, work, and even love with people of a different color. So why do tensions remain?

By Adam Goodheart

The rural Maryland county where I live, barely an hour from the Washington, D.C., Beltway, is a place whose soul is not just divided but fractured. There are still small towns here that feel like the Old South, where whites talk about "colored people" and blacks in their late 40s remember such things as farming with mules and horses and attending segregated schools. But there are newer communities, too: sprawling tracts of identical suburban houses whose middle-class residents—black as well as white—think little about the past and care even less. In their midst, a small but growing Hispanic population has started to thrive, drawn by the economic opportunities that change has brought.

Many parts of our country today look something like this. When President Lyndon Johnson's Kerner Commission famously prophesied in 1968 a future of "two societies, one black, one white," it was wrong. What we have now is a multiplicity of Americas, often sharing the same neighborhood, but rarely the same mindset.

The good news is that in the 50 years since the Supreme Court ruled in favor of school desegregation in the case of *Brown* v. *Board of Education*, there have been some dramatic changes in Americans' attitudes toward race and equality. Today, most Americans—55 percent—think that the state of race relations is either very or somewhat good, according to a landmark telephone survey of 2,002 people conducted last November and December by the Gallup Organization for AARP and the Leadership Conference on Civil Rights (LCCR). Yet disheartening divisions between the races persist. Such is the complicated picture painted by "Civil Rights and Race Relations," the largest and most comprehensive race-relations survey of blacks, Hispanics, and whites that Gallup has ever undertaken.

The most astonishing progress has been made in two areas that hit closest to home for most Americans: interracial relationships and the neighborhoods we live in. Consider that 70 percent of whites now say they approve of marriage between whites and blacks, up from just 4 percent in a 1958 Gallup poll. Such open-mindedness ex-

tends across racial lines: 80 percent of blacks and 77 percent of Hispanics also said they generally approve of interracial marriage. Perhaps even more remarkable, a large majority of white respondents—66 percent—say they would not object if their own child or grandchild chose a black spouse. Blacks (86 percent) and Hispanics (79 percent) were equally accepting about a child or grandchild's marrying someone of another race.

When it comes to choosing neighbors, an inclusive spirit again prevails: majorities of blacks, whites, and Hispanics all say they would rather live in racially mixed neighborhoods than surround themselves with only members of their own group. "It's hard now to imagine the level of fear and anxiety that Americans felt about these issues just a few decades ago," says Taylor Branch, who won a Pulitzer Prize in 1989 for his history of the Civil Rights Movement, *Parting the Waters: America in the King Years, 1954-1963*. "The idea [among whites] that you might have a black colleague or customer or neighbor has now become relatively commonplace except in a few scattered pockets." Similarly, slight majorities of whites and Hispanics and a little less than half of blacks think that minorities should try to blend in with the rest of American culture rather than maintain their own separate identities.

The data did show a significant generation gap: young Americans (ages 18-29) of all races were more likely than older respondents (65-plus) to favor the retention of distinctive cultures. But this is not necessarily a step backward. "Younger people are more likely to have been exposed in school to the idea that multiculturalism is a positive thing, that it's not necessarily bad when certain groups desire to be among their own kind," suggests the eminent Harvard sociologist William Julius Wilson. "This is a phenomenon of just the last couple of decades."

When it comes to future expectations, however, in certain respects the picture is as bleak as ever. Sixty-three percent of Americans think that race relations will always be a problem for our country—a view that varies little whether the respondents are white, black, or Hispanic.

Survey Insights

Our respondents told us that they...

1. Would not object to a child or grandchild's marrying someone of another race.

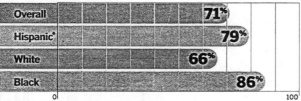

Overall	71%
Hispanic*	79%
White	66%
Black	86%

* Black Hispanics were asked about marrying whites; white Hispanics were asked about marrying blacks.

2. Prefer to live in a neighborhood that is mostly mixed.

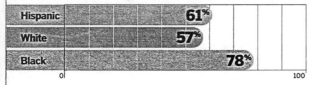

Hispanic	61%
White	57%
Black	78%

3. Believe race relations will always be a problem in the U.S.

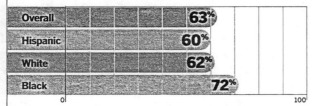

Overall	63%
Hispanic	60%
White	62%
Black	72%

4. Think all or most of the goals of Dr. Martin Luther King Jr. and the Civil Rights Movement have been achieved.

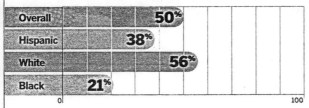

Overall	50%
Hispanic	38%
White	56%
Black	21%

5. Have been denied a rental or an opportunity to buy a home.

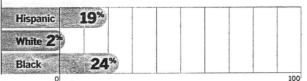

Hispanic	19%
White	2%
Black	24%

*Civil Rights and Race Relations," a study commissioned by AARP and the LCCR and conducted by the Gallup Oranization, is based on telephone interviews with 2,002 people 18 years of age or older from households in the continental United States. All polling was conducted between November 11 and December 14, 2003. The respondents included 915 whites and oversamples of 446 blacks and 551 Hispanics. In addition, 90 who belonged to other groups or gave no racial or ethnic affiliation were interviewed. The results were weighted to reflect the actual representation of each group in the U.S. population. ("Whites" refers to non-Hispanic whites; "black" refers to non-Hispanic blacks; and the "Hispanic" category includes all Hispanics, whether they identified as black or as white or did not specify a racial category.) The margin of error at the 95 percent confidence level for that total national sample is +/-5.1 percentage points. +/-6.7 percentage points for whites, +/-8.5 percentage points for blacks, and +/-6.2 percentage points for Hispanics.

That's up sharply from the 42 percent who felt similarly in a study done in 1963, when most Americans were seeing television images of African Americans withstanding police dogs and fire hoses but believed the Civil Rights Movement would eventually prevail. (Indeed, respondents over 65, who remember the 1960s well, were the ones most likely to remain optimistic, while those under 30—of all races—were the least hopeful.)

"There was a sense then that eventually truth and justice would win out," recalls Julian Bond, who as a founder of the Student Nonviolent Coordinating Committee (SNCC) led some of the earliest sit-ins and is now chairman of the National Association for the Advancement of Colored People (NAACP). "Maybe people are looking back and realizing we haven't come as far as we'd hoped."

A large majority of Americans of all ages and races does agree that the 20th-century crusade for civil rights was a watershed in our nation's history. In addition, most people of all backgrounds also believe that the movement has benefited not just blacks and other minorities but all Americans. This is a remarkable degree of unanimity for an issue that violently divided so many families and communities just a generation or two ago.

"The Civil Rights Movement has had enormous collateral effects for everyone from gays to members of religious minorities, and especially for women," Branch says. "These effects have been felt in every university, every corporation, and even, I'd venture to say, almost every American household, down to the level of who does the dishes and changes the diapers."

But when it comes to gauging the ultimate success or failure of the struggle, members of different races diverge sharply. While 56 percent of whites say they believe that "all or most" of the goals of Dr. Martin Luther King Jr. and the 1960s Civil Rights Movement have been achieved, only 21 percent of blacks agree with them. A similar margin divides whites' and blacks' opinions on how much of a role the movement will continue to have: 66 percent of blacks think it will be "extremely important" to the United States in the future, compared with only 23 percent of whites. "Many whites have a misconception of the Civil Rights Movement as something with a few limited goals that have already been achieved," Branch suggests.

Similarly, the AARP-LCCR survey found vast gulfs between different groups' perceptions of how minorities are treated today. Seventy-six percent of white respondents think that blacks are treated "very fairly" or "somewhat fairly," but only 38 percent of blacks agree with them; nearly one-third, in fact, say that members of their race are treated "very unfairly." (Hispanics fall in the middle: they are more or less evenly divided about the treatment of their own group as well as that of blacks.) And while 61 percent of whites believe that blacks have achieved equality in the realm of job opportunities, just 12 percent of African Americans concur.

How is it that we can all share the same land, the same history, and yet reach such different conclusions? The disparities start to make sense when you look at the most fundamental measure of each group's current happiness: economic prosperity.

Blacks are more than twice as likely as whites to say that their personal finances are in "poor shape"; they are also more than twice as likely to say they worry constantly about whether their family's income will be enough to pay the bills. Hispanics appear to be feeling similar or even greater degrees of financial stress. And indeed, their concerns are legitimate: nationally, the median household income is $35,500 among blacks, $40,000 among Hispanics, and $55,318 among whites, according to the most recent figures available from the U.S. Census Bureau.

"Were we to have solved all the problems that we tried to take on, there would be relative parity today," Bond says. "The fact that there is still an enormous wealth gap between blacks and whites is evidence of the continuing legacy of segregation and even of slavery."

What explains these persistent economic disparities? Continued prejudice, plain and simple. Half a century after *Brown*, a minuscule 8 percent of African Americans could claim that they had ever in their lives been denied admittance to a school on account of race. Yet other forms of discrimination persist. A third reported that they had been passed over for a job because they are black, a third said they had been blocked from promotion, and a quarter said they had been denied an opportunity to rent or buy housing. Only slightly fewer Hispanics said they had experienced similar forms of prejudice.

Even more than such dramatic instances of racism, it is the less obvious, day-to-day examples of prejudice that are a continuing, grinding burden on minorities in America. Nearly half of all blacks reported having experienced at least one form of discrimination in the last 30 days, in settings ranging from stores (26 percent) to restaurants and theaters (18 percent) to public transportation (10 per-

cent). The figures for Hispanics were at nearly the same level. Perhaps most troubling of all, a surprising 22 percent of blacks and 24 percent of Hispanics said they had, in the past month, been the victims of prejudice in an interaction with the police.

For the record, a significant number of white Americans maintain that they, too, are sometimes penalized on the basis of race: 21 percent report that they have been the victims of reverse discrimination, especially in the workplace. And many seem unaware or even dismissive of continuing prejudice against other groups: nearly half insist that society treats them no better than blacks. But the majority of whites—52 percent—say they support affirmative action for blacks, as do 81 percent of blacks and 66 percent of Hispanics. So while an uncomfortably large number of Americans remain in denial about persistent discrimination against minorities, an even larger percentage, it seems, want to do the right thing.

Like the American countryside, the AARP-LCCR survey results are a landscape of layers: old outlooks and new perceptions, 20th-century memories and 21st-century expectations. One of the most unexpected results came when the polltakers asked participants to consider the prediction that by 2050 the majority of Americans will be nonwhite. Only about 13 percent of each group said this would be a bad thing; most Americans said it simply won't matter.

So, as their country changes, perhaps Americans—more than they are often given credit for—are ready to change along with it. Indeed, the revolution that *Brown* started will likely continue through the next 50 years and beyond. "We did much," Bond says, "but there's much left to do."

Adam Goodheart is a fellow of the C. V. Starr Center for the Study of the American Experience at Washington College in Chestertown, Maryland.

From *AARP The Magazine*, May/June 2004. Copyright © 2004 by Adam Goodheart, reprinted with the permission of the Wylie Agency Inc.

THIN ICE:
"STEREOTYPE THREAT" AND
BLACK COLLEGE STUDENTS

When capable black college students fail to perform as well as their white counterparts, the explanation often has less to do with preparation or ability than with the threat of stereotypes about their capacity to succeed. Educators at Stanford who tested this hypothesis report their findings and propose solutions

by CLAUDE M. STEELE

THE buildings had hardly changed in the thirty years since I'd been there. "There" was a small liberal-arts school quite near the college that I attended. In my student days I had visited it many times to see friends. This time I was there to give a speech about how racial and gender stereotypes, floating and abstract though they might seem, can affect concrete things like grades, test scores, and academic identity. My talk was received warmly, and the next morning I met with a small group of African-American students. I have done this on many campuses. But this time, perhaps cued by the familiarity of the place, I had an experience of déjà vu. The students expressed a litany of complaints that could have come straight from the mouths of the black friends I had visited there thirty years earlier: the curriculum was too white, they heard too little black music, they were ignored in class, and too often they felt slighted by faculty members and other students. Despite the school's recruitment efforts, they were a small minority. The core of their social life was their own group. To relieve the dysphoria, they went home a lot on weekends.

I found myself giving them the same advice my father gave me when I was in college: lighten up on the politics, get the best education you can, and move on. But then I surprised myself by saying, "To do this you have to learn from people who part of yourself tells you are difficult to trust."

Over the past four decades African-American college students have been more in the spotlight than any other American students. This is because they aren't just college students; they are a cutting edge in America's effort to integrate itself in the thirty-five years since the passage of the Civil Rights Act. These students have borne much of the burden for our national experiment in racial inte-

gration. And to a significant degree the success of the experiment will be determined by their success.

Nonetheless, throughout the 1990s the national college-dropout rate for African-Americans has been 20 to 25 percent higher than that for whites. Among those who finish college, the grade-point average of black students is two thirds of a grade below that of whites.

The finger-pointing debate over the underperformance of black undergraduates has missed one big culprit—"stereotype threat." This is the threat of being viewed through the lens of a negative stereotype, or the fear of doing something that would inadvertently confirm that stereotype.

A recent study by William Bowen and Derek Bok, reported in their book *The Shape of the River*, brings some happy news: despite this underachievement in college, black students who attend the most selective schools in the country go on to do just as well in postgraduate programs and professional attainment as other students from those schools. This is a telling fact in support of affirmative action, since only these schools use affirmative action in admissions. Still, the underperformance of black undergraduates is an unsettling problem, one that may alter or hamper career development, especially among blacks not attending the most selective schools.

Attempts to explain the problem can sound like a debate about whether America is a good society, at least by the standard of racial fairness, and maybe even about whether racial integration is possible. It is an uncomfortably finger-pointing debate. Does the problem stem from something about black students themselves, such as poor motivation, a distracting peer culture, lack of family values, or—the unsettling suggestion of *The Bell Curve*—genes? Or does it stem from the conditions of blacks' lives: social and economic deprivation, a society that views blacks through the lens of diminishing stereotypes and low expectations, too much coddling, or too much neglect?

In recent years this debate has acquired a finer focus: the fate of middle-class black students. Americans have come to view the disadvantages associated with being black as disadvantages primarily of social and economic resources and opportunity. This assumption is often taken to imply that if you are black and come from a socioeconomically middle-class home, you no longer suffer a significant disadvantage of race. "Why should the son of a black physician be given an advantage in college admission over the son of a white delivery-truck driver?" This is a standard question in the controversy over affirmative action. And the assumption behind it is that surely in today's society the disadvantages of race are overcome when lower socioeconomic status is overcome.

But virtually all aspects of underperformance—lower standardized-test scores, lower college grades, lower graduation rates—persist among students from the African-American middle class. This situation forces on us an uncomfortable recognition: that beyond class, something racial is depressing the academic performance of these students.

Some time ago I and two colleagues, Joshua Aronson and Steven Spencer, tried to see the world from the standpoint of these students, concerning ourselves less with features of theirs that might explain their troubles than with features of the world they see. A story I was told recently depicts some of these. The storyteller was worried about his friend, a normally energetic black student who had broken up with his longtime girlfriend and had since learned that she, a Hispanic, was now dating a white student. This hit him hard. Not long after hearing about his girlfriend, he sat through an hour's discussion of *The Bell Curve* in his psychology class, during which the possible genetic inferiority of his race was openly considered. Then he overheard students at lunch arguing that affirmative action allowed in too many underqualified blacks. By his own account, this young man had experienced very little of what he thought of as racial discrimination on campus. Still, these were features of his world. Could they have a bearing on his academic life?

My colleagues and I have called such features "stereotype threat"—the threat of being viewed through the lens of a negative stereotype, or the fear of doing something that would inadvertently confirm that stereotype. Everyone experiences stereotype threat. We are all members of some group about which negative stereotypes exist, from white males and Methodists to women and the elderly.

And in a situation where one of those stereotypes applies—a man talking to women about pay equity, for example, or an aging faculty member trying to remember a number sequence in the middle of a lecture—we know that we may be judged by it.

Like the young man in the story, we can feel mistrustful and apprehensive in such situations. For him, as for African-American students generally, negative stereotypes apply in many situations, even personal ones. Why was that old roommate unfriendly to him? Did that young white woman who has been so nice to him in class not return his phone call because she's afraid he'll ask her for a date? Is it because of his race or something else about him? He cannot know the answers, but neither can his rational self fully dismiss the questions. Together they raise a deeper question: Will his race be a boundary to his experience, to his emotions, to his relationships?

With time he may be weary of the extra vigilance these situations require and of what the psychologists Jennifer Crocker and Brenda Major have called the "attributional ambiguity" of being on the receiving end of negative stereotypes. To reduce this stress he may learn to care less about the situations and activities that bring it about—to realign his self-regard so that it no longer depends on how he does in the situation. We have called this psychic adjustment "disidentification." Pain is lessened by ceasing to identify with the part of life in which the pain occurs. This withdrawal of psychic investment may be supported by other members of the stereotype-threatened group—even to the point of its becoming a group norm. But not caring can mean not being motivated. And this can have real costs. When stereotype threat affects school life, disidentification is a high price to pay for psychic comfort. Still, it is a price that groups contending with powerful negative stereotypes about their abilities—women in advanced math, African-Americans in all academic areas—may too often pay.

MEASURING STEREOTYPE THREAT

CAN stereotype threat be shown to affect academic performance? And if so, who would be most affected—stronger or weaker students? Which has a greater influence on academic success among black college students—the degree of threat or the level of preparation with which they enter college? Can the college experience be redesigned to lessen the threat? And if so, would that redesign help these students to succeed academically?

As we confronted these questions in the course of our research, we came in for some surprises. We began with what we took to be the hardest question: Could something as abstract as stereotype threat really affect something as irrepressible as intelligence? Ours is an individualistic culture; forward movement is seen to come from within. Against this cultural faith one needs evidence to argue that something as "sociological" as stereotype threat can repress something as "individualistic" as intelligence.

To acquire such evidence, Joshua Aronson and I (following a procedure developed with Steven Spencer) designed an experiment to test whether the stereotype threat that black students might experience when taking a difficult standardized test could depress their performance on the test to a statistically reliable degree. In this experiment we asked black and white Stanford students into our laboratory and gave them, one at a time, a thirty-minute verbal test made up of items from the advanced Graduate Record Examination in literature. Most of these students were sophomores, which meant that the test was particularly hard for them—precisely the feature, we reasoned, that would make this simple testing situation different for our black participants than for our white participants.

In matters of race we often assume that when a situation is objectively the same for different groups, it is *experienced* in the same way by each group. This assumption might seem especially reasonable in the case of "standardized" cognitive tests. But for black students, difficulty with the test makes the negative stereotype relevant as an interpretation of their performance, and of them. They know that they are especially likely to be seen as having limited ability. Groups not stereotyped in this way don't experience this extra intimidation. And it is a serious intimidation, implying as it does that they may not belong in walks of life where the tested abilities are important—walks of life in which they are heavily invested. Like many pressures, it may not be experienced in a fully conscious way, but it may impair their best thinking.

This is exactly what Aronson and I found. When the difficult verbal test was presented as a test of ability, black students performed dramatically less well than white students, even though we had statistically matched the two groups in ability level. Something other than ability was involved; we believed it was stereotype threat.

But maybe the black students performed less well than the white students because they were less motivated, or because their skills were somehow less applicable to the advanced material of this test. We needed some way to determine if it was indeed stereotype threat that depressed the black students' scores. We reasoned that if stereotype threat had impaired their performance on the test, then reducing this threat would allow their performance to improve. We presented the same test as a laboratory task that was used to study how certain problems are generally solved. We stressed that the task did not measure a person's level of intellectual ability. A simple instruction, yes, but it profoundly changed the meaning of the situation. In one stroke "spotlight anxiety," as the psychologist William Cross once called it, was turned off—and the black students' performance on the test rose to match that of equally qualified whites.

Aronson and I decided that what we needed next was direct evidence of the subjective state we call stereotype threat. To seek this, we looked into whether simply sitting down to take a difficult test of ability was enough to make black students mindful of their race and stereotypes about it. This may seem unlikely. White students I have taught over the years have sometimes said that they have hardly any sense of even having a race. But blacks have many experiences with the majority "other group" that make their race salient to them.

We again brought black and white students in to take a difficult verbal test. But just before the test began, we gave them a long list of words, each of which had two letters missing. They were told to complete the words on this list as fast as they could. We knew from a preliminary survey that twelve of the eighty words we had selected could be completed in such a way as to relate to the stereotype about blacks' intellectual ability. The fragment "—ce," for example, could become "race." If simply taking a difficult test of ability was enough to make black students mindful of stereotypes about their race, these students should complete more fragments with stereotype-related words. That is just what happened. When black students were told that the test would measure ability, they completed the fragments with significantly more stereotype-related words than when they were told that it was not a measure of ability. Whites made few stereotype-related completions in either case.

What kind of worry is signaled by this race consciousness? To find out, we used another probe. We asked participants on the brink of the difficult test to tell us their preferences in sports and music. Some of these, such as basketball, jazz, and hip-hop, are associated with African-American imagery, whereas others, such as tennis, swimming, and classical music, are not. Something striking emerged: when black students expected to take a test of ability, they spurned things African-American, reporting less interest in, for instance, basketball, jazz, and hip-hop than whites did. When the test was presented as unrelated to ability, black students strongly preferred things African-American. They eschewed these things only when preferring them would encourage a stereotypic view of themselves. It was the spotlight that they were trying to avoid.

STEREOTYPE THREAT VERSUS SELF-FULFILLING PROPHECY

ANOTHER question arises: Do the effects of stereotype threat come entirely from the fear of being stereotyped, or do they come from something internal to black students—self-doubt, for example?

Beginning with George Herbert Mead's idea of the "looking-glass self," social psychology has assumed that one's self-image derives in large part from how one is viewed by others—family, school, and the broader society. When those views are negative, people may internalize them, resulting in lower self-esteem—or self-hatred, as it has been called. This theory was first applied to the experience of Jews, by Sigmund Freud and Bruno Bettelheim, but it was also soon applied to the experience of African-Americans, by Gordon Allport, Frantz Fanon, Kenneth Clark, and others. According to the theory, black students internalize negative stereotypes as performance anxiety and low expectations for achievement, which they then fulfill. The "self-fulfilling prophecy" has become a commonplace about these students. Stereotype threat, however, is something different, something external: the situational threat of being negatively stereotyped. Which of these two processes, then, caused the results of our experiments?

Joshua Aronson, Michael Lustina, Kelli Keough, Joseph Brown, Catherine Good, and I devised a way to find out. Suppose we told white male students who were strong in math that a difficult math test they were about to take was one on which Asians generally did better than whites. White males should not have a sense of group inferiority about math, since no societal stereotype alleges such an inferiority. Yet this comment would put them under a form of stereotype threat: any faltering on the test could cause them to be seen negatively from the standpoint of the positive stereotype about Asians and math ability. If stereotype threat alone—in the absence of any internalized self-doubt—was capable of disrupting test performance, then white males taking the test after this comment should perform less well than white males taking the test without hearing the comment. That is just what happened. Stereotype threat impaired intellectual functioning in a group unlikely to have any sense of group inferiority.

In science, as in the rest of life, few things are definitive. But these results are pretty good evidence that stereotype threat's impairment of standardized-test performance does not depend on cueing a pre-existing anxiety. Steven Spencer, Diane Quinn, and I have shown how stereotype threat depresses the performance of accomplished female math students on a difficult math test, and how that performance improves dramatically when the threat is lifted. Jean-Claude Croizet, working in France with a stereotype that links poor verbal skills with lower-class status, found analogous results: lower-class college students performed less well than upper-class college students under the threat of a stereotype-based judgment, but performed as well when the threat was removed.

Is everyone equally threatened and disrupted by a stereotype? One might expect, for example, that it would affect the weakest students most. But in all our research the most achievement-oriented students, who were also the most skilled, motivated, and confident, were the most impaired by stereotype threat. This fact had been under our noses all along—in our data and even in our theory. A

person has to care about a domain in order to be disturbed by the prospect of being stereotyped in it. That is the whole idea of disidentification—protecting against stereotype threat by ceasing to care about the domain in which the stereotype applies. Our earlier experiments had selected black students who identified with verbal skills and women who identified with math. But when we tested participants who identified less with these domains, what had been under our noses hit us in the face. None of them showed any effect of stereotype threat whatsoever.

These weakly identified students did not perform well on the test: once they discovered its difficulty, they stopped trying very hard and got a low score. But their performance did not differ depending on whether they felt they were at risk of being judged stereotypically.

WHY STRONG STUDENTS ARE STEREOTYPE-THREATENED

THIS finding, I believe, tells us two important things. The first is that the poorer college performance of black students may have another source in addition to the one—lack of good preparation and, perhaps, of identification with school achievement—that is commonly understood. This additional source—the threat of being negatively stereotyped in the environment—has not been well understood. The distinction has important policy implications: different kinds of students may require different pedagogies of improvement.

The second thing is poignant: what exposes students to the pressure of stereotype threat is not weaker academic identity and skills but stronger academic identity and skills. They may have long seen themselves as good students—better than most. But led into the domain by their strengths, they pay an extra tax on their investment—vigilant worry that their future will be compromised by society's perception and treatment of their group.

This tax has a long tradition in the black community. The Jackie Robinson story is a central narrative of black life, literature, and journalism. *Ebony* magazine has run a page for fifty years featuring people who have broken down one or another racial barrier. Surely the academic vanguard among black college students today knows this tradition—and knows, therefore, that the thing to do, as my father told me, is to buckle down, pay whatever tax is required, and disprove the damn stereotype.

That, however, seems to be precisely what these students are trying to do. In some of our experiments we administered the test of ability by computer, so that we could see how long participants spent looking at different parts of the test questions. Black students taking the test under stereotype threat seemed to be trying too hard rather than not hard enough. They reread the questions, reread the multiple choices, rechecked their answers, more than when they were not under stereotype threat. The threat made them inefficient on a test that, like most standardized tests, is set up so that thinking long often means thinking wrong, especially on difficult items like the ones we used.

Philip Uri Treisman, an innovator in math workshops for minority students who is based at the University of Texas, saw something similar in his black calculus students at the University of California at Berkeley: they worked long hours alone but they worked inefficiently—for example, checking and rechecking their calculations against the correct answers at the back of the book, rather than focusing on the concepts involved. Of course, trying extra hard helps with some school tasks. But under stereotype threat this effort may be misdirected. Achievement at the frontier of one's skills may be furthered more by a relaxed, open concentration than by a strong desire to disprove a stereotype by not making mistakes.

Sadly, the effort that accompanies stereotype threat exacts an additional price. Led by James Blascovich, of the University of California at Santa Barbara, we found that the blood pressure of black students performing a difficult cognitive task under stereotype threat was elevated compared with that of black students not under stereotype threat or white students in either situation.

In the old song about the "steel-drivin' man," John Henry races the new steam-driven drill to see who can dig a hole faster. When the race is over, John Henry has prevailed by digging the deeper hole—only to drop dead. The social psychologist Sherman James uses the term "John Henryism" to describe a psychological syndrome that he found to be associated with hypertension in several samples of North Carolina blacks: holding too rigidly to the faith that discrimination and disadvantage can be overcome with hard work and persistence. Certainly this is the right attitude. But taken to extremes, it can backfire. A deterioration of performance under stereotype threat by the skilled, confident black students in our experiments may be rooted in John Henryism.

This last point can be disheartening. Our research, however, offers an interesting suggestion about what can be done to overcome stereotype threat and its detrimental effects. The success of black students may depend less on expectations and motivation—things that are thought to drive academic performance—than on trust that stereotypes about their group will not have a limiting effect in their school world.

HOW TO REDUCE STEREOTYPE THREAT

PUTTING this idea to the test, Joseph Brown and I asked, How can the usual detrimental effect of stereotype threat on the standardized-test performance of these students be reduced? By strengthening students' expectations and confidence, or by strengthening their trust that they are not at risk of being judged on the basis of stereotypes? In the ensuing experiment we strengthened or weakened participants' confidence in their verbal skills, by arranging for them to have either an impressive success or an impressive failure on a test of verbal skills, just before they took the same difficult verbal test we had used in our earlier research. When the second test was presented as a test of ability, the boosting or weakening of confidence in their verbal skills had no effect on performance: black participants performed less well than equally skilled white participants. What does this say about the commonsense idea that black students' academic problems are rooted in lack of self-confidence?

What did raise the level of black students' performance to that of equally qualified whites was reducing stereotype threat—in this case by explicitly presenting the test as racially fair. When this was done, blacks performed at the same high level as whites even if their self-confidence had been weakened by a prior failure.

These results suggest something that I think has not been made clear elsewhere: when strong black students sit down to take a difficult standardized test, the extra apprehension they feel in comparison with whites is less about their own ability than it is about having to perform on a test and in a situation that may be primed to treat them stereotypically. We discovered the extent of this apprehension when we tried to develop procedures that would make our black participants see the test as "race-fair." It wasn't easy. African-Americans have endured so much bad press about test scores for so long that, in our experience, they are instinctively wary about the tests' fairness. We were able to convince them that our test was race-fair only when we implied that the research generating the test had been done by blacks. When they felt trust, they performed well regardless of whether we had weakened their self-confidence beforehand. And when they didn't feel trust, no amount of bolstering of self-confidence helped.

Policies for helping black students rest in significant part on assumptions about their psychology. As noted, they are typically assumed to lack confidence, which spawns a policy of confidence-building. This may be useful for students at the academic rearguard of the group. But the psychology of the academic vanguard appears different—underperformance appears to be rooted less in self-doubt than in social mistrust.

Education policy relevant to non-Asian minorities might fruitfully shift its focus toward fostering racial trust in the schooling situation—at least among students who come to school with good skills and high expectations. But how should this be done? Without particulars this conclusion can fade into banality, suggesting, as Alan Ryan has wryly put it in *Liberal Anxieties and Liberal Education*, that these students "will hardly be able to work at all unless everyone else exercises the utmost sensitivity to [their] anxieties." Sensitivity is nice, but it is an awful lot to expect, and even then, would it instill trust?

That is exactly what Geoffrey Cohen, Lee Ross, and I wondered as we took up the question of how a teacher or a mentor could give critical feedback across the "racial divide" and have that feedback be trusted. We reasoned that an answer to this question might yield insights about how to instill trust more broadly in the schooling environment. Cohen's hunch was that niceness alone wouldn't be enough. But the first question had to be whether there was in fact a racial divide between teachers and students, especially in the elite college environment in which we worked.

We set up a simple experiment. Cohen asked black and white Stanford students one at a time to write essays about their favorite teachers, for possible publication in a journal on teaching. They were asked to return several days later for feedback on their essays. Before each student left the first writing session, Cohen put a Polaroid snapshot of the student on top of his or her essay. His ostensible purpose was to publish the picture if the essay was published. His real purpose was to let the essay writers know that the evaluator of their writing would be aware of their race. When they returned days later, they were given constructive but critical feedback. We looked at whether different ways of giving this feedback engendered different degrees of trust in it.

We found that neither straight feedback nor feedback preceded by the "niceness" of a cushioning statement ("There were many good things about your essay") was trusted by black students. They saw these criticisms as probably biased, and they were less motivated than white students to improve their essays. White students took the criticism at face value—even as an indication of interest in them. Black students, however, faced a different meaning: the "ambiguating" possibility that the criticism was motivated by negative stereotypes about their group as much as by the work itself. Herein lies the power of race to make one's world insecure—quite apart from whatever actual discrimination one may experience.

But this experiment also revealed a way to be critical across the racial divide: tell the students that you are using high standards (this signals that the criticism reflects standards rather than race), and that your reading of their essays leads you to believe that they can meet those standards (this signals that you do not view them stereotypically). This shouldn't be faked. High standards, at least in a relative sense, should be an inherent part of teaching, and critical feedback should be given in the belief that the recipient can reach those standards. These things go without saying for many students. But they have to be made explicit for students under stereotype threat. The good news of this study is that when they *are* made explicit, the students trust and respond to criticism. Black students who got this kind of feedback saw it as unbiased and were motivated to take their essays home and work on them even though this was not a class for credit. They were more motivated than any other group of students in the study—as if this combination of high standards and

assurance was like water on parched land, a much needed but seldom received balm.

REASSESSING THE TEST-SCORE GAP

THERE is, of course, another explanation for why black college students haven't fared well on predominantly white campuses: they aren't prepared for the competition. This has become an assumption of those who oppose affirmative action in college admissions. Racial preference, the argument goes, brings black students onto campuses where they simply aren't prepared to compete.

The fact most often cited in support of the underpreparation explanation is the lower SAT scores of black students, which sometimes average 200 points below those of other students on the same campus. The test-score gap has become shorthand for black students' achievement problems. But the gap must be assessed cautiously.

First, black students have better skills than the gap suggests. Most of the gap exists because the proportion of blacks with very high SAT scores is smaller than the corresponding proportions of whites and Asians. Thus when each group's scores are averaged, the black average will be lower than the white and Asian averages. This would be true even if the same admissions cut-off score were used for each group—even if, for example, affirmative action were eliminated entirely. Why a smaller proportion of blacks have very high scores is, of course, a complex question with multiple answers, involving, among other things, the effects of race on educational access and experience as well as the processes dwelt on in this article. The point, though, is that blacks' test-score deficits are taken as a sign of underpreparation, whereas in fact virtually all black students on a given campus have tested skills within the same range as the tested skills of other students on the campus.

In any case, the skills and preparation measured by these tests also turn out not to be good determinants of college success. As the makers of the SAT themselves tell us, although this test is among the best of its kind, it measures only about 18 percent of the skills that influence first-year grades, and even less of what influences subsequent grades, graduation rates, and professional success.

Indulge a basketball analogy that my colleagues Jay Rosner and Lee Ross and I have developed. Suppose that you were obliged to select a basketball team on the basis of how many of ten free throws a player makes. You'd regret having to select players on the basis of a single criterion. You'd know that free-throw shooting involves only a few of the skills that go into basketball—and, worse, you'd know that you'd never pick a Shaquille O'Neal.

You'd also wonder how to interpret a player's score. If he made ten out of ten or zero out of ten, you'd be fairly confident about making a judgment. But what about the kid who makes five, six, or seven? Middling scores like these could be influenced by many things other than underlying potential for free-throw shooting or basketball playing. How much practice was involved? Was the kid having a good or a bad day? Roughly the same is true, I suggest, for standardized-test scores. Are they inflated by middle-class advantages such as prep courses, private schools, and tours of European cathedrals? Are they deflated by race-linked experiences such as social segregation and being consistently assigned to the lower tracks in school?

In sum, black college students are not as underprepared in academic skills as their group score deficit is taken to suggest. The deficit can appear large, but it is not likely to be the sole cause of the troubles they have once they get on campus.

Showing the insufficiency of one cause, of course, does not prove the sufficiency of another. My colleagues and I believed that our laboratory experiments had brought to light an overlooked cause of poor college performance among non-Asian minorities: the threat to social trust brought about by the stereotypes of the larger society. But to know the real-life importance of this threat would require testing *in situ*, in the buzz of everyday life.

To this end Steven Spencer, Richard Nisbett, Kent Harber, Mary Hummel, and I undertook a program aimed at incoming first-year students at the University of Michigan. Like virtually all other institutions of higher learning, Michigan had evidence of black students' underachievement. Our mission was clear: to see if we could improve their achievement by focusing on their transition into college life.

We also wanted to see how little we could get away with—that is, to develop a program that would succeed broadly without special efforts. The program (which started in 1991 and is ongoing) created a racially integrated "living and learning" community in a 250-student wing of a large dormitory. It focused students on academic work (through weekly "challenge" workshops), provided an outlet for discussing the personal side of college life (through weekly rap sessions), and affirmed the students' abilities (through, for example, reminding them that their admission was a vote of confidence). The program lasted just one semester, although most students remained in the dormitory wing for the rest of their first year.

Still, it worked: it gave black students a significant academic jump start. Those in the program (about 15 percent of the entering class) got better first-year grades than black students outside the program, even after controlling for differences between these groups in the skills with which they entered college. Equally important, the program greatly reduced underperformance: black students in the program got first-year grades almost as high

as those of white students in the general Michigan population who entered with comparable test scores. This result signaled the achievement of an academic climate nearly as favorable to black students as to white students. And it was achieved through a concert of simple things that enabled black students to feel racially secure.

One tactic that worked surprisingly well was the weekly rap sessions—black and white students talking to one another in an informal dormitory setting, over pizza, about the personal side of their new lives in college. Participation in these sessions reduced students' feelings of stereotype threat and improved grades. Why? Perhaps when members of one racial group hear members of another racial group express the same concerns they have, the concerns seem less racial. Students may also learn that racial and gender stereotypes are either less at play than they might have feared or don't reflect the worst-feared prejudicial intent. Talking at a personal level across group lines can thus build trust in the larger campus community. The racial segregation besetting most college campuses can block this experience, allowing mistrust to build where cross-group communication would discourage it.

Our research bears a practical message: although stereotypes held by the larger society may be hard to change, it is possible to create educational niches in which negative stereotypes are not felt to apply—and which permit a sense of trust that would otherwise be difficult to sustain.

Our research bears a practical message: even though the stereotypes held by the larger society may be difficult to change, it is possible to create niches in which negative stereotypes are not felt to apply. In specific classrooms, within specific programs, even in the climate of entire schools, it is possible to weaken a group's sense of being threatened by negative stereotypes, to allow its members a trust that would otherwise be difficult to sustain. Thus when schools try to decide how important black-white test-score gaps are in determining the fate of black students on their campuses, they should keep something in mind: for the greatest portion of black students—those with strong academic identities—the degree of racial trust they feel in their campus life, rather than a few ticks on a standardized test, may be the key to their success.

Claude M. Steele is the Lucie Stern Professor in the Social Sciences at Stanford University. His articles have appeared in *The New York Times* and *The American Prospect*.

From *The Atlantic Monthly*, August 1999, pp. 44-47, 50-54. © 1999 by Claude M. Steele with permission of the author.

UNIT 8
Violence and Aggression

Unit Selections

Key Points to Consider

- What is violence? What is aggression? What is bullying? Do you think that these behaviors have increased in our society in the last decade? If yes, why? What are you doing to reduce violence that you see on the streets or in the media?

- Is there too much violence in the media in your opinion? Are there media, not mentioned in the anthology, that also contain violence (e.g. comic books)? How has the content of televised violence changed, and what are the effects of these changes? If you were a legislator, what laws would you want put into effect as related to media violence?

- What types of television programs are scheduled when young children are watching? Do you think children are more influenced by media violence than adults? If you were a parent, what types of programs would you want your child to watch? As a parent, how could you ensure that your child wasn't overexposed to media violence? If your child was attracted to violent programs, what would you as a parent do about it?

- Do you know the mock prison study? How does it explain the Iraqi prisoner abuse? How was the mock prison study different from what happened in Iraq? Do you think prisoner abuse is a common occurrence? What do you think could have been done differently to prevent the abuse in Iraq? How can prisons and staff be reformed so that abuse is less likely?

- What is a bully? Why do children bully? What are the consequences of bullying to the victim? Have you ever been the subject of bullying? Have you ever bullied anyone else? What can parents and teachers do to intercede between victim and bully?

- How can we reduce violence and aggression in our society? What is negotiation? How does it function? How does negotiation help participants better manage conflict? Are there situations where negotiation is appropriate? Inappropriate?

 **Links: www.dushkin.com/online/**
These sites are annotated in the World Wide Web pages.

MINCAVA: Minnesota Center Against Violence and Abuse
http://www.mincava.umn.edu

National Consortium on Violence Research
http://www.ncovr.heinz.cmu.edu/docs/data_mission.htm

Jacob was a quiet baby, but he was adorable with his full cheeks, blonde hair, and blue eyes. Jake was his parent's first child, and his mother lavished him with attention and affection. She was so proud of him when a shopper at the grocery store stopped her to take a closer look. At other times, his mother would sit in the park and watch all the toddlers playing. As she compared Jake to the other children, she thought he was the cutest and smartest of all.

Everything changed for Jake when he entered kindergarten. Not only was Jake smaller than the other children, he was younger and a bit slower. The teacher noticed this immediately and began giving Jake the extra attention he seemed to need. Although he was only five, the added help embarrassed him. The other children noticed, too. A few of them wondered out loud why Jake never seemed to get his projects finished on time or done well.

By the time Jake entered first grade, he had fallen hopelessly behind. Other children knew the alphabet and colors; Jake did not. In response to his needs, Jake's first grade teacher placed him in the "Sparrows" reading group. Other children were assigned to the "Robins" or the "Swallows" groups. Jake's classmates soon realized that the Sparrows were the slowest reading group of all. They read easier books and progressed less quickly than did the other two groups.

Some of the children taunted and bullied the Sparrows on the playground or refused to allow them to participate in projects. Jake was on the receiving end of the most hurtful behavior by his classmates. After occasionally admonishing her students, the teacher felt helpless to change the other children's negativity toward Jake.

When Jake started falling behind in school, his father became harsh and critical, especially when Jake was held back and repeated first grade. His mother tried to stand up to her husband on Jake's behalf but did not succeed so eventually withdrew from the dispute. The recurring criticism by his father made young Jake retreat to his room and cry. He did so as softly as possible so his father would not call him "a baby."

When Jake entered second grade, he was a different child. He was angry, sullen, and brooding. Jake seemed to smolder when the other children came near him, and he rejected any nurturing efforts on the part of his teacher and mother. Late one afternoon, when his mother was at the store, Jake once again brought home a failing report card. Not only were his grades low, his teacher had noted in several places Jake's lack of effort and lack of cooperation with the other children. Jake's father was furious and called him "stupid." Jake went upstairs, climbed to the top of his father's closet, pulled out the shotgun, and killed his father with a single blast. He then pumped ten more bullets into the lifeless body. Then Jake ran away.

Sadly, the above story is true. Why do children tease other children? How do humans become so angry that they kill one another? The issue of aggression is the primary subject of Unit 8. Four articles introduce you to the causes, consequences of, and solutions to violence and aggression in society.

The first article details research on media violence. Televisions, movies, video games, and other forms of media introduce violence every day to American homes. Nancy Signorielli, writing about prime-time violence, provides an excellent summary of the effects of media violence. She concludes that the amount of violence has not decreased much, but the type of brutality and its outcomes have changed—for the worse.

The second article is "How Psychology Can Help Explain the Iraqi Prisoner Abuse." After reviewing the types of abuse, the article summarizes the results of and likens the abuse to Zimbardo's now famous mock prison research. In the research, the behavior of guards became so atrocious that the investigation was terminated early.

Bullying by and of school children is another important form of abuse and is discussed in this unit. Why bullying occurs and how to intervene when it happens are the topics of "Bullying: It Isn't What it Used to Be."

Social psychologists are very concerned about the causes and consequences of violence and aggression. Their work would be incomplete if they did not also offer methods for managing these behaviors. Manning and Robertson in "Influencing, Negotiating, and Conflict Handling," review research that demonstrates not only is negotiation effective, it goes *beyond* simple conflict management.

Prime-Time Violence 1993-2001:

Has the Picture Really Changed?

Violence remained stable in prime-time network programs broadcast between the spring of 1993 and the fall of 2001 and similar to levels found in studies of the 1970s and 1980s. Violence appeared in 6 out of 10 programs, at a rate of 4.5 acts per program. Violence was context-free. There was little gratuitous or graphic violence, few characters were punished for their involvement in violence, and few overall consequences. The lack of context may teach that violence is "sanitary," not necessarily immoral, and that those who commit violence are not sorry for their actions, or punished for their transgressions.

Nancy Signorielli

Concerns about television violence have sparked intense debate since television's earliest days. There is general agreement that violence exists on television, but because of differences in the way violence is defined and measured, there is little agreement, and considerable controversy, about the degree or amount of violence (Signorielli, Gross, & Morgan, 1982; Signorielli, Gerbner, & Morgan, 1995; Lometti, 1995). The importance of the context in which violence on television is presented is a recent focus in this research (Kunkel et al., 1995; Smith et al., 1998). This analysis will update our knowledge of the portrayal of violence on television by examining weeklong samples of prime-time network programming broadcast between the spring of 1993 and the fall of 2001, looking for change in the amount of violence as well as more information about the context of violence. This study provides an opportunity to replicate some of the work of both the Cultural Indicators Project and the National Television Violence Study (NTVS). The sample spans 9 years of prime-time broadcast programming and includes variables that permit comparisons with studies conducted during the past 30 years.

The Policy Perspective

In the past forty years, public concern about television violence has fluctuated, almost cyclically. For the ten years between 1968 and 1978, there was considerable public concern and numerous Congressional Hearings about the amount of violence on television. Most, if not all, of these hearings did not result in substantive action (Hoerrner, 1999). Public debate subsided during the 1980s era of deregulation. Concern about television violence surfaced again in the early 1990s with the passing of the Television Violence Act (designed to protect the networks from antitrust action if they joined to talk about ways to reduce violence on television). Toward the end of 1992, when it appeared as though little had changed in regard to television violence, the close expiration date of the Television Violence Act prompted its author, Senator Paul Simon (Democrat-Illinois), to warn of harsher legislation. The result was a renewed promise by network executives that they would explore ways to reduce violence in prime time (Dustin, 1992). In 1993, for the first time since the late 1970s, Congressional hearings on television violence were held and a number of separate bills relating to television violence were introduced in Congress (Hoerrner, 1999). In response to Congressional concern, the television industry implemented parental "advisories" before those programs they designated as "violent." These advisories, however, did not adequately solve the problem and an amendment was added to the Telecommunications Act of 1996 that mandated all television sets 13 inches or larger, manufactured after 1999, be equipped with the V-Chip, an electronic device that enables parents to screen and block the programs their children watch on television. The television industry was asked to develop a rating system to use with the V-Chip to filter violent and sexually explicit programming (FCC, 2000). The result was the implementation of ratings (TV-G, TV-PG, TV-PG14, and TV-M), similar to those used by the motion picture industry, supplemented by advisories for content (V-violence, S-sexual situations, D-suggestive dialogue, and L-language).

The Theoretical Perspective

Numerous theories explain why the study of television violence is important and how it may affect viewers, especially children. Desensitization (see Potter, 1999) and social learning-social cognitive theory (Bandura, 1986), for example, examine the immediate and typically harmful effects of viewing violence. Cultivation theory, on the other hand, looks at viewing violence from a cumulative, long-term perspective, involving three areas: institutional-policy perspectives, messages about violence on television, and, ultimately, effects.

Cultivation theory argues that to understand the effects of viewing on attitudes, beliefs, and behaviors we must examine television as a collective symbolic environment with an underlying formulaic structure (Gerbner, Gross, Morgan, Signorielli, & Shannahan, 2002). Commercial constraints necessitate that common themes cut across all programs. These, in turn, cultivate common world views and stereotypes. Violence is one such theme and is especially important in the cultivation perspective because people are more likely to experience violence when they watch television (whether in news or entertainment programs) than in real life. Consequently, cultivation theory predicts that people's conceptions about violence are more likely to reflect the messages about violence they see, day in and day out, on television. Cultivation research has found that those who watch more television are more likely to view the world as a mean and scary place, to believe that crime and violence are more prevalent than they actually are, and to take precautions to protect themselves, their homes, and their families against crime (Gerbner, Gross, Morgan & Signorielli, 1994).

Violence on Television

While there were some studies in the 1950s and 1960s, most of our knowledge of violence on television comes from the Cultural Indicators Project and the National Television Violence Study. The Cultural Indicators Project examines and measures the amount of physical violence on television by monitoring prime-time and weekend daytime network broadcast television programming and studied relationships between television viewing and conceptions of social reality (Gerbner, Morgan, & Signorielli, 1994; Gerbner, Gross, Morgan & Signorieili, 1980a, 1980b, 1986; Gerbner & Signorielli, 1990; Signorielli, 1990; Gerbner, et al., 2002), periodically publishing the results as the Violence Profile.

One report (Gerbner, Morgan, & Signorielli, 1994) found, for samples of prime-time programs broadcast between 1973 and the fall of 1992, that violence appeared in seven out of 10 programs at the rate of 5.3 incidents per hour and 4.6 incidents per program and that half of the major characters in these programs were involved in violence. Moreover, the figures reported for the samples broadcast during the early 1990s were under the Project's 25-year averages. In the sample of programs from the 1992-93 season, while 65.0% of prime-time fictional dramatic programs contained violence and 45.6% of the characters were involved in violence, the average frequency of violent acts was 2.9 per hour, about three-fifths of the 25-year average.

The National Television Violence Study (NTVS) (Wilson, Kunkel, Linz, Potter, Donnerstein, Smith, Blumenthal, & Gray, 1997, 1998; Smith, et al., 1998) examined physical violence in three yearly samples (1994-95, 1995-96, and 1996-97) of three composite weeks of programming across 23 channels operating between 6:00 a.m. and 11:00 p.m. each day. The sample (N = 8,200) included broadcast (commercial networks, independent stations, and public television) and cable channels (basic and premium offerings). All genres except game shows, religious programs, "infomercials" or home shopping channels, sports, instructional programs, and news were included (Smith, et al., 1998).

In all of the programming sampled, the NTVS found no change in the prevalence of violence from the 1994-95 to the 1996-97 television seasons; 58% of the programs in the 1994-95 sample, 61% of the programs in the 1995-96 sample, and 61% of the programs in the 1996-97 sample contained violence. There was, however, in prime time (8:00 p.m. to 11:00 p.m.) an 8% increase in the overall level of violence in cable and broadcast programs; 59% of the programs in the 1994-95 sample, 66% of the programs in the 1995-96 sample, and 67% of the programs in the 1996-97 sample contained violence. The largest increase from 1994-95 to 1996-97 (14%) was found for those programs broadcast on the commercial networks. Thus, in prime time, the time of day that draws the largest share of viewers, particularly on the commercial networks (ABC, CBS, NBC, and FOX), the percentage of programs with violence increased.

A more recent examination of the 1996-1997 NTVS data (Smith, Nathanson, & Wilson, 2002), found that the amount of violence in prime-time programs was similar to that found in programs aired during other times of the day. Violence was found in six out of ten programs and the rate of violent interactions in prime time was 6.63 per hour, compared to 6.40 per hour during other times of the day. This analysis found that 67% of broadcast network programs contained violence that appeared at a rate of 5.16 violent interactions per hour, figures similar to those for programs on basic cable. Premium cable programming, on the other hand, had the most violence—88% of the programs at a rate of 12.40 violent interactions per hour.

There have been two other studies of television violence in 1990s programming. An industry (ABC, CBS, NBC, and FOX) funded study (Cole, 1995, 1998) monitored at least four episodes of every prime-time and Saturday morning (7:00 a.m. to noon) network program in each of three seasons (1994-95, 1995-96, and 1996-97) and two weeks of programs on independent stations, public television, and pay cable. While this analysis did not provide overall measures of the level of violence, there was a drop, between 1994-95 and 1996-97, in the number of television series that raised frequent concerns about the way violence was presented. The only programs that raised more concerns at the end of this three-year period were reality shows (e.g., World's Most Dangerous Animals and World's Scariest Police Chases).

The Center for Media and Public Affairs (Lichter & Amundson, 1992) isolated physical violence on 10 channels (network, independent, and cable) during one day. Violence appeared most frequently during the afternoon (2 to 5 p.m.) with 191 acts per hour, early morning (6 to 9 a.m.) 158 acts per hour, and during prime time with 102 acts per hour. In an update, Lichter, Lichter, and Amundson (1999) isolated acts of violence in two randomly selected, constructed weeks of prime-time network and cable fictional programs (N = 284) and 50 movies on cable and broadcast television during the 1998-99 season. They found 12 acts of violence per episode (half were "serious") in broadcast programs and 10 per episode (half were "serious") in cable programs.

The data from these studies, particularly the Cultural Indicators Project in the early 1990s and the National Televison Violence Study, are at odds with expectations given the posturing and promises made by network executives before, during, and after the 1993 round of congressional hearings (Hearings, 1993; Dustin, 1992). Consequently, this analysis will examine the level of violence in prime-time programs between the spring of 1993 and the fall of 2001.

RQ1: Has the amount of violence in samples of prime-time network programs broadcast decreased between the spring of 1993 and the fall of 2001?

Context of Violence

A second area of interest is the context in which violence is presented within storylines. The Cultural Indicators Project examined humor and program genre in relation to violence. During the 1970s, slightly more than a quarter of prime-time programs were comic in nature and less than half (45.5%) included violence at a rate of 2.0 incidents per program and 3.6 incidents per hour. In addition, close to half of the network prime-time programs were action-adventures, an exceptionally violent genre, with 94.5% containing some violence at a rate of 7.8 inci-

dents per program and 6.8 incidents per hour (Gerbner, Gross, Morgan, & Signorielli, 1980b). Similarly, Signorielli (1990) in an analysis through the fall 1985 sample, found that only one in five prime-time programs had humorous violence.

The National Television Violence Study advanced our understanding of the contextual elements in the portrayal of violence on television (Wilson, et al., 1997, 1998; Smith, et al., 1998). The NTVS examined the consequences of violence, whether or not humor was involved, the graphic nature of the violence, whether or not weapons were used, and the degree of realism. The analysis of data from the 1994-95 sample found that the context in which violence is presented poses risks for viewers (NTVS, 1994-1995). In particular, three-quarters of the violent scenes had unpunished perpetrators, negative consequences of violence were rarely presented, one-quarter of the violence incidents involved the use of a handgun, and less than one in 20 programs emphasized anti-violence themes. Yet, television violence was not particularly graphic. While the analysis found that broadcast network programs had less violence than cable channels, the context of violence on both broadcast and cable was similar.

The NTVS also examined year-to-year changes in the portrayal of the contextual elements of violence. Looking specifically at violent broadcast programming, only 35% of the prime-time programs in 1994-95, 23% of the programs in 1995-96, and 24% in 1996-97 had any long-term negative consequences of violence. At the same time, there was no display of remorse, regret, or sanctions in 6 out of 10 of the violent scenes in these samples. Similarly, while two-thirds of the violent interactions in the 1994-95 sample did not show any pain as a result of violence, this proportion dropped to slightly more than half of the violent interactions (54% in the 1995-96 sample and 53% in the 1996-97 sample). This analysis indicated that violence on television, examined at the program, scene, and interaction level, is antiseptic and devoid of pain and suffering. Interestingly, there were no substantial changes from year to year (Smith, et al., 1998).

Smith, et al., (2002) found that prime-time broadcast network programming and basic cable programming were less likely than premium cable programming to include violent interactions that depicted pain or harm. The violent interactions in premium cable programs also were more likely to show long-term consequences of violence than those in network broadcast programs or the basic cable programs. Consequently, this analysis also shows that prime-time network broadcast programs are relatively devoid of pain and suffering.

Potter and Smith (2000), in an analysis of data from the 2nd year of the NTVS (1995-96), examined the context of graphic portrayals of violence. This analysis found that most violence presents a low level of graphicness and that the violence in fantasy programs rarely exhibits graphicness. High levels are only found in one out of ten violent actions. Moreover, it tends to be presented with a high degree of realism such as the violence seen in live action programs (recreated reality programs) with human targets and perpetrators. The use of guns and knives (shooting or stabbing a victim) is also related to higher levels of graphic violence.

Potter, et al.'s, (1995) analysis of a composite week (6 p.m. to midnight) of programs broadcast on ABC, CBS, FOX, and NBC in the spring of 1994, also found that aggressive acts were context-less; fewer than one in six acts had any major consequences, only one in six acts was punished, while one-third were actually rewarded. Although Potter and Ware (1987) found that only one in ten acts of violence was punished and that heroes and villains were equally likely to commit antisocial acts, violence, at least from the perspective of the perpetrator, was seen as justified. Similarly, Lichter, Lichter, and Amundson (1999) found that most television violence did not have either psychological or physical consequences and occurred in a moral vacuum because heroes typically saw the violence they committed as justified (in self-defense, in a law enforcement context, etc.)

Given the potential importance of contextual elements in conveying messages about violence in society, this study will continue the examination of the context in which violence is portrayed on television. It will explore the degree of humorous violence whose importance can be understood from the perspective of cultivation theory. While some of the earliest research in the observational learning/social cognitive perspective (Bandura, 1986, 1990; Bandura, Ross, & Ross, 1963, 1961), along with other early studies of symbolic aggression (Lovas, 1961), found that youngsters often learn and reproduce violent behaviors after seeing cartoon/humorous violence, cultivation theory posits that humorous violence is an effective way to convey lessons of power. Although comic violence may appear less threatening, the actions are often mean-spirited with few realistic consequences, a sure formula for influence. These lessons typically translate to conceptions of living in a mean and dangerous world and overestimating chances of being involved in violence by those who watch more television. Specifically, those who watch more television, compared to those who watch less, tend to believe that most people "cannot be trusted," that most people are "just looking out for themselves" and overestimate how many people are involved in violence and the number of people who are involved in crime detection and law enforcement (Gerbner, et al., 1980a, 1994; Signorielli, 1990).

Cultivation theory also explains the importance of the significance of violence reflected in the complex social scenario illustrated by the patterns of committing violence and victimization in characterizations as well as the frequency of violence in the program. These elements ultimately cultivate a sense of fear, intimidation, and vulnerability reflected in the positive relationships between television viewing and scores on both the Mean World Index and the Index of Alienation and Gloom (Signorielli,

1990). In short, the more violence there is and the more important it is for the storyline, the more likely viewers believe that they live in a mean and dangerous world. Similarly, those who watch more television, particularly those who have been to college, are more likely to feel more bored, depressed, and lonely (Morgan, 1984).

The examination of graphic, immoral, intentional, and justified violence as well as the portrayal of the physical consequences of violence are also critical to the understanding of the context of television violence. Each of these elements is supported by several theories, including desensitization (Potter, 1999) and social learning/social cognitive theory (Bandura, 1986). Cultivation theory is also relevant because it explores how these elements relate to how different groups of viewers perceive their own vulnerability. Specifically, heavy viewers are more likely to believe they will be victims of violence and consequently more likely to buy more guns and locks as well as have watchdogs for protection (Gerbner, Gross, Signorielli, Morgan, b Jackson-Beeck, 1979).

In light of the above, this study will examine the context in which violence is portrayed, exploring humorous, significant, graphic, immoral, intentional, and justified violence as well as the physical consequences of violence. The analysis will also look for changes in contextual elements between the spring of 1993 and the fall of 2001 and how often multiple contexts of violence appear.

RQ2: What is the context of violence and have there been changes in the context of violence in samples of prime-time network programs broadcast between 1993 and 2001?

RQ3: How often does the storyline provide a context for violence and how many different contexts are seen within the same program?

The last area of focus for this analysis explores character involvement in violence. The cultivation perspective has shown that television violence illustrates and provides lessons about power. Violence shows who's on top and who's on the bottom, who gets hurt and who does the hurting. Studies have consistently found a demographic power structure, with women and minorities more likely to be hurt than to hurt others. Violence Profile No. 11 (Gerbner, et al., 1980a, 1980b), for example, found that between 1969 and 1979, 60% of the male major characters compared to 40% of the female major characters were involved in violence (either hurting others or being hurt themselves). Whites were more likely than minorities to be involved in violence; more than half of the minority men, compared to 60% of the white men and less than one-quarter of the minority women, compared to 40% of the white women either hurt others or were hurt themselves. During the 1970s these patterns favored victimization.

Gerbner, Morgan, and Signorielli (1994) found that, during the 1980s, male characters were slightly less likely to be involved in violence than in the 1970s. More than half of the male characters (56%) in the 1980s, compared to 60% in the 1970s either hurt others or were hurt themselves. The percentage of women involved in violence, on the other hand, increased slightly during the 1980s. In the 1970s 40% of the women were involved in violence while 44% were involved during the 1980s. Once again, characters were somewhat more likely to be victimized than to hurt others.

While the National Television Violence Study (Smith, et al., 1998) did not generate a profile of all characters on television, it did examine the demographic makeup of perpetrators and targets of violence. Most of the perpetrators (close to three-quarters) were men while only one in ten was a woman. Few perpetrators were categorized as heroes and most were white. More than four out of ten (43%) were "bad" while more than a quarter (28%) were "good" and one in ten were both "good and bad." Similarly, most of the targets were men (71%) while only 10% were women and most were white. Potter, et al. (1995) also found that men were more likely than women to perpetuate aggressive acts, particularly those of a serious nature. They note, however, that these higher rates of aggression, and hence the unrealistic nature of the portrayals, are due to the overrepresentation of men on television (Signorielli & Bacue, 1999). Potter, et al. (1995) also found that the television world typically presents an unrealistic picture of serious aggression in regard to the race of those who commit the acts as well as those who are victimized. In short, television overrepresents both white perpetrators and white victims of aggression.

Although Potter, et al.'s (1995) research as well as the NTVS and the CI reports differ considerably in how they isolate characters' involvement in violence, the patterns are similar—more men than women and more whites than minorities. This study will extend the analysis of those involved in violence, examining if they remain at the high levels of the 1970s and 1980s and if those involved in violence are more likely to be men than women and/or whites than nonwhites.

The patterns of violence and victimization clearly demonstrate power and cultivation theory posits that these depictions serve to intimidate rather than incite and to paralyze rather than trigger action (Gerbner, 2002). Those who watch more tend to overestimate their chances of being involved in violence, believe that their neighborhoods are unsafe, and believe that crime is a very serious problem and is rising, despite data to the contrary (Gerbner, Gross, Morgan, & Signorielli, 1984). This leads to the last research question.

RQ4: What are the demographic and contextual patterns of characters' involvement in violence between the spring of 1993 and the fall of 2001?

Method

The study builds upon Cultural Indicators research on television violence. The sample consists of 13 weeks of prime-time[1] network dramatic programming, broad cast between the spring of 1993 and the fall of 2001. The sample has 1,127 programs and 4,885 major and supporting characters. The analysis examined prime-time network programs because, despite the proliferation of cable channels and other media outlets and their availability, network prime-time programs remain the most readily available to most viewers. Prime-time programs are consistently seen by at least half of the population (Nielsen, 2000). The samples were analyzed as part of an ongoing class project at an Eastern university. There were two samples in 1993, 1997, 1998, and 1999—one collected in the spring and one in the fall; the remaining years only sampled fall programming. The weeks sampled were not selected during a sweeps period and only network programming (ABC, CBS, NBC, FOX, UPN and WB[2]) was included. The samples were drawn around the same time each year; the fall samples in late September and early October and the winter/early spring samples in January and March (February was omitted because it is a sweeps month). Numerous tests to assess the validity of week-long samples have found that a week of programming gives a fairly accurate description while being cost and time effective (Signorielli, et al., 1982).

The coders were junior and senior communication majors.[3] Their three-week training consisted of discussions to explain coding schemes as well as hands-on coding of programs that had been specifically selected and precoded for the training process. The recording instruments, although not identical, included many of the same variables. Those used in this study had identical coding schemes in each of the samples.

The television program and the major/supporting character were the units of analysis. The program unit consisted of television plays (sitcoms, dramas, and action programs), feature or made-for-television films, some animation (e.g., The Simpsons), reality, news/information, and award-type programs. The news/information and award programs were omitted from this analysis. The major/supporting characters were those roles essential to the story line; coders were instructed to include the character if their omission would have substantially changed the plot. All of the characters selected for coding were included in the sample.

The recording instruments isolated numerous dimensions of content. The definition of violence was that used in the Cultural Indicators Project: "The overt expression of physical force (with or without a weapon, against self or other) compelling action against one's will on pain of being hurt or killed, or actually hurting or killing" (Signorielli, et al., 1982, p. 163). To be coded, violence had to be plausible and credible; idle threats and verbal abuse were not coded. All acts of violence that fit the definition, regardless of conventional notions about types of violence that might have "serious" effects, were recorded. Violence in a humorous context was included. "Accidental" violence and "acts of nature" were also recorded because they are purposeful, claim victims, and demonstrate power. Coders counted all of the acts of violence (a scene of some violence confined to the same agents) within a program.

Context of Violence

The context of violence was examined from the perspective of the program and the character. There were eight variables describing the contexts in which violence was portrayed within the program's story line. The seriousness (or potential seriousness) of violence, isolated whether violence was always presented in a humorous/comic way, sometimes in a humorous way, or was mostly real, serious violence, even if in a cartoon or comedy. Humorous violence is included because humor is often an effective way to present serious lessons about violence in society (Gerbner, et al., 1980a). The significance of violence examined the importance of violence to the plot and main characters; violence was coded as not appearing, as minor or incidental to the plot, or significant to the plot. The intentionality of violence isolated whether the violence was mostly unintentional, both intentional and unintentional, or mostly intentional. Context variables at the program level also isolated the degree of immoral, justified, gratuitous, and graphic violence. Immoral violence was violence that was clearly and explicitly intended, within the story, to be seen as destructive, negative, or evil. Justified violence was violence that was clearly and explicitly intended, within the context of the story, to be seen as just or as a means to an end. Gratuitous/excessive violence was beyond that which would be essential to the plot. Graphic violence was descriptive, vivid, and/or gory in nature. Each of these four variables was coded using the following scheme: no violence in the program, no violence fitting the definition of intentional, immoral, justified, gratuitous, or graphic violence, and violence fitting the above definitions. The physical consequences of violence isolated whether or not viewers were shown the physical results/consequences of violence. Again, the coding scheme differentiated between having no violence at all, no violence with physical consequences, or if physical consequences were presented in the story line. In order to determine if contexts of violence were likely to occur within the same program, a summated measure of context was calculated by counting the number of separate contexts that appeared within each program. This measure had a high level of internal consistency (Cronbach's [alpha] = .94). Most of the variables measuring the context of violence within the program are similar to variables used in other studies of television violence (Potter, 1999), including the National Television Violence Study (Smith, et al., 1998).

Last, characters in major and supporting roles were coded on a number of demographic (gender, race, etc.) and descriptive variables relating to their involvement in violence and the context of violence within their characterization. Violence committed (coded at the highest degree of behavior) examined whether the character did not commit violence, hurt others, or killed. Similarly, victimization (coded at the highest degree) determined if the character did not get hurt, was hurt, or was killed. Four variables were added in the fall of 1997 and examined the context in which characters were involved in violence. Consequences of violent behavior isolated whether or not a character's violent behavior was rewarded or punished. The coding scheme included not engaging in violent behavior, violent behavior neither rewarded nor punished, violent behavior mostly rewarded, violent behavior mostly punished, or violent behavior both rewarded and punished. Justified violence was violence that was portrayed as just or as a means to an end. The scheme differentiated if the character did not engage in violent behavior, the violent behavior was not portrayed as justified, or the violent behavior was justified. Immoral violence was violence portrayed as immoral, destructive, negative, or evil, and each character was coded as committing no violent behavior, violent behavior that was not immoral, or violent behavior that was immoral. The recording instrument also examined the character's reaction to violence (whether or not the character exhibited remorse). This coding scheme differentiated characters by whether they did not engage in violent behavior, did not show remorse, or exhibited remorse. Again, Potter (1999) discusses most of these variables in relation to studies that measure the context of television violence.

Reliability and Data Analyses

Three-quarters or more of the programs in each of the samples were coded by two independent coders to provide a test of reliability. Roughly 80% of the characters in each sample were isolated by both coders. Reliability was measured for each variable in each sample by Krippendorff's (1980) alpha. The average value of alpha for the 13 samples was .95 for gender and .90 for race; the 13-sample average for the number of violent actions was .71, ranging from a low of .66 to a high of .87. The agreement coefficients for the program and character variables in each sample meet standards outlined by Krippendorff (1980); for simplicity, 13-sample averages are reported.[4]

Many of the data analyses are one-way analyses of variance in which the independent variable is the sample year and the dependent variable is the proportion of programs with the element being examined—for example, the proportion of programs with comic violence. These values, when presented in the text, are reported as percentages to simplify the discussion. Analyses reporting the average number of violent actions or the average number of contexts of violence also test for statistical significance with one-way analyses of variance in which the independent variable is the sample year and the dependent variable is the mean score (effect size = eta-squared). Tests for linear trends were conducted to determine if

Table 1
Average Number of Violent Actions (VA) and Percent of Programs with Violence (%V) from Spring 1993 to Fall 2001

Sample Year	N of Programs	Avg. N of VA	SD	% V
1993 Spring	79	3.48	6.24	63.3
1993 Fall	76	4.05	7.39	59.2
1994 Fall	79	4.48	7.87	77.2
1995 Fall	85	3.06	5.34	49.4
1996 Fall	78	4.65	7.60	65.4
1997 Spring	76	5.71	7.80	68.4
1997 Fall	110	3.29	5.66	56.9
1998 Spring	81	4.67	8.42	56.8
1998 Fall	90	3.66	6.27	66.7
1999 Spring	90	3.26	5.81	48.9
1999 Fall	96	8.20	17.25	69.8
2000 Fall	88	5.45	10.81	53.4
2001 Fall	100	4.82	8.86	63.0
Total	1127	4.53	8.81	61.2

there were either increases or decreases in the presentation of violence on prime time during the 1990s. The analysis of data for characters does not look for year-to-year trends and uses a cross-tab format, with statistical significance tested by chi-square.

Results

The percentage of programs with violence remained stable between the spring of 1993 and the fall of 2001 (Table 1). Approximately 60% of the programs in each year have some violence, with the smallest percentages in the fall of 1995 (49.4%) and the fall of 1999 (48.9%) and the largest in the fall of 1994 (77.2%). Also, from the spring of 1993 to the fall of 2001, the number of violent actions ranged from a low of 3.06 per program to a high of 8.20 per program. The analysis of variance shows a statistically significant difference from year to year in the average number of violent actions ($F = 2.36$, $df = 12,1116$, $p < .01$; Eta-Sq = .025) along with a significant linear trend ($F = 2.11$, df = 11,1116; $p < .05$). This finding, however, is due to the spike in violent actions in the fall 1999 sample (8.20 per program). The results of the Duncan Multiple Range Test indicate that the average number of violent actions in the fall of 1999 is significantly different from the average in each of the other samples except for the spring of 1997. There are no statistical differences between the other sample means. This spike is due to three reality programs with excessive numbers of violent actions; if these three programs are removed from the analysis there are no differences between the samples ($F = 1.31$, df = 12,1113, ns; Eta-sq = .014), no linear trend ($F = 1.20$, df = 11,1113, ns), and the average number of violent actions for the fall 1999 sample drops to 5.60 (SD = 9.20). Consequently, it is prudent to conclude that the amount of violence in the 1990s through the fall of 2001 has not increased or undergone any major changes. Violence appears in six out ten programs and with four to five acts of violence per program.

RQ2 asks about the context of violence and if there have been changes during the 1990s. One element of the context of television violence is how important (significant) violence is to the plot. Table 2 shows that violence was a significant or major element of the plot in one-third of the programs and a minor element is slightly more than a quarter of the programs. Once again, these distributions were fairly stable through the 1990s.

Another element of context is whether or not violence is presented as a serious or comic plot element. In these samples of prime-time network broadcasting, more than four out of ten programs have violence that is serious in nature while less than a quarter of the programs have violence that is humorous or somewhat humorous. The data in Table 3 indicate that these percentages were stable during the 1990s. One-way analyses of variance for humorous violence (F = 1.66, df = 12,1116, ns; Eta-sq = .018) and serious violence (F = 1.06, df = 12,1116, ns; Eta-sq = .011) were not statistically significant.

As can be seen in Table 4, the majority of the programs do not show many contextual elements for the violence. The context that appeared most frequently was intentional violence in four out of ten programs. Gratuitous and graphic violence each appeared in about a quarter of the programs, while justified violence, immoral violence, and showing the consequences of violence were found in about a third of the programs.

The one-way analyses of variance examining differences by sample year in the degree of immoral (F = 1.15, df = 12,1116; Eta-sq = .012), gratuitous (F = 1.37, df = 12,1116;

Table 2

Significance of Violence from Spring 1993 to Fall 2001

Sample	No Violence Row %	Minor Violence Row %	Major Violence Row %	N of Programs
1993 Spring	36.7	31.6	31.6	79
1993 Fall	40.8	23.7	35.5	76
1994 Fall	22.8	40.5	36.7	79
1995 Fall	50.6	22.4	27.1	85
1996 Fall	34.6	35.9	29.5	78
1997 Spring	31.6	25.0	43.4	76
1997 Fall	43.1	30.3	26.6	110
1998 Spring	43.2	30.9	25.9	81
1998 Fall	33.3	32.2	34.4	90
1999 Spring	51.1	21.1	27.8	90
1999 Fall	30.2	26.0	43.8	96
2000 Fall	46.6	19.3	34.1	88
2001 Fall	37.0	29.0	34.0	100
Total	38.8	29.0	34.0	1127

$x^2 = 42.46$, $df = 24$, $p < .01$; $V = .137$, $p < .01$

Table 3

Humorous and Serious Violence in Prime-Time Programs from Spring 1993 to Fall 2001

Sample	None Row %	Comic Row %	Mixed Row %	Serious Row %	N of Programs N
1993 Spring	35.4	22.8	3.8	38.0	79
1993 Fall	40.8	15.8	3.9	39.5	76
1994 Fall	22.8	25.3	7.6	44.3	79
1995 Fall	48.2	17.6	3.5	30.6	85
1996 Fall	33.3	25.6	3.8	37.2	78
1997 Spring	31.6	22.4	3.9	42.1	110
1997 Fall	42.7	18.2	8.2	30.9	81
1998 Spring	44.4	21.0	6.2	28.4	90
1998 Fall	33.3	25.6	4.4	36.7	90
1999 Spring	51.1	11.1	5.6	32.2	90
1999 Fall	30.2	16.7	10.4	42.7	96
2000 Fall	46.6	4.5	6.8	42.0	88
2001 Fall	36.6	14.9	6.9	41.6	100
Total	38.4	18.3	5.9	37.3	1128

$x^2 = 55.64$, $df = 36$, $p < .02$; $V = .128$, $p < .02$

Eta-sq = .015), and intentional violence (F = 1.74, df = 8,801; Eta-sq = .017) were not statistically significant. There were, however, significant year-to-year differences and linear trends for the consequences of violence, graphic and justified violence. For the consequences of violence (F = 2.94, df = 11,1038, p < .001; Eta-sq = .030) the differences were found primarily in three sample years: the fall of 1995

when only 18.8% of the programs showed any consequences of violence, the fall of 1994 when only 24.1% of the programs had consequences, and the fall of 1999 when almost half (49%) of the programs showed the consequences of violence. The pattern for the data in Table 4 for this variable indicates an increase in the percentage of programs showing the consequences of violence from the mid-1990s

Table 4

Context of Violence in Prime-Time Network Programs
from Spring 1993 to Fall 2001

Sample	Immoral Row%	Gratuitous Row %	Graphic Row %	Intention Row %	Justified Row %	Conseq Row %	None R%	Total Programs
1993 Spring	25.3	16.5	N/A	N/A	36.7	N/A	49.4	79
1993 Fall	31.6	25.0	N/A	N/A	30.3	31.6	46.1	76
1994 Fall	34.2	19.0	19.0	N/A	30.4	24.1	45.6	79
1995 Fall	25.9	24.7	16.5	N/A	25.9	18.8	54.1	85
1996 Fall	37.2	20.5	21.8	41.0	42.3	43.6	37.2	78
1997 Spring	42.1	34.2	28.9	51.3	40.8	46.1	40.8	76
1997 Fall	30.9	17.3	16.4	38.2	25.5	32.7	46.6	109
1998 Spring	27.2	28.4	14.8	30.9	32.1	30.9	46.9	81
1998 Fall	24.4	25.6	21.1	48.9	38.9	36.7	40.0	90
1999 Spring	32.2	26.7	21.1	34.4	26.7	40.0	51.1	90
1999 Fall	42.7	31.3	41.7	37.5	43.8	49.0	31.3	96
2000 Fall	36.4	20.5	33.0	40.9	36.4	35.2	48.9	88
2001 Fall	35.6	27.7	34.7	48.5	42.6	40.6	38.6	100
Total	33.6	24.4	24.6	41.2	34.7	35.9	44.2	1128

Immoral: $X^2 = 49.02$, $df = 24$, $p < .002$, $V = .147$, $p < .001$

Gratuitous: $X^2 = 54.21$, $df = 24$, $p < .001$, $V = .155$, $p < .00$

Graphic: $X^2 = 76.45$, $df = 20$, $p < .001$, $V = .198$, $p < .001$

Intentional: $X^2 = 44.60$, $df = 16$, $p < .01$, $V = .135$, $pp < .01$

Justified: $X^2 = 54.34$, $df = 24$, $p < .001$, $V = .155$, $p < .001$

Consequences: $X^2 = 77.94$, $df = 22$, $p < .001$, $V = .193$, $p < .001$

to the end of the 1990s, with a leveling off in the fall of 2000 and 2001. The percentage of programs with graphic violence also increased from the mid-1990s to the end of the decade. The year-to-year differences were statistically significant ($F = 3.98$, $df = 10, 963$, $p < .01$; Eta-sq = .040) and there was a significant linear trend ($F = 2.39$, $df = 9,963$, $p < .01$). The analysis for justified violence was barely significant ($F = 1.81$, $df = 12,1116$, $p < .05$; Eta-sq = .019) and there was no linear trend. Justified violence was least likely to be found in the fall of 1995 (25.9%) and the fall of 1997 (25.5%) and found most often in the fall of 1996, the fall of 1999, and the fall of 2001.

The summated measure of the context of violence found that 44.2% of the programs presented no context for the violence (Table 4). More than half of the programs in the fall of 1995, the spring of 1998, and the spring of 1999 samples did not have any context of violence while the sample from the fall of 1999 had the largest percentage of programs with a context for the violence. Interestingly, this was the sample with the highest number of violent incidents. Table 5 shows the average number of contexts for each year for the entire sample as well as only those programs with violence ($N = 690$). This analysis found, in programs with violence, that the average number of contexts per program was 2.88, ranging from 1.24 in the spring of 1993 to 3.78 in the fall of 2000. The differences from year to year were statistically significant ($F = 13.93$, $df = 12,676$, $p < .001$; Eta-sq = .198), with a statisti-

cally significant linear trend ($F = 3.60$, $df = 11,679$, $p < .001$). In the entire sample, there were, on average, 1.76 contexts per program, again with year to year statistically significant differences ($F = 6.46$, $df = 12,1116$, $p < .001$ Eta-sq = .065) and a significant linear trend ($F = 2.75$, $df = 11,1116$, $p < .01$). In general, these analyses show that the number of violent contexts increased during the 1990's.

Tables 6 and 7 provide the data to answer RQ4: What are the patterns of the characters' involvement in violence during the 1990s? This analysis does not break out the data by sample year but looks at overall differences between men and women, and whites and minorities. Table 6 examines the patterns of committing violence and being victimized. Only one-third of all the characters are involved in violence, either by hurting or killing others or being hurt or killed themselves. While more men than women are so involved—38.0% of the men compared to 27.3% of the women ([chi square] = 60.40, $df = 1$, $p < .001$; $V = .111$, $p < .001$), the proportions of whites and minorities are almost equal ([chi square] = 2.80, $df = 1$, ns; $V = .024$, ns). Men are more likely to both commit violence and to be victimized: 27.5% of the men commit violence compared to 19.0% of the women ([chi square] = 54.11, $df = 2$, $p < .001$; $V = .05$, $p < .001$) and 27.0% of the men are victimized compared to 17.4% of the women ([chi square] = 62.88, $df = 2$, $p < .001$; $V = .11$, $p < .001$). Again, there are no differences in the percent of whites and minorities who commit violence or who are victimized. Interestingly, during the 1990s the ratios of

Table 5

Average Number of Contexts per Program from Spring 1993 to Fall 2001

	All Programs			Programs With Violence		
Sample	N	Mean	SD	N	Mean	SD
1993 Spring	79	0.78	0.89	50	1.24	0.82
1993 Fall	76	1.18	1.39	45	2.00	1.28
1994 Fall	79	1.27	1.56	61	1.64	1.59
1995 Fall	85	1.12	1.52	42	2.21	1.49
1996 Fall	78	2.06	2.03	51	3.16	1.69
1997 Spring	76	2.43	2.37	52	3.56	2.06
1997 Fall	110	1.61	1.82	62	2.82	1.55
1998 Spring	81	1.64	2.11	46	2.89	2.05
1998 Fall	90	2.06	1.87	60	3.08	1.44
1999 Spring	90	1.81	2.22	44	3.70	1.75
1999 Fall	96	2.46	2.12	67	3.52	1.64
2000 Fall	88	2.02	2.24	47	3.78	1.63
2001 Fall	100	2.30	2.26	63	3.65	1.79
Total	1128	1.76	1.99	690	2.88	1.80

Table 6

Patterns of Committing Violence and Being Victimized in Prime-Time Programs
from Spring 1993 to Fall 2001

	Men		Women		Whites		Minorities		Total
	R%	C%	R%	C%	R%	C%	R%	C%	C%
Total N =		2859		2026		3953		889	4885
Violence									
Not Commit	55.7	72.6	44.3	81.1	82.0	76.5	18.0	74.7	76.1
Hurts others	65.0	20.8	35.0	15.7	79.8	18.1	20.2	20.5	18.6
Kills	74.2	6.7	25.8	3.3	83.1	5.3	16.9	4.8	5.3
Victimization									
Not Hurt	55.4	73.0	44.6	82.6	81.7	77.1	18.3	76.8	77.0
Gets Hurt	67.7	23.3	32.3	15.6	81.9	20.1	18.1	19.8	20.1
Is Killed	73.9	3.7	26.1	1.8	78.4	2.8	21.6	3.4	2.9
Involved Viol									
Not Involved	54.6	62.0	45.4	72.7	81.9	66.7	18.1	65.8	66.5
Involved	66.2	38.0	33.4	27.3	81.2	33.3	18.8	34.2	33.5
Involved Kill									
Not Involved	57.5	91.4	42.5	95.3	81.7	93.1	18.3	93.0	93.0
Involved	71.9	8.6	26.1	4.7	81.6	6.8	18.4	7.0	7.0

R% = Row Percentages; C% = Column Percentages
Violence: Gender: $X^2 = 54.11$, $df = 2$, $p < .001$, V = .105,
$p < .001$; Race: $X^2 = 2.80$, $df = 2$, ns, V = .024, ns
Victim: Gender: $X^2 = 62.88$, $df = 2$, $p < .001$, V = .114,
$p < .001$; Race: $X^2 = 1.02$, $df = 2$, ns, V = .014, ns
Involved: Gender: $X^2 = 60.40$, $df = 1$, $p < .001$, V = .111,
$p < .001$; Race: $X^2 = 0.29$, $df = 1$, ns, V = .008, ns
Killing: Gender: $X^2 = 27.22$, $df = 1$, $p < .001$, V = .075,
$p < .001$; Race: $X^2 = 0.01$, $df = 1$, ns, V = .001, ns

hurting to being hurt changed from the patterns seen in the 1970s and through the mid-1980s (Signorielli, 1990) for women but not for men. Today, for every 10 male characters who hurt or kill, 11 are victimized—the same ratio found in the earlier analysis. For women, however, instead of 16 women being victimized for each women who hurts or kills, the odds are even: women are equally likely to hurt or kill as be hurt or killed. Interestingly, while whites are a little more likely to be victimized than hurt others, minority characters are just as likely to hurt/ kill others as be hurt/killed themselves.

The analysis shows that there is not much information about the context in which characters commit violence (see Table 7). Only 12.9% of the men, 5.3% of the women, 9.4% of the whites, and 9.4% of the minorities who commit violence are either rewarded and/or punished for their behaviors. Similarly, 14.3% of the men, 11.1% of the women, 13.0% of the whites, and 12.5% of the minorities are presented as committing violence that is justified. Remorse is rarely found, exhibited by only 3.8% of the men, 3.3% of the women, 3.4% of the whites, and 4.4% of the minorities. And finally only 9.4% of the men, 4.6% of the women, 7.4% of the whites, and 6.8% of the minorities are portrayed as having committed immoral violence. Overall, gender differences were statistically significant but race differences were not.

Table 7
Context in Which Characters Are Involved in Violence in Prime-Time Programs from Spring 1993 to Fall 2001

	Men		Women		Whites		Minorities		Total
	R%	C%	R%	C%	R%	C%	R%	C%	C%
Total N =		1620		1162		2216		543	2782
Consequences									
No violence	55.1	71.6	44.9	81.2	80.2	75.7	19.8	76.4	75.6
No conseq	61.6	15.6	38.4	13.5	81.0	14.8	19.0	14.2	14.7
Rewarded	74.2	4.3	25.8	2.1	84.8	3.5	15.2	2.6	3.3
Punished	81.2	6.7	18.8	2.2	80.5	4.6	19.5	4.6	4.8
Both	72.1	1.9	27.9	1.0	70.7	1.3	29.3	2.2	1.5
Justification									
None given	55.2	71.7	44.8	81.2	80.1	85.7	19.9	76.8	75.7
Not justified	71.9	14.1	28.1	7.7	81.2	11.3	18.8	10.7	11.4
Justified	64.2	14.3	35.8	11.1	80.9	13.0	19.1	12.5	12.9
Morality									
None	58.2	71.8	44.8	81.3	80.2	75.9	19.8	76.6	75.8
Not immoral	65.2	18.8	34.8	14.0	80.5	16.7	19.5	16.6	16.8
Immoral	73.7	9.4	26.3	4.6	81.6	7.4	18.4	6.8	7.4
Remorse None	55.1	71.6	44.9	81.2	80.1	75.1	19.9	76.6	75.6
No remorse	68.9	24.6	31.1	15.5	81.8	20.9	18.2	19.0	20.8
Remorse	62.0	3.8	38.0	3.3	75.8	3.4	24.2	4.4	3.6

R% = Row Percentages; C% = Column Percentages
Consequences: Gender: $X^2 = 52.22$, $df = 4$, $p < .001$, V = .137, $p < .001$; Race: $X^2 = 3.69$, $df = 4$, ns, V = .037, ns
Justification: Gender: $X^2 = 37.80$, $df = 2$, $p < .001$, V = .117, $p < .001$; Race: $X^2 = 0.31$, $df = 2$, ns, V = .011, ns
Morality: Gender: $X^2 = 36.16$, $df = 2$, $p < .001$, V = .117, $p < .001$; Race: $X^2 = 0.25$, $df = 2$, ns, V = .009, ns
Remorse: Gender: $X^2 = 35.83$, $df = 2$, $p < .001$, V = .114, $p < .001$; Race: $X^2 = 2.18$, $df = 2$, ns, V = .028, ns

Discussion

The overall level of violence did not change between the spring of 1993 and the fall of 2001—six out of 10 network prime-time programs contain some violence. Although there were fewer acts of violence per program in the early 1990s, by the fall of 2001 violence had increased to the levels consistently found in the 1970s and the 1980s (Gerbner, et al., 1980a, 1980b, 1994; Gerbner & Signorielli, 1990). These findings also substantiate analyses of programming in the 1990s (Smith, et al., 1998, 2002; Lichter & Amundson, 1994). In short, for the past 30-plus years violence was found in 60% of prime-time network programs at a rate of 4.5 acts per program. Television violence is a pervasive thematic element. Thus, whether a light, moderate, or heavy viewer, most people encounter some violence when watching. From the standpoint of observational learning/social cognitive theory, the pervasiveness of violence on television may translate to the acceptance and/or implementation of violent solutions to problems, while from a cultivation theory .perspective, the steady diet of television violence may increase viewers' conceptions of a mean world and/or alienation and gloom.

This analysis isolated one important difference between the portrayal of violence in the 1970s and 1980s, compared to the 1990s and early 2000s—the involvement of fewer characters. In the 1970s and 1980s Gerbner, et al. (1980a, 1980b, 1986, 1994) consistently found about half of the major characters either hurt/killed others or were hurt/killed. During the 1990s, however, involvement dropped to one-third. Now the same amount of violence is committed by fewer characters who are essential to the story line.

Nevertheless, demographic differences remain. In the 1990s more whites than minorities committed violence or were victimized. These differences occur, however, because television programs have more white than minority characters. Similarly, more men than women are involved in violence, again because men consistently outnumber women on prime time (Signorielli & Bacue, 1999). Within-gender and within-race distributions show that the proportion of men involved in violence (about 4 in 10) is considerably larger than the proportion of women involved in violence (about 1 in 4). In addition, the patterns of committing violence and victimization still favor men over women. More men are likely to hurt or kill others (about a quarter) and to be hurt or killed themselves (also a quarter). Less than one in five women, on the other hand, harm others or are harmed themselves. Moreover, the same proportion of whites and minorities were involved in violence—roughly one in three. The findings for the gender distributions are similar to those of the NTVS (Smith, et al., 1998) but smaller than Gerbner, et al.'s (1980a, 1980b, 1986, 1994) studies in the 1970s and 1980s Thus, while gender differences remain, racial differences are smaller.

This analysis also corroborates the finding of the NTVS (Smith, et al., 1998) that violence is context-less and that most programs do not show any long-term consequences of violence, remorse, regret, or sanctions. Throughout the 1990s, almost half of the programs did not include any contextual elements of violence—physical consequences rarely appeared, violence was rarely seen as justified or immoral, and only one in four programs included intentional violence. On a more positive note, perhaps, fewer programs displayed violence that was gratuitous or graphic. But, few characters were punished for their involvement in violence. Fewer programs with gratuitous violence may be a positive factor in that violence is presented as a necessary plot element. Less graphic violence also reduces the amount of visual gore which may, in turn, reduce the degree of realism. But this may be a double-edged sword because realism is related to the development of schemas supporting aggressive behavior (Potter, 1999). Less realism, thus, could translate to more aggressive behavior.

Similarly, television today may not adequately support or reinforce the lesson that "crime does not pay." Indeed, the lack of an adequate context for violent behaviors on television may transmit the lesson that violence is "sanitary," is not necessarily immoral, and that those characters who commit violence are not typically sorry for their actions, and may not be punished for their transgressions. In short, there are few, if any, consequences for committing violence. From a social learning perspective these messages could result in viewers being more likely to learn and even accept aggressive behaviors. Thus, the environment of violent entertainment in which many people, particularly children, spend most of their free time may be potentially harmful for viewers (Smith, et al., 1998). Moreover, as Potter, et al. (1995) concluded, television's lack of realistic contexts for violence may signal that aggression and violence are acceptable. Thus, as many studies have shown, there are long-term causative effects of watching television violence that ultimately lead to a vicious cycle. Eron (1982), for example, has postulated that viewing leads to aggressive behavior and those who are more aggressive typically watch more violence.

Finally, as cultivation theory postulates, the ultimate long-term effects of watching television violence may pose threats for civil liberties and freedom. Cultivation studies have found that those who watch more television, compared to those who watch less, are more likely to overestimate their chances of being involved in violence, believe that fear of crime is an important personal problem, and assume that crime is rising. Those who spend more time watching television tend to believe that they are living in a mean and dangerous world as well as express feelings of alienation and gloom (Gerbner, et al., 2002; Signorielli, 1990). The problem is that violent images are almost impossible to avoid and, as a result, those who watch more television may become more fearful and alienated and may express sentiments of dependency and be willing to accept deceptively simple, strong, and hard-line political and religious positions if these beliefs seem to promise to relieve existing insecurities and anxieties. From the perspective of cultivation theory, the overall long-term effects of television violence may be the ready acceptance of repressive political and social environments that could translate into a loss of personal liberties.

Notes

1. Prime-time programs were those broadcast between 8 p.m. and 11 p.m. on Monday through Saturday and between 7 p.m. and 11 p.m. on Sunday.
2. WB and UPN were added in the 1997 sample of fall programming.
3. There were 13 different sets of coders who were predominantly white and middle-class; between two-thirds and three-quarters of the coders for each sample were women.
4. Average values of alpha for program variables: number of violent actions (.72), seriousness of violence, (.72), significance of violence (.69), intentionality of violence (.61), immoral violence (.69), justified violence (.66), gratuitous violence (.60), graphic violence (.67), and physical consequences of violence (.68). Average values of alpha for the character variables: gender (.95), race (.90), committing violence (.71), victimization (.66), physical consequences of violence (.73), justified violence (.71), immoral violence (.70), and reaction to violence (.68). While most of the variables exhibit robust reliability, some of the contextual elements were more difficult to isolate; these results should be viewed with some caution.

References

Bandura, A. (1986). Social foundations of thought and action: A social cognitive theory. Englewood Cliffs, NJ: Prentice Hall.

Bandura, A. (1990). Selective activation and disengagement of moral control. Journal of Social Issues, 46, 27-46.

Bandura, A., Ross, D., & Ross, S. A. (1961). Transmission of aggression through imitation of aggressive models. Journal of Abnormal and Social Psychology, 63, 575-582.

Bandura, A., Ross, D., & Ross, S. A. (1963). Imitation of film-mediated aggressive models. Journal of Abnormal and Social Psychology, 66, 3-11.

Cole, J. (1995). The UCLA television violence monitoring report. Los Angeles, CA: UCLA Center for Communication Policy.

Cole, J. (1998). The UCLA television violence monitoring report, year 3. Los Angeles, CA: UCLA Center for Communication Policy.

Dustin, D. (1992, Dec. 12). Three networks agree to standards governing violence on television. Philadelphia Inquirer.

Eton, L. D. (1982). Parent-child interaction, television violence and aggression of children. American Psychologist, 37, 197-211.

Federal Communications Commission (FCC). (Sept. 15, 2000). Viewing television responsibly: The V-Chip. V-Chip Homepage (http://www.fcc.gov/vchip/).

Gerbner, G. (2002). Mass media and dissent. In M. Morgan (Ed), Against the Mainstream: The selected works of George Gerbner (pp. 479-481). New York: Peter Lang Publishers.

Gerbner, G., Gross, L., Morgan, M., & Signorielli, N. (1980a). The "mainstreaming" of America: Violence profile no. 11. Journal of Communication, 30(3), 10-29.

Gerbner, G., Gross, L., Morgan, M., & Signorielli, N. (1980b). Violence profile no. 11: Trends in network television drama and viewer conceptions of social reality, 1967-1979. Philadelphia, PA: The Annenberg School for Communication.

Gerbner, G., Gross, L., Morgan M., & Signorielli, N. (1984). Political correlates of television viewing. Public Opinion Quarterly, 48(1), 283-300.

Gerbner, G., Gross, L., Morgan, M., & Signorielli, N. (1986). Television's mean world: Violence profile no. 14-15. Philadelphia, PA: The Annenberg School for Communication.

Gerbner, G., Gross, L., Morgan, M., & Signorielli, N. (1994). Growing up with television: The cultivation perspective. In J. Bryant & D. Zillmann (Eds.), Media effects: Advances in theory and research (pp. 17-42). Hillsdale, NJ: Erlbaum.

Gerbner, G., Gross, L., Morgan, M., Signorielli, N., & Shanahan, J. (2002). Growing up with television: The cultivation perspective. In J. Bryant & D. Zillmann (Eds.), Media effects: Advances in theory and research (pp. 43-68). Hillsdale, NJ: Erlbaum.

Gerbner, G., Gross, L., Signorielli, N., Morgan, M., & Jackson-Beeck, M. (1979). The demonstration of power: Violence profile no. 10. Journal of Communication, 29(3), 177-196.

Gerbner, G., Morgan, M., & Signorielli, N. (1994). Television violence profile No. 14: The turning point. Philadelphia, PA: The Annenberg School for Communication.

Gerbner, G., & Signorielli, N. (1990). Violence profile 1967 through 1988-89: Enduring patterns. Department of Communication, University of Delaware, Newark, DE.

Hearings before the Subcommittee on Telecommunications and Finance (1993). Violence on television. Washington, DC: Government Printing Office.

Hoerrner, K. L. (1999). Symbolic politics: Congressional interest in television violence from 1950 to 1996. Journalism and Mass Communication Quarterly, 76(4), 684-698.

Krippendorff, K. (1980). Content analysis. Beverly Hills, CA: Sage.

Kunkel, D., Wilson, B., Donnerstein, E., Linz, D., Smith, S., Gray, T., Blumenthal, E., & Potter, W. J. (1995). Measuring television violence: The importance of context. Journal of Broadcasting & Electronic Media, 39(2), 284-291.

Lichter, S. R., & Amundson, D. (1992). A day of television violence. Washington, DC: Center for Media and Public Affairs.

Lichter, S. R., & Amundson, D. (1994). A day of television violence: 1992 vs. 1994. Washington, DC: Center for Media and Public Affairs.

Lichter, S. R., Lichter, L. S., & Amundson, D. R. (1999). Merchandizing Mayhem: Violence in popular entertainment 1998-99. Washington, DC: Center for Media and Public Affairs.

Lometti, G. E. (1995). The measurement of televised violence. Journal of Broadcasting & Electronic Media, 39, 292-295.

Lovas, O. I. (1961). Effects of exposure to symbolic aggression on aggressive behavior. Child Development, 32, 37-44.

Morgan, M. (1984). Heavy television viewing and perceived quality of life. Journalism Quarterly, 61(3), 499-504, 740.

National Television Violence Study—Executive Summary (1994-1995). Studio City, CA: Media Scope, Inc.

Nielsen, A. C. (2000). Report on Television. New York: A. C. Nielsen Company.

Potter, W. J. (1999). On media violence. Thousand Oaks, CA: Sage.

Potter, W. J., & Smith, S. (2000). The context of graphic Portrayals of television violence. Journal of Broadcasting & Electronic Media, 44(2), 301-323.

Potter, W. J., Vaughan, M. W., Warren, R., Howley, K., Land, A., & Hagemeyer, J. C. (1995). How real is the portrayal of aggression in television entertainment programming? Journal of Broadcasting & Electronic Media, 39(4), 496-516.

Potter, W. J., & Ware, W. (1987). An analysis of the contexts of antisocial acts on prime-time television. Communication Research, 14, 116-124.

Signorielli, N. (1990). Television's mean and dangerous world: A continuation of the Cultural Indicators perspective. In N. Signorielli & M. Morgan (Eds.), Cultivation analysis: New directions in media effects research (pp. 85-106). Newbury Park, CA: Sage Publications.

Signorielli, N., & Bacue, A. (1999). Recognition and respect: A content analysis of prime-time television characters across three decades. Sex Roles, 40(7/8), 527-544.

Signorielli, N., Gerbner, G., & Morgan, M. (1995). Violence on television: The Cultural Indicators Project. Journal of Broadcasting & Electronic Media, 39(2), 278-283.

Signorielli, N., Gross, L. and Morgan, M. (1982). Violence in television programs: Ten years later. In D. Pearl, L. Bouthilet, and J. Lazar (eds.), Television and social behavior: Ten years of scientific progress and implications for the eighties (pp. 158-173). Rockville, MD: National Institute of Mental Health.

Smith, S. L., Nathanson, A. I., & Wilson, B. J. (2002). Prime-time television: Assessing violence during the most popular viewing hours. Journal of Communication, 52(1), 84-111.

Smith, S. L., Wilson, B. J., Kunkel, D., Linz, D., Potter, J., Colvin, C. M., & Donnerstein, E. (1998). Violence in television programming overall: University of California, Santa Barbara.

Study. In National television violence study, Vol. 3. Thousand Oaks, CA: Sage.

Wilson, B. J., Kunkel, D., Linz, D., Potter, J., Donnerstein, E., Smith, S. L., Blumenthal, E., & Gray, T. (1997). Television violence and its context: University of California, Santa Barbara study. In National television violence study, Vol. 1. Thousand Oaks, CA: Sage.

Wilson, B. J., Kunkel, D., Linz, D., Potter, J., Donnerstein, E., Smith, S. L., Blumenthal, E., & Berry, M. (1998). Violence in television programming overall: University of California, Santa Barbara study. In National television violence study, Vol. 2. Thousand Oaks, CA: Sage.

Nancy Signorielli (Ph.D., University of Pennsylvania) is a Professor of Mass Communication at the University of Delaware. Her research interests include the content and effects of mass media, particularly television.

How Psychology Can Help Explain The Iraqi Prisoner Abuse

Americans were shocked by the photos of U.S. soldiers abusing Iraqi prisoners, and now many want to know why "seemingly normal" people could behave so sadistically. Psychologists who study torture say most of us could behave this way under similar circumstances.

Q: **What can the Stanford prison and Milgram experiments tell us about what has been happening in Iraq? How do these experiments help to explain what we have seen in the photos out of the Abu Ghraib prison?**

A: Dr. Philip G. Zimbardo, who led the Stanford prison study in which two dozen college students were randomly selected to play the roles of prisoners or guards in a simulated jail, believes that his experiment has striking similarities to the Abu Gharib prison situation. "I have exact, parallel pictures of naked prisoners with bags over their heads who are being sexually humiliated by the prison guards from the 1971 study," he said. Professor Zimbardo explains that prisons offer an environment where the balance of power is so unequal that even normal people without any apparent prior psychological problems can become brutal and abusive unless great efforts are made by the institution to control the expression of guards' hostile impulses. Of the Stanford and Iraq prisons, he states, "It's not that we put bad apples in a good barrel. We put good apples in a bad barrel. The barrel corrupts anything that it touches."

Prison situations are examples of enormous power differentials, said Zimbardo. Guards have total power over prisoners who are powerless. Unless there is strict leadership and transparent oversight that prevent the abuse of power, that power will foster abuse. According to Zimbardo, in the case of Abu Ghraib, where everyone—guards and prisoners alike—was trapped in an alien setting and had neither a common language nor culture, the situation was likely to produce a classic case of abuse.

To the degree that the Abu Ghraib guards were following orders from intelligence officers as some reports say, another experiment performed 40 years ago by Dr. Stanley Milgram, who taught psychology at

Yale, also explains how people can end up abusing others in situations where one person has complete control over another.

Back in the early 1960s, while Milgram was teaching at Yale, he began studying the impact of authority on human behavior. He wanted to see whether ordinary people would follow an authority figure's orders to keep administering what they thought were increasingly painful and possibly lethal electric shocks to other people. In over a dozen studies, with both Yale college students and more than 1,000 ordinary citizens, Milgram's experiment assigned the subjects to be "teachers" who were to help "learners" improve their memories by punishing their mistakes with increasing levels of shock as they continued the learning task. The research director, who wore a white lab coat, made it clear that he was responsible for any harm to the "learners".

These experimental findings shocked Dr. Milgram and also shocked the public once the findings were released in the news. The findings illustrated how someone in charge, in this case a researcher in a white lab coat giving instructions, could cause two-thirds of the subjects to keep raising the voltage levels to the full level of 450 volts despite the screams (and soon silence) of a learner in the next room. Social scientists have learned that in research, when subjects first observe a peer following the instructions completely, they do the same when it becomes their turn. This was the case here, where almost 100 percent of those subjects were blindly obedient to the authority figures. The learner subjects were actually confederates who were not really shocked, but led the subjects to believe they were. Milgram later identified some key conditions for suspending human morality, many relevant to Abu Ghraib:

- There is given an acceptable justification for the behavior, akin to an ideology.

151

- The guards (or teachers or participants) develop a distorted sense of the victims (or participants) as not comparable to themselves. Dehumanizing them as animals would be an extreme example.
- Euphemisms, such as "learners" (instead of victims) are used.
- There is a gradual escalation of violence that starts with a small step.

Q: **What percentage of people can be expected to become abusive and sadistic when power is placed in their hands?**

A: According to Dr. Zimbardo and others who studied the issue, the overwhelming majority of soldiers do not commit abuses or atrocities, but a few will cross the line of human decency in any war or conflict. And, a majority of people will obey and conform to rules in a new situation. Moreover, in some cases, otherwise compassionate people will perform cruel acts at the behest of an authority figure. For example, in the original Milgram study, it was not merely the case that two thirds of the participants obeyed the experimenter's orders until the very end. It was also the case that nearly 100 percent of Milgram's participants delivered a very high level of shock to the victim. That is, even the most compassionate of Milgram's original participants (those who eventually refused to obey the experimenter's instructions) delivered what they thought was a 300-volt shock to the victim. No one in the study stopped as soon as we all would like to think any normal person would. So the Milgram study shows that some powerful situations can make anyone perpetrate a cruel act.

Q: **How can ordinary people commit brutal, humiliating acts like what we saw from the Abu Ghraib pictures?**

A: According to Dr. Robert Jay Lifton, a psychiatry professor at Harvard Medical School who has studied Nazi doctors and Vietnam veterans, everyone has the potential for sadism. He says that sadism is a reaction to the atrocities occurring in one's environment. "The foot soldiers, MPs and civilian contractors are all caught up in the atrocity-producing situation. They end up adapting to the group and joining in."

Because of the confusion in Iraq as to who the enemy is, said Lifton, the population and the U.S. military personnel experience a high level of fear, frustration and hostility, which creates a group process of atrocity rather than any kind of individual aberration. Moreover, because of our natural tendency to fear and distrust those whom we categorize as outsiders, this situation was bound to foster abuse. Both field studies of real groups and laboratory studies of newly created groups show that most people are naturally predisposed to distrust, compete with, and even attack others whom we categorize as outsiders (e.g., foreigners,

members of a social or ethnic group other than their own). So it is also useful to remember that the perpetrators of abuse at Abu Ghraib were not committing these acts against their fellow Americans (or even against Iraqis they encountered in the street). Abusers undoubtedly viewed their victims as "the enemy."

Dr. Zimbardo says that everyone has the potential to be good or evil. The human mind can guide us toward anything imaginable, to create heavens or hells on earth. It depends entirely on the special situations in which we might become enmeshed. These young men and women mistreating prisoners in the Abu Ghraib prison pictures were embedded in an evil barrel, says Zimbardo.

Q: **Is it inevitable, given the nature of war, that these things will happen no matter what rules or regulations exist?**

A: Experts say that it is not inevitable. When there is accountability, transparency, a clear chain of command and a respect for the enemy as a human combatant, this will prevent future atrocities like Abu Ghraib, said Zimbardo.

Q: **Is there something inherent in a captor–captive relationship that encourages this behavior?**

A: It is the power differential, with guards having total power over prisoners, and conditions that lead them to develop a dehumanized perception of the inmates as animals, said Zimbardo. It is also having no external institutional checks on that exercise of power. Of course, social labeling plays a role, too. It was probably easier for these soldiers to view foreigners as less than human than it might have been if the victims had looked and acted like Americans.

Q: **What are the most prevalent forces that influence or cause captors to abuse prisoners? Is failure of leadership always a factor?**

A: It can start with a failure of leadership, said Zimbardo, but includes a host of social psychological processes, such as, diffusion of responsibility, dehumanization of the enemy, secrecy of the operation, lack of personal accountability, conditions facilitating moral disengagement, relabeling evil as "necessary" and developing justifications for evil, social modeling, group pressures to conform in order to fit a macho cultural identity, emergent norms that establish what is acceptable to the group in that setting and obedience to emergent authorities or group leaders—in this case it may have been the CIA and civilian contractors who were the "interrogator-torturers". Also the guards' boredom, frustration, stress and revenge contribute to fostering negative outcomes.

Q: **How do we prevent these atrocities from occurring again?**

A: Zimbardo suggests bringing in experts in military corrections from the U.S. Navy and Airforce and model U.S. prisons. He also suggests releasing the detainees who are not clearly security threats or giving them access to lawyers and human rights services. Listed below are suggestions, according to military and psychological experts, to prevent future Abu Ghraib situations:

1. Training. According to news reports, the guards were reservists and most of them had not been trained to work in a prison or internment camp, had a low status in the military and had little or no training to interrogate terrorists or prisoners of war. Training also should include educating prison guards about how power, ambiguity, and a lack of personal accountability can so readily foster abuse.

2. Staffing. Most sources say there were too many prisoners and too few guards. Experts say this tends to encourage brutality as a crude means of inmate control. More planning is required to deal with this imbalance in creative ways.

3. Direction. The soldiers' basic charge was to guard prisoners, but that apparently became unclear when military intelligence officers came forward with vague requests to "soften up" prisoners and "set conditions" for interrogation. There must be clear chains of command, with superiors responsible for establishing "best practices" operating conditions—and enforcing them.

4. Supervision. Make sure the unit's commander visits the prison frequently and conducts unannounced random visits.

5. Accountability. In the absence of a clear line of command and being thousands of miles from home, oversight of the guards' behavior obviously fell short. Explicit procedures should be established for full accountability throughout the system, from the guards up through the entire hierarchy. Guards need to know that, both ethically and professionally, they are responsible for their own behavior. Most psychologists who study prisons believe that the veil of secrecy that shrouds many prisons must be lifted to prevent abuses like those the world has witnessed at Abu Ghraib.

Psychologists Philip Zimbardo, PhD, of Stanford University; Brett Pelham, PhD, Senior Scientist of the American Psychological Association; Steven J. Breckler, PhD, Executive Director of the Science Directorate of the American Psychological Association, contributed their expertise to the Fact Sheet

Bullying: It Isn't What It Used To Be

Janice Selekman
Judith A. Vessey

Many adults can remember a time during their childhood when either they felt like they were being bullied or they were bullies themselves. Others can remember the discomfort they felt knowing that classmates were being bullied, but doing nothing about it. While some will argue that bullying is just a rite of passage for children, most will now disagree based on the increase in violent behavior in today's society and the increased morbidity and mortality that result. This article will explore the current state of bullying behavior among today's youth and the role nurses play.

Defining Bullying

Before bullying can be addressed, it must be defined. Usually schools are the organizing force to address bullying, and it should be the responsibility of the "players" within the school environment to decide what they consider to be bullying behaviors. These "players" must include students, faculty (including the school nurse), administrators, and parents. Optional participants may be mental health care providers, social workers, and law enforcement.

The National Association of School Nurses (NASN) (2003) has defined bullying as "dynamic and repetitive persistent patterns of verbal and/or non-verbal behaviors directed by one or more children on another child that are *intended to deliberately inflict physical, verbal, or emotional abuse* in the presence of a real or perceived power differential." Compare the above definition to one from the United Kingdom. "Bullying is long-standing violence, physical or psychological, conducted by an individual or group and directed *against an individual who is not able to defend himself* in the actual situation, with a *conscious desire to hurt,* threaten or frighten that individual or put him under stress" (Thompson, Arora & Sharp, 2002, p. 4).

The concepts in italics are important, in that they appear in most definitions of bullying in some form. They include: (a) aggressive behavior or intentional "harm do-

ing" by one person or a group; (b) the behaviors are carried out repeatedly and over time; and (c) bullying is targeted towards someone less powerful (Nansel et al., 2001; Oleweus, 1997). No matter which way bullying behaviors are analyzed, the bottom line is that "bullying is violence."

The definitions should assist the "players" in identifying what is not bullying. Examples would include (a) students who just don't like each other; (b) playful teasing between friends; and (c) a physical fight between two students of equal stature and strength who are angry at each other. (Anger does not imply bullying.) It is important to differentiate bullying behaviors that occur only once from bullying, which is more chronic. Care should be taken to not label every child who displays the former as a bully.

The Bullying Spectrum of Behaviors

Teasing refers to "verbal and/or nonverbal behaviors among peers that are generally humorous and playful, but may be annoying to the recipient on another level" (Vessey, Swanson, & Hagedorn, 1995). It is often a healthy way for children to send useful messages or show interest in another student. When it is funny to both parties, it can help build interpersonal relationships. How a child responds to the teasing depends on his or her past relationship with the instigator. Children's interpretation of the teasing affects their response. If a child cannot see the humor in the comment or action, or if the victim feels intimidated by either a real or perceived power differential, even if it is unintended, then it may no longer be interpreted as teasing. Consequently, the impact of teasing is based on how the victim of the "tease" interprets what is said or done. Good-natured teasing can deteriorate into ridicule and mean-spirited taunts, or be interpreted that way, if the recipient feels threatened (Vessey, Carlson, & David, 2003). With playful teasing on one end of the spectrum, the continuum continues to bullying and then on to more severe violence.

Manifestations of Bullying

Familiar forms of bullying include physical or psycho-social/verbal acts, all of which have a psychological impact. Common physical acts of bullying include:

- actions causing physical injury (hitting, punching, kicking, tripping)
- taking money, lunch, or homework
- taking or damaging belongings of others
- engaging in extortion
- embarrassing by snapping the bra, lifting the skirt, pulling down pants

Psychosocial/verbal manifestations may be subtler. They include:

- using insults, name calling, or threats
- humiliating in front of peers; spreading rumors about the person or his/her family
- shunning or excluding
- slamming books
- gesturing
- setting one person against another ("You can join but you have to drop them as your friends.")

There is also the act of coercing others to steal from or bully a victim. This is referred to as "bully by proxy" and occurs when one bully tells another person what to do to a victim (Thompson et al., 2002).

The newest form of bullying is "online bullying." It can be extremely vicious. Those who use this medium often feel that they cannot be held accountable. Social inhibitions of face-to-face confrontation are eased allowing the bully to write things that they would never say to someone's face … and then to send it out for all to see. While the home was once a safe haven from bullying behaviors, online bullying can occur 24 hours a day and be shared with many more people. School officials often do little in these situations since they argue that the behaviors occurred off of school grounds; however, the messages are often passed around in school.

Regardless of the form, it must be recognized that all bullying is aggression, although not all aggression is bullying, and aggression is a form of violence.

Where Does Bullying Occur?

Bullying occurs anywhere there is an absence of adults. Kids learn to engage in these behaviors "under the radar" of adult supervision; the most common locations for bullying to occur include to and from school, on the bus, in the cafeteria, in the halls, at the lockers, in the gym locker room, and on the playground.

Who Are the Children Involved?

It is estimated that 3 out of 10 students are either bullies or victims of bullies. Thirteen percent are bullies; 11% are victims; and 6% are both (Fox, Elliott, Kerlikowske, Newman, & Christeson, 2003). For children in grades 6 through 10, this translates into 3.7 million children who bully other children each year and 3.2 million who are victims (Fox et al., 2003). Bullying occurs equally by children of both genders. Boys are more likely to be physical while girls resort to more "social toxicity."

Bullying occurs throughout the school-age years, starting in elementary school. "The prevalence of nasty teasing/ bullying has two peaks: in early elementary school (ages 7-8) and again in middle school (ages 11-14)" (NASN, 2003, p. 1). While bullying behaviors can certainly be seen in toddlers and preschoolers, they can only be considered bullying when the child reaches "a certain level of awareness and understanding" (Thompson et al., 2002, p. 18) of an intent to hurt. The child has to be aware that what they are doing is called bullying and that it is not an acceptable way to behave because of its consequences for the victim and others in the group. Early signs that a child is developing this awareness are seen in the child who forcefully takes possessions from another child or hurts another; shows pleasure at the child's reaction; and appears unconcerned when disciplined for the action.

Bullying decreases during the high school years, but it still occurs, often with very negative outcomes. The same behaviors seen in young people can also be seen in adults; however, in adulthood it is called harassment. Whatever it is called and whenever it occurs, its consequences can be devastating.

What Influences Bullying Behaviors

There is no difference in bullying behaviors based on geography or locale (e.g., urban, suburban, or rural settings), race/ethnicity, or socio-economic status. Bullies often come from homes where aggressive methods are used to manage difficult situations (Thompson et al., 2002). Certainly parental attitudes regarding bullying behaviors as well as parental disciplinary measures can send messages to children and teens about what behaviors are appropriate and which ones will get a response by the parent. Other influences include role models and violence on television and in the movies, as well as those portrayed in videogames. When bullies see that parents and teachers will not interfere in the bullying process, this is a message that the behaviors can continue.

Why Does Bullying Occur?

The need for perceived power and control results in a feeling of dominance and an achieved status, even if only in the eyes of the bully and those who watch and often fear him or her. Bullying is perceived as a demonstration of being "tough." Yet, for all of its violence, bullying is a social activity. Rarely is it just done on a one-to-one basis. While the victim may be alone, the bully often has a "fan club" around to share the "success."

Who Is the Victim?

Victims are often identified as being "different" from their peers (Bernstein & Watson, 1997). This may be in their height, stature, choice of clothes, mannerisms, be-liefs, lack of coordination, disabilities, craniofacial abnor-malities (i.e., big ears, braces, or glasses), or sexual orientation. These are frequently the children and adoles-cents who are described as "weird" by their peers, such as the computer geeks. They may be the ones who are highly disliked by their classmates or those who are nei-ther liked nor disliked. This latter group often holds no status in the peer group; it is as if they do not exist.

Victims may already be anxious and insecure and have a lowered self-esteem and poorer social skills. They ap-pear to be more annoyed by and less tolerant of teasing by their classmates (Vessey, 1999).

What About the Bystanders?

It was noted above that the bully rarely acts alone. Fre-quently there are "watchers" or bystanders who watch the process occur. As observers, they act as collaborators; they fuel the bully to show off to the peers and receive a vicarious thrill from watching, even though they do noth-ing. Some refer to them as "bully-assistants" or reinforc-ers; they are certainly accessories to the crime.

Watchers are reluctant to intervene because they be-lieve that the bully will come after them if they do, or they may be concerned that they would not be successful if they tried. Other reasons for lack of intervention on the part of "watchers" is "It's none of my business;" "I thought someone else was reporting it;" or they may ac-tually believe that the victim deserves the abuse. Those who do stand up for the victim underestimate how im-portant their contribution is.

The Sequelae of Being a Bully

"Bullying is an early warning that bullies may be headed toward more serious antisocial behavior" (Fox et al., 2003, p. 1). Bullies were found to be seven times more likely to carry a weapon to school than non-bullies. In ad-dition, nearly 60% of boys who were classified as bullies in grades 6 through 9 were convicted of at least one crime by the age of 24; 40% of them had three or more convic-tions by age 24 (Fox et al.). Children who are bullies also are more likely to engage in criminal activities after reach-ing adulthood—everything from simple assault to rape and murder. Because bullying is violence, there are legal consequences of being involved in violent acts that may involve the police.

The Sequelae of Being a Victim

Those who are bullied often suffer the psychological complications that result (Hawker & Boulton, 2000). These may include sleep disturbances (e.g., nightmares); psychosomatic complaints; irritability; increased fre-quency of illness and disease related to chronic stress; and regression to younger behaviors, such as enuresis, com-fort habits, and nail biting. Within the school environ-ment, the victim may have impaired concentration,

decreased academic performance, truancy from school (to prevent bullying from occurring), or absence from special school activities or certain classes. They may fear rejection, being excluded or ignored, feeling betrayed, or being ridiculed in class with the spread of nasty rumors.

They may feel lonely and isolated from their friends and classmates. Peers can provide a sense of acceptance and belonging; close friendships can result in intimacy, loyalty, and emotional support. The victim may feel they are without any of this support. They have lowered self-esteem, increased anxiety, and increased depression. They may actually suffer from post traumatic stress dis-order (PTSD) (Thompson et al., 2002). Young people who are bullied are five times more likely to be depressed than those who were not (Fox et al, 2003). This may result in suicidal thoughts. Bullied boys are four times more likely to be suicidal, whereas bullied girls are eight times more likely to be suicidal (Fox et al.).

Seventy-five percent of the school shootings over the past decade have been related to bullying and feeling per-secuted, threatened, attacked, or injured prior to the inci-dent (Fox et al., 2003).

What Interventions Do NOT Work?

The worst thing anyone can do is to do nothing or as-sume that bullying behaviors are harmless. Equally harm-ful is instructing youths to fight back. Responsible adults cannot discount or minimize these behaviors or reports of them. Comments such as "Just ignore them," "Stand up and fight," "Kids will be kids," "Kids sure can be cruel," "It's just a small minority of kids," or "This will prepare you for the real world" are neither helpful nor supportive to the victim and allow bullying to continue. Equally dam-aging are comments such as, "You must have done some-thing to bring it on yourself" or "You deserved it."

Certain school approaches are also ineffective. These include the misinterpretation of bullying behavior as an-ger and using anger management strategies as a way of coping. When two children do not like each other, it may be helpful to use lines such as, "If you can't say anything nice, don't say it at all" or "Stay away from each other." It might also be helpful to assist in displacing anger by punching a pillow or punching bag. However, these are inappropriate strategies for bullying.

Also inappropriate are peer mediation approaches—unless there is significant adult input and support. There is too much stress on the victim to be in these situations. Zero tolerance policies with no other programs in place are also not effective, as they do not address the behaviors and give direction as to how to change them. Lastly, dis-ciplining the bully without providing adequate safe-guards for the victim often place the victim at greater risk.

Helpful Interventions

The best intervention is communication. Parents should be encouraged to talk to their children to discuss the child's view of bullying, what causes people to bully each other, how it feels to be bullied or to bully others, and the effects bullying behaviors have on students who are victims and the bystanders. Parents also can offer suggestions as to how to handle bullies or role play responses.

Schools can incorporate discussions of bullying behaviors in classes that discuss history and laws. Examples from history and politics, including information on prejudice can help student explore what society would be like if bullying behavior was acceptable. Schools can have group discussions about how to stop bullying and the moral dilemmas faced when encountering bullying behavior (Thompson et al., 2002).

All school personnel as well as parents need to promote trust—trust that the adult will be there for them and protect them and trust that they will do something about the problem. Adults need to be aware that bullying occurs. Children do not want their parents and teachers to over-react or take control, which may be one of the reasons that they do not share details of the problem with adults.

All environments that respond to children need to be intolerant of bullying behaviors. Adults need to be positive role models in managing relationships. They can emphasize sharing, helping, and caring. They can demonstrate and mandate of others that they respect others and others' property. Even the Golden Rule can be used—Do unto others as you would have others do unto you.

Schools should adopt "codes of behavior" for all members of the school community. For classroom exercises that require teams or partners, teachers should assign students to groups to prevent someone from always being the last to be chosen. Care must be taken to assure that the bully and victim are not paired together. Students need to learn conflict resolution, both through formal lessons and informally at the time of untoward incidents. Whenever possible, the victim should be surrounded by supportive students. Lastly, strategies need to be developed that encourage students to tell a staff member or the school nurse when bullying is occurring; the same principles can be used as when the students find weapons.

The victim can be empowered to keep logs or diaries of what happened, where it happened, who was present, what was said or done, and how they felt. This assists the student to stay calmer and make mental notes about what is happening. The victims can be assisted with assertiveness training as well as rehearsal skills; scripts can be used to help the victim know how to respond. If they are open to it, give them ideas of how to decrease their vulnerability, whether it is how to dress or how they carry themselves. Involve them with peers and promote attachment to others.

It is especially important to promote positive self-esteem and enhance resiliency. One school nurse reported that a fifth grade girl who was being bullied would often come to the school nurse's office for respite. The school nurse applauded her for her smile and told her that every day she wanted the girl to stop in the office and smile so that she, the nurse, could start her day smiling back.

When dealing with the bully, it is important to have a clear direct honest message to avoid interactions. Make a basic simple statement of what you do or do not want to happen. Establish ground rules so that the bully and victim can coexist, although they never have to become friends.

Teach all children, especially the "watchers," that everyone has the responsibility to help and that no one has the right to hurt others. Children need to understand their role in promoting or preventing these behaviors. They may also need to be empowered to band together and protect their classmates. They can be the buffers or the defenders of the student being bullied and can distract the bully so that the victim can escape or can surround the victim to offer protection and support. Thompson et al. (2002) calls them the "befrienders."

The watchers should not provide an audience for the bully. it is hard to bully without the support from peers, and their absence will reduce his power base. Students should also sign an agreement regarding the ethical use of the Internet and make sure that they define bullying to include actions that are either on or off school grounds, in writing or in person.

Bullying first must be tackled at the group level and involve the whole school community, since it is a collective responsibility. Curricula that emphasize conflict resolution and empathy training may be of help. Policies also must be in place with consequences for bullying clearly

HRSA's Stop Bullying Now Campaign

Because of the extent of bullying among today's youths, the United States Department of Health and Human Services, the Health Resources Administration, and the Maternal Child Health Bureau have recently launched the largest bullying prevention effort and media campaign ever. Specifically geared to reach middle school youths between the ages of 9-13 years of age, a variety of materials are available for youths, parents, and other interested adults. Materials include:

- Public Service Announcements for print, radio, and TV that target youths or adults
- An interactive Web site for middle-school children
- "Webisodes": animated stories about bullying and appropriate responses to it
- Tip Sheets for Adults

All materials are free for your use and are available through: www.StopBullyingNow.hrsa.gov

articulated and be consistently applied in response to specific bullying incidents. "School staff retain the ultimate responsibility for ensuring the welfare of pupils" (Thompson et al., 2002, p. 128).

Conclusion

Bullying is abuse and abuse is not tolerated. It is present in every school in America. Some children say that it is a bigger problem than drugs and alcohol. Every child has a right to be protected from oppression. The goal for children is to promote success in school, social ties, and productive lives. They need to be taught that everyone has the responsibility to help and that no one has the right to hurt others.

References

Bernstein, J.Y., & Watson, M.W. (1997). Children who are targets of bullying: A victim pattern. *Journal of Interpersonal Violence, 124*, 483-498.

Fox, J., Elliott, D., Kerlikowske, R., Newman, S., & Christeson, W. (2003). *Bullying prevention is crime prevention*. Washington, DC: Fight Crime: Invest in Kids.

Hawker, S.J., & Boulton, M.J. (2000). Twenty years research on peer victimization and psychosocial maladjustment: A meta-analytic review of cross sectional studies. *Journal of Child Psychology and Psychiatry, 41*, 441-455.

Nansel, R., Overpeck, M., Pilla, R., Ruan, W., Simons-Morton, B., & Scheidt, P. (2001). Bully behaviors among U.S. youth: Prevalence and association with psychosocial adjustment. *Journal of the American Medical Association, 285*(16), 2094-2100.

National Association of School Nurses (NASN). (2003). *Peer bullying. Issue brief: School health nursing services role in health care*. Retrieved September 7, 2003, from www.nasn.org/briefs/bullying.htm.

Oleweus, D. (1997). Bully/victim problems in school: Facts and intervention. *European Journal of Psychology of Education, 12*, 495-510.

Thompson, D., Arora, T., & Sharp, S. (2002). *Bullying: Effective strategies for long term improvement*, London: Routledge/Falmer.

Vessey, J. (March, 1999). Bully-proof your child. *The Johns Hopkins Health Insider, 2*(4), 8.

Vessey, J.A., Carlson, K., & David, J. (2003). Helping children who are being teased or bullied. *Nursing Spectrum, 7*, 14-16.

Vessey, J.A., Swanson, M.N., & Hagedorn, M.I. (1995). Teasing: Who says names will never hurt you? *Pediatric Nursing, 21*, 297-300.

Janice Selekman, DNSc, RN, is Professor, Department of Nursing, University of Delaware, Newark, DE.

Judith A. Vessey, PhD, MBA, PNP, FAAN, is the Lelia Holden Carroll Professor, Boston College, William F. Connell School of Nursing, Chestnut Hill, MA.

Reprinted from *Pediatric Nursing*, May/June 2004, Vol. 30, No. 3, pp. 246-249. Reprinted with permission of the publisher, Jannetti Publications, Inc., East Holly Avenue Box 56, Pitman, NJ 08071-0056; Phone (856) 256-2300; FAX (856) 589-7463. For a sample copy of the journal, please contact the publisher.

Influencing, negotiating skills and conflict-handling: some additional research and reflections

This paper examines the connection between influencing, negotiation and conflict-handling. Using newly gathered data, it develops earlier articles on the relationships between negotiation and influencing by linking them to the associated area of conflict-handling. The new data confirm the authors' view that negotiation is best seen as an aspect of influencing and that, although both are associated with conflict-handling, they go beyond this. The new findings reinforce concerns about the role of negotiation and suggest some situations in which negotiation may be appropriate and some where it may not be suitable. As earlier, these findings have implications for the way training in these areas is carried out and how managers can make effective use of influencing, negotiation and conflict-handling.

Tony Manning and Bob Robertson

Introduction

This paper looks at some of the ways in which approaches to both influencing and negotiation are related to conflict-handling. In particular, it develops the findings of an earlier pair of articles (Manning and Robertson, 2003) on the connection between influencing and negotiation. These were based on the analysis of data collected by the authors, in their capacity as training and development practitioners, and concluded that it is beneficial to see negotiation as one type of influencing. One implication of this, for both training and managerial effectiveness, was the danger of assuming that negotiating skills are appropriate to all influencing situations. This raised further questions about the key ways in which influence situations vary and the skills that are appropriate, and inappropriate, to the different situations.

These issues can be further explored by looking at the relationship between conflict-handling and influencing, which in line with the above, can be taken to include negotiation. Conflict-handling, influencing and negotiating are inter-linked concepts. It is, therefore, informative to investigate the inter-relationships through further empirical research as this may throw further light on the approaches to different types of influencing situations.

Additional data have been collected by one of the authors, Tony Manning, on the use by individuals of various conflict-handling modes, along with their influencing strategies and styles, and negotiating skills. The data are based on the responses to three established psychometric instruments: the

Thomas-Kilmann conflict mode instrument (Thomas and Kilmann, 1974); the influencing strategies and styles profile (ISSP) developed by Tony Manning (Manning and Robertson, 2003); the negotiating skills questionnaire (NSQ) prepared by Manning and Robertson (2003). The Thomas-Kilmann model is outlined in Figure 1. The latter two instruments were described in the previous articles and are summarised below.

The ISSP

The six influencing strategies are as follows.

1. *Reason* – using reason, information and logic to justify a request,
2. *Assertion* – making a direct request for what we want,
3. *Exchange* – working together for the best overall result – offering an exchange of benefits,
4. *Courting favour* – bringing oneself into favour with the other person,
5. *Coercion* – threatening to use, or actually using, some kind of sanction,
6. *Partnership* – getting the support of others at all levels.

The three dimensions of influence are as follows.

1. *Strategist-opportunist. Strategists* tend to use reason, assertion and partnership to influence others, but avoid courting favour and exchange. They are likely to be clear about what they want to achieve, to have thought about why

Figure 1 The Thomas-Kilmann model of conflict-handling

This model is concerned with an individual's behaviour in conflict situations, using the definition of conflict noted above Thomas and Kilmann identify two dimensions to describe a person's behaviour in a conflict situation:

- *Assertiveness* – the extent to which the individual attempts to satisfy his or her own concerns
- *Cooperativeness* – the extent to which the individual attempts to satisfy the other person's concerns.

These two dimensions are used to define five specific methods of dealing with conflicts or conflict-handling modes:

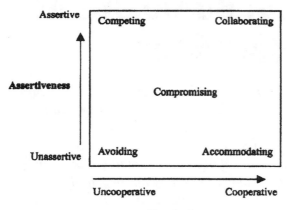

The five conflict-handling modes described by Thomas and Kilmann are outlined briefly below:-

1. *Competing* – assertive and uncooperative: pursues own concerns at the other person's expense; power-oriented: uses whatever power seems appropriate to win one's own position.

2. *Collaborating* – assertive and co-operative: attempts to work with the other person to find some solution which fully satisfies both parties; involves identifying the underlying concerns of both parties.

3. *Compromising* – intermediate in both assertiveness and cooperatives: seeks to find a mutually acceptable solution which partially satisfies both sides without fully meeting all concerns to everyone's satisfaction.

4. *Avoiding* – unassertive and uncooperative: the individual pursues neither their own goal nor the other person's goals; involves not addressing the issue.

5. *Accommodating* – unassertive and cooperative: neglects their own concerns to satisfy the concerns of the other person

they want it and to have identified who they need to influence to get it.

Opportunists tend to use courting favour and exchange to influence others, but avoid reason, assertion and partnership. They are likely to be less clear about who they need to influence, about what and why and respond more opportunistically in the face-to-face situation.

2. *Collaborator-battler.* Collaborators tend to use partnership, reason, exchange and courting favour to influence others but not coercion and assertion. They engage collaboratively in a rational partnership with others for the overall good. Battlers tend to use coercion and assertion but not partnership, reason, exchange and courting favour. They concentrate on getting across exactly what they want to achieve and the sanctions they are prepared to use if they do not achieve it.

3. *Bystander-shotgun.* In addition to the two independent dimensions of influence described above, statistical analysis shows there is a third factor that is independent of the other two dimensions and relates to the overall level or frequency of influence attempts strategies. Using terms derived from Kipnis and Schmidt (1998), although in a slightly different way, we refer to this dimension as the "Bystander versus Shotgun" scale. Bystanders engage in relatively few influence attempts, using little of any influence strategies. This may be associated with a low need to influence others at work and/or limited power to influence. However, it may also involve the more judicious use of influence strategies

4. *Shotguns* engage in a relatively large number of influence attempts, using a lot of all strategies. This may be associated with a high need to engage in influence attempts and/or the possession of significant and varied sources of power.

However, it may also be associated with the non-judicious use of influence strategies.

NSQ

This measure allows respondents to compare their negotiating skills against a model of good negotiating practice. The following are the main *stages in the process* of negotiation.

1. *Preparation* – establishing the issues, getting quality information, preparing the case and preparing for the encounter.
2. *The opening phase* – creating a positive climate, stating your case and finding out their case.
3. *Getting movement to reach agreement* – challenging their case, responding to challenges on your case, making concessions, trading or linking and moving to reach agreement.
4. *Closure* – summarising and recording agreements, establishing monitoring and review procedures and building for the future.

Within these four stages, there are a number of issues which run through the whole process of negotiation. They are as follows.

1. *Clarity of focus.* Defining the issues, having a clear and simple case, using different types of information from a variety of sources, taking time before making decisions, agreeing the outcome, monitoring and reviewing.
2. *Flexibility of strategy.* Finding out about the other party and what they want, taking a long term perspective, planning around issues rather than in a strict sequence and using concessions, adjournments and whatever is necessary to reach an agreement.
3. *Win-win-values.* Having respect for the other party and what they want, considering a wide range of options and outcomes, ensuring both parties clearly present their case, and cooperating openly to achieve mutually acceptable outcomes.
4. *Win-win-interactive skills.* Showing personal warmth, seeking information and clarification throughout, summarising and testing understanding of what is said, and being open and non-defensive. This paper begins by examining the relationship between conflict-handling, influencing and negotiation. This sets the scene for a more detailed examination of the links between conflict-handling and influencing and conflict-handling and negotiation. This reinforces the view that negotiation is only one method of influencing and, once again, highlights the dangers of assuming that negotiating skills are appropriate to all influence situations. It also illustrates that negotiation may not be appropriate in all conflict situations. It may be appropriate in certain circumstances, but there are also situations in which it is likely to be inappropriate.

Conflict-handling, influencing and negotiation

Conflict-handling is defined by Thomas and Kilmann (1974) as situations in which the concerns of two people appear to be incompatible. This suggests a clear link with influencing and negotiation as both can be seen as possible means by which any

conflict could be resolved. By definition, influencing involves trying to get another person to do what they might otherwise not do. As such, it can contribute to reducing the apparent incompatibility between those involved in a conflict. Negotiation is one form of influencing and is about trying to achieve win-win. It is a process of compromise, involving parties with different sets of objectives and values, based on their different vested interests. It is, by its vary nature, a process intended to decrease the incompatibility between the parties involved.

The above refers to a situation where conflict can be said to be overt in that both parties recognise that their concerns are not compatible. This seems to be the situation envisaged by Thomas and Kilmann (1974). Conflict in their model is overt at least to the extent that both parties accept that, at a particular moment, their concerns seem to be incompatible.

However, the use of influencing and negotiation is not confined to this state of affairs. Both can be used where the parties believe their concerns to be consistent with each other. Each of the two sides in a negotiation, for example, may believe that the other wishes to reach an agreement and that the purpose of the negotiation is to settle the terms of the agreement. In these circumstances, however, influencing and negotiation have the potential to cause conflict. Any attempt to persuade someone to do something, which they might not otherwise do, for instance, must carry the risk that it will expose concerns "which appear to be incompatible".

It is clear that the concepts of conflict-handling, influencing and negotiating are inter-linked. However, this only tells us a certain amount about how they are inter-related and further empirical research is needed to investigate the relationships further. The following discussion attempts to do this.

Influencing and conflict-handling

The framework for looking at influencing strategies and styles is described by Manning and Robertson (2003). It identifies six influencing strategies and two dimensions of style, each with two polar extremes, although in this paper we also include an additional dimension of influencing style also with two polar extremes. Figure 1 provides some further information on this instrument.

Thirty-three individuals, all participants on training courses concerned with influencing skills, completed both the Thomas-Kilmann conflict mode instrument and the ISSP. It was, therefore, possible to establish the relationships between these two sets of variables. Appendix 1 shows the correlation matrix for conflict-handling modes and influencing strategies and styles.

Some tentative conclusions can be drawn from this about the relationship between conflict-handling and influencing. With respect to the six *influencing strategies,* it appears to confirm the view that different strategies relate to different circumstances. Coercion, for example, is strongly associated with competition as an approach to handling conflict; and exchange is related to collaboration.

It also suggests that the various approaches to conflict-handling can be treated as aspects of influencing. Reason, for example, unlike all other influencing strategies, is not related to any particular conflict-handling mode which implies that influencing strategies go beyond handling conflict. Some strategies like partnership and courting favour are associated with avoidance of conflict and thus, cover situations where incompatible concerns may not surface. They approach this situation differently, however. Partnership is about friendly cooperation and collaboration while courting favour may be linked to grasping an opportunity to "get into someone's good books".

Similar points can be made in terms of the *influencing styles*. For example, collaborators tend to use a lot of collaboration but not competition, whereas battlers do the opposite and tend to use a competition most but lack collaboration. This confirms that different people prefer to act in different ways and, in line with the argument that different strategies are appropriate in different circumstances, can help to explain why, in some cases, influencing attempts can result in successful conflict-handling, but may not succeed in others, where a different approach would be appropriate.

It also appears that shotguns tend to use avoidance and, to a lesser extent, a lack of compromise, while bystanders tend not to use avoidance, but show some willingness to compromise. This suggests that more attempts at influence do not mean more facing up to and dealing with conflicts but less, along with less willingness to compromise on such issues. This adds further support to the view that it is the strategy of influencing which is chosen that is likely to be important in any situation. Again, influencing may be the broader category as it covers both overt conflict and situations where conflict may not necessarily follow an attempt at influencing.

Negotiating and conflict-handling

Thirty-one individuals, all participants on training courses concerned with negotiating skills, completed both the Thomas-Kilmann conflict mode instrument and the NSQ. Once again, it was, therefore, possible to establish the relationships between these two sets of variables. Appendix 2 shows the correlation matrix for conflict-handling modes and stages and issues in negotiating.

The results provide some support for the behaviours associated with a win-win approach to negotiation. One example is that the conflict-handling mode of collaboration is related to the preparation and opening phases of the negotiation: it is here when the most significant attempts to find a solution acceptable to both parties are likely to be made. Further, this mode is directly linked to the key issue of a win-win approach. The conflict-handling mode of avoidance is negatively related to all four stages of negotiation, which is consistent with the notion that skilled negotiators do attempt to address explicitly the issues in a negotiation. This idea is reinforced by the fact that low avoidance is also associated with a flexibility of approach to negotiation.

The general pattern of relationships between an individual's approach to negotiating and his or her approach to conflict-handling, therefore, is very clear: skilled negotiators tend to use low avoidance and high collaboration modes of conflict-handling. To a lesser extent, skilled negotiators also show a preparedness to use accommodation and compromise, whilst avoiding competition.

Overall, therefore, only some of the modes of conflict-handling (collaborating, compromising and accommodation)

appear to be consistent with negotiation. Further, Appendix 1 suggests a link between the influencing strategy of assertion and the conflict-handling mode of avoidance. Once again, there seems to be a support for the notion that negotiation can be seen as a subset of influencing.

Thomas and Kilmann (1974) make it clear that there is no "one best" approach to handling conflict and that all approaches might be effective in particular circumstances. They also provide some guidance on the appropriate use of each of the five modes. In the light of the finding that skilled negotiators tend to use certain conflict-handling modes but not others, it may be useful to look at the three conflict-handling modes which are used successfully in negotiation and consider both when they may be appropriate. Effectively, this develops the guidance provided by Thomas and Kilmann.

Negotiation is fundamentally a collaborative, win-win approach to conflict resolution. Collaboration is likely to be particularly useful:

- to find integrative solutions without compromising either sets of concerns;
- when your objective is to learn and find out the other party's views;
- to merge insights from people with different perspectives on a problem;
- to gain commitment by incorporating the other's concerns into a consensual decision; and
- to work through hard feelings which have interfered with interpersonal relationships.

Negotiation may involve accommodating as an element of conflict-handling. Accommodating is likely to be useful:

- when you realise you are wrong;
- to avoid further damage in a situation which is not going well;
- when the issues are more important to the other party than to you;
- as a goodwill gesture, to build-up credit points for later issues which are important to you; and when preserving harmony and avoiding disruption are important.

Negotiation may also involve compromising as an element conflict-handling. Compromise is likely to be useful:

- when your goals are only moderately important;
- when there is an equal balance of power and strong commitment to mutually exclusive goals; and
- as a temporary settlement, expedient solution or back up mode.

The other two modes of conflict-handling, avoiding and competing are not used by skilled negotiators. However, if negotiation is seen as one possible approach among several options to any situation, both may be appropriate in certain circumstances. Avoiding is likely to be useful:

- when the issue is trivial or symptomatic of another more basic issue;
- when you perceive no possibility of satisfying your concerns, perhaps because of an adverse balance of power;
- when the potential damage of confronting an issue outweighs its resolution;

Appendix 1.

Table AI Correlation matrix for conflict-handling modes and influencing strategies and styles (*N* = 33)

	Competition	Collaboration	TKCM Compromise	Avoidance	Accommodation
ISSP strategies					
Reason	−0.06	−0.04	0.08	0.06	−0.06
Assertion	−0.06	−0.05	−0.11	0.19	0.00
Exchange	−0.10	0.28	−0.21	0.11	−0.02
Courting favour	0.04	−0.12	−0.17	0.16	0.03
Coercion	0.31	−0.22	−0.07	−0.03	−0.15
Partnership	−0.25	0.11	−0.09	0.30	−0.04
ISSP style dimensions					
Total (bystander-shotgun)	−0.05	−0.01	−0.15	0.22	−0.07
AF1 (strategist-opportunist)	0.10	0.07	−0.20	−0.01	0.05
AF2 (collaborator-battler)	0.37	−0.24	−0.12	0.05	−0.11

Appendix 2.

Table AII Correlation matrix for conflict-handling modes and negotiating stages and issues (*N* = 31)

NSQ	Competition	Collaboration	TKCM Compromise	Avoidance	Accommodation
Stages in the process					
Preparation	−0.26	0.22	−0.04	−0.11	0.26
Opening phase	0.05	0.36	0.01	−0.41	−0.01
Movement	−0.02	0.12	−0.09	−0.12	0.09
Closure	−0.08	−0.02	0.08	−0.01	0.05
Key issues throughout the process					
Clarity of focus	−0.04	0.29	−0.11	−0.21	0.10
Flexibility of approach	−0.04	0.12	0.17	−0.32	0.06
Win-win values and approach	−0.09	0.17	0.14	−0.25	0.06
Win-win interpersonal skills	0.02	0.04	−0.14	−0.04	0.11
Negotiating skills – total score	−0.10	0.25	−0.04	−0.23	0.14

• to let people cool down, reduce tensions, regain perspective and composure; and when gathering more information is more important than making an immediate decision.

Competition is likely to be useful:

• when quick, decisive action is vital, e.g. emergencies;
• when issues are important and where unpopular courses of action need implementing;
• when issues are vital to organisation welfare, when you know you are right; and
• to protect yourself against people who take advantage of non-competitive behaviour.

Conclusion

The conclusions drawn from the analysis of the research data presented above reinforce the conclusion arrived at in our previous pair of articles, that it is important for those providing training and development activities to recognise that negotiating is not a paradigm for all influence situations. Negotiating is an appropriate method of influencing and conflict-handling in certain conditions and situations, although other methods of influencing and conflict-handling are likely to be more appropriate in contrasting conditions and situations. Training and development activities should reflect the legitimacy of a variety of approaches to interpersonal influence and conflict-handling, and give due consideration to an equal diversity of situations and the particular skills appropriate to each other. Negotiation has a place, is fine in its place but is best kept in its place.

References

Kipnis, D. and Schmidt, S.M. (1988), "Upward-influence styles: relationships with performance evaluations, salary and stress", *Administrative Science* Quarterly. Vol. 33, pp. 528-42.

Manning, T. and Robertson, B. (2003), Influencing and negotiating skills: some research and reflections—Part I: influencing strategies and styles. Part II: influencing styles and negotiating skills, *Industrial and Commercial Training*, Vol. 35 Nos 1/2, pp. 60-6, pp. 11-15.

Thomas, K. (1976), "Conflict and conflict management", in Dunnette, M.D. (Ed.), *Handbook of Industrial and Organisational Psychology*. Wiley, New York, NY.

Thomas, K.W. and Kilmann, R.H. (1974), *Thomas-Kilmann Conflict Mode Instrument*, Xicom.

UNIT 9

Altruism, Helping and Cooperation

Unit Selections

Key Points to Consider

- Are you generally a helpful and cooperative person? How regularly do you help others in small ways such as holding a door open or when asked, telling a stranger what time it is? How often do you engage in larger positive social behaviors such as donating money or time to charities?

- Have you ever been in a situation where you or someone else was victimized? How did you react? If you were the victim, did anyone come to your assistance?

- Are you familiar with other cases where someone had an emergency or compelling need for aid? Did anyone respond? If yes, what were the characteristics of the helper(s)? If no one helped, can you identify situational circumstances that prohibited helping? What was the eventual outcome of the incident? Did helping substantially alter the course of events?

- Do you think helping is part of the natural evolution of most species? That is, do you think most animals, including humans, help their own kind? Can you think of any examples of interspecies helping? For example, have humans ever come to the aid of a pet? Do pets ever help their owners? On what basis is this assistance granted?

- How does culture advance altruism? How does it inhibit altruism? Do you know any cases of lost children in our society? Does our culture encourage or discourage strangers' helping children?

- What is bystander apathy? When do bystanders help or not help? Why is it important to replicate in the real world any laboratory results on bystander behavior? If someone is having an emergency, what advice would you offer them? What would you tell nearby bystanders?

- What is social justice? What are cooperation and its alternate, competition? When does cooperation occur? When does competition occur? In both situations, what dictates most people's sense of fairness? Given past research on social justice, where do you think researchers should head next?

 **Links: www.dushkin.com/online/**
These sites are annotated in the World Wide Web pages.

Americans With Disabilities Act Document Center
http://www.jan.wvu.edu/links/adalinks.htm
Give Five
http://www.independentsector.org/give5/givefive.html
University of Maryland Diversity Database
http://www.inform.umd.edu/EdRes/Topic/Diversity/

While her coworkers gathered at a local pub to discuss the latest gossip at work, a young woman believed in regular exercise and doing something to relax after work. She would go home, grab a bottle of water and her MP3 player and go for a brisk walk. She generally followed the same itinerary, but on this particular day, she decided to cross a large park because one of the roads on her usual route was under construction. She wanted to avoid the noise, the dust, and snarled traffic.

Because she had earphones on, she did not hear the man sprinting up behind her. The next thing she knew, she was hurled to the ground. Her headphones had fallen off but she still clutched the water bottle. As the man began to tear at her clothes, she pummeled him with the bottle, but she had drunk too much water for the bottle to be effective. When the bottle didn't stop him, she started screaming, "Help me; help me, please."

Would anyone come she worried? Would this man get what he wanted? Would he leave her dead or alive? As she screamed for the second time, her assailant tried to cover her mouth with his hand. The grip of his other hand momentarily released so that she could push him off. She got up and started to run. He just as quickly pursued her. As she ran, she screamed again until he caught her and threw her to the ground. As she fell, she remembered what she had learned in a women's self-defense course—to yell loudly "I don't know you; get away."

This time the struggling pair was seen by several people in the park. A young man walking a dog nearby heard her desperate screams and ran to her. The young man pulled the attacker off the woman. The rescuer's big dog snarled and barked and bit at the stranger, who finally ran off. The young man asked if the victim was all right, called 911 on his cell phone, and grabbed his dog. Together they awaited the arrival of the medics and the police.

Is this story usual or unusual, not so much in regard to the woman's assault, but because someone actually responded to cries her for help? Every day someone somewhere needs help in our society, but just how helpful are people? Who are the helpers and rescuers? Which victims will they help? Why do some people not respond to the pleas of others? Under what circumstances will people help rather than just watch?

The topic of this unit is helping, altruism, and cooperation—positive social behaviors. "Helping" and "cooperation" are readily understood terms by the average American. But what is altruism? Most social psychologists define *altruism* as helping another *at a cost to the helper*. The cost might be lost time, threats to personal safety, money donated, or anything else that the helper offers up.

The first article in this series is "The Nature of Human Altruism." The authors discuss the origins of altruism. Many studies utilizing animal models have found that humans are not the only altruistic specie. The authors propose, however, that socialization, especially in terms of cultural expectations, plays a large role in promoting human altruism. They conclude that a combination of the two factors, heredity and culture, both influence human altruism.

In a second and provocative essay titled "Cause of Death: Uncertain(ty)," Robert Cialdini details information on helping. He reviews Darley and Latane's landmark studies on *bystander apathy* which occurs when bystanders do not intervene to aid a person in need. The bystander studies were conducted first in the laboratory and then in real settings. After the analysis of Darley and Latane's work, Cialdini offers specific advice on what to do in emergency situations similar to the one about the assault of the young woman described above.

The last article in this unit explores a related concept—social justice. *Social justice* essentially means a person's perception that the outcomes or rewards of his or her effort are fair and just. Most people have an acute sense of fairness when they interact with others, although what they perceive as fair for themselves may not be what they interpret as fair for others. Skitka and Crosby analyze past research on fairness and cooperation as well as point future researchers in new directions.

The nature of human altruism

Some of the most fundamental questions concerning our evolutionary origins, our social relations, and the organization of society are centred around issues of altruism and selfishness. Experimental evidence indicates that human altruism is a powerful force and is unique in the animal world. However, there is much individual heterogeneity and the interaction between altruists and selfish individuals is vital to human cooperation. Depending on the environment, a minority of altruists can force a majority of selfish individuals to cooperate or, conversely, a few egoists can induce a large number of altruists to defect. Current gene-based evolutionary theories cannot explain important patterns of human altruism, pointing towards the importance of both theories of cultural evolution as well as gene–culture co-evolution.

ERNST FEHR AND URS FISCHBACHER

Human societies represent a huge anomaly in the animal world[1]. They are based on a detailed division of labour and cooperation between genetically unrelated individuals in large groups. This is obviously true for modern societies with their large organizations and nation states, but it also holds for hunter-gatherers, who typically have dense networks of exchange relations and practise sophisticated forms of food-sharing, cooperative hunting, and collective warfare[2, 3]. In contrast, most animal species exhibit little division of labour and cooperation is limited to small groups. Even in other primate societies, cooperation is orders of magnitude less developed than it is among humans, despite our close, common ancestry. Exceptions are social insects such as ants and bees, or the naked mole rat; however, their cooperation is based on a substantial amount of genetic relatedness.

Why are humans so unusual among animals in this respect? We propose that quantitatively, and probably even qualitatively, unique patterns of human altruism provide the answer to this question. Human altruism goes far beyond that which has been observed in the animal world. Among animals, fitness-reducing acts that confer fitness benefits on other individuals are largely restricted to kin groups; despite several decades of research, evidence for reciprocal altruism in pair-wise repeated encounters[4, 5] remains scarce[6–8]. Likewise, there is little evidence so far that individual reputation building affects cooperation in animals, which contrasts strongly with what we find in humans. If we randomly pick two human strangers from a modern society and give them the chance to engage in repeated anonymous exchanges in a laboratory experiment, there is a high probability that reciprocally altruistic behaviour will emerge spontaneously[9, 10].

However, human altruism extends far beyond reciprocal altruism and reputation-based cooperation, taking the form of strong reciprocity[11, 12]. Strong reciprocity is a combination of altruistic rewarding, which is a predisposition to reward others for cooperative, norm-abiding behaviours, and altruistic punishment, which is a propensity to impose sanctions on others for norm violations. Strong reciprocators bear the cost of rewarding or punishing even if they gain no individual economic benefit whatsoever from their acts. In contrast, reciprocal altruists, as they have been defined in the biological literature[4, 5], reward and punish only if this is in their long-term self-interest. Strong reciprocity thus constitutes a powerful incentive for cooperation even in non-repeated interactions and when reputation gains are absent, because strong reciprocators will reward those who cooperate and punish those who defect.

The first part of this review is devoted to the experimental evidence documenting the relative importance of repeated encounters, reputation formation, and strong reciprocity in human altruism. Throughout the paper we rely on a behavioural—in contrast to a psychological[13]—definition of altruism as being costly acts that confer economic benefits on other individuals. The role of kinship in human altruism is not discussed because it is well-known that humans share kin-driven altruism with many other animals[14, 15]. We will show that the interaction between selfish and strongly reciprocal individuals is essential for understanding of human cooperation. We identify conditions under which selfish individuals trigger the breakdown of cooperation, and conditions under which strongly reciprocal individuals have the power to ensure widespread cooperation. Next we discuss the limits of human altruism that arise from the costs of altruistic acts. Finally, we discuss the evolutionary origins of the different forms of human altruism. We are particularly interested in whether current evolutionary models can explain why humans, but not other animals, exhibit large-scale cooperation among genetically unrelated individuals, and to what extent the evidence supports the key aspects of these models.

Proximate patterns

Altruistic behaviour in real-life circumstances can almost always be attributed to different motives. Therefore, sound knowledge about the specific motives behind altruistic acts predominantly stems from laboratory experiments. In the following, we first discuss experiments in which interactions among kin, repeated encounters, and reputation formation have been ruled out. Next, we document how the possibility of future encounters and individual reputation formation changes subjects' behaviour. In all experiments discussed below, real money, sometimes up to three months' income[16-18], was at stake. Subjects never knew the personal identities of those with whom they interacted and they had full knowledge about the structure of the experiment—the available sequence of actions and the prevailing information conditions. If, for example, the experiment ruled out future encounters between the same individuals, subjects were fully informed about this. To rule out any kind of social pressure, the design of the experiment even ensured in several instances that the experimenter could not observe subjects' individual actions but only the statistical distribution of actions[19,20].

Altruistic punishment

The ultimatum game[21] nicely illustrates that a sizeable number of people from a wide variety of cultures[22,23] even when facing high monetary stakes[16,17], are willing to punish others at a cost to themselves to prevent unfair outcomes or to sanction unfair behaviour. In this game, two subjects have to agree on the division of a fixed sum of money. Person A, the proposer, can make exactly one proposal of how to divide the money. Then person B, the responder, can accept or reject the proposed division. In the case of rejection, both receive nothing, whereas in the case of acceptance, the proposal is implemented. A robust result in this experiment is that proposals giving the responder shares below 25% of the available money are rejected with a very high probability. This shows that responders do not behave to maximize self-interest, because a selfish responder would accept any positive share. In general, the motive indicated for the rejection of positive, yet 'low', offers is that responders view them as unfair. Most proposers seem to understand that low offers will be rejected. Therefore, the equal split is often the modal offer in the ultimatum game. The decisive role of rejections is indicated by the dictator game, in which the proposer unilaterally dictates the division of the money because the responder cannot reject the offer. The average amount given to the responders in the dictator game is much lower than that in the ultimatum game[20, 24].

Rejections in the ultimatum game can be viewed as altruistic acts because most people view the equal split as the fair outcome. Thus, a rejection of a low offer is costly for the responder and it punishes the proposer for the violation of a social norm. As a consequence, the proposer is likely to obey the norm in the future by making less greedy offers. For the purpose of this review, we ran an experiment with ten proposers who met a different responder in ten successive rounds. We observed that proposers who experienced a rejection in the previous round increased their offers in the current round by 7% of the available sum of money.

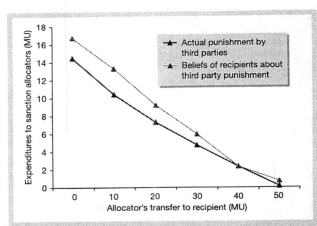

Figure 1 Altruistic punishment by third parties who are not directly affected by the violation of a fairness norm (based on ref. 27). The fair transfer level is given by 50 MUs. The more the allocator's transfer falls short of the fair level of 50 MUs, the more third parties punish the allocator. The recipients of the transfer also expect that the allocators will be punished for unfair transfers.

In the ultimatum game, the proposer's action directly affects the responder. However, a key element of the enforcement of many social norms, such as food-sharing norms in hunter-gatherer societies[2,3], is that people punish norm violators not for what they did to the punisher but for what they did to others[25,26]. Norm enforcement involves the punishment of norm violations even by those who are not economically affected by the violation. To study this question experimentally, we conducted a third-party punishment game involving three subjects—an allocator, a recipient, and a third party[27]. The allocator is endowed with 100 monetary units (MUs), the recipient has no endowment, and the third party is endowed with 50 MUs. The allocator is free to give whatever he wants to the 'poor' recipient. After the third party has been informed about the allocator's transfer to the recipient, he can spend money to punish the allocator. Every MU spent on punishment reduces the allocator's income by three MUs. Because it is costly to punish, no selfish third party will ever punish. But if a fairness norm applies to the situation, altruistic punishers are expected to punish unfair transfers. In fact, 55% of the third parties punish the allocator for transfers below 50, and the lower the transfer, the higher the punishment (Fig. 1). Moreover, between 70 and 80% of the recipients expect that allocators will be punished for unfairly low transfers. Similar results have been observed when third parties are given the chance to punish subjects in a 'prisoners' dilemma'[27]. In this case, they frequently punish a defector if his opponent cooperated. If it is anticipated, the punishment by third parties thus deters non-cooperation.

Altruistic rewarding

Sequentially played social dilemmas are a powerful tool for the study of altruistic rewarding. They come in various forms—as gift exchange games[28], trust games[29] or sequentially played prisoners' dilemmas[30]—but the basic structure is captured by the following example. There is a truster and a trustee, both of whom are endowed with 10 MUs. First, the truster decides how many, if any, MUs to transfer to the trustee. Then the trustee decides how much of his endowment to send to the truster. The experimenter doubles any amount sent to the other subject so that, collectively, the two subjects are best off if both transfer their whole endowment: if both keep what they have, each one earns 10; if both transfer their whole endowment, each earns 20. However, a selfish trustee will transfer nothing regardless of how much he received and, therefore, a selfish truster who anticipates this behaviour will never transfer anything in the first place.

This experiment mimics the essence of a vast number of real-life situations. A similar structure characterizes any sequential exchange that takes place in the absence of contracts that are enforced by the courts. In these situations, both players are better off exchanging their goods and favours but there is also a strong temptation to cheat. Despite the incentive to cheat, however, more than 50% of the trustees transfer money and their transfers are the higher the more the truster transferred initially[28–30]. Like altruistic punishment, the presence of altruistic rewarding has also been documented in many different countries[31], in populations with varying demographic characteristics[32], and under stake levels approaching 2—3 months' income[18].

Strong reciprocity and multilateral cooperation

A decisive feature of hunter-gatherer societies is that cooperation is not restricted to bilateral interactions. Food-sharing, cooperative hunting, and warfare involve large groups of dozens or hundreds of individuals[1]. To what extent does strong reciprocity contribute to cooperation in public goods situations involving larger groups of individuals? By definition, a public good can be consumed by every group member regardless of the member's contribution to the good. Therefore, each member has an incentive to free-ride on the contributions of others. Altruistic rewarding in this situation implies that an individual's contributions increase if the expected contributions from the other group members increase. Individuals reward others if the latter are expected to raise their cooperation.

In public goods experiments that are played only once, subjects typically contribute between 40 and 60% of their endowment, although selfish individuals are predicted to contribute nothing[33]. There is also strong evidence that higher expectations about others' contributions induce individual subjects to contribute more[33–35]. Cooperation is, however, rarely stable and deteriorates to rather low levels if the game is played repeatedly (and anonymously) for ten rounds[36, 37].

The most plausible interpretation of the decay of cooperation is based on the fact that a large percentage of the subjects are strong reciprocators but that there are also many total free-riders who never contribute anything[35]. Owing to the existence of strong reciprocators, the 'average' subject increases his contribution levels in response to expected increases in the average contribution of other group members. Yet, owing to the existence of selfish subjects, the intercept and the steepness of this relationship is insufficient to establish an equilibrium with high cooperation (Fig. 2). In round one, subjects typically have optimistic expectations about others' cooperation but, given the aggregate pattern of behaviours, this expectation will necessarily be disappointed, leading to a breakdown of cooperation over time.

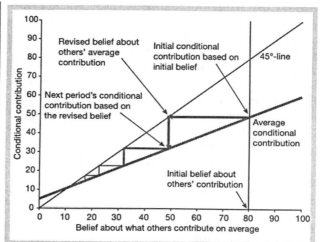

Figure 2 The decay of cooperation over time. Subjects are heterogeneous with regard to their willingness to reward altruistically. This results in the relationship between the expected average contribution of other group members to the public good and the contribution of a representative individual (the average conditional contribution indicated by the purple line). Initially, individuals expect high average contribution rates, say 80% of the endowment. On average, this induces them to contribute 50%. Therefore, expectations are disappointed which leads to a downwards revision of expectations to say, 50% of the endowment. Yet, if individuals expect 50% they will in fact only contribute roughly 30%, causing a further downwards revision of expectations. The process stops at the intersection point with the 45° line, which determines the equilibrium level of altruistic cooperation in this setting.

This breakdown of cooperation provides an important lesson. Despite the fact that there are a large number of strong reciprocators, they cannot prevent the decay of cooperation under these circumstances. In fact, it can be shown theoretically that in a population with a clear majority of strong reciprocators, a small minority of selfish individuals suffices to render zero cooperation the unique equilibrium[38]. This implies that it is not possible to infer the absence of altruistic individuals from a situation in which we observe little cooperation. If strong reciprocators believe that no one else will cooperate, they will also not cooperate. To maintain cooperation in *n*-person interactions, the upholding of the belief that all or most members of the group will cooperate is thus decisive.

Any mechanism that generates such a belief has to provide cooperation incentives for the selfish individuals. The punishment of non-cooperators in repeated interactions[39–41] or altruistic punishment[27, 42] provide two such possibilities. If cooperators have the opportunity to target their punishment directly towards those who defect they impose strong sanctions on the defectors. Thus, in the presence of targeted punishment opportunities, strong reciprocators are capable of enforcing widespread cooperation by deterring potential non-cooperators[39,40,42]. In fact, it can be shown theoretically that even a minority of strong reciprocators suffices to discipline a majority of selfish individuals when direct punishment is possible[38].

Repeated interactions and reputation formation

A reputation for behaving altruistically is another powerful mechanism for the enforcement of cooperation in public goods situations. If people are engaged in bilateral encounters as well as in *n*-person public goods interactions, a defection in the public goods situation, if known by others, may decrease others' willingness to help in bilateral interactions[43]. Suppose that after each round of interaction in a public goods experiment, subjects play an indirect reciprocity game[44]. In this game, subjects are matched in pairs and one subject is randomly placed in the role of a donor and the other in the role of a recipient. The donor can help the recipient, and the donor's costs of helping are lower than the benefits for the recipient. The recipient's reputation is established by his decision in the previous public goods round and his history of helping decisions in the indirect reciprocity game. It turns out that the recipients' reputations in the public goods game are an important determinant for the donors' decisions. Donors punish the recipients by being significantly less likely to help when the recipients defected in the previous public goods game. This, in turn, has powerful cooperation-enhancing effects in the future rounds of the public goods game.

Helping behaviour in indirect reciprocity experiments has also been documented in the absence of interactions in public goods games[45,46]. A crucial element in these experiments is that direct reciprocity is ruled out because no recipient will ever be put in a position where he can give to one of his previous donors. Helping rates between 50 and 90% have been achieved and recipients with a history of generous helping decisions are significantly more likely to receive help themselves. This suggests that the donors' behaviour may be driven by the desire to acquire a good reputation. However, it is also possible that altruistic rewarding drives helping behaviour. A recent study examines this question by allowing only half of the subjects in the experiment to acquire a reputation[47]. This means that one can compare the behaviour of donors who cannot gain a reputation with the behaviour of those who can. The data show that both altruistic rewarding and reputation-seeking are powerful determinants of donors' behaviour. Donors who cannot acquire a reputation help in 37% of the cases whereas those who can gain a reputation help in 74% of the cases. These results indicate that humans are very attentive to possibilities of individual reputation formation in the domain of rewarding behaviours. They exhibit a sizeable baseline level of altruistic rewarding, and when given the opportunity to gain a reputation for being generous, helping rates increase strongly. Humans are similarly attentive to the possibility of repeated interactions with the same individual (reciprocal altruism). The cooperation rate is much higher in social dilemmas if subjects know that there is a possibility of meeting the same partners again in future periods[10].

Little is known about repetition and reputation effects in the domain of punishing behaviours. We conducted a series of ten ultimatum games in two conditions for this purpose—a reputation condition and a baseline condition. In both conditions, 10 MUs have to be divided in every period and every proposer is matched with a new responder in each of the ten games. In the reputation condition, the proposers are informed about the current responder's past rejection behaviour, whereas this knowledge is absent in the baseline condition. This means that the responders in the reputation condition can gain an individual reputation for being tough bargainers by rejecting even high offers. A responder who incurs the short-term cost of a rejection can gain the long-term benefits of a 'good' reputation by inducing future proposers to make him better offers. Because this

economic benefit is absent in the baseline condition, subjects who understand the logic of reputation formation will exhibit higher acceptance standards in the reputation condition.

In both conditions, the responders indicated an acceptance threshold in each period, that is, the smallest amount they were willing to accept. The results show that when the subjects were in the baseline condition first, the average acceptance threshold was about 3 MUs, whereas if they entered the reputation condition, their thresholds immediately jumped to more than 4 MUs (Fig. 3a). This jump in the thresholds forced the proposers to increase their offers. Similarly, if the reputation condition took place first, the average thresholds immediately decreased when subjects entered the baseline condition (Fig. 3a). Moreover, this change in the average thresholds is not an artefact of aggregation. It is explained by the fact that the vast majority of responders (82%, $n = 94$) increase the

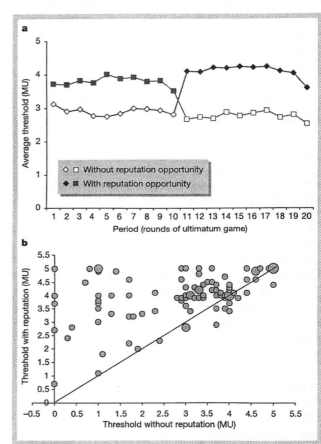

Figure 3 Responders' acceptance thresholds in the ultimatum game with and without reputation opportunities. **a**, Time trend of acceptance thresholds. If the control treatment without the opportunity to build an individual reputation for toughness is conducted first, the responders reject offers below 3 MUs (open blue symbols). Immediately after the implementation of reputation building opportunities in period 11, the acceptance thresholds jump up to more than 4 MUs, indicating the desire to be known as a 'tough' responder (solid blue symbols). If the reputation treatment comes first (purple symbols) the removal of the opportunity to acquire a reputation immediately causes a decrease in responders' acceptance thresholds. **b**, Individual level changes in responders' average acceptance thresholds. The relative size of the circles represents the frequency of observations behind a circle. Responders who increase their average acceptance threshold in the reputation condition relative to the baseline condition generate a data point above the 45° line. The vast majority of responders increase their thresholds when they can gain a reputation for toughness. Only a small minority lowers the thresholds or keeps them roughly constant.

threshold in the reputation condition relative to the baseline (Fig. 3b) while the remaining minority keep the thresholds roughly constant. These results suggest that altruistic punishers clearly understand that if individual reputation building is possible, it pays to acquire a reputation as a tough bargainer. This also means that their rejections in the baseline condition cannot be attributed to cognitive problems in understanding when individual reputation matters and when it does not.

Limits of human altruism

Strongly reciprocal individuals reward and punish in anonymous one-shot interactions. Yet they increase their rewards and punishment in repeated interactions or when their reputation is at stake. This suggests that a combination of altruistic and selfish concerns motivates them. Their altruistic motives induce them to cooperate and punish in one-shot interactions and their selfish motives induce them to increase rewards and punishment in repeated interactions or when reputation-building is possible. If this argument is correct, we should also observe that altruistic acts become less frequent as their costs increase. At a higher cost, individuals have to give up more of their own payoff to help others, so that the individuals will exhibit less altruistic behaviour for a given combination of selfish and altruistic motives. The evidence from dictator games and public good games confirms this prediction. If the own payoff that needs to be invested to produce one unit of the public good increases, subjects invest less into the public good[36, 37]. Likewise, if the cost of transferring one MU to the recipient in the dictator game increases, the dictators give less money to the recipients[48].

Proximate theories

Altruistic rewards and punishment imply that individuals have proximate motives beyond their economic self-interest—their subjective evaluations of economic payoffs differ from the economic payoffs. Although this is an old idea[49], formal theories of non-selfish motives with predictive power in a wide range of circumstances have only recently been developed. These theories formalize notions of inequity aversion[38, 50] and reciprocal fairness[51–53]. They predict, for example, that many subjects in the prisoners' dilemma prefer mutual cooperation over unilateral defection, even though it is in their economic self-interest to defect regardless of what the other player does. This prediction is supported by the evidence[30, 54] and has wide-ranging implications. If the players have such preferences, the game is no longer a prisoners' dilemma but an assurance game in which both mutual defection as well as mutual cooperation are equilibria. The crucial point is that such subjects are willing to cooperate if they believe that their opponent will cooperate and, therefore, mutual cooperation is an equilibrium. However, because mutual defection is also an equilibrium, it depends on the individuals' beliefs about the other players' actions as to whether the mutual cooperation or the mutual defection equilibrium is played.

Recent results on the neurobiology of cooperation in the prisoners' dilemma support the view that individuals experience particular subjective rewards from mutual cooperation[55]. If subjects achieve the mutual cooperation outcome with another human subject, the brain's reward circuit (components of the mesolimbic dopamine system including the striatum and the orbitofrontal cortex) is activated relative to a situation in which subjects achieve mutual cooperation with a programmed computer. Moreover, there is also evidence indicating a negative response of the dopamine system if a subject cooperates but the opponent defects.

Evolutionary origins

What are the ultimate origins behind the rich patterns of human altruism described above? It must be emphasized in the context of this question that a convincing explanation of the distinct features of human altruism should be based on capacities which are distinctly human—otherwise there is the risk of merely explaining animal, not human, altruism.

Reciprocal altruism

Reciprocal altruism[4,5] in the form of tit-for-tat or similar cooperation-sustaining strategies in the repeated prisoners' dilemma is a powerful ultimate explanation for human altruism in small and stable groups. The experimental evidence unambiguously shows that subjects cooperate more in two-person interactions if future interactions are more likely[9,10]. There are, however, several aspects of human interactions that point towards the need to go beyond reciprocal altruism: first, with a few exceptions[26,56], the evolutionary analysis of repeated encounters has been largely restricted to two-person interactions but the human case clearly demands the analysis of larger groups. Unfortunately, the evolutionary success of tit-for-tat-like strategies of conditional cooperation is extremely limited even in relatively small groups of 4–8 individuals. It turns out that in a repeated n-person prisoners' dilemma, the only conditionally cooperative, evolutionarily stable strategy prescribes cooperation only if all other group members cooperated in the previous period. The basin of attraction of this strategy is extremely small because a few selfish players suffice to undermine the cooperation of the conditional cooperators.[56]

Second, the interacting individuals are forced to stay together for a random number of periods[6]. This assumption is not only violated by many, if not most, animal interactions but it is also clearly violated in the case of humans. Throughout evolutionary history, humans almost always had the option to stop interacting with genetically unrelated individuals. Thus, the choice of cooperation partners has to be modelled explicitly, which brings issues of reputation formation to the forefront of the analysis. Recent experiments indicate that endogenous partner choice and the associated incentives for reputation formation have powerful effects on human cooperation[57].

Third, reciprocal altruism relies on the idea that altruistic behaviour creates economic benefits for the altruist in the future. Therefore, it has difficulties explaining strongly reciprocal behaviour, which is characterized by the absence of future net benefits. Reciprocal altruism could only explain strong reciprocity if humans behave as if cooperation provides future net benefits, although there are none objectively. The ethnographic evidence suggests that—depending on the interaction partner—humans faced many different probabilities of repeated encounters so that situations often arose in which defection was the best strategy[58]. Indeed, the very fact that humans seem to have excellent cheating detection abilities[59] suggests that, despite many repeated interactions, cheating has been a major problem throughout human evolution. Therefore, humans' behavioural rules are likely to be fine-tuned to the variations in cheating opportunities, casting doubt on the assumption that humans systematically overestimate the future benefits from current altruistic behaviours.

Reputation-seeking

Evolutionary approaches to reputation-based cooperation[44,60-64] represent important steps beyond reciprocal altruism. The indirect reciprocity model[44,60,61] relies on the idea that third parties reward individuals with an altruistic reputation if they can acquire a good reputation themselves by rewarding. It has been shown that aspects of the food-sharing pattern of the Ache of Paraguay can be explained by this logic[65]. The experimental evidence also strongly suggests that a considerable part of human altruism is driven by concerns about reputation. Yet there are still some unsolved theoretical problems that point towards the need for further research. First, the indirect reciprocity approach produces long-run helping rates of roughly 40% if the recipient's benefit is four times the donor's cost, provided that all individuals live in isolated groups without any migration. If, however, genetic mixing between the groups occurs, helping rates decline dramatically and approach zero[61]. It would be an important step forward if the indirect reciprocity approach could be modified in such a way that significant helping rates could be maintained under reasonable assumptions about migration between groups. Second, the question of how to model the concept of a good reputation remains open. For example, should an individual who does not help a person with a bad reputation lose his good reputation? Currently the image-scoring approach[44] gives an affirmative answer to this question while others do not[61].

Third, reputation formation among humans is based on our language capabilities. However, we can use our language to tell the truth or to lie. Thus, what ensures that individuals' reputations provide a reasonably accurate picture of their past behaviours? Fourth, the indirect reciprocity approach is limited to dyadic cooperation. Therefore, it cannot currently explain cooperation in larger groups. But recent experiments that connect the n-person public good game with an indirect reciprocity game do point towards a potential solution[43]. Finally, reputation-based approaches cannot account for strong reciprocity unless one assumes that humans behave as if they systematically overestimate the future gains from current altruistic acts—an assumption that is dubious in view of the experimental evidence.

Costly signalling theory also provides a reputation-based ultimate explanation for altruistic behaviour[62,63]. According to this approach, individuals signal favourable, yet unobservable, traits with altruistic acts, rendering them preferred mating partners or helping in the recruitment of coalition partners in conflicts. The assumption behind this theory is that individuals with better traits have lower marginal signalling costs, that is, lower costs of altruistic acts. Thus, those with better traits are more likely to signal, which allows the inference that those who signal have better traits on average. The advantage of this approach is that it could, in principle, explain contributions to n-person public goods. The weakness is that the signalling of unobservable traits need not occur by altruistic acts but can also take other forms. The approach, therefore, generates multiple equilibria—in some equilibria, signalling occurs via altruistic behaviour; in others, signalling does not involve any altruistic acts. Therefore, this theory has difficulties explaining human altruism unless it is supplemented with some other mechanisms. One such mechanism might be cultural group selection[63]. If groups where signalling takes place via altruistic behaviour have better survival prospects, selection between groups favours those groups which have settled at a pro-social within-group equilibrium. Since there is no within-group selection against the altruists at the pro-social equilibrium, only weak effects of cultural selection between groups are required here. There is evidence[66] from Meriam turtle hunters that is consistent with costly signalling theory but so far there is no experimental evidence for altruistic costly signalling.

Gene–culture coevolution

The birth of modern sociobiology is associated with scepticism against genetic group selection[67]; although it is possible in theory, and in spite of a few plausible cases[25], genetic group selection has generally been deemed unlikely to occur empirically. The main argument has been that it can at best be relevant in small isolated groups because migration in combination with within-group selection against altruists is a much stronger force than selection between groups. The migration of defectors to groups with a comparatively large number of altruists plus the within-group fitness advantage of defectors quickly removes the genetic differences between groups so that group selection has little effect on the overall selection of altruistic traits[68]. Consistent with this argument, genetic differences between groups in populations of mobile vertebrates such as humans are roughly what one would expect if groups were randomly mixed[69]. Thus, purely genetic group selection is, like the gene-based approaches of reciprocal altruism and indirect reciprocity, unlikely to provide a satisfactory explanation for strong reciprocity and large-scale cooperation among humans. However, the arguments against genetic group selection are far less persuasive when applied to the selection of culturally transmitted traits. Cultural transmission occurs through imitation and teaching, that is, through social learning. There are apparent large differences in cultural practices of different groups around the world and ethnographic evidence indicates that even neighbouring groups are often characterized by very different cultures and institutions[70]. In addition, a culture-based approach makes use of the human capacity to establish and transmit behavioural norms through social learning—a capacity that is quantitatively, and probably even qualitatively, distinctly human[1,71].

Recent theoretical models of cultural group selection[72,73] or of gene–culture coevolution[71,74] could provide a solution to the puzzle of strong reciprocity and large-scale human cooperation. They are based on the idea that norms and institutions—such as food-sharing norms or monogamy—are sustained by punishment and decisively weaken the within-group selection against the altruistic trait. If altruistic punishment is ruled out, cultural group selection is not capable of generating cooperation in large groups (Fig. 4). Yet, when punishment of non-cooperators and non-punishers is possible, punishment evolves and cooperation in much larger groups can be maintained[73]. This is due to the fact that the altruistic punishment of non-cooperators in combination with the imitation of economically successful behaviours prevents the erosion of group differences with regard to the relative frequency of cooperating members. If there are a sufficient number of altruistic punishers, the cooperators do better than the defectors because the latter are punished. Therefore, cooperative behaviour is more likely to be imitated. Moreover, when cooperation in a group is widespread, altruistic punishers have only a small or no within-group disadvantage relative to pure cooperators who do not punish. At the limit, when everybody cooperates, punishers incur no punishment costs at all and thus have no disadvantage. Thus, small cultural group selection effects suffice to overcome the small cost disadvantage of altruistic punishers that arises from the necessity of punishing mutant defectors.

To what extent is there evidence for the role of culture and group selection in human altruism? There is strong evidence from intergenerational ultimatum and trust games that advice from players who previously participated in the experiment increases

altruistic punishment and altruistic rewarding[75]. Recent intergenerational public good games where advice is given indicate that later generations achieve significantly higher cooperation levels even in the absence of punishment opportunities[76]. Ultimatum and dictator games with children of different ages show that older children are more generous and more willing to punish altruistically[77]. Although these changes in children's behaviour could be a result of genetic developmental processes, it seems at least as plausible to assume that they are also a product of socialization by parents and peers. Why, after all, do parents invest so much time and energy into the proper socialization of their children if this effort is futile? Perhaps the strongest evidence for the role of cultural norms comes from a series of experiments in 15 small-scale societies[23], showing decisive differences across societies in the behaviour of proposers and responders in the ultimatum game. Some tribes like the Hazda from Tanzania exhibit a considerable amount of altruistic punishment whereas the Machiguenga from Peru show little concern about fair sharing. Thus, taken together, there is fairly convincing evidence that cultural forces exert a significant impact on human altruism.

Yet, what is the evidence for cultural group selection? There is quite strong evidence that group conflict and warfare were widespread in foraging societies[78,79]. There are also examples[70,80] suggesting that group conflict contributes to the cultural extinction of groups because the winning groups force their cultural norms and institutions on the losing groups. However, although these examples are suggestive, they are not conclusive, so further evidence is needed.

If cultural group selection was a significant force in evolution, then the human propensity to reward and punish altruistically should be systematically affected by inter-group conflicts. In particular, altruistic cooperation should be more prevalent if cooperative acts contribute to success in a group conflict. Likewise, people should be more willing to punish defectors if defection occurs in the context of a group conflict. There is evidence from inter-group conflict games indicating that altruistic cooperation in prisoners' dilemmas indeed increases if the game is embedded in an inter-group conflict[81]. However, there is no evidence so far showing that inter-group conflicts increase altruistic punishment.

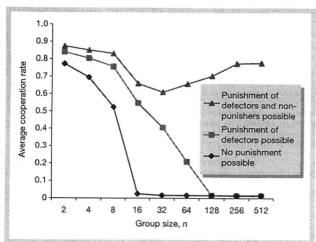

Figure 4 Simulations of the evolution of cooperation in multi-person prisoners' dilemmas with group conflicts and different degrees of altruistic punishment. The simulations are based on the model of ref. 73 but we added the possibility of punishing the non-punishers. There are 64 groups of fixed size n with n ranging from 2 to 512. The figure shows the average cooperation rate in 100 independent simulations over the last 1,000 of 2,000 generations. If the altruistic punishment of defectors is ruled out, cooperation already breaks down for groups of size 16 and larger. If altruistic punishment of defectors is possible, groups of size 32 can still maintain a cooperation rate of 40%. However, the biggest impact from altruistic punishment prevails if non-punishers can also be punished. In this case, even groups of several hundred individuals can establish cooperation rates of between 70 and 80%.

Open questions

We now know a lot more about human altruism than we did one decade ago. There is experimental evidence indicating that repeated interactions, reputation-formation, and strong reciprocity are powerful determinants of human behaviour. There are formal models that capture the subtleties of interactions between selfish and strongly reciprocal individuals, and there is a much better understanding about the nature of the evolutionary forces that probably shaped human altruism. However, there are still a considerable number of open questions. In view of the relevance of cultural evolution, it is necessary to study the relationship between cultural and economic institutions and the prevailing patterns of human altruism. Although recent evidence[23] suggests that market integration and the potential gains from cooperation are important factors, our knowledge is still extremely limited. This limitation is partly due to the fact that far too many experiments use students from developed countries as participants. Instead, we need experiments with participants that are representative of whole countries or cultures and we need to combine behavioural measures of altruism with individual-level demographic data and group-level data about cultural and economic institutions. In view of the theoretical importance of group conflicts and group reputation, much more evidence on how these affect altruistic rewarding and punishment is necessary. We also need more empirical knowledge about the characteristics of the individual reputation acquired by people and how others respond to this reputation.

At the ultimate level, the evolution and role of altruistic rewarding for cooperation in larger groups remains in the dark. Likewise, the empirical study of altruistic rewarding has been largely limited to dyadic interactions and little is known about how cooperation in *n*-person public good situations is affected if subjects have the opportunity to altruistically reward others after having observed each others' contribution choices. Evolutionary explanations of this kind of altruistic rewarding are likely to be much more difficult than explanations of altruistic punishment because, when cooperation is frequent, rewarding causes high costs for the altruists whereas a credible punishment threat renders actual punishment unnecessary. Finally, to enhance the study of the evolution of human altruism, there is a great need for empirically testable predictions that are rigorously derived from the evolutionary models.

References

1. Boyd, R. & Richerson, P. *The Nature of Cultures* (Univ. Chicago Press, Chicago, in the press).
2. Kaplan, H., Hill, J., Lancaster, J. & Hurtado, A. M. A theory of human life history evolution: diet, intelligence, and longevity. *Evol. Anthropol.* **9**, 156–185 (2000).
3. Hill, K. Altruistic cooperation during foraging by the Ache, and the evolved human predisposition to cooperate. *Hum. Nat.* **13**, 105–128 (2002).
4. Trivers, R. L. Evolution of reciprocal altruism. *Q. Rev. Biol.* **46**, 35–57 (1971).
5. Axelrod, R. & Hamilton, W. D. The evolution of cooperation. *Science* **211**, 1390–1396 (1981).
6. Hammerstein, P. in *Genetic and Cultural Evolution of Cooperation. Dahlem Workshop Report 90.* (ed. Hammerstein, P.) 1–11 (MIT Press, Cambridge, MA, 2003).
7. Stephens, D. W., McLinn, C. M. & Stevens, J. R. Discounting and reciprocity in an iterated prisoner's dilemma. *Science* **298**, 2216–2218 (2002).
8. Hauser, M. D., Chen, K. M., Frances, C. & Chuang, E. Give unto others: Genetically unrelated cotton-tamarin monkeys preferentially give food to those who altruistically give food back. *Proc. R. Soc. Lond. B* (in the press).
9. Andreoni, J. & Miller, J. Rational cooperation in the finitely repeated prisoner's dilemma: experimental evidence. *Econ. J.* **103**, 570–585 (1993).
10. Gächter, S. & Falk, A. Reputation and reciprocity: consequences for the labour relation. *Scand. J. Econ.* **104**, 1–26 (2002).
11. Fehr, E., Fischbacher, U. & Gächter, S. Strong reciprocity, human cooperation, and the enforcement of social norms. *Hum. Nat.* **13**, 1–25 (2002).
12. Gintis, H. Strong reciprocity and human sociality. *J. Theor. Biol.* **206**, 169–179 (2000).
13. Batson, D. C. *The Altruism Question* (Lawrence Erlbaum Associates, Hillsdale, NJ, 1991).
14. Silk, J. B. Adoption and kinship in Oceania. *Am. Anthropol.* **82**, 799–820 (1980).
15. Daly, M. & Wilson, M. Evolutionary social-psychology and family homicide. *Science* **242**, 519–524 (1988).
16. Cameron, L. A. Raising the stakes in the ultimatum game: Experimental evidence from Indonesia. *Econ. Inq* **37**, 47–59 (1999).
17. Slonim, R. & Roth, A. E. Learning in high stakes ultimatum games: An experiment in the Slovak republic. *Econometrica* **66**, 569–596 (1998).
18. Fehr, F., Tougareva, E. & Fischbacher, U. *Do High Stakes and Competition Undermine Fairness?* Working Paper 125 (Institute for Empirical Research in Economics, Univ. Zurich, 2002).
19. Bolton, G. & Zwick, R. Anonymity versus punishment in ultimatum bargaining. *Game Econ. Behav.* **10**, 95–121 (1995).
20. Hoffman, E., McCabe, K., Shachat, K. & Smith, V. Preferences, property rights and anonymity in bargaining games. *Game Econ. Behav.* **7**, 346–380 (1994).
21. Güth, W., Schmittberger, R. & Schwarze, B. An experimental analysis of ultimatum bargaining. *J. Econ. Behav. Organ.* **3**, 367–388 (1982).
22. Roth, A., Prasnikar, V., Okuno-Fujiwara, M. & Zamir, S. Bargaining and market behavior in Jerusalem, Ljubljana, Pittsburgh and Tokyo: An experimental study. *Am. Econ. Rev.* **81**, 1068–1095 (1991).
23. Henrich, J. *et al.* In search of *Homo economicus:* behavioral experiments in 15 small-scale societies. *Am. Econ. Rev.* **91**, 73–78 (2001).
24. Forsythe, R., Horowitz, J. L., Savin, N. E. & Sefton, M. Fairness in simple bargaining experiments. *Game Econ. Behav.* **6**, 347–369 (1994).
25. Sober, E. & Wilson, D. S. *Unto Others—the Evolution and Psychology of Unselfish Behavior* (Harvard Univ. Press, Cambridge, MA, 1998).
26. Bendor, J. & Swistak, P. The evolution of norms. *Am. J. Sociol.* **106**, 1493–1545 (2001).
27. Fehr, E. & Fischbacher, U. Third party punishment and social norms. *Evol. Hum. Behav.* (in the press).
28. Fehr, E., Kirchsteiger, G. & Riedl, A. Does fairness prevent market clearing? An experimental investigation. *Q. J. Econ.* **108**, 437–459 (1993).
29. Berg, J., Dickhaut, J. & McCabe, K. Trust, reciprocity and social history. *Game Econ. Behav.* **10**, 122–142 (1995).
30. Hayashi, N., Ostrom, E., Walker, J. & Yamagishi, T. Reciprocity, trust, and the sense of control—a cross-societal study. *Rational. Soc.* **11**, 27–46 (1999).
31. Buchan, N. R., Croson, R. T. A. & Dawes, R. M. Swift neighbors and persistent strangers: a cross-cultural investigation of trust and reciprocity in social exchange. *Am. J. Sociol.* **108**, 168–206 (2002).
32. Fehr, E., Fischbacher, U., Rosenblatt, B., Schupp, J. & Wagner, G. A nationwide laboratory—examining trust and trustworthiness by integrating behavioural experiments into representative surveys. *Schmoller Jahrbuch* **122**, 519–542 (2002).
33. Dawes, R. M. Social dilemmas. *Annu. Rev. Psychol.* **31**, 169–193 (1980).
34. Messick, D. & Brewer, M. in *Review of Personality and Social Psychology* (ed. Wheeler, L.) (Sage Publ., Beverly Hills, 1983).
35. Fischbacher, U., Gächter, S. & Fehr, E. Are people conditionally cooperative? Evidence from a public goods experiment. *Econ. Lett.* **71**, 397–404 (2001).
36. Isaac, R. M. & Walker, J. M. Group-size effects in public-goods provision—the voluntary contributions mechanism. *Q. J. Econ.* **103**, 179–199 (1988).

37. Ledyard, J. in *Handbook of Experimental Economics* (eds Kagel, J. & Roth, A.) 111–194 (Princeton Univ. Press, 1995).
38. Fehr, E. & Schmidt, K. M. A theory of fairness, competition, and cooperation. *Q. J. Econ.* **114**, 817–868 (1999).
39. Yamagishi, T. The provision of a sanctioning system as a public good. *Pers. Soc. Psychol.* **51** 110–116 (1986).
40. Ostrom, E., Walker, J. & Gardner, R. Covenants with and without a sword: self-governance is possible. *Am. Polit. Sci. Rev.* **86**, 404–417 (1992).
41. Sethi, R. & Somanathan, E. The evolution of social norms in common property resource use. *Am. Econ. Rev.* **86**, 766–788 (1996).
42. Fehr, E. & Gächter, S. Altruistic punishment in humans. *Nature* **415**, 137–140 (2002).
43. Milinski, M., Semmann, D. & Krambeck, H. J. Reputation helps solve the 'tragedy of the commons'. *Nature* **415**, 424–426 (2002).
44. Nowak, M. A. & Sigmund, K. Evolution of indirect reciprocity by image scoring. *Nature* **393**, 573–577 (1998).
45. Wedekind, C. & Milinski, M. Cooperation through image scoring in humans. *Science* **288**, 850–852 (2000).
46. Milinski, M., Semmann, D., Bakker, T. C. M. & Krambeck, H. J. Cooperation through indirect reciprocity: Image scoring or standing strategy? Proc. *R. Soc. Lond. B* **268**, 2495–2501 (2001).
47. Engelmann, D. & Fischbacher, U. *Indirect Reciprocity and Strategic Reputation Building in an Experimental Helping Game* (Working Paper 132, Institute for Empirical Research in Economics, Univ. Zurich, 2002).
48. Andreoni, J. & Miller, J. Giving according to Garp: an experimental test of the consistency of preferences for altruism. *Econometrica* **70**, 737–753 (2002).
49. Thibaut, J. W. & Kelley, H. H. *The Social Psychology of* (Wiley, New York, 1959).
50. Bolton, G. E. & Ockenfels, A. Erc: A theory of equity, reciprocity, and competition. *Am. Econ. Rev.* **90**, 166–193 (2000).
51. Rabin, M. Incorporating fairness into game theory and economics. *Am. Econ. Rev.* **83**, 1281–1302 (1993).
52. Levine, D. K. Modeling altruism and spitefulness in experiments. *Rev. Econ. Dynam.* **1**, 593–622 (1998).
53. Falk, A. & Fischbacher, U. Distributional consequences and intentions in a model of reciprocity. *Ann. Econ. Stat.* **63**, 111–129 (2001).
54. Kiyonari, T., Tanida, S. & Yamagishi, T. Social exchange and reciprocity: confusion or a heuristic. *Evol. Hum. Behav.* **21**, 411–427 (2000).
55. Rilling, J. K. *et al.* A neural basis for social cooperation. *Neuron* **35**, 395–405 (2002).
56. Boyd, R. & Richerson, P. J. The evolution of reciprocity in sizable groups. *J. Theor. Biol.* **132**, 337–356 (1988).
57. Brown, M., Falk, A. & Fehr, E. Relational contracts and the nature of market interactions. *Econometrica* (in the press).
58. Fehr, E. & Henrich, J. in *Genetic and Cultural Evolution of Cooperation. Dahlem Workshop Report 90* (ed. Hammerstein, P.) 55–82 (MIT Press, Cambridge, MA, 2003).
59. Cosmides, L. & Tooby, J. in *The Adapted Mind* (eds Barkow, J., Cosmides, L. & Tooby, J.) (Oxford Univ. Press, New York, 1992).
60. Alexander, R. D. *The Biology of Moral Systems* (Aldine De Gruyter, New York, 1987).
61. Leimar, O. & Hammerstein, P. Evolution of cooperation through indirect reciprocity. *Proc. R. Soc Lond. B* **268**, 745–753 (2001).
62. Zahavi, A. Altruism as a handicap—the limitations of kin selection and reciprocity. *J. Avian Biol.* **26**, 1–3 (1995).
63. Gintis, H., Smith, E. A. & Bowles, S. Costly signaling and cooperation. *J. Theor. Biol.* **213**, 103–119 (2001).
64. Nowak, M. A., Page, K. M. & Sigmund, K. Fairness versus reason in the ultimatum game. *Science* **289**, 1773–1775 (2000).
65. Gurven, M., Allen-Arave, W., Hill, K. & Hurtado, M. It's a wonderful life: Signaling generosity among the Ache of Paraguay. *Evol. Hum. Behav.* **21**, 263–282 (2000).
66. Smith, E. A., Bliege Bird, R. L. & Bird, D. W. The benefits of costly signalling: Meriam turtle hunters. *Behav. Ecol.* **14**, 116–126 (2003).
67. Williams, G. D. *Adaption and Natural Selection: A Critique of Some Current Evolutionary Thought* (Princeton Univ. Press, Princeton, 1966).
68. Aoki, M. A condition for group selection to prevail over counteracting individual selection. *Evolution* **36**, 832–842 (1982).
69. Long, J. C. The allelic correlation structure of Gainj and Kalam speaking peoples and interpretation of Wright's *f*-statistics. *Genetics* **112**, 629–647 (1986).
70. Kelly, R. C. *The Nuer Conquest: The Structure and Development of an Expansionist System* (Univ. Michigan Press, Ann Arbor, 1985).
71. Bowles, S., Choi, J.-K. & Hopfensitz, A. The co-evolution of individual behaviours and social institutions. *J. Theor. Biol.* (in the press).
72. Henrich, J. & Boyd, R. Why people punish defectors—weak conformist transmission can stabilize costly enforcement of norms in cooperative dilemmas. *J. Theor. Biol.* **208**, 79–89 (2001).
73. Boyd, R., Gintis, H., Bowles, S. & Richerson, P. J. The evolution of altruistic punishment. *Proc. Natl Acad. Sci. USA* **100**, 3531–3535 (2003).
74. Gintis, H. The hitchhiker's guide to altruism: Gene-culture co-evolution and the internalization of norms. *J. Theor. Biol.* **220**, 407–418 (2003).
75. Schotter, A. Decision making with naive advice. *Am. Econ. Rev.* **3**, 196–201 (2003).
76. Chaudhuri, A. & Graziano, S. *Evolution of Conventions in an Experimental Public Goods Game with Private and Public Knowledge of Advice* (Working Paper, Department of Economics, Univ. Auckland, 2003).
77. Harbaugh, W. T., Krause, K. & Liday, S. *Children's Bargaining Behavior: Differences by Age, Gender, and Height* (Working Paper, Department of Economics, Univ. Oregon, 2000).
78. Jorgensen, J. G. *Western Indians: Comparative Environments, Languages, and Cultures of 172 Western American Indian Tribes* (W. H. Freeman, San Francisco, 1980).
79. Otterbein, K. F. *The Evolution of War: A Cross-Cultural Study* (Human Relations Area Files Press, New Haven, 1985).
80. Soltis, J., Boyd, R. & Richerson, P. J. Can group-functional behaviors evolve by cultural-group selection—an empirical-test. *Curr. Anthropol.* **36**, 473–494 (1995).
81. Bornstein, G. & Ben-Yossef, M. Cooperation in intergroup and single-group social dilemmas. *J. Exp. Soc. Psychol* **30**, 52–67 (1994).

Acknowledgements We gratefully acknowledge support by the Ludwig Boltzmann Institute for the Analysis of Economic Growth, by the Swiss National Science Foundation and by the MacArthur Foundation Network on Economic Environments and the Evolution of Individual Preferences and Social Norms. We thank G. Bornstein, S. Bowles, R. Boyd, M. Brewer, J. Carpenter, S. Gächter, H. Gintis, J. Henrich, K. Hill, M. Milinski, P. Richerson, A. Riedl, K. Sigmund, E. A. Smith, D. S. Wilson and T. Yamagichi for comments on the manuscript, and M. Naef, D. Reding and M. Jörg for their research assistance.

Competing interest statement The authors declare that they have no competing financial interests.

Correspondence and requests for materials should be addressed to E.F. (efehr@iew.unizh.ch).

Ernst Fehr & Urs Fischbacher—University of Zürich, Institute for Empirical Research in Economics, Blümlisalpstrasse 10, CH-8006 Zürich, Switzerland

Cause of Death: Uncertain(ty)

Robert B. Cialdini

Arizona State University

All the weapons of influence discussed in this book* work better under some conditions than under others. If we are to defend ourselves adequately against any such weapon, it is vital that we know its optimal operating conditions in order to recognize when we are most vulnerable to its influence. We have already had a hint of one time when the principle of social proof worked best with the Chicago believers. It was a sense of shaken confidence that triggered their craving for converts. In general, *when we are unsure of ourselves, when the situation is unclear or ambiguous, when uncertainty reigns, we are most likely to look to and accept the actions of others as correct* (Tesser, Campbell, & Mickler, 1983).

In the process of examining the reactions of other people to resolve our uncertainty, however, we are likely to overlook a subtle, but important fact: Those people are probably examining the social evidence, too. Especially in an ambiguous situation, the tendency for everyone to be looking to see what everyone else is doing can lead to a fascinating phenomenon called *pluralistic ignorance.*A thorough understanding of the pluralistic ignorance phenomenon helps explain a regular occurrence in our country that has been termed both a riddle and a national disgrace: the failure of entire groups of bystanders to aid victims in agonizing need of help.

The classic example of such bystander inaction and the one that has produced the most debate in journalistic, political, and scientific circles began as an ordinary homicide case in New York City's borough of Queens. A woman in her late twenties, Catherine Genovese, was killed in a late-night attack on her street as she returned from work. Murder is never an act to be passed off lightly, but in a city the size and tenor of New York, the Genovese incident warranted no more space than a fraction of a column in the *New York Times.* Catherine Genovese's story would have died with her on that day in March 1964 if it hadn't been for a mistake.

The metropolitan editor of the *Times,* A. M. Rosenthal, happened to be having lunch with the city police commissioner a week later. Rosenthal asked the commissioner about a different Queens-based homicide,and the commissioner, thinking he was being questioned about the Genovese case, revealed something staggering that had been uncovered by the police investigation. It was something that left everyone who heard it, the commissioner included, aghast and grasping for explanations. Catherine Genovese had not experienced a quick, muffled death. It had been a long, loud, tortured, *public* event. Her assailant had chased and attacked her in the street three times over a period of 35 minutes before his knife finally silenced her cries for help. Incredibly, 38 of her neighbors watched from the safety of their apartment windows without so much as lifting a finger to call the police.

Rosenthal, a former Pulitzer Prize winner reporter, knew a story when he heard one. On the day of his lunch with the commissioner, he assigned a reporter to investigate the "bystander angle" of the Genovese incident. Within a week, the *Times* published a long, front-page article that was to create a swirl of controversy and speculation. The initial paragraphs of that report provided the tone and focus of the story:

> For more than half an hour 38 respectable, law-abiding citizens in Queens watched a killer stalk and stab a woman in three separate attacks in Kew Gardens.
>
> Twice the sound of their voices and the sudden glow of their bedroom lights interrupted him and frightened him off. Each time he returned, sought her out, and stabbed her again. Not one person telephoned the police during the assault; one witness called after the woman was dead.
>
> That was two weeks ago today. But Assistant Chief Inspector Frederick M. Lussen, in charge of the borough's detectives and a veteran of 25 years of homicide investigations, is still shocked.
>
> He can give a matter-of-fact recitation of many murders. But the Kew Gardens slaying baffles him—not because it is a murder, but because "good people" failed to call the police. (Ganzberg,1964)

As with Assistant Chief Inspector Lussen, shock and bafflement were the standard reactions of almost everyone who learned the story's details. The shock struck first, leaving the police, the news people, and the reading public stunned. The bafflement followed quickly. How could 38 "good people" fail to act under those circumstances? No one could understand it. Even the murder witnesses themselves were bewildered. "I don't know," they answered one after another. "I just don't know." A few offered weak reasons for their inaction. For example, two or three people explained that they were "afraid" or "did not want to get involved." These reasons, however, do not stand up to close scrutiny: A simple anonymous call to the police could have saved Catherine Genovese without threatening the witnesses' future safety or free time. No, it wasn't the observers' fear or reluctance to complicate their lives that explained their lack of action; something else was going on there that even they could not fathom.

Confusion, though, does not make for good news copy. So the press as well as the other media—several papers, TV stations, and magazines that were pursuing follow up stories—emphasized the only explanation available at the time: The witnesses, no different from the rest of us, hadn't cared enough to get involved. Americans were becoming a nation of selfish, insensitive people. The rigors of modern life, especially city life, were hardening them. They were becoming "The Cold Society," unfeeling and indifferent to the plight of their fellow citizens.

In support of this interpretation, news stories began appearing regularly in which various kinds of public apathy were detailed. Also supporting such an interpretation were the remarks of a range of armchair social commentators, who, as a breed, seem never to admit to bafflement when speaking to the press. They, too, saw the Genovese case as having large-scale social significance. All used the word *apathy,* which, it is interesting to note, had been in the headline of the *Times's* front-page story, although they accounted for the apathy differently. One attributed it to the effects of TV violence, another to repressed aggressiveness, but most implicated the "depersonalization" of urban life with its "megalopolitan societies" and its "alienation of the individual from the group." Even Rosenthal, the newsman who first broke the story and who ultimately made it the subject of a book, subscribed to the city-caused apathy theory.

Nobody can say why the 38 did not lift the phone while Miss Genovese was being attacked, since they cannot say themselves. It can be assumed, however, that their apathy was indeed one of the big-city variety. It is almost a matter of psychological survival, if one is surrounded and pressed by millions of people, to prevent them from constantly impinging on you, and the only way to do this is to ignore them as often as possible. Indifference to one's neighbor and his troubles is a conditioned reflex in life in New York as it is in other big cities. (A. M. Rosenthal, 1964)

As the Genovese story grew—aside from Rosenthal's book, it became the focus of numerous newspaper and magazine pieces, several television news documentaries, and an off-Broadway play—it attracted the professional attention of a pair of New York-based psychology professors, Bibb Latané and John Darley (1968b). They examined the reports of the Genovese incident and, on the basis of their knowledge of social psychology, hit on what had seemed like the most unlikely explanation of all—the fact that 38 witnesses were present. Previous accounts of the story had invariably emphasized that no action was taken, *even though* 38 individuals had looked on. Latané and Darley suggested that no one had helped precisely *because* there were so many observers.

The psychologists speculated that, for at least two reasons, a bystander to an emergency will be unlikely to help when there are a number of other bystanders present. The first reason is fairly straightforward. *With several potential helpers around, the personal responsibility of each individual is reduced:* "Perhaps someone else will give or call for aid, perhaps someone else already has." So with everyone thinking that someone else will help or has helped, no one does. The second reason is the more psychologically intriguing one; it is founded on the principle of social proof and involves the pluralistic ignorance effect. Very often an emergency is not obviously an emergency. Is the man lying in the alley a heart-attack victim or a drunk sleeping one off? Is the commotion next door an assault requiring the police or an especially loud marital spat where intervention would be inappropriate and unwelcome? What is going on? In times of such uncertainty, the natural tendency is to look around at the actions of others for clues. We can learn from the way the other witnesses are reacting whether the event is or is not an emergency.

What is easy to forget, though, is that everybody else observing the event is likely to be looking for social evidence, too. Because we all prefer to appear poised and unflustered among others, we are likely to search for that evidence placidly, with brief, camouflaged glances at those around us. Therefore everyone is likely to see everyone else looking unruffled and failing to act. As a result, and by the principle of social proof, the event will be roundly interpreted as a nonemergency. This, according to Latané and Darley (1968b) is the state of pluralistic ignorance "in which each person decided that since nobody is concerned, nothing is wrong. Meanwhile, the danger may be mounting to the point where a single individual, uninfluenced by the seeming clam of others, *would* react."[1]

A Scientific Approach

The fascinating upshot of Latané and Darley's reasoning is that, for an emergency victim, the idea of "safety in numbers" may often be completely wrong. It might be that someone in need of emergency aid would have a better chance of survival if a single bystander, rather than a crowd, were present. To test this unusual thesis, Darley, Latané, their students, and colleagues performed a systematic and impressive program of research that produced a clear set of findings (for a review, see Latané & Nida, 1981). Their basic procedure was to stage emergency events that were observed by a single individual or by a group of people. They then recorded the number of times the emergency victim received help under those circumstances. In their first experiment (Darley & Latané, 1968), a New York college student who appeared to be having an epileptic seizure received help 85 percent of the time when there was a single bystander present but only 31 percent of time with five bystanders present. With almost all the single bystanders helping, it becomes difficult to argue that ours is "The Cold Society" where no one cares for suffering others. Obviously it was something about the presence of other bystanders that reduced helping to shameful levels.

Other studies have examined the importance of social proof in causing widespread witness "apathy." They have done so by planting within a group of witnesses to a possible emergency people who are rehearsed to act as if no emergency were occurring. For instance, in another New York-based experiment (Latané & Darley, 1968a), 75 percent of lone individuals who observed smoke seeping from under a door reported the leak; however, when similar leaks were observed by three-person groups, the smoke was reported only 38 percent of the time. The smallest number of bystanders took action, though, when the three-person groups included two individuals who had been coached to ignore the smoke; under those conditions, the leaks were reported only 10 percent of time. In a similar study conducted in Toronto (A.S. Ross, 1971), single bystanders provided emergency aid 90 percent of the time, whereas such aid occurred in only 16 percent of the cases when a bystander was in the presence of two passive bystanders.

After more than a decade of reserach, social scientists now have a good idea of when bystanders will offer emergency aid. First, and contrary to the view that we have become a society of callous, uncaring people, once witnesses are convinced that an emergency situation exists, aid is very likely. Under these conditions, the number of bystanders who either intervene themselves or summon help is quite comforting. For example, in four separate experiments done in Florida (R. D. Clark & Word, 1972, 1974), accident scenes involving a maintenance man were staged. When it was clear that the man was hurt and required assistance, he was helped 100 percent of the time in two of the experiments. In the other two experiments, where helping involved contact with potentially dangerous electric wires, the victim still received bystander aid in 90 percent of the instances. In addition, these extremely high levels of assistance occurred whether the witnesses observed the event singly or in groups.

The situation becomes very different when, as in many cases, bystanders cannot be sure that the event they are witnessing is an emergency. Then a victim is much more likely to be helped by a lone bystander than by a group, especially if the people in the group are strangers to one another (Latané & Rodin, 1969). It seems that the pluralistic ignorance effect is strongest among strangers: Because we like to look graceful and sophisticated in public and because we are unfamiliar with the reactions of those we do not know, we are unlikely to give off or correctly read expressions of concern when in a group of strangers.Therefore, a possible emergency is viewed as a nonemergency and a victim suffers.

A close look at this set of research findings reveals an enlightening pattern. All the conditions that decrease an emergency victim's chances for bystander aid exist normally and innocently in the city, in contrast to rural areas:

1. Cities are more clamorous, distracting, rapidly changing places where it is difficult to be certain of the nature of the events one encounters.
2. Urban environments are more populous; consequently, people are more likely to be with others when witnessing a potential emergency situation.
3. City dwellers know a much smaller percentage of fellow residents than do people who live in small towns; therefore, city dwellers are more likely to find themselves in a group of strangers when observing an emergency.

These three natural characteristics of urban environments—their confusion, their populousness, and their low levels of acquaintanceship—fit in very well with the factors shown by research to decrease bystander aid. Without ever having to resort to such sinister concepts as "urban depersonalization" and "megalopolitan alienation," then,we can explain why so many instances of bystander inaction occur in our cities.

Devictimizing Yourself

Explaining the dangers of modern urban life in less ominous terms does not dispel them. Furthermore, as the world's populations move increasingly to the cities—half of all humanity will be city dwellers within a decade—there will be a growing need to reduce those dangers. Fortunately, our newfound understanding of the bystander "apathy" process offers real hope. Armed with this scientific knowledge, an emergency victim can increase enormously the chances of receiving aid from others. The key is the realization that groups of bystanders fail to help because the bystanders are unsure rather than unkind. They don't help because they are unsure an emergency actually exists and whether they are responsible for taking action.When they are sure of their responsibilities for intervening in a clear emergency, people are exceedingly responsive!

Once it is understood that the enemy is the simple state of uncertainty, it becomes possible for emergency victims to reduce this uncertainty, thereby protecting themselves. Imagine, for example, you are spending a summer afternoon at a music concert in a park. As the concert ends and people begin leaving, you notice a slight numbness in one arm but dismiss it as nothing to be alarmed about. Yet, while moving with the crowd to the distant parking areas, you feel the numbness spreading down to your hand and up one side of your face. Feeling disoriented, you decide to sit against a tree for a moment to rest. Soon you realize that something is drastically wrong. Sitting down has not helped; in fact, the control and coordination of your muscles has worsened, and you are starting to have difficulty moving your mouth and tongue to speak. You try to get up but can't. A terrifying thought rushes to mind: "Oh, God, I'm having a stroke!" Groups of people are passing by and most are paying no attention. The few who notice the odd way you are slumped against the tree or the strange look on your face check the social evidence around them and, seeing that no one else is reacting with concern, walk on convinced that nothing is wrong.

Were you to find yourself in such a predicament, what could you do to overcome the odds against receiving help? Because your physical abilities would be deteriorating, time would be crucial. If, before you could summon aid, you lost your speech or mobility or consciousness, your chances for assistance and for recovery would plunge drastically. It would be essential to try to request help quickly. What would be the most effective form of that request? Moans, groans, or out cries probably would not do. They might bring you some attention, but they would not provide enough information to assure passersby that a true emergency existed.

If mere outcries are unlikely to produce help from the passing crowd, perhaps you should be more specific. Indeed, you need to do more than try to gain attention; you should call out clearly your need for assistance. You must not allow bystanders to define your situation as a nonemergency. Use the word "Help" to show your need for emergency aid, and don't worry about being wrong. Embarrassment is a villain to be crushed. If you think you are having a stroke, you cannot afford to be worried about the possibility of overestimating your problem. The difference is that between a moment of embarrassment and possible death or lifelong paralysis.

Even a resounding call for help is not your most effective tactic. Although it may reduce bystanders' doubts that a real emergency exists, it will not remove several other important uncertainties within each onlooker's mind: What kind of aid is required? Should I be the one to provide the aid, or should someone more qualified do it? Has someone else already gone to get professional help, or is it my responsibility? While the bystanders stand gawking at you and grappling with these questions, time vital to your survival could be slipping away.

Clearly, then, as a victim you must do more than alert bystanders to your need for emergency assistance; you must also remove their uncertainties about how that assistance should be provided and who should provide it. What would be the most efficient and reliable way to do so?

Many Are Called But Only One Should Be Chosen

Based on the research findings we have seen, my advice would be to isolate one individual from the crowd: Stare, speak, and point directly at that person and no one else: "You, sir, in the blue jacket, I need help. Call an ambulance." With that one utterance you would dispel all the uncertainties that might prevent or delay help. With that one statement you will have put the man in the blue jacket in the role of "rescuer." He should now understand that emergency aid is needed; he should understand that he, not someone else, is responsible for providing the aid; and, finally, he should understand exactly how to provide it. All the scientific evidence indicates that the result should be quick, effective assistance.

In general, then, your best strategy when in need of emergency help is to reduce the uncertainties of those around you concerning your condition and their responsibilities. Be as precise as possible about your need for aid. Do not allow bystanders to come to their own conclusions because, especially in a crowd, the principle of social proof and the consequent pluralistic ignorance effect might well cause them to view your situation as a nonemergency. Of all the techniques in this book designed to produce compliance with a request, this one is the most important to remember. After all, the failure of your request for emergency aid could mean your life. . . .

Footnotes

1. The potentially tragic consequences of the pluralistic ignorance phenomenon are starkly illustrated in a UPI news release from Chicago: *A university coed was beaten and strangled in daylight hours near one of the most popular tourist attractions in the city, police said Saturday. The nude body of Lee Alexis Wilson, 23, was found Friday in dense shrubbery alongside the wall of the Art Institute by a 12-year-old boy playing in the bushes. Police theorized she may have been sitting or standing by a fountain in the Art Institute's south plaza when she was attacked. The assailant apparently then dragged her into the bushes. She apparently was sexually assaulted, police said. Police said thousands of persons must have passed the site and one man told them he heard a scream about 2 P.M. but did not investigate because no one else seemed to be paying attention.*

Trends in the Social Psychological Study of Justice

Linda J. Skitka
Department of Psychology
University of Illinois at Chicago

Faye J. Crosby
Department of Psychology
University of California, Santa Cruz

Justice is one of the most basic and potentially important social psychological areas of inquiry. The assumption that others will be fair is what makes social cooperation possible. This article provides a brief review of trends, both historical and current, in the social psychological study of justice and provides an introduction for a special issue of Personality and Social Psychology Review devoted to social psychological theorizing and research on the role that justice plays in human affairs. This overview highlights some exciting new directions injustice theorizing and research, including new uses of identity's ties to justice reasoning, increased attention to negative justice and moral emotion, as well as a greater emphasis on integrative and contingent, rather than competing, social psychological models of justice.

Justice research has a rich history in social psychology. Social psychologists cannot determine what is just or unjust, but we can document how people think and feel about justice issues. We can study people's behavior, and chart how matters of fairness are associated with various thoughts, feelings, and actions on the part of individual and groups.

In the four decades that social psychologists have been conducting research on social justice, a number of changes have occurred. During the 1960s and 1970s, the primary guiding metaphor of justice research was that of *homo economics*. Equity theorists assumed that people's concern with justice was primarily rooted in a desire to maximize their long- or short-term self-interests. Social interactions were conceptualized as forms of exchange and the focus was on distributions. Early challenges to the hegemony of equity theory—including Melvin Lerner's (1971) path-breaking work on the justice motive and Morton Deutsch's (1975) insistence that proportionality was only one of several basics for determining justice—exposed some of the limitations of equity theory but still conceived of justice in terms of allocations. The same implicit focus on allocations may be said of Susan Opotow's (e.g.. 1994, 1996) important work on the "scope of justice," work that described how fair-minded people can be cruel to those outside their moral community.

It was during the late 1970s and the 1980s that a concern with procedural justice replaced the exclusive focus on distributive justice. As Thibaut and Walker (1975), Deutsch (1979), and Leventhal (1980; Leventhal, Karoza, & Fry, 1980) were among the first to note, people care not only about the content of decisions, they also care about how the decisions are made. A number of studies showed that people will remain attached to their groups and satisfied with the authority figures if they think the authorities have followed fair procedures, even if the authorities have rendered a decision that adversely affects them (see Tyler & Smith, 1998, for a review).

Considerable justice research during the 1970s, 1980s, and 1990s primarily sought to gauge the relative importance of distributive and procedural justice concerns for people in a variety of settings. Meanwhile, other research looked instead at the reasons why procedural justice matters. Under the strong leadership of Tom Tyler and Alan Lind (e.g., Lind & Tyler, 1988; Tyler, 1989; Tyler & Lind, 1992), many researchers documented that procedures communicate important information about social worth and value to involved parties. People need to feel they are valued and respected members of the group, and they need to take pride in their group membership. A number of studies have found that people feel that even unfavorable outcomes are fair so long as they are treated with courtesy and respect.

Now, in the new millennium, more shifts in justice theorizing and research appear to be underway. Several researchers have become cognizant of the contingent nature of procedural justice. As happened earlier with equity theory, procedural justice studies have increasingly come to recognize that procedural fairness matters in some situations and for some subjects and not in or for others. Meanwhile, other researchers are seeking to enumerate the properties of procedural justice. Still other researchers are moving beyond what might be called positive justice to examine the reactions of people to situations in which a harm has been done or an injustice has been committed. How people react cognitively, emotionally, and behaviorally to unfairness is currently a topic of intense research activity.

The goal of this special issue of *Personality and Social Psychology Review* is to present samples of some of the current theorizing in the social psychology of justice. The issue includes some newcomers to the field, like Julie Exline and her colleagues, some established scholars, like Carolyn Hafer and Linda Skitka, and some of the pioneers, like Melvin Lerner, Faye Crosby, Tom Tyler, and John Darley. In a sense, then, our issue contains the current conceptualizations of three generations of scholars.

When do people care about social justice? The article by Linda Skitka (this issue) attempts to answer this and other basic questions. Specifically, she proposes an Accessible Identity Model (AIM) that predicts that people will be more likely to think about justice when identity concerns are particularly salient The AIM also posits that people's definitions of what is fair or unfair depends on which aspect of identity—the material, social, or personal or moral—dominates their working self-concept. Different justice norms, values, and expectations are predicted to be linked in memory to different aspects of identity, and therefore will be more cognitively accessible in contexts that prime different identity-relevant goals or values.

Like Skitka, Susan Clayton and Susan Opotow (this issue) similarly focus on the links between justice and identity concerns. Clayton and Optotow argue that "who" is included in one's scope of justice will shape people's justice reasoning in important ways. Whereas Skitka focuses on different levels of individual identity (how people see themselves as individuals with material, social, and personal standing), Clayton and Optotow focus instead on differences that arise from conceiving of oneself as an individual or as a representative of a broader group (e.g., as a rancher or environmentalist). Their article explores the contours of justice reasoning when one's individual interests might be at odds with one's sense of self as part of a larger group. Just as it is important to consider differences in individual perspective, Clayton and Optotow review evidence that to understand how people reason about fairness, it is important to know whether people are taking the perspective of themselves as individuals or of as more mor-

ally inclusive groups (e.g., women, all of humanity, or all living things).

Carolyn Hafer and Jim Olson (this issue) review research on the scope of justice, or the boundaries people seem to draw between those who are covered by considerations of justice and those who are not As a construct, the "scope of justice" has been invoked to help account for a host of phenomena such as mass internment, genocide, and slavery. Experimental evidence has seemed to corroborate models about the scope of justice. Hafer and Olson point to a number of possible alternative explanations, however, for these experimental findings and articulate other interpretations of the historical evidence than the ones originally articulated by Opotow (e.g., 1994, 1996). Hafer and Olson note that people outside the scope of justice sometimes receive positive outcomes, and people within the scope of justice sometimes are harmed—and moreover, are harmed in the name of justice. In short, conceptions of justice also involve punishment, vengeance, and harm, regardless of where the lines of the scope of justice are drawn. Hafer and Olson present an agenda for future research that can help to tease apart when harm is done because the harmed ones lie outside the harmdoer's moral community and when harm is done because, on the contrary, the harmed ones lie within it.

What about when harm has already been done? John Darley and Thane Pittman's article (this issue) presents a review of the retributive justice literature, an area of inquiry that is gaining increasing momentum in the justice literature. Their review of the literature leads to an integrated model of retributive justice. Specifically, their model proposes that the attribution people make for why a perpetrator inflicted harm will lead to different levels of moral outrage. Accidental, negligent, and intentional harm will lead to respectively higher levels of moral outrage. People's level of moral outrage in response to harm is used as a psychological barometer that predicts what is needed for justice to be done. Darley and Pittman's model predicts that low levels of moral outrage lead to low perceived need for punishment, whereas moderate levels of moral outrage lead people to demand compensatory reactions to make the victim "whole," or to return him or her to a preharm state. High levels of moral outrage lead people to feel that justice requires not only compensation, but also retribution, such as payment of punitive in addition to compensatory damages.

Retribution is not the only possible reaction to harm. Research on forgiveness represents another emerging area of psychological inquiry that has been gaining momentum in recent years. Julie Exline, Everett Worthington, Jr., Peter Hill, and Michael McCullough (this issue) review recent trends in law, management, philosophy, theology, and psychology that point to forgiveness as being increasingly discussed as a viable alternative to retribution. Although the very young field of forgiveness studies can be a minefield that can conflate "ought" with "is," and prescription with description, these authors provide an objective review of the research to date on the precursors and consequences of forgiveness, and outline five questions important for future research, including the following: (a) the development of a clear and consistent definition of forgiveness; (b) exploration of whether forgiveness encourages or deters future offenses; (c) whether people believe there are some offenses that cannot, or perhaps should not, be forgiven; (d) exploration of the motivational underpinnings of the desire to forgive; and (e) exploring whether variables that affect perceptions of justice or injustice similarly relate to people's desire to forgive.

The article by Tom Tyler and Steven Blader (this issue) looks at justice issues less from the point of view of the actor and more from the point of view of those who are, as it were "acted upon." Tyler and Blader review the current literature on procedural justice and integrate the insights of that now vast literature into a revised model of procedural fairness, the Group Engagement Model This version of the model, like its predecessors, focuses on the role of fair treatment in validating people's social identities. Whether people's social identities are validated or invalidated by fair or unfair procedures, in turn, plays an important role in people's subsequent thoughts, feelings, and behavior. Tyler and Blader's article extends previous work on procedural justice by differentiating between the consequences of procedural treatment for voluntary and involuntary cooperation with authorities. It also proposes that people's reactions to material outcomes do not directly affect variables like cooperation, but rather influence social identity that, in turn, affects cooperation.

Much of the vitality of social justice research derives from the pan-disciplinary nature of the research. Since the days of J. Stacy Adams (1965), justice researchers have combined organizational with social psychology. For example, scholars like Alan Lind and Tom Tyler (e.g., Lind & Tyler, 1988). Gerald Greenberg (e.g., Greenberg, 1993: Greenberg & Wiethoff, 2001), and Rob Folger and Russell Cropanzano (e.g., Folger & Cropanzano, 1998). have stepped outside the ivory tower and gathered data from legal settings, businesses, and other organizational contexts to test various hypotheses about the psychology of justice. In the tradition of pan-disciplinary research on justice. Faye Crosby and Jamie Franco (this issue) seek to develop insights into social justice theorizing by looking closely at the field of public policy. Rather than working deductively from theory to generate predictions for research, furthermore. Crosby and Franco work inductively from a controversial social problem to arrive at important new insights that can guide subsequent justice theorizing and research. Specifically, Crosby and Franco note that for all the attention lavished on issues of procedural justice, little thought has been given to what may be the most basic question of all: How can those who have been privileged by a system accommodate to changes in system roles, given that neither they nor anyone else is operating in the Rawlsian "veil of ignorance" when the rules are changed?

Like Crosby and Franco (this issue), Dave Schroeder, Julie Steel, Andria Woodell, and Alicia Bembenek (this is-

sue) provide a novel perspective on justice theorizing and research by bridging different areas of substantive inquiry. Specifically, Schroeder et al. see the conflict between individual and group outcomes that lies at the heart of social dilemmas as prime examples of the contexts where questions of justice and fairness are especially likely to emerge. Their review of the social dilemma literature provides important insight into the conditions when people will be more likely to be concerned about distributive, procedural, retributive, and restorative justice. Their review illustrates the benefits of studying justice in contexts that allow relationships to emerge and that include opportunities for the social and interactive aspects of justice decision making to unfold, rather than relying exclusively on single-shot encounters or decisions to inform justice theorizing and research.

Finally, the capstone article of this special issue is one by Melvin Lerner, who provides a historical review and critique of the justice literature from his unique position as one of the field's senior statesmen. His article outlines some cautionary messages for justice researchers. Specifically, he argues that justice theorists need to take a more nuanced look at whether experimental manipulations or measures arouse or tap a set of justice-based cognitions, or instead, simply elicit impression-managed adherence to normative conventions.

Visible Shifts in Justice Theorizing and Research

Taken together, the articles included in this special issue illustrate some developments in the social psychological study of justice. One clear trend is the concern with identity. Another is the attention to what might be called *negative justice*—that is, what happens after wrongs have occurred. A third is increased attention given to contingent models, that is, to models that specify the boundary conditions when different considerations are likely to be especially important in people's conceptions of justice. A fourth development that is discernable is the return to emotion For a while, all of social psychology appeared to concentrate on cold cognitions; today, feelings about justice (and about the self and others in justice-related situations) are understood as representing important components of the social psychology of justice. For example, the articles by Darley and Pittman and Exline et al. clearly reveal the important role of moral emotions in how people think about justice. Gaining a better understanding of moral emotion more generally as well as how it relates to the social psychology of justice, is an exciting new frontier for justice researchers to explore.

The articles in this issue also reveal important intersections between justice theorizing and other areas of social psychological inquiry, and illustrate how greater cross-boundary research can facilitate work in justice, as well as other areas of social psychology. For example, research and theorizing that focuses on contemporary social problems, like affirmative action, are especially important in revealing new insights into both the psychological foundations of people's objections to affirmative action, and because it can reveal important and previously neglected gaps in theory, such as rule change as a procedural justice issue. Relating social dilemma research and theories to justice provides another excellent example of how bridging different areas of inquiry can do much to inform each one.

Our ultimate goal in putting together this issue was to fan the flames of interest in social psychological justice theory and research, and to showcase the many new developments that are emerging in the social psychological study of questions relating to justice and fairness. We hope for a two-fold outcome. First, we hope that the research agendas of social psychologists currently doing research injustice will benefit from incorporating some of the innovations in justice theorizing that this issue presents into their current thinking and work. Second, we hope that social psychologists working in other areas will have an increased recognition of the importance of justice as an area of social psychological inquiry. To a considerable degree, negotiating how the benefits and burdens of social cooperation are to be allocated across persons—the fundamental focus of justice theory and research—is one of the most central of all social psychological questions. We therefore hope that this special issue facilitates a broader recognition of the importance of justice as a social psychological construct worthy of both additional study and inclusion as a chapter in social psychology textbooks.

References

Adams. S. I. (1965). Inequity in social exchange. In L. Berkowiltz (Ed.), *Advances in experimental social psychology, Vol 2* (pp. 267-299). New York: Academic.

Clayton, S., & Opotow, S. (2003). Justice and identity: Changing perspectives on what is fair. *Personality and Social Psychology Review 7,* 298-310.

Crosby. F. J., & Franco. J. L (2003). Connections between the ivory tower and the multicolored world: Linking abstract theories of social justice to the rough and tumble of affirmative action. *Personality and Social Psychology Review, 7,* 362-373.

Darley, J. M., & Pittman, T. S. (2003). The psychology of compesatory and retributive justice. *Personality and Social Psychology Review, 7,* 324-336.

Deutsch, M. (1975). Equity, equality, and need: What determines which value win be used as the basis of distributive justice? *Journal of Social Issues, 31*(4), 137-149.

Deutsch, M. (1979). Education and distributive justice: Some reflections on grading systems. *American Psychologist, 34,* 391-401.

Exline, J. J., Worthington. E. L., Jr., Hill, P., & McCullough. M. E. (2003). Forgiveness and justice: A research agenda for social and personality psychology. *Personality and Social Psychology Review, 7,* 337-348.

Folger, R., & Cropanzano, R. (1998). *Organizational justice and human resource management.* Thousand Oaks, CA: Sage

Greenberg, J. (1993). Justice and organizational citizenship: A commentary on the state of the science. *Employee Responsibilities and Rights Journal, 6,* 249-256.

Greenberg, J., & Wietholf, C. (2001). Organizational justice as proaction and reaction: Implications for research and application. In R. Cropanzano (Ed). *Justice in the workplace: From theory to practice, Vol. 2* (pp. 271-302). Mahwah, NJ: Lawrence Erlbaum Associates, Inc.

Hafer, C. L., & Olson, J. M. (2003). An analysis of empirical research on the scope of justice. *Personality and Social Psychology Review, 7,* 311-323.

Lerner. M. J. (1971). Justified self-interest and responsibility for suffering: A replication and extension. *Journal of Human Relations, 19,* 550-559.

Lerner, M. J. (2003). The justice motive: Where social psychologists found it, how they lost it, and why they may not find it again. *Personality and Social Psychology Review, 7,* 388-399.

Leventhal, G. S. (1980). What should be done with equity theory? In K. J. Gergen. M. S. Greenberg, & R. H. Willis (Eds.). *Social exchange: Advances in theory and research* (pp. 27-55). New York: Plenum.

Leventhal, G. S., Karuza, J., & Fry, W. R. (1980). Beyond fairness: A theory of allocation preferences. In G. Mikula (Ed.). *Justice and social interaction* (pp. 167-218). New York: Springer-Verlag.

Lind, E. A., & Tyler, T. R. (1988). *The social psychology of procedural justice.* New York Plenum.

Opotow, S. (1994). Predicting protection: Scope of justice and the natural world. *Journal of Social Issues, 50,* 49-63.

Opotow, S. (1996). Is justice finite? The case of environmental inclusion. In L. Montada & M. Lerner (Eds.), *Social justice in human relations: Current societal concerns about justice. Vol. 3* (pp. 213-230). New York Plenum.

Schroeder, D. A., Steel. J. E., Woodell, A. J., & Bembenek, A. F. (2003). Justice within social dilemmas, *Personality and Social Psychology Review, 7,* 374-387.

Skitka, L. J. (2003). Of different minds: An accessible identity model of justice reasoning. *Personality and Social Psychology Review, 7,* 286-297.

Thibaut, J., & Walker. L. (1975). *Procedural justice: A psychological analysis.* Hillside. NJ: Lawrence Erlbaum Associates, Inc.

Tyler, T. R. (1989). The psychology of procedural justice: A test of the group-value model. *Journal of Personality and Social Psychology, 57,* 830-838.

Tyler, T. R., & Blader, S. L. (2003). The Group Engagement Model: Procedural justice, social identity, and cooperative behavior. *Personality and Social Psychology Review, 7,* 349-361.

Tyler, T. R., & Lind, E. A. (1992). A relational model of authority in groups. In M. Zanna (Ed.), *Advances in experimental social psychology, Vol. 4* (pp. 595-629). Boston: McGraw-Hill.

Tyler, T., & Smith. H. J. (1998). Social justice and social movements. In D. T. Gilbert & S. T. Fiske (Eds.), *The handbook of social psychology, Vol. 2* (4th ed., pp. 595-629). New York McGraw-Hill.

UNIT 10
Group Processes

Unit Selections

Key Points to Consider

- How is leadership defined by social psychologists? Would you add anything to this definition? Can a leader lead no matter what the situation? Does the situation play any role in determining who will be leader and whether the leader will be effective?

- Have you ever been a leader? What characteristics do you possess that make you a candidate for leadership? What traits do other leaders possess? Do you think that leaders share a common set of characteristics? Do men and women who lead share common traits or is each different from the other in terms of leadership style?

- What is emotional intelligence? How is it related to leadership? Do you think emotional intelligence is the most important leader attribute? Can emotional intelligence be learned if an individual is placed in a leadership position but has not yet cultivated it? What other attributes must good leaders possess?

- What role does culture play in leader behavior? Is being a leader desirable in all cultures? Are there some cultures where it is better to fit into the crowd or not stand out?

- Why do some people prefer to be followers rather than leaders? Can followers become toxic for their groups? For their leaders? How so? Leaders use various strategies to keep followers compliant, inspired, and effective. What tactics do followers use to manipulate leaders? Can you provide some examples of your own life? When followers only tell the leader what he or she wants to hear, how can leaders determine what they really need to know, including any negatives?

- What are interpersonal skills and why are they so important to everyday life? What are some of the skills needed by an individual to function successfully in a group? How important is communication to group processes? Are most people good communicators? Can communication skills be improved? How?

- Can you define groupthink? Is there anything you would add to the typical definition of this group process? How does groupthink evolve? What are some of its symptoms? How can groups avoid or overcome groupthink? When groupthink does occur, what are the typical outcomes? Can you supply some historic examples of groupthink?

 **Links: www.dushkin.com/online/**
These sites are annotated in the World Wide Web pages.

Center for the Study of Group Processes
http://www.uiowa.edu/~grpproc/
Collaborative Organizations
http://www.workteams.unt.edu

In American schools, all too often cliques form, children are ostracized, and fights break out. Popularity, fitting in, and recognition by other students, teachers, and coaches dominate the thinking of many junior and senior high school students.

An experienced eighth grade teacher became concerned with the exclusion of her only Asian student from groups in her classroom. Despite her best efforts at teaching about diversity and cultural sensitivity, her other students just did not put any of the information into practice. She spoke to other teachers and the principle about her Asian student's situation. The teacher reported that Ho was chosen last for student teams, was not invited to play with the other boys at recess, was teased by some of his classmates for his accent, and was generally ignored by the girls, although some had begun flirting with other boys. No one to whom the teacher spoke had any helpful advice; in fact, each listener complained that the same conditions prevailed in other classrooms.

One night at dinner, the distressed and frustrated teacher grumbled to her family that the situation was absolutely exasperating. The teacher's daughter who was studying social psychology at the nearby community college sympathized and then shared information about noted psychologist Elliott Aronson's jigsaw classroom technique.

In a jigsaw classroom, master groups learn pieces of material about a particular topic. A likely topic might be Passover. One master group would learn about the general teachings of Judaism. Another master group would learn about specific reasons Passover is celebrated. A third group might learn how Passover is celebrated by contemporary Jews and so on.

The master groups next break into jigsaw groups comprised of one member from each master group such that every aspect learned by the master groups about Passover is represented. In the jigsaw groups, if a member does not contribute or has trouble expressing him- or herself, it is incumbent on the remaining members to improve that member's performance or all will fail. The jigsaw classroom scientifically has been confirmed to enhance children's cooperation, increase interactions with less popular children, and improve classroom climate.

The teacher was happy to hear about this method! She questioned why so few teachers knew or practiced this teaching approach. She could not wait to learn more and implement the jigsaw technique in her classroom.

Groups not only play a special role in students' lives, they are a significant part of all of our lives. Groups surround us at work, places of worship, on the streets, and even in our homes. While families are our primary groups, there certainly are other groups—formal and informal, large and small—that considerably impact us.

In this final unit of the anthology, we will contemplate group dynamics. Because there are at least two major components of most groups—leader and followers—we will consider both. In the first subsection of this unit, the emphasis is on leadership. In "Putting Leaders on the Couch," the author Diane Coutu discusses why some leaders are successful and others fail, what role culture plays in leader success, and how various personal attributes such as emotional intelligence influence leader emergence and effectiveness.

The second selection on leadership discusses how followers affect leaders. Lynn Offerman presents information and advice to leaders about how their followers might try to influence the leader. Sycophants, for example, use flattery or agreement with the leader to attract approval from the leader.

The second part of this unit pertains to group dynamics, especially the members of a group. Two additional articles round out the collection of essays. Interpersonal skills—namely communication ability—are extremely important to group functioning. Author Charles McConnell explains that most people, despite believing they are excellent communicators, are not. The average group participant needs to improve communication with others so that interactions can be effective.

Other circumstances besides poor communication can make groups ineffectual. Groupthink, a well-established phenomenon in the social psychology literature, results in poor and sometimes disastrous decision making. During groupthink, group members become self-righteous, exclude outside opinions, and make no alternate plans if their plan fails. Groupthink is the theme of the final selection by Vicki Kemper. Kemper reveals that groupthink may well have triggered the decision to invade Iraq and instigated the miscalculations about the aftermath of the invasion.

Putting Leaders on the Couch

A Conversation with Manfred F. R. Kets de Vries

Diane L. Coutu

LEADERSHIP IS THE GLOBAL OBSESSION. Thousands of recent books—many of them best sellers—have dissected the leadership styles of great leaders from Jesus to Jefferson. Business writers, too, have joined the frenzy. The trouble is, much of the business literature on leadership unlike the broader literature on the subject—starts with the assumption that leaders are rational beings. In part, that's because readers come to these business books for advice, so they get suggestions on how to imitate the conscious motivations, behaviors, and choices of role models. Advice books are hardly likely to focus heavily on leaders' irrational side—and still less likely to suggest that the role models' successes may even stem from their psychological frailties. Yet irrationality is integral to human nature, and psychological conflict can contribute in significant ways to the drive to succeed. Surely, therefore, we can benefit from putting CEOs on the couch, to explore how their early personal experiences shaped subsequent behaviors and to understand how these leaders deal with setbacks and pain.

Great leaders are capable, visionary, and inspiring. That doesn't mean they're rational.

Although a number of business scholars—most notably Harvard's Abraham Zaleznik and Harry Levinson—have explored the psychology of executives, only one has made the analysis of CEOs his life's work: Manfred F.R. Kets de Vries, the Raoul de Vitry d'Avaucourt Chaired Professor of Leadership Development at Insead in Fontainebleau, France, and the director of Insead's Global Leadership Center. Kets de Vries is also a practicing psychoanalyst whose research has provided rich pickings:

He has authored or edited some 20 books on the psychology of leaders and organizations, including best sellers such as *Life and Death in the Executive Fast Lane, The Leadership Mystique,* and *The Neurotic Organization.* Kets de Vries's work has brought him close to many of the world's leading corporations: The executives of such firms as Heineken, BP, and Nokia have drawn on his expertise. Indeed, it's probably fair to say that no other leadership scholar has had as much exposure to the mind of the business leader.

So it was to Kets de Vries that HBR turned for insight into what really goes on inside the mind of the leader. In this edited version of a wide-ranging discussion at his office in Paris, Kets de Vries draws on three decades of experience and study to describe the psychological profile of successful CEOs. He explores top executives' vulnerabilities, which are often intensified by the ways followers try to manipulate their leaders. Kets de Vries also explains just how these vulnerabilities play out in organizations and suggests how leaders might overcome them. His prescription for healthy leadership? Self-awareness and a well-rounded personal life, as well as an ability to suffer fools and laugh at yourself.

You've studied the psychology of leaders your whole life. How do you identify the successful ones?

The first thing I look for is emotional intelligence—basically, how self-reflective is the person? Of course, emotional intelligence involves a lot more than just being introspective. It also involves what I call the teddy bear factor: Do people feel comfortable with you? Do they want to be close to you? An emotionally intelligent leader also knows how to single people out and say, "Hey, Deborah, you're special. I've looked a long time for you, and I really want you to be part of my team." In general, emotionally intelligent leaders tend to make better team players, and they are more effective at motivating themselves and others.

Unfortunately, the right side of the brain—the part responsible for more intuitive processes—is not stimulated in business school. As a result, few students work to develop the skill of emotional intelligence. Furthermore, leaders do not always learn it on the job. This is particularly true today as more and more CEOs come from the financial sector, where emotional insight and people skills are often underrated. Of course, over the years, I've met highly successful executives who are not self-reflective at all. They're total doers. You have to be a doer to make it in business; navel-gazers do not make great leaders. Nevertheless, in my experience, the most effective leaders are able to both act and reflect, which prepares them to manage for the long term. These individuals not only run, they also take the time to ask themselves where they are going and why.

Do the backgrounds of the successful leaders you've studied have anything in common?

There is evidence that many successful male leaders had strong, supportive mothers and rather remote, absent fathers. This is beautifully exemplified by Jack Welch, who, in his autobiography, describes his attachment to a powerhouse of a mother and depicts his father, a train conductor, as pleasant enough but not very present. The same was true of a very different leader—Virgin's Richard Branson, whose mother told everyone she knew that Richard would become prime minister one day. It was Branson's mother who convinced him that he could do whatever he set his mind to do; his father played a much smaller role in his life. Former President Bill Clinton is yet another product of an adoring mom and a missing dad (he died before Clinton was born). Indeed, it seems to me that there is a lot of truth in Freud's famous statement that there is nothing as conducive to success as being your mother's favorite. When it comes to women, though, it's harder to explain what makes for success—there still aren't enough women leaders in business for researchers to make any real generalizations. But it does seem that the model for great women leaders is more complicated than that for great male leaders. As with the men, some strong women leaders had powerful, supportive mothers. But others had powerful fathers. Indeed, a successful woman often has been her father's favorite son.

Would you say that culture plays a role in determining what type of leader you are?

Certainly, different cultures have very different expectations of leaders. In America, for instance, a leader is a big shot. He takes himself very seriously, and other people put him on a pedestal. In the Dutch language, however,

the word for "leader" can have two meanings, one of which is "martyr." In other words, a leader is someone who suffers. To put yourself on display and blow your own trumpet would never be acceptable in the Dutch world of work (and otherwise). It would show exceedingly bad taste.

The link between leadership and culture is very complex. Let me approach it through a hypothetical situation, admittedly a difficult one. Imagine that you're in a boat with your child, your spouse, and your mother. It's sinking, and you're the only one who can swim. Who do you choose to save? When this question is posed across a spectrum of cultures, 60% of the respondents in Western Europe and America (men and women) say they would save the child, and 40% say they would save the spouse. In most Islamic societies, 90% of respondents (men only) say they would save the mother. Recently I was in Saudi Arabia giving a leadership workshop. In response to this question, 100% of the participants (all were male) said they would save their mothers. Officially, the logic here is that you can always remarry and have another child, but you can never have another mother. But psychologically, the fact is that women are not allowed to do much in Saudi Arabia. They are very handicapped. So the only way they can live and get glory is through their sons (their daughters are also demeaned). What develops is an incredibly intense relationship between the mother and the son, so there is no wife—or child, for that matter—who can ever live up to the gratifications the mother provided.

> "People in mental hospitals are easy to understand because they suffer from extreme conditions. The mental health of senior executives is much more subtle."

This story has many implications, but to me it underscores the cultural complexity of leadership. It's not always easy to appreciate or understand that what people do, mean, and say varies from one culture to the next, and without that understanding, it is impossible to lead in another culture. A leadership style that would be effective in Sweden, for example, might be quite dysfunctional in Russia, whose business elite I have been studying for some time. Of course, I'm talking now about the national culture, not a corporate culture. But corporate culture varies enormously as well, and companies differ in how they regard factors such as power, status, and hierarchy. There are also great differences in the way executives from various national cultures look at control and authority. There are numerous explanations for this, but as the story illustrates, the differences often derive from variations in child rearing.

By the way, of all the national leadership styles I've studied, the Finnish is one I admire very much. Unlike the Swedes or the English, the Finns never had kings or queens except when they were imported, so they have this element of democracy and a strong belief that working hard makes things happen. The Finns also have a straightforward, plain honesty, which is very good in a leader. And unlike many American leaders, the Finns have a strong sense of humility. When things are going too well for them, they throw up their hands and groan, "My God, the sky is going to fall down on us." That touch of creative paranoia can make for very good leadership.

You often write that executives are irrational. What do you mean by that?

If you study executives, you quickly see that they don't behave rationally all the time. Indeed, irrational behavior is common in organizational life. It was my realization of this—and my desire to understand that irrationality—that led me into the fields of psychiatry and psychoanalysis. Once I started, I found that business leaders were much more complex than the subjects most psychologists studied. People in mental hospitals are actually easy to understand because they suffer from extreme conditions. The mental health of senior executives is much more subtle. They can't be too crazy or they generally don't make it to senior positions, but they are nonetheless extremely driven people. And when I analyze them, I usually find that their drives spring from childhood patterns and experiences that have carried over into adulthood. Executives don't like to hear this; they like to think they're totally in control. They're insulted to hear that certain things in their minds are unconscious. But like it or not, people have blind spots, and the nonrational personality needs of decision makers can seriously affect the management process.

What are these blind spots, and how do they play out in the organization?

I'm struggling with a case right now involving an entrepreneur. Part of his problem is that he has great difficulty with authority. However simplistic this may sound, his troubles really do originate in a difficult relationship with his father. On top of that, he had a mother who was quite controlling. Not surprisingly, after he had started his company, he had a very hard time delegating; he micromanaged. For example, he opened all the mail that came to the company, and he insisted that everybody's e-mails be forwarded to him! This level of control was manageable as long as the company was in the start-up phase, but once it had become a $20 million operation, the entrepreneur's lack of trust in others' capabilities had a stifling effect. Predictably, the entrepreneur just couldn't keep good people. There was high turnover as people bristled under his exceedingly rigid control. Recently, this entrepreneur came to see me about hiring a large number of MBAs. I'm sure I could find many outstanding MBAs for his company, but I know they wouldn't stay with him. They would surely cite different excuses for their dissat-

isfaction and resignations, but the real reason would be that the entrepreneur is a control freak, a failing of which he remains largely unconscious. And because he is unconscious of it, he can't take responsibility for it, which means that nothing can change. Unfortunately, I am inclined to say that even if this entrepreneur could acknowledge his obsessive need for control, he would most likely come up with many elaborate rationalizations for his behavior. I believe it would take a great number of interventions before his destructive patterns could be brought to his conscious awareness.

In my work with CEOs, I also find that many executives are trying to compensate for narcissistic wounds—blows to their self-esteem that were inflicted in childhood by parents who were either too distant or too indulgent. (A child in an extremely indulgent household cannot develop a balanced sense of his own personality.) Typically, people with narcissistic injuries have a great hunger for recognition and external affirmation. To combat their feelings of helplessness and lack of self-worth, they are always in search of an admiring audience. In my work with leaders, I have found that CEOs generally have no idea that narcissistic wounds underlie their behavior. To make executives aware of their vulnerabilities, I sometimes ask them to describe the most critical negative voice that still plays in their heads from childhood. Even highly successful executives admit to saying things to themselves like, "You're not as good as you pretend to be. You're an imposter." This is a parental voice that has lingered into adulthood. Larry Ellison is a very good example. I never met the man, but I once wrote a case about him. I found out that his stepfather used to tell him repeatedly: "You'll never amount to anything. You will never be a success." Of course, this affects his leadership style today. Ellison is always trying to prove the bastards wrong. Not surprisingly, he has created a very aggressive organization. In organizations, we often find strong links between the personality of the leader, his leadership style, and the general culture—especially in companies where power is centralized.

Can you expand on the narcissism of leaders? There's been a lot of talk about the subject lately. Why is it so problematic?

We need to be careful here. Narcissism has a terrible reputation, often rightly so. But all people—especially leaders—need a healthy dose of narcissism in order to survive. It's the engine that drives leadership. Assertiveness, self-confidence, tenacity, and creativity just can't exist without it. But once a narcissist gets into a position of leadership, funny things start to happen. Because narcissistic leaders are often charismatic, employees start to project their own grandiose fantasies onto the narcissistic leader. And suddenly everything becomes surreal.

I remember being in a meeting once in southern Europe. Thirty senior executives were gathered for a presentation about the future of the organization. The president was a very wealthy man who used to brag that he would need ten lifetimes to spend all his money. Not surprisingly, his office was filled with enormous statues and paintings of himself. He arrived 20 minutes late for the meeting, and he came in talking on a mobile phone. Nobody acted annoyed. Eventually the presentation started, and the CEO's phone rang. He picked it up and talked for 15 minutes while everybody sat there, waiting. Suddenly the CEO got up and said he had to go. This was the most important meeting of the year, and he just walked out. But no one, not one person, objected. Everyone told him what he wanted to hear. It was as if the CEO were in a hall of mirrors.

> "To be effective, organizations need people with a health, disrespect for the boss—people…who can engage in active give-and-take."

This reaction on the part of followers is hardly unusual. Do you remember the Peter Sellers film *Being There*? It looks at the life of an illiterate and slow-witted gardener named Chance, who is standing in the street one day when a limousine backs into him. Hoping to avoid publicity, the woman in the car takes Chance home to be seen by a doctor who is caring for her husband, a big-shot financier and friend of the president. When the president asks Chance what he thinks about the economy, the poor man hasn't a clue. Taking refuge in what he knows best—gardening—he says: "As long as the roots are not severed, all is well." The president interprets this simple statement as a great revelation. The results are inevitable: Chance is eventually pushed to run for the presidency. It was George Bernard Shaw who said, "Kings are not born: They are made by artificial hallucination." There's a lot of truth to that. The problem with many so-called narcissistic leaders is that they both deliberately and inadvertently activate the latent narcissism of their followers. These followers are often ideal-hungry personalities who idealize wildly and uncritically. And if the leader happens to like being positively mirrored by others, he can become addicted to the followers' idealization of him. Tragically, some leaders get to the point where they fire individuals who don't praise them sufficiently.

Why are followers so prone to idealizing?

It has its roots in what Freud called transference. Transference is probably the most important concept in psychotherapy; it was one of Freud's great discoveries. After he started working with patients, Freud found to his great consternation that patients kept falling in love with him. To his immense credit, Freud realized that it couldn't be his own wonderful personality that was stirring up such deep feelings of admiration. Instead, he realized that in their dealings with him, patients were interacting with powerful figures from their own internal theaters, usually important childhood figures like parents, teachers, and siblings. Transference is the term for this continuity between early childhood and adult behavior. What Freud meant is that we all bring to our current relationships a map of past relationships that we transfer onto the present. This particularly happens during times of stress and in hierarchical situations, which are reminiscent of the parent-child constellation. Indeed, people in positions of authority have an uncanny ability to reawaken transferential processes in themselves and others. And these transferential reactions can present themselves in a number of ways—positively or negatively. One employee, for example, may relate to her boss as if he were her favorite brother, and thus she idealizes him. But that boss may relate to her as if she were his withholding mother! It is precisely this confusion of time and place that results in the psychic "noise" of the workplace. Sadly, Freud was not interested in business, so he never studied it. But it would have been fascinating to see what sense he would have made of everyone's tendency in business to relate to people as if they were someone else.

Doesn't all this put followers in a vulnerable position as well?

It certainly does. I discovered this when I was about 14 years old. I was with my brother in a youth camp in the Netherlands where we went every summer. Most children were sent to this camp for only three weeks, but we were sent there for the whole summer. After three weeks, there was always a transition between the old group and the new, and one year my brother and I decided to liven up the changeover with an initiation ritual. We placed a bathtub filled with freezing water in the middle of a field and announced that according to an old camp tradition, all the newcomers had to dunk themselves in the tub. I can still clearly remember more than 60 boys (most of them much bigger than us) lining up and, one after another, obediently immersing themselves in the cold water. Everything went well until the headmaster of the camp passed by. He was dumbfounded. He broke our spell by inciting the newcomers to rebel, pointing out that there were 60 of them against the two of us. Eventually, my brother and I got what was coming to us. But for me, the scene remained etched on my mind as a testament to just how far people are willing to go to obey what they perceive as authority.

> "I happen to believe that those who accept the madness in themselves may be the healthiest leaders of all."

The fact is that even scant authority can get away with murder, both literally and figuratively. Indeed, I would say that some organizations are so political and unsafe that they resemble concentration camps. Everyone kowtows to authority out of tremendous fear. And you can see why. I once met an executive who told me, "Every day I walk into the office, I can make the lives of l0,000 people completely miserable by doing very, very little." His company was probably not a very healthy workplace—why wouldn't he say instead: "By doing very, very little, I can make the lives of l0,000 people much easier"? That's why at Insead I try to introduce CEOs to a kind of applied psychoanalysis in an organizational setting. In each of my workshops, there are around 20 individuals who together might be responsible for 100,000 people. My hope is that by helping leaders to become a little more self-reflective, we can make their organizations a bit less like concentration camps.

But with all the psychic noise in organizations, how can leaders ever get honest feedback and criticism?

Today there is a lot of talk about using 360-degree feedback. I use it quite a bit in my leadership workshops. When I use it for coaching purposes, I gather information not only from people at the workplace but also from people close to the leader in his or her private life. This helps me get a sense of who the leader really is. But people at very high levels are usually considered much too important to go through 360-degree feedback. And even if they do go through it, they often don't get honest comments. That's because it's not very difficult for the person being evaluated to figure out who said what on the feedback forms. So the people giving feedback skew their answers out of fear of retaliation. But even if they did give genuine feedback, it's unlikely they could express it in a way that would pierce the leader's narcissistic armor. That's why I like to make the case for having an organizational fool.

What do you mean?

The fool I'm talking about is a foil for the leader—and every leader needs one. Down through the ages, the fool has played a traditional role as the stabilizer of kings and queens (and other leaders). This is the wise fool of *King Lear*—the guardian of reality. The fool shows the leader his reflection and reminds him of the transience of power. He uses antics and humor to prevent foolish action and groupthink. Let's not forget: Humor humbles. It creates insights. That makes it a very powerful instrument for change. Let me explain the importance of the fool through an anecdote. A couple goes to a fair where there's a large, impressive-looking machine. The husband puts in a coin and receives a card telling him his age and what kind of person he is. He reads it and gets excited. It says: "You're brilliant and charming. Women fall all over you." His wife grabs the card from him and turns it over. "Aha!" she says, "they got your age wrong, too." Leaders in all

organizations need someone like this who is willing to speak out and tell the leader how things really are. That's precisely the role of the fool. He offers the king a delicious sandwich, and between the slices of bread he shoves in a little piece of reality.

To be effective, organizations need people with a healthy disrespect for the boss—people who feel free to express emotions and opinions openly, who can engage in active give-and-take. Sadly, this typically happens only after a leader is out of power. As former President George Bush once remarked when he was asked what had changed since he left office: "Well, for one thing, I no longer win every golf game I play." In a well-run organization, the CEO wouldn't win every golf game either. And if a leader wants honest feedback, he should ask himself whether or not he's created an organization in which there's a place for a fool.

You've often observed that leaders get caught up in a whirl of hyperactivity. What's behind that?

Anxiety is one reason. Action is a typical human response to anxiety, and executives tend to be an anxious bunch. At any given time, there are many things going on that the executives feel they have little control over. So, like anyone else, they tend to look for some form of support, and one well-accepted response in the business world is the retreat into action. Another reason is that many top executives suffer from depression. I see it all the time. The chief cause for executive depression is that people usually don't join the ranks of senior executives until they're middle aged. And in middle age, people start to feel desperate about coming to terms with unfulfilled dreams before it's too late. The Germans have a term for this—*Torschlusspanik*, the panic that strikes because of the closing of the gates, the closing down of possibilities. Midlife prompts a reappraisal of career identity; it raises concerns about burnout and loss of effectiveness. By the time a leader is a CEO, an existential crisis is often imminent. This can happen with anyone, but the probability is higher with CEOs and senior executives, because so many of them have been devoting their lives almost exclusively to work.

I tell you honestly that very, very few executives lead balanced lives. They delude themselves about it, too. If you ask them how much time they spend with their wives and children, they give you numbers that are completely at odds with the numbers the families give. I worked for two years as a consultant and coach with about 150 managing directors of a large, well-known investment bank to help them be more effective as leaders in their organization. These were people who worked 70, 80 hours a week, and they worked very efficiently, very successfully. What's more, they were typically smart, pleasant, and insightful—very sure of themselves. But because they were such workaholics, these investment bankers were not secure about their personal lives. They had tremendous guilt over their families, whom they never saw. When I began my work with them, all they talked about at first was problems in the organization and conflicts they were having with one another. Eventually, however, as our conversations continued—often one-on-one—they began to acknowledge that the roots of their problems lay elsewhere, in some internal conflicts.

As I dug around, I found that these investment bankers, like many top executives who are obsessed with work and money, often had experienced deprivation of some kind early in life. They work for large salaries and option packages as a way of obtaining what is sometimes crudely described as "fuck you money," to be independent. It is their way of having more control over a world they often perceive (given their early experiences in life) as uncontrollable. The trouble is that once they've proved they're successful, they can't get off the treadmill. All they know how to do is work. In the meantime, their personal relationships have become a mess. So they feel stuck and bored, and that makes them more depressed. Unfortunately, in business you are not allowed to show pain. So to liven himself up a bit, the CEO might find a new wife, a trophy wife. Or he might try to pull off some really big, aggressive deal, like a takeover. Now that provides some excitement. What better way to cure boredom than by becoming a modern day Viking, raping and plundering? Mergers and marriages both help to mask CEO's psychic pain. But at some point, all leaders have to slow down. Retirement looms. When that happens, the depression that has never been resolved starts to become apparent.

Let's conclude by looking at the glass as half full. What makes a leader healthy?

Healthy leaders are able to live intensely. They're passionate about what they do. That's because they are able to experience the full range of their feelings—without any color blindness to any particular emotion. At the same time, healthy leaders strongly believe in their ability to control (or at least affect) the events that impact their lives. They're able to take personal responsibility; they are not always scapegoating or blaming other people for what goes wrong. Healthy leaders don't easily lose control or resort to impulsive acts. They can work through their own anxiety and ambivalence. As we saw earlier, healthy leaders are very talented in self-observation and self analysis; the best leaders are highly motivated to spend time on self-reflection. Another factor is that healthy leaders, unlike the less healthy ones, have the ability to deal with the disappointments of life. They can acknowledge their depression and work it through. Very importantly, they have the capacity to establish and maintain relationships (including satisfactory sexual relationships). Their lives are in balance, and they can play. They are creative and inventive and have the capacity to be nonconformist. These are the things that are fundamental, but I would also hope (after having said all of this!) that we can accept that we need a little madness in our leaders, because I happen to believe that those who accept the madness in themselves may be the healthiest leaders of all. To quote Shaw once again, "We want a few mad people now. See where the sane ones have landed us!"

Diane L. Coutu, dcoutu@hbsp.harvard.edu, *is a senior editor at HBR specializing in psychology and business.*

When Followers Become Toxic

Few leaders realize how susceptible they are to their followers' influence.
A good set of values, some trusted friends, and a little paranoia can
prevent them from being led astray.

by Lynn R. Offermann

Douglas MacArthur once said, "A general is just as good or just as bad as the troops under his command make him." Almost as he made that remark, his country's president was proving the point. For in late 1961, John F. Kennedy, bowing to pressure from his advisers, agreed to the escalation of American intervention in Vietnam. Among the advisers pressuring him was the senior author of a report recommending military intervention. And that adviser's trusted friend—an American general—was chosen by the president to lead the new U. S. command in Saigon. Given his loyalties, the general wanted to make sure things looked good on the surface, so he stifled evidence from the field about potential setbacks and obstacles in Vietnam, making it tough for the president to discern the truth.

That, according to author and journalist David Halberstam, was how President Kennedy and his advisers led the United States into Vietnam. The story starkly illustrates just how easily, and with the best of intentions, loyal and able followers can get their leaders into trouble. If an accomplished politician like Kennedy could be misled in this way, it's no surprise that today's business leaders often fall into the same trap. No matter who we are, we are all influenced by those around us. Some of us are leaders, but we are *all* followers. Indeed, Ken Lay, the disgraced ex-chairman of Enron, may not be entirely wrong in blaming unscrupulous subordinates and advisers for his company's demise. As an executive coach to senior leaders in a variety of industries for more than 20 years, I've seen firsthand just how easily followers can derail executive careers.

How does it happen? In the following pages, I draw both on my experience as a consultant and executive coach and on decades of research in organizational psychology to describe when and why leaders become vulnerable to being led astray by their followers. In some cases, as the Kennedy story illustrates, effective leaders can end up making poor decisions because able and well-meaning followers are united and persuasive about a course of action. This is a particular problem for leaders who attract and empower strong followers; these leaders need to become more skeptical and set boundaries. At other times, leaders get into trouble because they are surrounded by followers who fool them with flattery and isolate them from uncomfortable realities. Charismatic leaders, who are most susceptible to this problem, need to make an extra effort to unearth disagreement and to find followers who are not afraid to pose hard questions. Charismatic or not, all leaders run the risk of delegating to unscrupulous followers. There's probably little they can do to completely guard against a determined corporate Iago, but leaders who communicate and live a positive set of values will find themselves better protected.

When the Majority Rules

Although many leaders pride themselves on their willingness to take unpopular stands, research has consistently demonstrated that most people—including leaders—prefer conformity to controversy. And the pressure to conform rises with the degree of agreement among those around you. Even if widespread agreement doesn't actually exist, the very appearance of it can be hard to resist.

One of the most striking pieces of evidence for this was a series of experiments conducted in the 1950s by psychologist Solomon Asch. Asch showed participants a vertical line and then asked them to judge which of three other lines was most similar in length to the test line. Participants who made judgments on their own chose the correct answer 99% of the time. Yet when other participants answered as part of a group in which fake respondents had been coached to pick a particular incorrect line, almost three-quarters of the unknowing participants made at least one wrong choice and one-third of them conformed to the group choice half the time.

It's worth noting that the participants conformed without any pressure from the fake respondents. Indeed, the fake respondents were strangers whom the participants were unlikely to see ever again. In workplace situations where continued interactions are expected and where there may be concern about possible loss of face, one would reasonably expect conformity to be even more marked. What's more, most business decisions are urgent, complex, and ambiguous, which encourages people to depend on the views of others. We should hardly be surprised, therefore, to find that the ethical and capable individuals who served on the boards of companies like WorldCom and Enron turned "into credulous, compliant apparatchiks more focused on maintaining collegiality than maximizing long-term profitability," as the *Washington Post* put it.

What happens is that leaders faced with a united opposition can start to question their own judgment. And they should question themselves—the reason that unanimity is such a powerful influencing force is simply that the majority often is right. In general, research shows that using social proof—what others think or do—to determine our behavior leads us to make fewer mistakes than opposing the majority view does. But as even the smartest leaders have had to learn the hard way, the majority can be spectacularly wrong.

> People tend to be what psychologists call "cognitive misers," preferring the shortcuts of automatic thinking over considered examination.

One reason that even well-informed experts so often follow the crowd is that people by nature tend to be what psychologists call "cognitive misers," preferring the shortcuts of automatic thinking over considered examination. These shortcuts can help us to process information more quickly but can also lead to monumental errors. For instance, product designers may assume that if they like a product, everyone will. Yet the flop of Dell's Olympic line of desktop and workstation computers taught managers there that products must appeal to more than the company's own technically savvy workforce. As Michael Dell put it, "We had gone ahead and created a product that was, for all intents and purposes, technology for technology's sake rather than technology for the customer's sake."

Cognitive miserliness can be reinforced by culture. In the United States, for instance, Americans have long tolerated—even encouraged—people who form and express quick opinions. It is not a reflective society. Americans like to brainstorm and move on. That shortcut mentality can be particularly dangerous if the opinions are presented publicly, because people will then advance their views tenaciously.

In such public forums, it falls to the leader to push followers to examine their opinions more closely. Alfred P. Sloan, the former chairman of GM, understood this very well. He once said at the close of an executive meeting: "Gentlemen, I take it we are all in complete agreement on the decision here. I propose we postpone further discussion until our next meeting to give ourselves time to develop disagreement and perhaps gain some understanding of what the decision is all about."

Another factor contributing to the power of the majority is that leaders worry about undermining their employees' commitment. This is a reasonable concern. Leaders do need to be careful about spending their political capital, and overruling employees one too many times can demotivate them. Indeed, there are times when going along with the majority to win commitment is more important than making the "right" decision. (For more on when it's wise to go along with the majority, see the box "Joining the Opposition") But other times, leaders need to listen instead to the single, shy voice in the background, or even to their own internal doubts. As Rosalynn Carter once said," A leader takes people where they want to go. A great leader takes people where they don't necessarily want to go but ought to be." In going against the tide, the leader will sometimes boost rather than undermine his or her credibility.

Fooled by Flattery

Being swept along by their followers isn't the only form of influence that leaders need to be wary of. Sometimes, follower influence takes the subtler and gentler form of ingratiation. Most people learn very early in life that a good way to get people to like you is to show that you like them. Flattery, favors, and frequent compliments all tend to win people over. Leaders, naturally, like those who like them and are more apt to let those they are fond of influence them.

For their part, followers think that being on the boss's good side gives them some measure of job security. To an extent, they're probably right; even a recent *Forbes* guide to surviving office parties recommends: "Try to ingratiate yourself. In this market, people are hired and kept at their companies for their personal skills." Indeed, a recent study indicated that successful ingratiators gained a 5% edge over other employees in performance evaluations. This kind of margin by itself won't get someone ahead, but in a competitive market, it might well tip the scale toward one of two people up for a promotion.

Everyone loves a sincere compliment, but those who already think highly of themselves are most susceptible to flattery's charms. In particular, leaders predisposed toward narcissism may find their narcissistic tendencies pushed to unhealthy levels when they are given heavy doses of follower ingratiation. Gratuitous ingratiation can create a subtle shift in a leader's attitude toward power. Instead of viewing power as something to be used in the

Joining the Opposition

The leader who automatically rejects his followers' opinions can be as unwise as one who unthinkingly goes along with them. In fact, there are times when it is advisable to go along with followers who are plainly wrong.

A senior executive in the health care field recently faced a united front of followers in an acquired facility. The followers wanted the executive to retain a popular manager despite an outside consultant's report that strongly recommended the manager's dismissal. Staff members felt that the manager had been wrongly blamed for the unit's problems and that the unit had been mishandled, underfunded, and generally "done in" by previous management.

Although the senior executive was under pressure from her COO to dismiss the manager, she chose to keep and support him—and watch carefully. By choosing this course, the executive won the support and confidence of hundreds of employees who saw procedural justice in her willingness to give the manager a chance. With the full support of her staff, the executive then went on to lead a turnaround of the facility in short order, exceeding the COO's expectations. Indeed, the executive built so much credibility through her actions that she was eventually able to dismiss the manager, with the staff understanding that he had had a fair chance but had failed.

The executive recognized not only the unanimity of employees but also the importance of winning their buy in and commitment. She chose, intentionally, to defer to the staff's wishes in order to demonstrate her fairness and openness. After all, the employees could have been correct in their assessment. Even though that didn't turn out to be the case, the leader's considered decision to go along with her reports likely resulted in a better outcome than if she had summarily rejected their opinions.

service of the organization, clients, and stakeholders, the leader treats it as a tool to further personal interests, sometimes at the expense of others in and outside the organization. This happens as a leader starts to truly believe his press and comes to feel more entitled to privileges than others. People often cite Jack Welch's retirement deal as an example of executive entitlement gone haywire. The resulting furor drew public scorn for a longstanding corporate icon.

But one of the most serious problems for leaders who invite flattery is that they insulate themselves from the bad news they need to know. In her memoir, Nancy Reagan relates how then—Vice President George Bush approached her with concerns about Chief of Staff Donald Regan. Mrs. Reagan said she wished he'd tell her husband, but Bush replied that it was not his role to do so. "That's exactly your role," she snapped. Yet followers who have witnessed the killing of previous messengers of unwelcome news will be unlikely to volunteer for the role. Samuel Goldwyn's words resonate strongly: "I want you to tell me exactly what's wrong with me and with MGM even if it means losing your job." As more staff ingratiate or hold back criticism, the perception of staff unanimity, often at the expense of the organization's health, increases as well.

The rare individual who won't join an ingratiating inner circle of followers is typically seen as a bad apple by both the leader and her peers. Even when this perception problem is acknowledged, it is tough to fix. Despite widespread publicity after the 1986 space shuttle *Challenger* disaster about the dangers of failing to attend to negative news, NASA is once again facing charges of having downplayed possible liftoff problems just before the *Columbia* disaster. In both cases, engineers allegedly did not inform senior NASA executives of safety concerns; they either withheld information or presented it in ways that diminished its importance or feasibility. Obviously, this tendency to withhold information is not limited to government agencies. Bill Ford, the new CEO of Ford Motor Company, believes that isolation at the top has been a big problem at Ford—a problem he has spent considerable time trying to rectify by a variety of means, including forcing debate and discussion among executives and having informal, impromptu discussions with employees at all levels.

In dealing with ingratiation, leaders need to begin by reflecting on how they respond to both flattery and criticism. In considering a follower's advice or opinion, ask yourself if you would respond differently if a staff member you disliked made the same comment, and why. Are followers really free to voice their honest assessments, or are they jumped on whenever they deviate from your opinions? Bill Ford makes a point of thanking people whom he has overruled because he wants them to know that their honesty is appreciated. One simple test of whether you're getting the feedback you need is to count how many employees challenge you at your next staff meeting. As Steven Kerr, chief learning officer of Goldman Sachs, says: "If you're not taking flak, you're not over the target."

Organizational mechanisms can also help. Greater exposure to external feedback from clients, well-run 360-degree feedback programs, and executive coaching may be more likely to reveal the full truth. It's hard to lead from a pedestal; open channels of communication can keep a leader far better grounded.

For honest feedback, some CEOs rely on longtime associates or family members, people who may even take pleasure at times in letting some of the air out of the executive's balloon. (Your teenage children might particularly

Six Ways to Counter Wayward Influences

There's no guaranteed means of ensuring that you won't be misled by your followers. But adhering to these principles may help.

1. **Keep vision and values front and center.** It's much easier to get sidetracked when you're unclear about what the main track is.
2. **Make sure people disagree.** Remember that most of us form opinions too quickly and give them up too slowly.
3. **Cultivate truth tellers.** Make sure there are people in your world you can trust to tell you what you need to hear, no matter how unpopular or unpalatable it is.
4. **Do as you would have done to you.** Followers look to what you do rather than what you say. Set a good ethical climate for your team to be sure your followers have clear boundaries for their actions.
5. **Honor your intuition.** If you think you're being manipulated, you're probably right.
6. **Delegate, don't desert.** It's important to share control and empower your staff, but remember who's ultimately responsible for the outcome. As they say in politics, "Trust, but verify."

enjoy this, though they might not have as much insight into your business). Bill Gates, for instance, has said that he talks to his wife, Melinda, every night about work-related issues. In particular, he credits her with helping him handle the transition period when he turned over the Microsoft CEO title to his old friend Steve Ballmer. Ballmer, too, has been one of Gates's closest advisers. Gates says of this peer relationship with Ballmer: "It's important to have someone whom you totally trust, who is totally committed, who shares your vision, and yet who has a little bit different set of skills and who also acts as something of a check on you." And Gates's well-known friendship with fellow billionaire and bridge buddy Warren Buffer serves as a sounding board for both men. Disney's Michael Eisner had a similar relationship with Frank Wells, until Wells's death in 1994, with Wells enjoying the role of devil's advocate, challenging Eisner to ensure that the best decisions got made.

> It's worth remembering the words of cartoonist Hank Ketchum: "Flattery is like chewing gum. Enjoy it, but don't swallow it."

In his book *You're Too Kind*, journalist Richard Stengel gives an account of flattery through the ages, noting that "the history of how ministers have used flattery to control leaders did not begin with Henry Kissinger's relentless and unctuous toadying to Richard Nixon. ... Cardinal Richelieu was a famous user of flattery ... and he was a famous sucker for it himself." Stengel argues that corporate VPs who suck up to their bosses are no different than the less powerful chimpanzees who subordinate themselves to more powerful ones in the animal world. Though it may feel great at the time, stroking a leader's ego too much, and protecting him or her from needed information, can have negative consequences for both the leader and the organization. It's worth remembering the words of cartoonist Hank Ketchum: "Flattery is like chewing gum. Enjoy it, but don't swallow it."

Powers Behind the Throne

Caught between the Scylla of follower unanimity and the Charybdis of flattery, leaders might be tempted to keep their followers at a distance. But in today's world, this is simply not an option. CEOs of major firms cannot know everything about their own organizations. In coaching senior executives, I often hear them lamenting that they don't have full knowledge of what's happening in their companies. They report sleepless nights because they've been forced to make decisions based on incomplete information. They must rely on others for full, accurate, and unbiased input as well as for many operational decisions.

From the follower's point of view, this presents wonderful opportunities. He can learn and practice new skills as the leader relies on him more and more, and he may be presented with new opportunities for advancement and reward. At the same time, however, it opens the door for the occasional follower who uses his newfound power to serve his own interests more than the company's.

So how can leaders guard against that problem? They can begin by keeping ethical values and corporate vision front and center when delegating and monitoring work. Only then can they be certain that followers have a clear framework and boundaries for their actions. As Baxter CEO Harry Kraemer says, the key to ensuring that followers do the right thing is "open communication of values ... over and over and over again."

Leaders can also protect themselves and their companies by setting good examples. Followers—especially ingratiators—tend to model themselves after their leaders. Thus, straightforward leaders are less likely to be manipulated than manipulative leaders are. And a leader who is seen to condone or encourage unethical behavior will almost certainly get unethical behavior in his ranks. Take the case of former WorldCom CEO Bernie Ebbers, who allegedly ridiculed attempts to institute a corporate code of conduct as a waste of time even as he pressed his followers to deliver double-digit growth. He shouldn't have been surprised to find that junior WorldCom executives cooked the books or at least turned a blind eye when others did.

Although competency is generally a good basis on which to grant followers greater influence, leaders need to avoid letting followers influence them based on competency alone. As W. Michael Blumenthal, former chairman and CEO of Unisys, once said, "When did I make my greatest hiring mistakes? When I put intelligence and energy ahead of morality." The danger here is that astute but unscrupulous followers can find ways of pushing their leaders in unethical directions and may even use the leader's stated values against him. Suggestions like "I know you like saving money, so you'll love the idea of...," followed by a shady proposal, force leaders into the position of having to choose between eating their words and accepting the proposal.

At the end of the day, leaders have to rely on their instincts about people. Fortunately, there is good news in this respect. Research by psychologist Robert Zajonc suggests that we process information both affectively and cognitively and that we experience our feeling toward something a split second before we intellectualize it. If leaders are attentive, therefore, they may be able to tune in to a fleeting feeling that something is not quite right or that they are being manipulated before they rationalize and accept what they would be better off rejecting. For example, one tactic favored by manipulative followers is to create a false sense of urgency to rush the leader into an uninformed decision. Recognizing that you're being pushed too fast and reserving judgment for a time may save you from an action you may regret.

> ## One simple test of whether you're getting the feedback you need is to count how many employees challenge you at your next staff meeting.

It's not only the people you delegate to that you have to watch, it's also *what* you delegate. Clearly, leaders can never delegate their own responsibilities without peril. Smart leaders understand that even well-intentioned followers have their own ambitions and may try to usurp tasks that properly belong to their leaders. Harry Stonecipher, former president and COO of Boeing, likes to point to the great polar explorer Ernest Shackleton as an example of a leader who knew what responsibilities he could and couldn't afford to delegate. Stranded on an ice pack and crossing 800 miles of stormy seas in an open boat, Shackleton knew the deadly consequences of dissension and therefore focused his attention on preserving his team's unity. He was happy to delegate many essential tasks to subordinates, even putting one man in charge of 22 others at a camp while he sailed off with the remainder of the crew to get assistance. But the one task he reserved for himself was the management of malcontents, whom he kept close by at all times. Amazingly, the entire crew survived the more than 15-month ordeal in fairly good health, and eight members even joined Shackleton on a subsequent expedition.

* * *

By understanding how followers are capable of influencing them, top executives can improve their leadership skills. They can choose to lead by steadfastly refusing to fall prey to manipulative forces and try to guide the way toward more open and appropriate communications.

Followers, for their part, can better understand their power to inappropriately influence leaders. Once they recognize the danger they pose to their leaders—and ultimately to themselves ingratiators may come to realize that isolating leaders from reality can be as costly to themselves as to the company's shareholders. Realizing the value of dissent may force followers to take more care in forming and promoting their opinions.

Understanding that some tasks are best left to a leader may help followers to know where to stop and leaders to know what not to give away. In the final analysis, honest followers have just as great an investment in unmasking manipulative colleagues as their leaders do.

Lynn R. Offermann is a professor of organizational sciences and psychology at George Washington University in Washington, DC, and the director of the university's doctoral program in industrial and organizational psychology.

Interpersonal Skills

What they are, and how to improve them, and how to apply them.

Charles R. McConnell

Interpersonal skills are those essential skills involved in dealing with and relating to other people largely on a one-on-one basis. The interpersonal communication behavior of many people suggests hey assume to have the ability to communicate effectively, which they do not possess and which they take for granted. One must work conscientiously to develop interpersonal competence by doing the fight things at all times and doing them repeatedly until they become ingrained. As with any human skills, interpersonal skills can be improved through conscious effort. Successful interpersonal communication involves shaping the behavior of others, often while countering their shaping behavior. To have a chance of being successful, every interpersonal contact must have an objective and every effort must be made to avoid creating win-lose transactions whenever possible.

INTERPERSONAL SKILLS ARE those particular communication skills that are used when we are behaving in a manner intended to achieve certain results or objectives in face-to-face encounters. Common interpersonal situations on the job include numerous contacts with direct-reporting employees, such as directing, coaching, counseling, praising, disciplining or reprimanding, training, problem-solving, and many others. For the department manager, common interpersonal situations also include one-on-one contacts with peers, higher management, and other employees and persons external to the organization. A truly exhaustive list of potential one-on-one situations would likely be extremely lengthy.

Everyone possesses interpersonal "skills" as such; however, while a few individuals may exhibit exceptional interpersonal skills, a great many others may demonstrate weak or negative or virtually nonexistent interpersonal skills. Such considerable difficulty as we know exists with interpersonal communication seems to exist because most individuals do not believe there is anything wrong with the way they communicate face to face. In general, we take a certain facility with interpersonal communication for glanted. As a result, most persons inherently believe they are better communicators than they actually are.

In any given face-to-face encounter, one is organizing one's own behavior for the accomplishment of some specific objective.

Shaping and Enhancing Behavior

Our behavior consists of what we say along with the things we do that are overt and observable and thus become part of the message being communicated. Our behavior in communication encompasses the words we use, the manner in which we apply the words we use, and the nonverbal indicators that we apply both consciously and unconsciously. The latter, the nonverbal indicators, can encompass reflex muscle movements,

those motor habits, gestures, and movements we make without conscious thought, along with other physical movement accompanying a verbal communication, which, when taken together, become the indicators that comprise what we frequently refer to as body language.

Body language is behavior that is largely conveyed unconsciously, but this may also be accompanied by deliberate actions, both verbal and nonverbal, such that the intended result is the intentional arranging of behavior so as to increase the chances of achieving specific communication objectives. Simple example of such behavior shaping might include yawning or overtly examining one's wristwatch during a lengthy explanation or presentation (nonverbal) or asking a specific leading question or deliberately open-ended question during an interview (verbal).

Our individual behavior matters considerably in face-to-face communication, because it has effects on others and, sometimes to a considerable extent, influences what others think and do. And that individual behavior is proscribed largely by that complex sum of traits, characteristics, capabilities, beliefs, and tendencies that we refer to as personality. One might have a personality that lends itself to effective interpersonal communication with others; one might exhibit personality traits and characteristics that impede effective interpersonal communication.

It is likely that the most important factors in interpersonal communication are personal credibility and interpersonal competence. Of lesser importance, although still at times significant, are technical expertise, temperament, and attitudes toward others. Motives, feelings, and attitudes, although often influencing behavior, are ordinarily less visible than immediate behavior. Thus, interpersonal competence, supported by personal credibility, will frequently be the strongest determinant of success at interpersonal communication.

Acquiring Interpersonal Competence

There are two equally important sides to the matter of interpersonal competence. On one hand, it is necessary to become skilled in the behavior necessary for effective face-to-face interactions. On the other hand, it is essential to learn how to interpret the behavior of others so that our own behavior can be adjusted accordingly. To acquire or enhance interpersonal competence, we must continually observe others and interpret their actions and arrange our behavior to suit the objectives of any particular interaction.

What is initially required for the acquisition of interpersonal competence is repetition—that is, of the proper sort; deliberate repetition through contact after contact after contact, in which one relates to others with thoughtfulness and respect. Said repetition is necessary for two reasons: fast, it is no secret to anyone that any skill is improved through practice; and second, repetition also serves to temper and eventually overcome the fears and apprehensions that so many people experience concerning face-to-face contacts with others. Take the first reason as a given, or at least a statement backed by the common-sense knowledge that most activities improve with practice, and look more closely at the second reason.

Consider, for instance, some of the contacts a department manager experi-

ences in the normal course of duty. When one is new to supervision, there is probably some reluctance felt and some minor measure of discomfort experienced when it is necessary to announce an unpopular decision or perhaps even just to provide an employee with direction contrary to what might have been expected. Surely, there was apprehension to be experienced the first time or two that the new supervisor realized that an employee had to be reprimanded or disciplined. However, anyone who has managed others for an appreciable time knows that these particular tasks become easier with repetition. One might always approach disciplinary action with a certain amount of trepidation—actually, some apprehension concerning disciplinary action is a healthy, if not essential, adjunct to the process—but it cannot be denied that one becomes better at these tasks through conscientious practice.

As managers have been discovering since time immemorial, it is easier to pass along good news than it is to disseminate bad news, and it is surely easier to dispense praise than it is to reprimand or dispense criticism. The way one gets better at handling the interpersonal contacts that inspire hesitation and apprehension is to just do it. And do it, and do it, until a workable level of competence is attained and one is able to address necessary negatives kindly but respectfully, thoroughly, and constructively. The supervisor or manager who, through fear and apprehension, shies away from disciplining or disciplines too late or in watered-down fashion is severely limiting his or her growth in management. Facing the apprehension again and again, however, will enhance personal growth and contribute to interpersonal competence. Repetition is as essential as saying and doing the correct things.

Consider, for a moment, the matter of conducting a performance appraisal interview. Perhaps one has had occasion to wonder why performance appraisals seem to be far from the average manager's favorite task. A manager's dislike of—and apprehension concerning—performance appraisals is probably owing to two areas of cause. First, there is the knowledge that this process is important to the employee, perhaps affecting pay increases, promotional opportunities, maybe even continued employment itself, all of which, in addition to the possibility of having to criticize, conspire to raise a manager's level of apprehension.

Second, the manager may have limited opportunity to acquire competence through repetition. Each employee is a unique individual, and each must be dealt with in a manner that is, in some ways, different from how the manager deals with all others. However, within most appraisal systems, the formal appraisal occurs but once per year, hardly a frequency that permits building interpersonal competence with each individual employee. So the performance appraisal is likely to remain a source of dislike for some managers, especially for those who have little or no other performance-related contact with the employee throughout the year (surely, a serious error of omission for some managers, but unfortunately a practice encountered all too often in the work force).

One also becomes skilled in face-to-face interactions by observing others and interpreting their actions and arranging one's own behavior to suit the objective of any particular interaction. In interpreting the behavior of others, however, it is necessary to be mindful that we are usually speculating, because we see only the outer indications of behavior and we have to infer feelings and motives from this behavior. Our interpretation of others' behavior is conditioned by our past experiences with others, and it is necessary to accept the likelihood of often being wrong in assessing another's behavior. This suggests why it is extremely important for a manager to truly know each employee in the group as an individual; the better the manager is acquainted with a person's moods and tendencies and personality characteristics, the better the manager will be at interpreting the person's behavior.

Interpersonal competence, then, comes with time and practice. It comes to those who can accept the truth of the statement noted earlier: most persons inherently believe they are better communicators than they actually are. Those who can believe that they are not nearly as good at communication as they could be are those best situated to seek the improvement necessary to gain interpersonal competence.

Improving Interpersonal Skills

A great deal can be offered concerning various means of improving one's interpersonal skills. However, there is a single factor that is probably central to ensuring the success of any face-to-face interaction, and that is the presence of a clearly understood objective.

Why objectives?

Setting an objective for any particular interaction may not change the interaction at all. Surely, we can—and frequently do—have interactions without objectives. However, having a specific objective requires that something arise from the interaction to serve that objective. Objectives require that something be done to achieve them. More often than not, interactions without objectives are unproductive. Interactions without objectives leave one with feelings like: "Three hours in a meeting and I can't see what we accomplished" or "Pleasant conversation, but was anything really decided?"

Going into an interpersonal exchange knowing in advance what one wishes to get from it will set the exchange on a potentially productive track. The objective may be modified or completely changed along the way as information is exchanged, but even a changing objective is more likely than no objective at all to keep an interchange on track. Managers consume a great deal of time meeting with others both one-on-one and in groups. The manager who enters every communication situation with a specific objective in mind will, in the long run, be more productive while spending less time communicating.

What is an objective, anyway?

An objective is a specific prediction of circumstances that you wish to attain at some specific time in the future. Simply described, an objective is a target. As far as a particular interpersonal contact is concerned, the objective is the state of things that you intend to exist at the conclusion of the interchange or perhaps a statement describing the outcome you desire for a situation. In on-the-job situations, objectives frequently refer to reaching agreement on something, determining a plan of action, making or affirming a decision, or resolving a particular issue. For example, one might wish to convince an employee of a necessary policy change (reaching agreement on something), spell out how to go about protesting an apparently faulty policy (determining a plan of action), establishing mutual agreement on how to pro-

ceed (making or affirming a decision), or solving a scheduling problem (resolving a particular issue).

Even the simplest of objectives must possess two essential elements: a description of the outcome one wishes to achieve (always both desirable and realistic) and some means by which success is to be measured. Going into any interaction, it is necessary to know what you wish to accomplish and how you will know it has been accomplished. An objective may be altered as it is pursued; this is often the case because the interaction can produce information that can suggest a change in direction or emphasis. However, to proceed with no specific objective in mind is to run the considerable risk of accomplishing nothing: if you do not know where you are going, you will never know when you arrive there. Even pursuing an objective that you feel is shaky and will undoubtedly change to some extent before you get there is better than having no objective at all—at least you know you are pointed in the right general direction.

Setting an objective in any interaction clarifies what you have to do; you can compare the outcome with the prediction and gauge the extent of success or failure. And fully as important as knowing where you are going, having a specific objective helps you in communicating to others what you want to accomplish.

Some guidelines to keep in mind when setting objectives for face-to-face interaction are the following:

• Formulate your objectives, taking into account what you know about the individuals with whom you are dealing. Every individual is unique in some respects, and the better you know those you are interacting with—whether employees, peers, superiors, or others—the better you can focus your objectives.

• Know specifically what you need to accomplish with any specific interaction. In other words, avoid overall objectives that are too large for accomplishment within the context of a single interaction.

• Although you cannot know in advance whether you will succeed in reaching a particular objective, you should have decided in advance what sort of results would constitute success or failure.

• Have a clear idea of the likely directions open to you depending on the results of a given interaction. That is, what might you do next if your immediate objective is achieved as envisioned? If the objective is missed altogether? If the results of the interaction indicate the need for an entirely different approach?

Why and how to set objectives for interaction

Through the conscientious and repeated analysis of interactive behavior, we gradually become proficient at monitoring our own behavior and that of others. This should lead to an improved ability to adapt any particular style of behavior as may be most appropriate to the achievement of our objectives. We come to know ourselves, and we come to know others and how they are likely to react in interaction with us, and thus we pattern our own behavior accordingly.

Quite simply, having an objective in any particular interaction gives you a specific target for which to aim. This target may have to be modified as you acquire new information through the interaction, but it still provides valid direction. The assessment of behavior provides you with essential guidance in choosing how to approach that objective.

We hear much about the desirability of pursuing win-win outcomes as opposed to dealing in win-lose situations. Most working managers would likely profess a preference for win-win outcomes for most interactions; however, many unconsciously structure their interactions as win-lose scenarios. Without necessarily realizing they are doing so, many individuals approach interpersonal communication as though most interchanges end with someone "winning" and someone "losing."

To some people, communication appears to be a game or a serious competition in which one must always endeavor to "win." These, of course, are the individuals who will prolong a discussion until they get their way or who will become emotional and resort to argument, perhaps using the deadly weapons of sarcasm, ridicule, name-calling, and blaming, the illegitimate tools of communication that serve to inflame and alienate. Many people exhibiting the win-lose mentality enter their interactions with narrowly defined objectives in mind, literally premade decisions that leave no room for negotiation, and they tend to take every "loss" as a personal affront.

We set objectives to conceptualize in advance the results we would like to achieve. However, if the objectives are narrow and rigidly defined and take into account only what the initiator of the interaction wants to accomplish, unmindful of the feelings and needs of the other party, the interaction will play out in a win-lose scenario. Should the other party be one of those who must "win" to maintain a sense of self-worth, the stage is set for conflict.

Surely, a genuine win-win situation is not always possible given the variety of communications situations a department manager is likely to become involved in. There are those occasions when one party cannot realistically expect to "win." Consider, for example, the following situation in which disciplinary action or at least serious criticism is warranted.

The nurse manager of a medical/surgical nursing unit entered the workroom of the unit just in time to see Sally, a nursing assistant whom the manager considered a usually careful worker, commit an act that could only be described as horseplay. Sally's behavior caused another employee to be startled into dropping and breaking two pieces of glassware. In addition to Sally and the person who dropped the glassware, there were two other staff members present.

Since the manager personally saw Sally commit the act, there is no room available for Sally to "win" in the inevitable interaction with the manager. The manager can, however, limit Sally's losses to what is absolutely necessary and can do so in a reasonable manner. Should the manager verbally take off on Sally right on the spot and promise punishment for her action, Sally would find herself criticized in the presence of others (an error for any manager to commit) and would thus "lose" additionally by being berated in the presence of her colleagues. This would suggest that the manager's hastily formulated objective for the interaction was: "Punish Sally and make an example of her for others." This objective violates 2 of the fundamental principles of fair and effective disciplinary action: discipline only in private, never in the presence of others; and never make an example of anyone.

If, along the lines of criticism or disciplinary action properly addressed, the manager were to get Sally alone, describe what was seen, and ask Sally for her version of the incident, stress precisely why Sally's behavior was inappropriate, provide advice for future behavior, and explain how this incident stands in contrast to Sally's usually good performance, the manager's implied objective becomes: "Correct Sally's behavior so that similar incidents are avoided in the future." In pursuing this objective, the manager has stayed focused on Sally's behavior in this specific instance, addressed the problem constructively, and did so in a way that ensures Sally "loses" no more than absolutely necessary. Being disciplined in the presence of others and being held up as an example would constitute personal "losses" for Sally well beyond that which is necessary to inspire correction of behavior.

Objectives, then, should be established such that they

- Focus specifically on what must be accomplished, avoiding the likelihood of peripheral "losses" that can result when objectives are harshly win-lose in character;
- Employ win-win scenarios when possible,
- Limit any party's perceived "losses" to the essential minimum;
- Respect and protect the dignity of any and every party to an interaction.

Using Interpersonal Skills

Some opening assumptions

Given that any particular interaction properly approached begins with certain end-of-interaction objectives in mind, without stretching too far, we can safely proceed with the following assumptions about interpersonal communication:

- There is a connection between the behavior of one party and that of the other; what one says or does will influence what the other says or does.
- It is possible to arrange one's outward behavior to influence or shape the behavior of the other party; this may be done unconsciously or it may be done deliberately.
- Only the other party's overt or visible behavior is directly accessible; it is not possible to know precisely what another is thinking or feeling.
- There is no win-lose scenario, no struggle for dominance in an inter-

change, if both parties to an interaction have equivalent objectives.

- Interpersonal skills are far more effective when applied in one-on-one interactions than when applied in a one-on-several or one-on-many situation, where the opportunities for effective behavior shaping are far less available.

Shaping behavior

Necessarily a two-way process

The manager who is communicating to convince another person to do something, believe something, or change something is attempting to shape that individual's behavior. Behavior shaping, however, is frequently a two-way process, so the person who is attempting to shape another's behavior may in turn have his or her behavior shaped by the other party. There is in fact nothing wrong with this turnabout behavior shaping; this is in part how one learns, how one acquires new information and forms new attitudes, and thus legitimately modifies objectives during an interaction.

Frequently, the language of an interaction bears a direct relationship to the behaviors experienced. For example, harsh, accusatory language, name-calling, and blame-casting signal belligerent, arbitrary, harsh behavior that suggests the interaction is on its way to a win-lose conclusion. This is highly likely to inspire strongly defensive behavior on the other person's part, setting up a situation in which the likelihood of any meaningful communication occurring is dramatically diminished. Since our behavioral activity is likely to trigger corresponding reactions in response, the initiator of an interaction—we will continue to assume this is the department manager—must be sufficiently disciplined to avoid projecting an overbearing or threatening posture that is likely to turn the interaction into an argument or an exchange of charges and countercharges.

Strong behavior shapers

Some particular behaviors are more powerful than others in their effectiveness as shapers of the behavior of other people. It will perhaps come as no surprise that these stronger behavior shapers are generally those that provide maximum opportunity for inclusion or participation by the other party. The department manager will surely recognize among the following a number of frequently offered suggestions for eliciting employee cooperation and participation:

- Seeking suggestions: asking for suggestions, perhaps even inviting the other party to propose a direction or solution, in effect offering to open the interaction so that it is less likely to be viewed as a one-way contact.
- Offering suggestions: actively offering suggestions and inviting the other party to respond or make counter-offerings.
- Extending proposals: offering a tentative proposal, complete with both process and intended result, and again encouraging the other party to accept, reject, or modify what is presented.
- Soliciting clarification: asking for the other party's understanding of the issue of mutual concern to them to ensure that both parties are "on the same page."

If dealing with direct-reporting employees, in using any of the foregoing behaviors, make every reasonable effort to tap into the employees' knowledge of the work of the department. The manager's knowledge of the department's work may be superior to that of the individual employees in the macro sense of knowing how all elements fit together in fulfilling the department's overall objectives, but the manager cannot reasonably expect to know the interior working details of every job in the department. It is always worth remembering that no one has better knowledge of the detailed requirements of a job better than the person who does that job every day.

Countering another's shaping behavior

In the majority of face-to-face interactions, each party will have an objective that he or she would like to attain, and whether consciously or unconsciously, each party will be attempting to shape the other's behavior such that a personal objective can be achieved. As an example, consider a particular face-to-face encounter between a manager and an employee on the subject of a proposal to change the individual's daily shift to start and end an hour earlier than previously. The manager's objective is to convince the employee that the new starting time is appropriate; the employee's objective, we shall say, is to retain her present hours and make no change.

Given the employee's objective, she will likely counter whatever the manager has to say with arguments in favor of making no change. Perhaps, she pleads transportation problems associated with the proposed change; perhaps, she cites disruption of child-care arrangements in a manner that suggests the new hours would create hardship for her. Perhaps, her behavior even suggests that she believes she is being picked on or punished by being forced to change her hours.

If the manager buys in to the employee's arguments and reconsiders the change, the manager has given in to the other's shaping behavior. This suggests the presence of one of three possibilities: the proposed change was not really needed and thus could not be "sold"; the employee is the stronger personality and simply overpowered the manager; or the manager was not adequately prepared for the interaction.

There are essentially three ways in which to go about getting employees to adopt a given change: the manager can tell them what to do, sell them on what must be done, or involve them in determining what must be done. In manager-to-employee interactions, the first way, telling them, is likely to generate resistance; it might get done, but there will likely be resentment and less than whole-hearted cooperation. With anyone, and especially with direct reporting employees, the telling route will most likely trigger significant shaping behavior. When the manager in our example says, in effect, "Here's your new schedule, like it or not," this manager can expect significant resistance and thus significant shaping behavior from the employee. Should the manager try to convince the employee—"We need to change your starting and quitting times by one hour because ... ," resistance may be less than under the telling route and the employee's shaping behavior will be less. If the manager can go into the interaction without offering a preconceived solution—say, for example, "We're having a problem with adequate coverage because of some significant changes in client arrival patterns, let's put our heads together and see if we can fix it"—resistance is avoided, and shaping behavior by the employee is avoided because the manager and employee acquire a common objective: solve the problem. And—who knows?—once drawn into a common objective, the employee may help formulate a more appropriate solution

than indicated by the manager's pre-made decision.

Therefore, successfully countering shaping behavior requires

- Advancing one's ideas as suggestions or possibilities, not as proposals and certainly not as orders or edicts.
- Avoiding argument.
- Differentiating between legitimate feedback and emotional reaction (legitimate feedback contributes to problem-solving; emotional reaction associates with shaping behavior).
- Utilizing constructive "idea-building" (as in brainstorming) to generate ideas and explore possible paths toward solution.
- Permitting maximum possible participation and involvement of the other party.

Changing another's behavior

This reference to changing another's behavior concerns behavior change in a planned interaction, action-oriented and undertaken to achieve a specific objective. This is a considerably narrower view of behavior change than that which we would associate with routine disciplinary action. In most instances, the primary purpose of disciplinary action is the correction of behavior; for example, if the manager disciplines an employee for chronic tardiness, the primary purpose of the action is to encourage the employee to no longer be tardy. However, behavior change within the context of an interpersonal contact requires an exclusive focus on the behavior of the other party during that specific interaction.

Changing another's behavior begins with carefully observing the person's behavior and feeding back observations that can make the other party aware of the behavioral characteristics coming across in the interaction. If, for example, the other party is told that he or she is "beginning to speak faster and louder and is starting to show signs of agitation," that may be all that is needed to bring the communication back into balance. This is eminently workable in the manager-employee relationship, in which the manager controls (or should control) the interaction and can provide feedback that may sound corrective in nature. Diplomatically approached, this process may also be fully appropriate in interactions between peers, as in, say, a manager-to-manager interaction.

Another's behavior is changed by providing the person with constructive feedback, keeping the interaction on track toward its intended objective and providing whatever support and encouragement may be necessary to ensure the other party's active participation.

Factors Reducing Interpersonal Effectiveness

The most commonly encountered reasons for reduced effectiveness of one-on-one interactions are conflicting objectives, shortage of time, emotional arousal, and inadequate listening.

Conflicting objectives

There is an age-old exercise in improvisation that involves a one-on-one interaction in which the two parties each receive their instructions in private and are then required to play out a scene based on what they have been told. Each is to react extemporaneously to what the other says. Example: The scene is to involve a manager and an employee. The instructions to the "manager" are that this generally valued employee is to be released as part of a company-wide cutback, and must be told so as diplomatically as possible. However, the "employee" is told that he or she is most likely being called in to be given a promotion and modest pay increase. One can imagine the confusion that can develop ha this sort of interaction and can perhaps also envision the extremes to which two enthusiastic participants could take this scene.

This example illustrates sharply different objectives in a one-on-one interaction. The "manager" wishes to humanely effect a termination; the "employee" wishes to receive official word of the expected promotion and increase. Although rarely will the objectives in any ordinary workaday interaction be as diverse as those in the example, it is common for the objectives of the two parties to differ. Say, the manager's objective is to solve a particular problem by any reasonable means, while the employee's objective is to help solve the problem without acquiring an added assignment. Or perhaps, the manager's objective is to resolve an apparent quality problem, while the employee's immediate objective is to avoid being blamed for the problem.

One party to the interaction must be in a position to exercise control and influence and remain aware of the need to get both participants "on the same page." This is ordinarily the person who initiates the interaction for some particular reason. In a manager-employee relationship, it will usually be the manager who must accept responsibility for the interaction and for making every reasonable attempt to ensure a common objective.

Shortage of time

Shortage of time—or, perhaps more appropriately expressed, time not committed to the extent necessary for effective communication—is a significant cause of ineffective one-on-one communication. Involved with this matter of time is the necessity for feedback in any interaction, feedback that is necessary if only to ensure that the message communicated by one party is properly understood by the other party. Feedback is required to ensure that any interaction constitutes two-way communication; without feedback, we are left with one-way communication, which, if we can accept a simple definition of communication as the transfer of meaning, is not communication at all.

Conflicting objectives generally foster frustration and wasted time as participants circle about in search of common ground. Inadequate time devoted to face-to-face communication, especially insufficient time devoted to offering, receiving, and responding to feedback, fosters misunderstanding. It happens more often than one might imagine: person A says something to person B, person B nods and moves on; A believes that B has received the message as intended, and B believes that he or she has understood the message as intended; yet they part with each having completely different meanings in mind. Such results occur time and again, especially in the work situation, simply because someone does not take the time to obtain verification via feedback.

In most present-day work settings, and especially in health care given its present trend toward leaner staffing, managers and employees alike are usually extremely busy. Busy people feel pressured to make the most of their time, and as they move from problem to problem and issue to issue, they tend not to linger over supposedly "simple" matters; they ask, instruct, order, and move

on to the next concern. Many times, the absence of feedback causes no problems and messages are received properly. Many other times, however, without feedback, misunderstanding results and problem arise, and the time that was supposedly saved by being "efficient" in communication must be spent, often several times over, in correcting the results of misunderstanding. There is perhaps a certain wisdom in the old, anonymous question: "How come there is never enough time to do it right the first time, but we can always find the time to do it over?"

Time and the pressures of time will forever be the enemies of effective interpersonal communication.

Emotional arousal

The presence of emotion, primarily the negative emotions—anger and all of its variants—reduces the effectiveness of interpersonal communication, often so much so that long-lasting damage results. The latter can occur when someone, usually in the heat of anger, says something that upsets another by causing pain or distress. Doing so is likely to ensure that nothing helpful results from the current interaction, and this behavior can also create a degree of alienation that hampers interactions between these people for some time to come. Although it can perhaps be said that, on rare occasions, a bit of righteous anger, carefully controlled, can be effective in certain kinds of situations; by and large, anger is destructive in interpersonal communication. We can safely say that in the overwhelming majority of interactions, as the level of anger increases, the chances of meaningful communication occurring decrease.

There often seems to be no ready means of overcoming another's anger in an interaction. Much will of course depend on the style and temperament of the individuals involved. Frequently, anger inspires anger, and an escalating argument ensues. However, it should be recognized that the party who is ostensibly in control of the interaction should assume the responsibility for remaining calm in the face of anger, refusing to be baited and refusing to engage in argument, and doing everything reasonably possible to defuse the other's anger. In addition to not offering argument, this also means avoiding criticizing, blaming, or contradicting what is said. More often than not, the best course of action in the face of anger is to terminate the interaction until such time as tempers cool and rational behavior can prevail.

Inadequate listening

In interpersonal communication, one can be fully effective in imparting information or reaching an agreement only if the other party is listening effectively. Here lies the greatest shortcoming to be encountered in communicating in the one-on-one relationship: one parry can be doing everything right, can be saying the proper things in the right way and behaving respectfully, perhaps even deferentially, and all can be for little or nothing, if the other person is not listening.

Listening can be described as communication along one of the four basic communication channels, the others being reading, writing, and speaking. Two are for incoming information—listening and reading; two are for outgoing information—writing and speaking. Listening, however, differs from the other three means in one important respect. The others are inherently active processes; one cannot read, write, or speak without making a decision to do so and consciously taking the necessary steps. Lis-

tening, however, is not inherently active. That is, because one can "hear" without taking any steps to make it possible and because there is often no subsequent effort to make listening active, what is being said is taken in superficially with no effort expended to truly understand the message.

The best defense against inadequate listening is, once again, the required use of feedback. If you wish to be certain your message has gotten across, the kind of question not to ask is, "Do you understand?" Many people, especially employees in interaction with managers, will answer "yes" whether they fully understand or not. (It is a sad fact of business life to know that there are occasional managers who take offense if it seems as though employees have not understood the great pronouncements upon initial hearing.)

The kind of request to make of the other party: "Tell me in your own words what I just asked you to do, so I can make sure we both see it the same way." The forthcoming response will be the sort of deliberately solicited, focused feedback that will reveal the extent to which the person has been listening—as well as allowing the requestor to supplement or clarify the message if necessary. En-

forced feedback is the primary defense against inadequate listening.

Conclusion: Practice, Practice

The way to become proficient at just about anything is to make the right moves and make them again and again. Proficiency in one-on-one interactions—interpersonal competence, if you will—is one of the hallmarks of the successful manager of people. Some managers spend as much as three-fourths or more of every workday in face-to-face contacts with others, be they employees, peers, superiors, clients, visitors, suppliers, or whoever. Those managers who may have occasion to feel that all of the people-contact that seems to consume the days to the extent of keeping them from the "real work" have yet to recognize that many of the most important elements of a manager's "real work" involve face-to-face, one-on-one interactions.

Interpersonal skills are not to be assumed; they are not to be taken for granted. Like any other skills employed in business in general and health care in particular, proficiency in their use requires conscientious application and practice.

SENATE INTELLIGENCE REPORT

Groupthink Viewed as Culprit in Move to War

By Vicki Kemper

WASHINGTON—The 1961 Bay of Pigs invasion. The escalation of the Vietnam War. The go-ahead for launching the space shuttle Challenger.

Groupthink, an insular style of policy-making, has been identified as a chief culprit in all. And Friday, the Senate Intelligence Committee added to those the process leading to the 2003 decision to attack Saddam Hussein.

Irving Janis, a Yale psychologist, coined the term in 1972 to describe a decision-making process in which officials are so wedded to the same assumptions and beliefs that they ignore, discount or even ridicule information to the contrary. When members of a cohesive, homogeneous group value unanimity and agreement on one course of action more than a realistic appraisal of alternatives, they are engaging in groupthink.

Experts said Friday that groupthink was not entirely responsible for the acceptance of faulty intelligence information on Iraq, but that the Bush administration was, by design, particularly susceptible to that dangerous style of decision-making.

"Groupthink is more likely to arise when there is a strong premium on loyalty and when there is not a lot of intellectual range or diversity within a decision-making body," said Stephen M. Walt, academic dean of Harvard University's Kennedy School of Government.

All organizations and presidential administrations face the same risk, Walt said. He added that the report specifically indicted the intelligence community, but that others, including Democratic lawmakers and the media, also failed to challenge basic assumptions about Iraq's weapons capability.

"When a president makes a decision about something, there is a tendency to get on the train rather than throwing yourself in front of it," Walt said. "Whatever Bush's flaws may be, indecision is not one of them."

Business schools and political scientists are among those who warn would-be policy-makers and managers of the dangers of groupthink. CRM Learning, a company specializing in developing products for leadership and management development, has been selling its popular Groupthink video program since the 1970s.

The commonly cited "symptoms" of groupthink are a fundamental overconfidence that gives members an illusion of invulnerability and a belief in the inherent morality of the group.

The groupthink dynamic also is characterized by a pressure to conform that often leads group members with different ideas to censor themselves. But groupthink is most likely to occur when all or most members of a group already share the same views.

In that sense, it is the opposite of collective wisdom, said James Surowiecki, a financial writer for the New Yorker and author of the recent book, "The Wisdom of Crowds."

What's really striking about groupthink is not so much that dissenting opinions are crushed or shouted down, but they come to seem improbable," he said. "Everyone operates on the idea that this is true, so everyone goes out to prove that it's true."

Surowiecki, who concludes in his book that "under the right circumstances, most groups are remarkably intelligent," said it's when leaders surround themselves with like-minded people that groupthink is a danger.

"Collective wisdom," by contrast, comes when "each person in the group is offering his or her best independent forecast," he said. "It's not at all about compromise or consensus."

He said a guiding principle of the Bush administration seems to be that "everyone needs to be on the same page to reach a decision." To reach good decisions, he said, "I think it's exactly the opposite."

Test Your Knowledge Form

We encourage you to photocopy and use this page as a tool to assess how the articles in *Annual Editions* expand on the information in your textbook. By reflecting on the articles you will gain enhanced text information. You can also access this useful form on a product's book support Web site at *http://www.dushkin.com/online/*.

NAME: DATE:

TITLE AND NUMBER OF ARTICLE:

BRIEFLY STATE THE MAIN IDEA OF THIS ARTICLE:

LIST THREE IMPORTANT FACTS THAT THE AUTHOR USES TO SUPPORT THE MAIN IDEA:

WHAT INFORMATION OR IDEAS DISCUSSED IN THIS ARTICLE ARE ALSO DISCUSSED IN YOUR TEXTBOOK OR OTHER READINGS THAT YOU HAVE DONE? LIST THE TEXTBOOK CHAPTERS AND PAGE NUMBERS:

LIST ANY EXAMPLES OF BIAS OR FAULTY REASONING THAT YOU FOUND IN THE ARTICLE:

LIST ANY NEW TERMS/CONCEPTS THAT WERE DISCUSSED IN THE ARTICLE, AND WRITE A SHORT DEFINITION:

We Want Your Advice

ANNUAL EDITIONS revisions depend on two major opinion sources: one is our Advisory Board, listed in the front of this volume, which works with us in scanning the thousands of articles published in the public press each year; the other is you—the person actually using the book. Please help us and the users of the next edition by completing the prepaid article rating form on this page and returning it to us. Thank you for your help!

ANNUAL EDITIONS: Social Psychology 05/06

ARTICLE RATING FORM

Here is an opportunity for you to have direct input into the next revision of this volume.
We would like you to rate each of the articles listed below, using the following scale:

1. **Excellent: should definitely be retained**
2. **Above average: should probably be retained**
3. **Below average: should probably be deleted**
4. **Poor: should definitely be deleted**

Your ratings will play a vital part in the next revision.
Please mail this prepaid form to us as soon as possible.
Thanks for your help!

RATING	ARTICLE
_____	1. Stupid Human Tricks
_____	2. Research Synthesis: Protection of Human Subjects of Research: Recent Developments and Future Prospects for the Social Sciences
_____	3. Something From Nothing: Seeking a Sense of Self
_____	4. Self-Concordance and Subjective Well-Being in Four Cultures
_____	5. Making Sense of Self-Esteem
_____	6. Why We Overestimate Our Competence
_____	7. How Social Perception Can Automatically Influence Behavior
_____	8. Make-Believe Memories
_____	9. How Culture Molds Habits of Thought
_____	10. More Than One Way to Make an Impression: Exploring Profiles of Impression Management
_____	11. Sources of Implicit Attitudes
_____	12. The Science and Practice of Persuasion
_____	13. Overcoming Terror
_____	14. Abu Ghraib Brings A Cruel Reawakening
_____	15. Liking: The Friendly Thief
_____	16. Persuasion: What Will It Take to Convince You?
_____	17. Beyond Shyness and Stage Fright: Social Anxiety Disorder
_____	18. Linking Up Online
_____	19. Isn't She Lovely?
_____	20. If It's Easy Access That Really Makes You Click, Log On Here
_____	21. The Marriage Savers
_____	22. The Self-Protective Properties of Stigma: Evolution of a Modern Classic
_____	23. Change of Heart
_____	24. Thin Ice: "Stereotype Threat" and Black College Students
_____	25. Prime-Time Violence 1993–2001: Has The Picture Really Changed?
_____	26. How Psychology Can Help Explain The Iraqi Prisoner Abuse
_____	27. Bullying: It Isn't What It Used to Be

RATING	ARTICLE
_____	28. Influencing, Negotiating Skills, and Conflict-Handling: Some Additional Research and Reflections
_____	29. The Nature of Human Altruism
_____	30. Cause of Death: Uncertain(ty)
_____	31. Trends in the Social Psychological Study of Justice
_____	32. Putting Leaders on the Couch
_____	33. When Followers Become Toxic
_____	34. Interpersonal Skills: What They Are, How to Improve Them, and How to Apply Them
_____	35. Senate Intelligence Report: Groupthink Viewed as Culprit in Move to War

(Continued on next page)

BUSINESS REPLY MAIL
FIRST CLASS MAIL PERMIT NO. 551 DUBUQUE IA

POSTAGE WILL BE PAID BY ADDRESEE

McGraw-Hill/Dushkin
2460 KERPER BLVD
DUBUQUE, IA 52001-9902

|ı.ıl..ıı.l.ıllll.ıı.ıll..ıı...ıllll.ıl.ı.lı.ıll..ıı.lı.ılıll|

- -

ABOUT YOU

Name _____ Date _____

Are you a teacher? ❏   A student? ❏
Your school's name _____

Department _____

Address _____ City _____ State _____ Zip _____

School telephone # _____

YOUR COMMENTS ARE IMPORTANT TO US!

Please fill in the following information:
For which course did you use this book?

_____

Did you use a text with this ANNUAL EDITION?   ❏ yes   ❏ no
What was the title of the text?

_____

What are your general reactions to the *Annual Editions* concept?

_____

Have you read any pertinent articles recently that you think should be included in the next edition? Explain.

_____

Are there any articles that you feel should be replaced in the next edition? Why?

_____

Are there any World Wide Web sites that you feel should be included in the next edition? Please annotate.

_____

May we contact you for editorial input?   ❏ yes   ❏ no
May we quote your comments?   ❏ yes   ❏ no